THE NEW
GOLDEN RULE

THE NEW
GOLDEN RULE

Community and Morality in
a Democratic Society

AMITAI ETZIONI

BasicBooks
A Division of HarperCollins*Publishers*

Designed by Elliott Beard

FIRST EDITION

Library of Congress Cataloging-in Publication Data

Etzioni, Amitai.
    The new golden rule : community and morality in a democratic society / by Amitai Etzioni. —1st ed.
      p. cm.
    Includes bibliographical references and index.
    ISBN 0-465-05297-5
    1. Social ethics. 2. Social values. 3. Communitarianism.
  4. Democracy. I. Title.
  HM216.E85   1997
  303.3'72—dc20
                                         96-21192
                                            CIP

97 98 99 00 ❖/RRD 10 9 8 7 6 5

For Shira and Eli, the youngest Etzionis, and for the young researchers who worked for me in recent years, to be heard of all on their own:

Linda Abdel-Malek
Michael Bocian
Laura Brodbeck
David Brown
David E. Carney
Daniel Doherty
Brandt Goldstein
Suzanne Goldstein
Gayton Gomez
Ryan J. Hagemann
Steven Helland
Vanessa Hoffman
Sarah Horton
Zubin Khambatta
Barry Kreiswirth

Alexandra Lahav
Darin Levine
Lauren Levy
Frank Lovett
Judith Lurie
Jeremy Mallory
William Mathias
Jessica Mayer
Dana Mitra
Nora B. Pollock
Sharon Pressner
Alyssa Qualls
Janet Shope
W. Bradford Wilcox
Benjamin Wittes

In small groups in which everyone feels that a great deal depends upon his actions, and learns to act upon his own responsibility instead of losing himself in the anonymity of the mass, social patterns grow up in which individuality can almost certainly develop.

—KARL MANNHEIM

America! America!
God mend thine every flaw,
Confirm thy soul in self-control
Thy liberty in law!

—KATHARINE LEE BATES, "AMERICA THE BEAUTIFUL"

Contents

Acknowledgments

In launching the work on this book, I benefited from profound suggestions from William A. Galston, Alan Wolfe, and Daniel A. Bell. Numerous detailed criticisms of drafts were made by Ronald Beiner and David M. Anderson. Mark Gould was particularly critical and helpful. I am most grateful for various suggestions by Paul Golob, my BasicBooks editor.

I am especially grateful to a team of research assistants who did much more than the usual research chores, tasks they discharged exceedingly well. They served as my sounding board and first critics, unfailingly posed challenges, questioned assumptions, and made numerous editorial suggestions. The team included Michael Bocian, Ryan J. Hagemann, Frank Lovett, Jeremy Mallory, Matthew L. Schwartz, Nora B. Pollock—and David E. Carney, who coordinated the work as well. He worked with me with great dedication from the day the book was first envisioned until it was sent to press. I am particularly indebted to him. Daniel Doherty, the managing editor of the *Responsive Community*, served as another major source of suggestions and criticisms. I am grateful to Laura Brodbeck for comments on several of the chapters and to David Karp, Andy Altman, Seth Jaffo, and Tamara Watts for their discussions. Pat Kellogg not only put up with me as I was writing the book, but made it significantly better.

The work was conducted under the auspices of the George Washington University Center for Communitarian Policy Studies and the Center for Policy Research, Inc. I am grateful to the Walter and Elise Haas Fund and its executive director, Bruce R. Sievers, and the Stuart Foudations and its president, Theodore E. Lobman, for small grants that helped bring the book to conclusion. For information on The Communitarian Network, see www.gwu.edu/~ccps. E-mail: comnet@gwis2.circ.gwu.edu.

Preface:
Virtue in a Free Society

In 1992, Antioch College issued a lengthy, detailed, written list of instructions that students, faculty, and staff are expected to follow when they proposition one another.[1] Members of the Antioch community are required to ask permission explicitly from their prospective partners at every step and move of courtship, and are warned not to proceed until and unless explicit and unambiguous consent to advance has been granted. Antioch explains the policy to incoming students (who are required to participate in sexual consent workshops) as follows: "Each step of the way, you have to ask. . . . If you want to take her blouse off, you have to ask. If you want to touch her breast, you have to ask. If you want to move your hand down to her genitals, you have to ask. If you want to put your finger. . . ."[2] All students are warned that if they violate the code, they will be subject to significant penalties, including expulsion from the college.[3]

The popular press had a field day with these guidelines. They were considered "a menace to spontaneity," political correctness gone mad, and were otherwise widely derided. However, to this sociologist they represent a near-desperate attempt to restore rules of conduct to an area that has been subject to a great deal of moral confusion, resulting in much conflict and abuse. The guidelines bespeak a much greater deficit than merely the lack of mores (specifications of values) concerning sexual conduct. At the same time, the guidelines point to the need for an approach to the regeneration of moral values and commitments that is markedly different from enforced codes.

The Antioch guidelines are best seen in a historical context. During the 1950s, there were relatively clear mores concerning intimate relations. Premarital sex was considered morally inappropriate. Young men, not young women, were expected to take the initiative. Women were supposed to "resist" and to feel and exhibit less interest in sexual relations than men. Boys who had heterosexual relations were viewed with an admiration mixed with mild disapproval, while girls who did so were castigated. Same-sex relations were taboo. Behaviorally, some of these mores were less honored than others, but expectations were rather clear. The same held for most other relationships—those among the races, between the individual and the state (patriotism, especially in the form of anticommunism, ran high), with authority figures (they were respected), and so on. Whether or not one judges these traditional mores as morally compelling, one notes that, up to a point, they provided order.

In the 1960s, this order was undermined. By the late 1980s, rules of conduct, expectations, and notions of what is right and wrong in sexual conduct, as in many other areas, were diminished. Many mores were stretched, challenged, or abandoned; others were bitterly contested. The current mores concerning gender roles provide a good case in point. Conduct that many men consider proper, or at least harmless (e.g., wolf whistles, ogling, the display of pinups), many women consider sexual harassment. Some men interpret invitations to a woman's bedroom and to foreplay as an invitation to engage in intercourse; many women believe that they may call a halt at any time. Much else has become subject to misunderstanding and haggling, such as the question of who will pay for the date, who is responsible for the myriad of possible consequences, at what point (indeed, whether) one partner informs the other about transmissible diseases, and so on. What was originally conceived as sexual liberation, enhanced freedom, and growing sexual equality ended up being experienced by many as troubling uncertainty and confusion.

EXCESSIVE LIBERTY

The notions of sexual liberation, and the awkward attempts of Antioch to deal with them, deserve attention because they cast doubt on a widely held notion in the West: that more freedom is better than less. This notion ignores a major sociological observation: movement from a high level of social restriction to a greater measure of choice, and hence enhancement of individual liberties, at some point becomes onerous for the actors involved and undermines the social order upon which liberties are ultimately based. Gerald Dworkin, in a masterly essay entitled "Is More Choice Better Than Less?," provides a wide array of reasons for preferring some measure of order, and hence some limits on one's choices.[4] These reasons for limitations include the economic and psychological costs of comparing numerous options; the focusing of responsibilities that arise when one forgoes some options (we are responsible only for that which we can affect); the danger of opening ourselves to new temptations (if there is no liquor in my house . . .); and the fact that by forgoing some choices, one can signal one's commitments both to other people and to values.[5] Sociologists would add to this list heightened tendencies toward conflict including violence, when there are too few shared moral convictions. (Noel Epstein notes that the Pilgrims sailed for America to escape not the authoritarianism of the British monarchy and its established church—but rather the openness of Holland. The Dissenters feared that their children would embrace lifestyles that they believed were beyond the pale.[6])

Above all, people abhor an ethical vacuum, one in which all choices have the same standing and are equally legitimate, when all they face are directions among which they may choose but no compass to guide them. In short, after a point, the quest for ever greater liberty does not make for a good society.[7] Much, I shall argue, follows from this observation.

The preceding brief discussion indicates two levels on which this book unfolds. One is sociological. I ask what constitutes a good society: Does it shy away from collective conceptions of virtue and instead nourish individualism and pluralism as the mainsprings of freedom? Or does a good society, following the model of several in Asia, build on tightly knit social webs to ensure respect for virtues that make the society good? Are there ways to combine these two approaches?

The second level is historical. I ask where our societies find themselves currently, and which directions they need to consider if they are to maintain or regain their inner balance and normative course. For the West, especially the United States, the issue is whether the time has come to stress the shoring up of shared values and to set some new limits on autonomy.

A SPECIAL ORDER

Once one recognizes the full significance of the deep-seated sociological and historical need for order, one must ask: What *kind* of order is it to be? On which bases will this order rest? Does a society that seeks to reestablish order need new laws and regulations, stronger penalties, and more law enforcement? Or can it build primarily on recommitment to moral values, on people reaffirming values they share and embody in their lives? And, are procedural virtues, such as tolerance for one another, commitment to the democratic process, and willingness to be civil and to compromise, sufficient? Or does the good society require a set of shared substantive, affirmative moral commitments? Do these commitments have to be monolithic (e.g., it has been argued that American society is Christian and that our moral code therefore should be based on Christianity, and that secular humanism is to be rejected) or is there room for a pluralism of virtues, albeit one confined within the framework of a core of shared substantive values? And how will the values to which the society commits itself be sorted out? Are new forms of public discourse needed, or can we rely on the kind of deliberation we are told characterized the Greek polis and New England town meetings?

While the Antioch guidelines serve as a telling indicator of the social need for a moral paradigm, they also raise grave questions about the ways to proceed when a society or a smaller community seeks to regenerate values; they point to roads that best remain less traveled. These guidelines are based on assumptions of which the drafters were perhaps not fully cognizant, but which a communitarian regeneration of values cannot ignore. The Antioch guidelines assume that consent is the basis of morality. (As long as the couple agrees, there is no limit to what they may do.) The guidelines rely on cognitive, explicit, formal, and above all ad hoc negotiations between the parties, instead of on shared values and established understandings. The college undergirds the new mores with strong penalties rather than relying on moral censure. It is easy to criticize this approach; it is much more taxing to develop an approach that avoids these failings and is compelling in its own right. Here, I face this challenge.

A BLEND OF TRADITION AND MODERNITY

On the highest level of generalization the issue with which this volume grapples is the synthesis of some elements of traditionalism with some elements of modernity, recasting both in the process. Until the beginning of modernity, bodies of thought (often folded into religious writings) were largely preoccupied with maintaining the legitimacy of order and the claims of appropriate social virtues. The ancient Greeks laid some foundations for individual autonomy, but this autonomy was rather restrained and available to only a limited and specific class in an otherwise rigid social order. There are good reasons for the fact that many consider Plato authoritarian or that Aristotle's prevailing political concern was maintaining order and preventing rebellion. Still, by the standards of the Middle Ages, the ancient Greeks were rather "modern." Much of the religious doctrine that prevailed in the Middle Ages extolled monolithic virtues and legitimated an established, and rather rigid, hierarchical, and pervasive social order.

Within this context, modern thinking—with its emphasis on universal individual rights (rather than those of a particular estate) and the virtue of autonomy, of voluntary action and consensual agreements—is best seen as a grand corrective to the social formations of the Middle Ages (the controlling feudal lords, monarchs, and churches) and the paradigms that legitimated them.

Viewed in this way, this volume argues that after the forces of modernity rolled back the forces of traditionalism, these forces did not come to a halt; instead, in the last generation (roughly, from 1960 on), they pushed ahead relentlessly, eroding the much weakened foundations of social virtue and order while seeking to expand liberty ever more.

As a result, we shall see that some societies have lost their equilibrium, and are heavily burdened with antisocial consequences of *excessive* liberty (not a concept libertarians or liberals often use). (In contrast, some contemporary societies, such as some in Asia and the Middle East, show the dangers of excessive order—the loss of equilibrium in the other direction.)

If this observation is a valid one, the next historical phase will need to find ways to blend the virtues of tradition with the liberation of modernity.

Two generations ago, it was widely believed that the world progressed from tradition to modernity; this notion is currently viewed by many as naively optimistic. On the other hand, there are those who

despair of the modern world altogether and seek a return to the traditions of the past. They are led by religious fundamentalists of both the
Islamic and Christian right and by their secular social conservative allies.
The communitarian quest, as I see it, is to seek a way to blend elements
of tradition (order based on virtues) with elements of modernity (well-
protected autonomy). This, in turn, entails finding an equilibrium
between universal individual rights and the common good (too often
viewed as incompatible concepts), between self and community, and
above all how such an equilibrium can be achieved and sustained.

The old golden rule (actually, *rules,* because this precept appears in
many cultures, albeit in somewhat different versions) contains an
unspoken tension between what ego would prefer to do to others, and
that which the golden rule urges ego to recognize as the right course of
action. And the old rule is merely interpersonal. The new golden rule
proposed here seeks to greatly reduce the distance between ego's preferred course and the virtuous one, while recognizing that this profound source of social and personal struggle cannot be eliminated. And
it seeks a good part of the solution on the macro, societal level rather
than merely, or firstly, on the personal one. I shall argue that a new
golden rule should read: Respect and uphold society's moral order as
you would have society respect and uphold your autonomy.

BEYOND THE WEST: A GENERIC PARADIGM

The challenge to form a paradigm for a good, communitarian society
has been posed so far largely in the particular historical and cultural
context of Western societies. These are the societies whose social order
has weakened, particularly from the 1960s to the 1990s. These societies
are entering a stage in which they are actively seeking to restore order
while attempting to change it at the same time. However, this volume
aspires to reach beyond the given historical context; it seeks to provide
a generic understanding of what is required to form and sustain a communitarian society—a generic paradigm for a sociology of virtue.

The paradigm advanced on the following pages is also applied to societies that already command a high, if not excessive, level of order.
These include ones whose order is based chiefly on shared social values
rather than on coercion, but are severely lacking in autonomy—China,
for instance. For these societies, the *same* generic paradigm is applied
the *other way* around: How do we expand and enhance the autonomy of
individuals and subgroups (women, minorities, ethnic groups) while

maintaining order? To put it differently, quests for either more order or more autonomy may seem at first as fundamentally unrelated, indeed diametrically opposed, until one realizes that these are two approaches to the same basic state of equilibrium, albeit from two opposing sides. (Many have written about communitarianism as though it were a concept of social order; I seek to stress that the concept of community, and hence the paradigm built around it, entails a combination of social order and autonomy. Without the first, anarchy prevails; without the second, communities turn into authoritarian villages, if not gulags or slave colonies.)

To determine the direction in which a specific communitarian society needs to move, the generic paradigm must be applied to a specific historical context. And this dynamic, as the following pages show, is not that of a universal march of progress from the dark ages of imposed order to a world full of liberties, but a quest to formulate the elements that a society is lacking so as to bring it closer to a virtuous equilibrium, the golden rule.

While it may seem outlandish to suggest that anyone would argue otherwise, a critical examination of libertarian, liberal, and social conservative writings in the following pages regrettably shows that, *au contraire*, many theories centered around the virtues of liberty *or* order advocate these virtues with insufficient attention to the historical and cultural context in which they are applied. Social philosophies promoting more license, which were well suited to the eighteenth-century world of Adam Smith, are applied to the contemporary United States. And champions of order never find that the punitive measures they just added to previously existing ones are quite sufficient. (Steve Forbes called for "one strike and you're out" during his 1996 presidential election campaign.[8])

This point cannot be stressed enough. There are those who posit that a good society requires a vigilant championing of individual rights, of liberty. They charge communitarians with trying to put a human face on conservative ideals.[9] There are those who argue that a good society requires a strong set of preordained values, values preferably based on religious commitment but imposed by theocratic law if necessary (sometimes referred to as "dominion theology"). They charge communitarians with attempting to put a false normative hue on liberal secular ideals. Each group sees one part of the elephant.

A good, communitarian society, we shall see, requires more than seeing the whole; it calls on those who are socially aware and active, people of insight and conscience, to throw themselves to the side opposite that *toward* which history is tilting. This is not because all virtue is on that opposite side, but because if the element that the society is neglecting will continue to be deprived of support, the society will become either oppressive or anarchic, ceasing to be a good society, if it does not collapse altogether.

Once the communitarian checklist (what is lacking, and to what extent?) of a particular society is drawn up, the specifics required for its return to equilibrium must be examined. For instance, if the society seeks to preserve the family, should its efforts be focused on attempts to restore the traditional family, or on peer marriage (of two persons equal in rights and responsibility), on a revival of the extended family, or on some other pattern? Will the recommitment to values be religious, spiritual, secular-ethical, or some blend of these? And so on.

A METHODOLOGICAL NOTE

The methodology brought to bear here attempts to advance a positive doctrine, the development of a communitarian paradigm, rather than add to the elaborate and rich communitarian literature that grew from debate with liberals. And the methodology is sociological and pragmatic in the sense that the work of Martin Buber and John Dewey is, rather than following the pattern of formal philosophy or political theory.[10] My main concern is with public philosophy, the treatment of the social thought of philosophers such as John Locke, John Stuart Mill, and Jean-Jacques Rousseau, not in its own right but insofar as it has influenced public thinking and been incorporated into social practices and public policies. Such public philosophies are more focused and less elaborate than the volumes of scholarship on which they are based, but it deeply influences our lives.

THE PLAN OF THE BOOK

The discussion opens in chapter 1 with an exploration of the two cardinal founding principles and core virtues of the good society: social order (based on moral values) and autonomy (or "thick" liberty). In chapter 2, it turns to an examination of the rather unusual relationship between these two core elements. The generic paradigm developed in the first two chapters is then applied, in chapter 3, to the West, examining where it is headed and where it must go if some form of communitarian equilibrium is to be achieved. A discussion of the need for shared virtues and how they are to be found brings me to explore, in chapter 4, a form of public discourse I refer to as moral dialogue (as distinct from rational deliberation and culture war), which, in chapter 5, leads me to an examination of the role played by the moral voice, as opposed to the voice of the law, in the regeneration of the social order.

Chapter 6 turns to human nature, a concept taken as self-evident by many but avoided by large segments of the social sciences. Given that human nature is much less tractable than many champions of progress have assumed (although hardly as fallible as many social conservatives and authoritarians presume), one must consider its implications for the application of the communitarian paradigm. What are the limits and opportunities it poses? And above all, what are the normative implications of these observations—to what extent should one fight human nature and when is it legitimate to yield, and then to what extent?

Having focused so far on one society or community at a time, the discussion turns, in chapter 7, to an exploration of ways communities relate to one another. This applies both to the relationships among the diverse ethnic, racial, and regional groups (among others) that make up a national society, where such a social milieu exists, and to societies that seek to form more encompassing communities, like that which the Europeans are attempting.

Each of the first seven chapters of the book concludes with a discussion of the implications of the ideas laid out in each chapter for community practice and for public policies. These discussions have two purposes: to provide material illustrating abstract ideas, and to suggest directions in which members of communities and policy makers may wish to proceed as they embrace the communitarian paradigm.

The discussions, while brief, vary according to the relative familiarity of particular policies. Thus, there is no need to explain crime watch (a neighbors' agreement to watch each other's property) with more than a short phrase, but a more innovative idea, for instance the introduction of community jobs, is laid out in more detail. The focus, however, is still on introducing policy ideas rather than exploring the various difficulties that might arise, how these might be dealt with, and so on. The policy suggestions are meant to serve as food for thought, as ideas that seem to deserve study, rather than policy analyses.

The phrase "implications for practice and policy" is used to stress that these discussions do not provide detailed policy analysis or "wonking"; they only suggest directions in which such answers may be found. They

are akin to making a case that it is time to move West rather than providing a road map of the prairies.

The toughest questions are left for the closing chapter: What criteria
do we rely on when judging a particular set of values that a community
affirms? Can one grant final moral authority to a community? What if
it violates individual rights, turns racist or violent? If metacommunity
values have to be drawn upon in forming such judgments, how can
these in turn be justified?

A.E.
Washington, D.C., October 1996

THE NEW
GOLDEN RULE

ONE

The Elements of a Good Society

VOLUNTARY ORDER AND BOUNDED AUTONOMY

A COMMUNITARIAN AGENDA

The age-old debate about what constitutes a good society has reintensified in the last decades. Religious fundamentalism has risen throughout the world, including in the West. Its champions are deeply concerned about the moral decay of their societies, which they often attribute to the influence of Western, or more generally modern, secular forces. To their way of thinking, individual rights have little or no standing. Fundamentalists argue that people thrive when they closely heed given religious laws. More moderate religious leaders and secular social conservatives are much more respectful of individual rights, but are nevertheless greatly and primarily concerned with the loss of virtues. They fear that barbarians are not at the gates but inside.[1] For instance, they protest lurid rap songs much more than the severe beating of several African Americans by the police.

At the same time, libertarians and laissez-faire conservatives see the

world awash with threats to individual liberties from expansive governments, religious fanatics, or power elites. Many of these individualists
reject the very notion of a good society. Societies, they maintain, flourish when individuals are granted as much autonomy as possible. (The
idea is expressed in more popular terms, in the often-repeated statement indicating that individuals should not be interfered with: "Don't
mess with me.") They are much more likely to protest an unnecessary
government regulation than face the moral issues raised by children
having children.

It has been previously noted that these bodies of thought tend to center around the virtue of either liberty or order. Charles Taylor, for
instance, points to a range of positions that "at one end give primacy to
individual rights and freedom and, at the other, give highest priority to
community life and the good of collectivities."[2]

Among those ideologues and intellectuals largely concerned with
social order (or their version of virtue), there are quite a few who are
also concerned with liberty, and vice versa—among those whose thinking is focused on the defense of liberty, there are quite a few who are
concerned with the social order. Both camps, however, tend to imply
that the best way to sustain the "other" virtue is to attend to the one
with which they are most concerned. They argue either that liberty is
best sustained when order is firm, or that society is best ordered when
liberty is maximized.

In contrast, the communitarian paradigm advanced here applies the
notion of the golden rule at the societal level, to characterize the good
society as one that nourishes both social virtues and individual rights. I
argue that a good society requires a carefully maintained equilibrium of
order and autonomy, rather than the "maximization" of either.

To build my case, the following questions need to be answered:

1: Even if one ignores the extremists, what are the significant bodies
of thought that center around order or autonomy but do not marry
both? What are their arguments, and how may they be countered?

2: If one grants that all societies need to concern themselves with
social order, one still must ask if the good society requires a special kind
of order. If the answer is in the affirmative, what is that good order?

3: If one recognizes that all societies need to provide social foundations to sustain a significant measure of autonomy, what are the distinctive characteristics of autonomy in a good society?

4: What are the implications of the dual virtues of social order and autonomy for the old intellectual and ideological debate, which raged over the last 150 years, between those who champion free economies and those who favor extensive government controls, between conservatives and liberals?

5: To suggest that social order and autonomy must be held in a carefully crafted equilibrium still leaves open many questions concerning the relationship between these dual virtues. Is it true, as is often implied, that the more social order there is, the less liberty the members of the society have? And that the more liberties they take, the less social order there is? Can a society gain both more order and more liberty?

Many books have a subtext, often one that reflects a position with which they quarrel or from which they seek to differentiate themselves. Most communitarians have debated liberals, stressing that individuals are socially embedded and the inevitability of the social formulation of the good, and much that follows from that. I share this perspective. However, I am equally keen to engage the social conservatives. They pay insufficient attention, to put it mildly, to social and moral risks one faces when one promotes—above all, seeks to impose—virtue and conformity. The same charge had been previously made against communitarians ranging from Tönnies to contemporary Asian communitarians. (When in 1990 a new communitarian group was formed, many of those convened were concerned that they will be confused with previous conservative or collectivistic communitarians—hence the term "responsive communitarians" [responsive to individuals, that is] was created.[3]) The communication position advanced here is deeply concerned with the balance between individual rights and social responsibilities, individuality and community, and autonomy and social order.

METHODOLOGICAL NOTES

The paradigm developed here to explore the good society differs from many others in that it is more sociological, and thus empirical, and less normative (less prescriptive). While the discussion draws on political theory and social philosophy, these are not the main foundations of the argument. The sociological and empirical nature of my approach is similar to earlier statements by communitarians who pointed to the unrealistic assumptions made by libertarians (and those whom political theorists call "liberals") about the nature of the individual. In contrast to the libertarian perspective, communitarians have shown that individuals do not exist outside particular social contexts, and that it is erroneous to depict individuals as free agents. We are social animals, members in one another.[4]

In the same sociological-empirical vein, it should be noted that while the term "communitarian" often brings to mind communities, and especially villages and small towns, this is a study of what makes any social entity, from a village to a group of nations, into more of a community. Community is a set of attributes, not a concrete place.

In trying to explore the nature of a good, communitarian society, the term "societal need" plays a pivotal role in the following discussion; it deserves a brief explication. The notion that societies have needs that must be addressed reflects the specific sociological approach applied here, which is known as functionalism. It explains the working of society by the contributions of the parts to the needs of the whole and the requirements a society must meet to maintain itself. For example, a society "needs" arrangements to ensure that as resources are depleted, they will be replenished.

We are used to thinking in terms of causality, and hence are often interested in what preceded what. In contrast, functional explanations tend to be ahistorical and therefore unconcerned with the originating circumstances of present conditions; they deal with factors that are contemporaneous, such as the observation that gated communities experience less violent crime. This is a valid observation even if one does not have the slightest notion about who erected the gates or why. Functional explanations rely primarily on elements that sustain one another, like bricks that hang together in an arch, instead of on cause-and-effect sequences.

Early functionalism was open to the charge that it contained a bias in favor of the status quo.[5] It was assumed that whenever people did not conform to the dictates of their socially prescribed roles, they were "deviants." In this way, all innovation and dissent could be characterized as endangering societal well-being. The functional paradigm applied in this book assumes that while certain *needs* are universal to all societies, there are always alternative *responses*. Instead of putting up gates, a community may fight crime by inviting those estranged from it to become members, and so on. True, these *alternatives* are never equivalent—they differ in their effectiveness. Societal needs do not dictate the specific ways a society must be designed; they only serve to indicate that satisfying basic societal needs—in one way or another—cannot be ignored, and that some ways make for a better society than others.

REARRANGING THE INTELLECTUAL-POLITICAL MAP

Before I can proceed, I must reluctantly suggest a redrawing of the intellectual-political map. In the process, I support the claim that communitarian thinking leapfrogs the old debate between left-wing and right-wing thinking and suggests a third social philosophy.[6] The basic reason this rearrangement is required is that the old map centers around the role of the government versus that of the private sector, and the authority of the state versus that of the individual. The current axis is the relationship between the individual and the *community,* and between freedom and order.

Given this different framework, it makes sense to view libertarians, liberals, laissez-faire conservatives, neoconservatives (usually considered right-wing), and civil libertarians (often considered liberal, if not left[7]) as belonging in various positions on one *side* (not pole) of the intellectual-political space because they all focus—albeit to varying degrees—on the need for autonomy, and pay relatively less direct attention to the needs for social order. When it is necessary to refer to all these lines of thinking together, I refer to them as individualist.[8] On the other side of the space are social conservatives (often lumped with libertarians and laissez-faire conservatives), who are relatively less directly concerned with autonomy, often focusing more on the need to shore up the moral order, and if necessary have it undergirded by the state.

Before I proceed to support the merit of the suggested rearrangement by referring to some specific works, I should reiterate that this is not another review of literature, or a discussion of nuances and differences in each camp. The only purpose of referring here to a few select libertarians, liberals, and social conservatives—of the many that could be cited—is to point to overarching themes as a background on which the paradigm I seek to advance can be etched.

In the process, I face a difficulty in that those scholars I cite have written extensively, have often modified their position over the years, and have been subject to rather extensive scholarship. Thus, any statement about a particular author is properly subject to divergent interpretations. For instance, when I suggested that Friedrich Hayek's work is centered around the virtue of liberty rather than that of social order, a colleague reminded me that Hayek opposed only *imposed* order but recognized the merit of spontaneous order. I could then respond to this valid observation by stating that in effect it further supports my point that Hayek was preoccupied with liberty. But my purpose here is not to try to add to this kind of very worthy scholarship. I choose instead to rely on readers to take into account that my purpose is not to explore these philosophies in their own right, but strictly to place the paradigm advanced here next to these others.

One group that belongs in the individualist camp are classical liberals, such as John Locke, John Stuart Mill (mainly in *On Liberty*),[9] and Adam Smith, and such classical liberals of the modern era as John Rawls, Ronald Dworkin, T. M. Scanlon, Stephen Holmes, and Thomas Nagel. "Liberal" is a particularly confusing term for those who are not members of the political science community or well versed in intellectual history because in contemporary common parlance the term "liberal" is generally applied to those who champion social causes—for example, those who call attention to the needs of the poor, children, mental patients, and other vulnerable members of society, and who favor considerable reliance on the state. (Hubert H. Humphrey, Mario Cuomo, Arthur Schlesinger Jr., John Kenneth Galbraith, Roger Wilkins, and Jacob Weisberg come to mind.[10]) This is generally not those whom political theorists refer to as "liberals."

Various attempts have been made to call attention to the fact that political scientists use the term "liberal" somewhat uniquely, by adding various adjectives, but each of these poses its own difficulties. "Classical" liberals run into trouble because there are contemporary liberals. "Contemporary classical liberals" has been tried, but this is a mouthful and a bit of an oxymoron. None of these terms has gained much currency. As a result, poor communication prevails, as I am hardly the first to observe.[11] "It's annoying to be called a conservative when you aren't. . . . [I]n fact, I am a liberal—or I would be a liberal if that perfectly good word had not been hijacked by people who should be more properly described . . . as socialists, social democrats or progressives," writes James K. Glassman. He goes on to report that the "saint" of the right, Friedrich Hayek, was forced to explain, for the same reasons, "Why I Am Not a Conservative" in a 1960 essay of that title.[12] Michael Oakeshott has written, "What may now be meant by the word 'liberal' is anyone's guess."[13] Paul Gottfried opens his forthcoming book by writing, "The history of liberalism in the twentieth century has been one of growing semantic confusion,"[14] and documents this point well. Thus, a need for clarification has been well established. To avoid this confusion,

I use "individualists" to refer to proponents of these lines of thinking. (When it is necessary to refer specifically to those whom political theorists call liberals, I will speak about "liberal individualists"; I will use the term "welfare liberals" to refer to those whom the members of the general public think about when they use the term "liberals.")

A related change is needed, at least for the purposes at hand, for the term "conservative." Conservatives were considered a small and marginal group intellectually in the early 1960s.[15] Hence there was little inclination to draw distinctions among them. This intellectual habit continued long after the importance of the conservative camp grew greatly. But even now, many write about "conservatives" as if social conservatives and laissez-faire conservatives—those who seek to shore up order by controlling social behavior and those who seek to enhance autonomy by promoting free choice in the marketplace—have much in common.[16] E. J. Dionne Jr. deals with this issue by distinguishing "libertarian conservatives" from others.[17]

I suggest that intellectual and political discourse would be served if we treated the laissez-faire conservative as one kind of individualist and viewed social conservatives as a camp unto themselves. Leading secular social conservatives include Gertrude Himmelfarb, Michael Oakeshott, Samuel Huntington, Diane Ravitch, Russell Kirk, Harvey Mansfield, and Linda Chavez. Among those who draw on both religious and secular sources are Paul Weyrich, Stanley Hauerwas, and Richard John Neuhaus. A particularly moderate but powerful articulation of the importance of virtues is found in the work of Alasdair MacIntyre.[18] Among the more popular social conservatives are William J. Bennett and George F. Will; David Brooks is one of the young writers in this school.[19]

Between individualists, who champion autonomy, and social conservatives, who champion social order, lies communitarian thinking, which characterizes a good society as one that achieves balance between social order and autonomy.

Within each camp there are significant differences. It might be useful to think about the more diehard advocates in each camp as constituting its core and the more moderate members as closer to its edge—and hence closer to the moderate members of the other camps. It is thus not surprising that Alasdair MacIntyre, a moderate social conservative, is often said to be a communitarian—despite the fact he himself rejects the application of this term to his work.[20] And several communitarians (Philip Selznick, for instance) view themselves as either liberal communitarians or communitarian liberals. However, despite the fact that the edges of each camp are fuzzy and that the camps shade into each other, the differences at the core are quite clearly etched.[21]

THICK SOCIAL ORDER—FULLY RESPECTFUL OF AUTONOMY

THE NEED FOR A THICK SOCIAL ORDER

All societies, whatever their virtue or lack thereof, must maintain some modicum of social order or they risk extinction. However, this is widely understood to mean the prevention of internal hostilities, ranging from violence among individuals to civil war among subgroups. In effect, all societies have a need for a much thicker social order, reflecting the fact that all societies promote some shared values, such as establishing a homeland (Israel for the Jews at its founding), seeking to develop a modern economy while sustaining socialism (Communist China in the early 1990s), or fostering its religion (Iran in the late 1980s). Hence, integral to the social order of all societies are at least some processes that mobilize some of their members' time, assets, energies, and loyalties to the *service of one or more common purposes.* (No assumption is made that a particular society is aware of these arrangements and makes them deliberately. A Spartan tribe, set on maintaining its warrior status, may not necessarily have a war mobilization board.)

Many of the old ideological and policy debates have been, in effect, about the question of how thick the social order ought to be. Social scientists keen on measuring thickness might use, as a first approximation, indicators such as the amount of tax exacted (as a proportion of the GNP); the size of the civil service as compared to the total labor force; the amount of time one is expected to spend serving the public (from performing jury duty to serving in the armed forces) and the community (for example, joining in anticrime patrols); and the scope of regulations advanced in the name of the public good (e.g., do they encompass personal matters such as abortion or sodomy? do they also mandate certain private economic conduct?).[22] We shall look at the proportion of values that are considered an integral part of the social order (and hence violating them is considered as undermining order) to those which members of the society are free to choose following their own normative commitments; this ratio is a particularly important indicator for differentiating various kinds of societies and paradigms.

The argument that there is a basic need for a thick social order may seem rather unremarkable, but it is contested by many individualists.[23] Some libertarians challenge the very notions of a collective actor and societal needs. Jeremy Bentham wrote that society is a fiction.[24] Margaret Thatcher proudly repeated this libertarian nostrum.[25] Others seek to maximize liberty and minimize restrictions on it in name of the social order. James K. Glassman writes, "The big idea is to place human freedom above everything else."[26] Lord Acton argued that "[l]iberty is not a means to a higher political end. It is itself the highest political end."[27] Robert P. George notes critically that libertarians take an important truth, that freedom is essential to human dignity, and stretch it until it becomes a falsehood.[28]

Most important, many libertarians and liberal individualists are troubled by social formulations of the common good that are a core part of thick social orders. They argue that each person should formulate his or her own virtue, and that public policies and mores should reflect only agreements that individuals voluntarily form.[29]

Libertarians' and liberal individualists' subtext is a fear that collective formulations of morality will lead to judging as morally inferior those who are less able to live up to them. Libertarians often fear that this, in turn, will lead to discrimination, if not laws enforcing commitment to the shared good—i.e., to a violation of liberty, libertarianism's cardinal value.

A strong presentation of this approach by a contemporary philosopher is found in an influential book by Robert Nozick, *Anarchy, State, and Utopia*. Nozick writes: "[T]here is no *social entity* with a good that undergoes some sacrifice for its own good. There are only individual people, different individual people, with their own individual lives."[30] Similarly, Ronald Dworkin defines liberalism as the conviction that "political decisions must be, so far as possible, independent of any particular conception of the good life, or of what gives value to life."[31]

And John Rawls writes at one point:

[I]ndividuals find their good in different ways, and many things may be good for one person that would not be good for another. . . . In a well-ordered society [one that applies Rawls's theory of justice], then, the plans of life of individuals are different in the sense that these plans give prominence to different aims, and persons are left free to determine their good, the view of others being counted as merely advisory.[32]

These points have been elaborated on often, especially in the debate between communitarians and liberal individualists. They have been the subject of an important and voluminous literature.[33] They are not reiterated here. (For example, no attempt is made to revisit the often-visited debate of communitarians with John Rawls.) The main point relevant to the discussion here is that while libertarians and liberal individualists do not ignore the need for social order, they not only champion a thin order but seek to limit the social order to one that is derived from and legitimated by individuals acting as free agents. In contrast, communitarians see a need for a social order that contains a set of shared values, to which individuals are taught they are obligated. Individuals may later question, challenge, rebel against, or even transform a given social order, but their starting point is a shared set of definitions of what is right versus what is wrong.[34]

COMMUNITARIAN ORDER: LARGELY VOLUNTARY

Almost any form of social order may seem attractive to people engulfed by social anarchy, whether it stems from violent crime, tribal warfare, gangs, or widespread moral disorientation. People who have experienced civil war in Lebanon, Bosnia, or Sri Lanka, or who live in the crime-ridden parts of Moscow or Washington, D.C., are rather articulate supporters of this observation. A 1996 poll found that 77 percent of Russians think order is more important than democracy, while only 9 percent endorsed the opposite view.[35] But not every social order makes for a good society. *A good society requires an order that is aligned with the moral commitments of the members.* Other forms of social order generate high social and individual costs (such as withdrawal from work, abuse of alcohol and drugs, or a high incidence of psychosomatic illnesses), and lead to numerous attempts to evade, change, or escape such order.

The challenge for those who aspire to a good society is to form and sustain—or, if it has been lost, to regenerate—a social order that is considered legitimate by its members, not merely when it is established (as contract libertarians would have it) but continuously. The new golden rule requires that the tension between one's preferences and one's social commitments be reduced by increasing the realm of duties one affirms as moral responsibilities—not the realm of duties that are forcibly imposed but the realm of responsibilities one believes one should discharge and that one believes one is fairly called upon to assume. Much of what follows is dedicated to the question of how such a unique social order, one that is ultimately based on its members' voluntary compliance, can be sustained. I should say here by way of introduction that a voluntary order is not an oxymoron. If I believe firmly that a decent human being drives safely, respectful of the community mores—and many other members of my community share this belief—the traffic will be largely orderly, relying on our moral commitments. Several colleagues suggested that I avoid the term "order" and refer instead to "community"; they suggested that the former term has a disconcerting or conservative aura to it. Some particular forms of orders do, but not those, we shall see, that are an integral part of the good society.

The starting point for such an examination is the factual observation that all forms of social order draw to some extent on coercive means (such as police and jails), "utilitarian" means (economic incentives generated by public expenditures or subsidies), and normative means (appeals to values, moral education).[36] Societies differ greatly, however, in the mix of means they employ. Totalitarian societies draw heavily on coercive means in ordering a very wide range of behavior; authoritarian societies maintain order in a similar manner, but for a significantly narrower range of behavior. Libertarian societies, which minimize the scope of the social order and seek to draw on the market even for public services (e.g., by privatizing garbage collection, welfare, schools, and even prison management), draw heavily on utilitarian means.[37] The order of good communitarian societies relies heavily on normative means (education, leadership, consensus, peer pressure, pointing out role models, exhortation, and, above all, the moral voices of communities). In this sense, the social order of good societies is a moral order.

For a social order to be able to rely heavily on normative means requires that most members of the society, most of the time, *share a commitment to a set of core values*, and that most members, most of the time, will abide by the behavioral implications of these values because they believe in them, rather than being *forced* to comply with them. It is rather self-evident that high levels of violent crime and other forms of antisocial behavior are indications that a society's order is lacking; it is much less often recognized that *a large number of police officers, tax auditors, and inspectors also indicates a deficient moral order,* even if antisocial behavior is low. Indeed, this is exactly the point at which the kind of order implied by the phrase "law and order" and the communitarian notion of a social order differ most.

The needed good order will be served by restoration of the civil (or civic) society that many have called for recently,[38] and is of merit in its own right, but by itself will not suffice to provide the kind of order a good society requires. "Civic order" is used to mean that people are civil to one another (that they do not demonize their opponents, are willing to compromise, conduct reasoned rather than impassioned discussions) and/or that a society should maintain a fabric of mediating institutions to protect individuals from the government. Or—that the government should heed the citizens' preferences. I agree that the civic order is part of the good order, but it is far too thin a concept; the civic order is often defined mainly in terms of procedure, limited to the political arena, or otherwise devoid of substantive values, as distinct from the concepts of good around which the social order of good societies is centered.[39]

Once one grants that a good society requires a social order based on commitments to and the embodiment of specific virtues, one may well ask: How does such a conception of order differ from that championed by social conservatives? We shall see that the answer lies in the status of autonomy, in the scope of conduct that the social formulation of the good seeks to encompass, and in the means of enforcement.

SOCIAL CONSERVATIVE ORDER: VIRTUE FOCUSED

The difference in approach to social order by communitarians and social conservatives can be highlighted by spelling out the latter's position. Social conservatives tend to treat social order the way individualists treat autonomy, as the primary social good. They tend not to view autonomy as if it had the same principled, primary standing as order and virtue, a key assumption of the communitarian paradigm of a good society. Ronald Beiner writes:

> The central purpose of a society, understood as a moral community, is not the maximization of autonomy, or protection of the broadest scope for the design of self-elected plans of life, but the cultivation of virtue, interpreted as excellence or as a variety of excellences, moral and intellectual.[40]

"Conservatism has been a theory of social and political order," writes Rodney Barker. He adds: "Conservatives have often distinguished their own beliefs as committed to order in preference to other values such as progress, or equality, or liberty."[41]

At the same time, social conservatives differ significantly among themselves in the extent to which they are unmindful of autonomy. Joseph de Maistre, for instance, was much less attentive to autonomy than Edmund Burke.[42] The underlying theme, though, remains, by definition, that social philosophers who do not accord primacy to social order are not considered social conservatives.

Cultural Conservatism: Toward a New National Agenda, published by the Institute for Cultural Conservatism, closes with a statement entitled "A Cultural Conservative Bill of Rights."[43] However, most of the bill consists of items that few would consider rights. The list includes Americans' "rights" to "a government that recognizes traditional culture's vital role,"[44] to "a government that respects traditional values," and to one that actively supports the family and the proper kind of education.[45]

Social conservatives tend to favor a smaller state (not involved in social welfare, not regulatory) but also a stronger state, one that is able to enforce moral codes. Robert P. George argues for using the law to enforce morality in public *and* private matters (for instance, to prohibit homosexual acts between consenting adults, even in private). He recognizes "prudential" limitations on such prohibitions, but not principled ones.[46] George's main argument is that while a decline of morality may not lead to a full-fledged disintegration of society, the decline will weaken the society as a moral and social community. One can argue whether or not the laws George favors will help sustain the moral order, but foster autonomy they do not.

Among the more moderate social conservatives is Alasdair MacIntyre. MacIntyre sees the institutions to which the Enlightenment gave birth as crumbling. The modern world, obsessed with liberty, has slain virtue, leaving us morally bereft, in a world of darkness. With modernity, MacIntyre argues, came an impulse to liberate the individual from "external morality" and to replace it with an inner moral voice. "Each moral agent now spoke unconstrained by the externalities of divine law, natural teleology or hierarchical authority; but why should anyone else now listen to him?"[47]

We try to give our opinions moral weight by asserting rights claims, but, as MacIntyre writes, "the truth is plain: *there are no such rights*, and belief in them is one with belief in witches and in unicorns."[48] As a result, he concludes: "[T]he barbarians are not waiting beyond the frontiers; they have already been governing us for quite some time."[49]

George F. Will argues that conservatives who favor a weaker government are off the mark; the promotion of virtue requires a strong government, strong enough to be able to help people deny themselves, restrain themselves against their desires. He writes: "[T]he central political problem for conservatives is to get the public to consent to government that censors their desires, refusing to fulfill many of them."[50]

Nationalism has long been a powerful, often overpowering, source of secular conservative ideologies that legitimated strong governments and order- and virtue-centered paradigms. Citizens are expected to make sacrifices and accept limitations on their liberties for one national purpose or another, often destiny. In the United States in the 1950s, for instance, social conservatives—keen to keep communism at bay—supported requiring loyalty oaths from university faculty members, blacklisting employees who were suspected of having Communist views, and firing government employees who were said to have "subversive" viewpoints.[51]

Many social conservatives base their position on religion. They hold that social order should be based on virtues prescribed by God and those who represent Him on earth, and that the dictates of religious values ought to take priority over considerations of autonomy. The hierarchical nature of the Catholic Church and much of its theology is probably the best-known example. Father Richard John Neuhaus repeated the often-expressed religious idea that people are free to choose, as long as they choose the Lord's way. Thus one cardinal difference between the social conservative and the communitarian paradigm advanced here is the standing of autonomy. It is basic to the communitarian paradigm; it is secondary or derivative in social conservative paradigms.

PERVASIVE VERSUS CORE; IMPOSED VERSUS VOLUNTARY

Aside from the status of autonomy, a major difference between social conservatives and communitarians (and among social conservatives) exists in their views regarding the legitimate ways to sustain virtue. While communitarians basically have faith in faith and seek to convince people of the value of their position, relying on the moral voice of the community, education, persuasion, and exhortation, social conservatives are much more inclined to rely on the law to promote values in which they believe. Moreover, while many social conservatives seek to remain within the confines of constitutional democracy—as they seek massive legislation to institute the virtues to which they are committed—strong conservatives, and above all authoritarians and fundamentalists, appeal to what they consider higher laws than those made by "man," and are willing to establish theocracies.[52]

Another major difference is that although communitarians, at least in terms of the paradigm advanced here, limit the virtues the society favors to a set of core values while legitimating differences on other normative matters, the scope of values social conservatives promote is much more pervasive and unitary. Social conservatives see few areas of behavior which they are willing to leave open to personal and subgroup choice. If the individualists are virtue-avoiders, strong social conservatives are virtue-monopolizers. What one eats, drinks, and reads are all morally infused.

Paul Weyrich, striking a relatively moderate position, writes, "We are talking about Christianizing America. We are talking about simply spreading the Gospel in a political context."[53] Georgia Republican Joseph Morecraft's agenda is even more pervasive: "The only hope for the United States is the total Christianization of the country at all levels—a thoroughly Christian republic."[54]

Less moderate is a group that preaches dominion theology. It "holds that Christians . . . have inherited the Old Testament mandates, one of the most fundamental of which is in Genesis 1:28, where God says to Adam and Eve 'have dominion over . . . *every living thing that moveth upon the earth* [emphasis added].'" Dominion theologians interpret this passage to mean that believers are entitled to control all the world's major institutions.[55] Such control may entail enforcing Mosaic Law instead of a legislature's, churches and families taking over education and welfare completely, or even using stoning as a punishment. At the extreme, other religions become heresy, and heresy becomes treason. Morecraft states: "Jesus Christ is the unrivaled monarch of the political process of the United States of America. Christians . . . may not rest until His divine rights and absolute authority are recognized and submitted to in the executive, legislative, and judicial branches of our civil government at the national, state, and local levels."[56]

In short, all social conservative paradigms differ from the communitarian paradigm as advanced here in that they are more order-focused and less concerned with autonomy as a primary virtue, have a much more pervasive and unitary normative agenda, and are more inclined to rely on the state than on the moral voice for the ultimate enforcement of values. As each of these propositions raises important issues, it should be noted that they are stated here merely by way of introduction. They are fully treated below.[57]

AUTONOMY FULLY RESPECTFUL OF ORDER

INDIVIDUALISTS AND UNBOUNDED AUTONOMY

Individualists' view that autonomy is the core virtue, not to be trumped by any other, mirrors their arguments against social formulation of the good: Individuals should be free to make their own choices (unless they harm other individuals).[58] Reference is typically made to legal rights and freedom from government. Special significance is attributed to individuals' rights to have their lives protected and to control and use their property. This position is most explicitly embraced by libertarians and laissez-faire conservatives.[59] While individualists do not deny in principle the need for curbing individuals, especially not when these limits are set socially and not by the government, in effect they tend to treat most specific claims on the individual with suspicion, if not hostility, at best with benign neglect, as we shall see.

Large parts of several social sciences are based in individualistic assumptions. These sciences assume that one can and should explain social phenomena in terms of the attributes and actions of individuals, and ignore or explicitly deny the importance of macro, historical, or cultural factors and forces. Individualism in social science is not a passing fad or a small branch. It has played a major role in psychology. Much of neoclassical economics, especially in the United States, is individualistic; so are public choice theory in political science, exchange sociology, and a significant part of legal studies (law and economics). The University of Chicago is a center for social science conducted within such an individualist paradigm; among the most often cited are Richard A. Epstein and Richard A. Posner. Terry Eastland is also referred to in this context, as is David Frum among younger writers.

Although individualists vary a great deal (for instance, even Mill's own position varies considerably from book to book), the rather familiar public philosophy and policy recommendations built on these divergent individualists' ideas are focused on one overarching concern:[60] Can more of the public business (social security, public schools, police departments, prisons, tax collections) be privatized? Can private business be further deregulated? Can taxes be reduced and funds returned to private hands? Among the more radical libertarian ideas of ways to further curtail the state role are the abolition of border controls on immigration and a shutdown of the Food and Drug Administration. Some even suggest that criminal justice be replaced by civil justice, in which considerations of moral and social values are ignored and violators are punished by having to compensate their victims who bring suits against them.[61] There is much less concern with the question of whether individual tastes and ambitions need to be balanced with concerns for the social order, either because it is assumed that such an order will arise automatically from the aggregation of individual acts (the invisible hand) or that, if individuals put their minds to it, they would heed the proper self-limitation. But there is no principled need for socially provided mores.

Civil libertarians are not usually considered in the same breath as other libertarians,[62] although like other individualists they are strong champions of autonomy and are uncomfortable with the concept of social responsibility. Civil libertarians are concerned with rights and not duties; with entitlements and not with national service, tithes, and taxes. Above all, they oppose guidance by the government and, more indirectly by others, as to what one ought to do. The ACLU Briefing Paper on Freedom of Expression states: "Governments by nature are always seeking to expand their powers beyond proscribed boundaries, the government of the United States being no exception. . . . "[63] The paper, which depicts the ACLU as the "Guardian of Liberty," states: "In every era of American history, the government has tried to expand its authority at the expense of individual rights. . . . The mission of the ACLU is to assure that the Bill of Rights—amendments to the Constitution that guard against unwarranted governmental control—are preserved for each new generation."[64] Ira Glasser, the executive director of the ACLU, adds: "The timeless tendency for government to overstep its constitutional bounds demands a permanent counterforce of citizens. For liberty is fragile, and forever vulnerable to the encroachments of illegitimate power."[65] F. LaGard Smith, a critic who has studied the ACLU for years, observes: "[W]hat the ACLU does share with the militant fringe of the extreme right is a perverse, deep-seated distrust of government. Merely mention . . . the FBI . . . and the ACLU's blood pressure jumps by a factor of ten. . . . This shared distrust of federal government largely explains why—despite vastly different ideologies—the extreme Right and the extreme Left have reacted almost in unison to warn against threatening government incursions into civil liberties."[66]

Most often, if faced with measures that enhance public order, civil libertarians demur. Over the last decades, the ACLU has objected to the following measures that aim to restore public order: metal detectors in airports to stop skyjackings and terrorism (one of the ACLU's arguments was that metal detectors would condition Americans to a police state);[67] drug testing of school bus drivers, train engineers, pilots, and police; roadblocks to screen for drunken drivers; use of lie detectors, even for those who were notified in advance of employment that their jobs (for example, in highly sensitive national security positions) require such tests; and keeping data banks on criminals. The ACLU refused to support measures to restrict in any manner the use of any kind of guns, including assault rifles and machine guns; it opposed school uniforms, AIDS tests (even for prostitutes), and numerous measures to reform campaign finances.

The ACLU has also strongly opposed measures that might help the moral elements of the social order, for example by curbing the production of child pornography (which the ACLU argued will have a "chilling" effect on movie producers); it fought to allow lawyers the right to file false bills ("legislation is too broadly crafted . . . "); and it opposes the V-chip, a piece of technology that enables *parents* to control what their children see on their home televisions. The ACLU fought for the rights of the North American Man/Boy Love Association (NAMBLA), which seeks to abolish laws concerning the age of consent for sex and advocates pedophilia, to meet in a public library,[68] and to fight for the right of a vice president of NAMBLA's New York chapter, who was actively promoting pedophilia, to teach in a public school. In short, both civil and other libertarians share a strong commitment to autonomy and less concern with policies whose direct purpose is to foster the social context individualism requires, to shore up a social order.

Strong individualists often define liberty as the right to choose. The same individualists, as an indication that they are not unmindful of the social order, tend to add that an individual is free to act only as long as he or she is causing no harm to others. However, the concept of harm is not a reliable guide. It is unclear whether it refers only to physical harm (in which cases violating someone's right to free speech, for instance, is not a "harm") or also includes psychological harm (in which case breaking up a romance might be prohibited). The level of harm that is to be avoided is also an unanswered issue. If all harm is to be avoided, individuals would lose practically all ability to act. For example, my operating an automobile might harm your ability to breathe pristine air. To the extent that the principle is interpreted to mean that the harm to others should not exceed the gain to ego, or not affect some Pareto, or some other theoretical distribution in an unfavorable manner, such determinations are impossible to make under most circumstances.

To examine the capacity of the calculus of harm to reach principled conclusions about the legitimacy of actions, the following anecdote may serve. In the late 1980s, a professor at the Harvard Business School used Braniff Airlines as a case study. In the case, the head of Braniff was asked by a customer if the airline would still be in business five months hence. He answered that he was not sure. The class felt that he should have lied because the harm to workers, creditors, and stockholders resulting from his honesty was likely to exceed the benefits to the customers. This led to a yearlong seminar of senior faculty to explore the issue. As a participant in that seminar, I found that the outcome of such calculations depends on the weight one assigns to the interests of the different groups. If one counted all groups as equal, lying was called for according to the calculus of harm because there are more groups to be hurt by truth telling than would benefit from not telling the truth. If one assigned a high weight to the customers, the result would be the opposite. But the determination of which weights one assigns is either arbitrary or reflects one's ideology. Moreover, the suggestion by some seminar members that the CEO should not have lied, because lying would have diminished the social fund of trust, is even less measurable.

Most profoundly, there are not now and never were freestanding individuals of the kind individualists envision. People are socially constituted and continually penetrated by culture, by social and moral influences, and by one another. Businesses advertise products in ways that motivational research has shown will appeal to their customers' infantile and impulsive urges. The youth culture promotes risky, irrational behavior. Social bonds tug at people unconsciously. In short, the choices made by individuals are not free from cultural and social factors. To remove, on libertarian grounds, limits set by the public, far from enhancing autonomy, merely leaves individuals subject to all the other influences, which reach them not as information or environmental factors they can analyze and cope with, but as invisible messages of which they are unaware and that sway them in nonrational ways.

The indefensibility of the individualists' notion of unbounded autonomy stands out in their interpretation of the Fifth Amendment clause against takings. They argue that it implies that if the government imposes any regulations on a private property owner, compensation should be made to that owner.[69] This notion disregards that we are not only owners but also members of one or more communities. For instance, if ego pours toxic waste into a river that runs through his property, he has obligations to those who are downriver, just as those who are upriver have obligations to him. The government acts here merely as an enforcer of community norms. True, there is room to ask if the government is going overboard when it acts as such an enforcer, or if it has been captured by special interests when it imposes such rules, as George J. Stigler argues.[70] But the fact that the government occasionally does extend its reach beyond reason or is captured, does not legitimate the notion that, in principle, individuals should be free to do with their private property as they wish, or must be compensated if they are to be attentive to the most elementary needs of their fellow human beings and community.

Libertarians may argue that if someone owns private property, that person is free to act as he or she deems fit on that property, and if others in the community do not approve, they may stay away (or pay enough to change the undesired behavior). If the roads are privately owned, the owners may test all those who drive for driving under the influence of intoxicants, and those who object need not drive on these particular roads. But this is a legalistic answer that is morally blind. The moral issue stands: Is the owner of the road doing the right thing (as distinct from having a right) in testing people? The same issue informs all the other moral claims that are put on individuals in the name of others and the community, from being tested for HIV if they are sexually active to being tested for drugs if they drive school buses, from allowing them to be searched for guns before entering schools to requiring people to be vaccinated.

Isaiah Berlin's often-cited discussion of negative and positive liberty is sometimes considered as reaching beyond the individualist mold. Actually, he provides a rather unbounded definition for *both* kinds of liberty. Negative liberty, Berlin writes, in the typically individualist mode, "is simply the area within which a man can act unobstructed by others."[71] (Note that no limits, including the concern for the rights of others, let alone the far-reaching implications of honoring these rights, are mentioned.) Positive liberty is one's right to do things one affirmatively seeks to do. Writes Berlin:

> The "positive" sense of the word "liberty" derives from the wish on the part of the individual to be his own master. . . . I wish, above all, to be conscious of myself as a thinking, willing, active being, bearing responsibility for my choices and able to explain them by reference to my own ideas and purposes.[72]

This definition relies on the actor's internal reason to decide whether or not he or she will be other-minded, and if so, what this entails. However, it still presumes unbounded autonomy. Hence, as I see it, at this point Berlin exemplifies a position individualists often embrace.

SOCIALLY CONSTRUCTED AUTONOMY

The characterization of autonomy the good society requires does not treat it, as is often the case, as merely an individual virtue of persons who cherish freedom and who conduct themselves in ways that sustain that virtue. Reference here is to a societal attribute, an attribute of a society that provides structured opportunities and legitimation for individual and subgroup expression of their particular values, needs, and preferences. To signify that I deal with virtue as a societal and not a personal attribute, I will use the term "social virtue."

Socially constructed autonomy enhances the ability of the society to adapt to change, to be metastable. Providing structured opportunities for individual and subgroup expression balances a tendency of those in power to avoid making needed changes in social formations and public policies following changes in the external environment or in internal societal compositions. For societies to be stable, they must be metastable, that is, to keep the same overarching pattern, they must continue to remake themselves. (The difference between plain stability and metastability is often overlooked. It is akin to the difference between making repairs on a sailboat and converting a sailboat into a steamboat: It is still a boat which fulfills the same function and may have the same destination, but has a different structure. Thus, while a society needs some form of constructed autonomy if it is to successfully adapt and balance the dual virtues, the society may change profoundly the specific ways autonomy is constructed.)

Societies that exert high pressure on their members to conform, and thus constrict their members' autonomy, tend to suffer from a lack of adaptation. Japan is often reported to be a society that is highly conformist as well as one that has generated relatively few scientific or artistic breakthroughs as compared to Western societies.[73] I will not try to determine whether these observations about Japan are valid; whatever the final data, the very debate serves to highlight the need for autonomy.

Totalitarian societies, which allow for even less autonomy, are typically even less adaptive. They tend to find out much later than those of democracies when their policies are erroneous. (While I apply terms that are often employed to characterize political regimes, such as democratic and authoritarian, they apply here to societal patterns. Thus, at issue is not merely the role of elections, legislatures, and such in the polity, but also the role of voluntary associations, and religious organizations, the treatment of the family, and many other societal factors.)

Furthermore, institutionalized autonomy allows a society to take into account that the members of society differ greatly in their capabilities and their specific environmental circumstances. To try to force them all to abide by the same rules (for instance, to insist that they all need to study calculus or a particular foreign language) sharply undercuts their ability to serve the society, aside from diminishing what they can do for themselves. This issue often arises in the area of education. Some societies control, on a national basis, the details of school curricula, while good societies leave much more room for local autonomy. The same issue is faced in numerous other areas of social policy.

Similar in importance is the opportunity for the expression of subgroup differences, whether these are mainly differences in values or are chiefly based on economic or power interests. Among the forms of governments, federalism has been touted as being more conducive to accommodating differences among subgroups than a unitary state. Discussions of devolution and of constitutional revisions to enhance federalism, suggestions to introduce a regional parliament in Scotland, and to enhance the rights of provinces in Canada and in many other countries—typically couched in legal, political, and institutional terms—are, in effect, discussions of how much autonomy to grant to various subgroups instead of holding them all to the same unitary, national standards. Moreover, the lines of subgroup autonomy are not limited to geographical or legal entities, such as states and local governments. Religious, racial, ethnic, or other subgroups all seek a measure of autonomy. The right not to work on Saturdays rather than on Sundays is a well-known case in point.

American public philosophy tends to base respect for autonomy not on societal needs but on the inalienable rights or the legal rights of the members of society, and the term "liberty" or "freedom" rather than autonomy is typically employed. I use the term "autonomy" to stress that it encompasses both what is typically considered as individual freedom and the needs for self-expression, innovation, creativity, and self-government as well as legitimation of the expression of subgroup differences.

AUTONOMY IN THE GOOD SOCIETY

Generals are often said to prepare to fight the last war rather than the next one. Western intellectuals, with long experience in confronting first authoritarianism, then totalitarianism, and more recently religious fundamentalism, are quite keenly aware of the dangers of excessive order, especially of the coercive variety. These intellectuals are less prepared to face the danger that ideologization of unbounded autonomy poses, as the champions of choice and self-expression undermine the moral taboos on antisocial behavior. A discussion of the difference between socially bounded and anarchic, unbounded autonomy highlights the kind of autonomy a good society requires.

While it is possible to think abstractly about individuals apart from a community, it must be noted that if individuals are actually deprived of the stable and positive affective attachments communities best provide, they exhibit very few of the attributes commonly associated with the notion of a freestanding person presumed by the individualist paradigm. Such individuals are unable to be reasonable and reasoning members of a civil society. Residents of large cities who live an isolated life in high-rise buildings and have no other sources of social attachments (e.g., at work) have been found to tend to be mentally unstable, impulsive, prone to suicide, and otherwise predisposed to mental and psychosomatic illnesses.[74] Studies of inmates who have been isolated from the general prison population (compared to those who are allowed to remain integrated into the inmate groups and culture), and of people isolated in psychological experiments, further highlight the importance of the social fabric—of communal attachments—for individuality in general and the ability to reason and act freely in particular.[75]

One needs to go a step beyond the well-taken and often-cited observations by Michael Sandel in his criticisms of individualist liberals and by Charles Taylor in his powerful criticism of atomism. Sandel points out that individuals have "encumbered selves" and defines those encumbrances as "those loyalties and convictions whose moral force consists partly in the fact that living by them is inseparable from understanding ourselves as the particular persons we are. . . . "[76] This is in opposition to individualist liberals who "insist that we view ourselves as independent selves, independent in the sense that our identity is never tied to our aims and attachments."[77]

Charles Taylor argues that atomists hold the ontological position that:

[I]n (a), the order of explanation, you can and ought to account for social actions, structures, and conditions in terms of properties of the constituent individuals; and in (b), the order of deliberation, you can and ought to account for social goods in terms of concatenations of individual goods.[78]

He critiques this view, arguing that "an instrumental stance to our own feelings divides us within, splits reason from sense. And the atomistic focus on our individual goals dissolves community and divides us from each other."[79] He further argues:

[T]he very definition of a republican regime as classically understood requires an ontology different from atomism, and which falls outside atomism-infected common sense. It requires that we probe the relations of identity and community, and distinguish the different possibilities, in particular, the possible place of we-identities as against merely convergent I-identities, and the consequent role of common as against convergent goods.[80]

The question has been raised whether these valid communitarian observations are merely ontological observations or also normative ones, "is" or also "ought" statements. As Michael Mosher points out:

[Sandel] has cast doubt on the foundational fact of an earlier generation of liberal arguments about rights: persons are *not* always separate. Whether, however, persons *ought* to be separate for certain purposes (self-appraisal, the capacity to honor duties to strangers, the possibility of living in a plural and adjudicative world) is still open to question.[81]

The extra step one needs to undertake is to note that not only are human beings social by nature but also that their sociability enhances their human and moral potential. Social thinking has to cease viewing communal attachments as cannonballs chained to inmates' legs, needed to maintain their stability but "encumbering." The social fabric sustains, nourishes, and enables individuality rather than diminishes it. True, as with all good things, from food to medications, an excess of sociability can cause major problems of its own. These include curtailing individual rights in the name of community needs; suppressing creativity in the name of conformity; and even suppresing a sense of self, losing individuality in a mesh of familial or communal relations.[82] But in good measure, communal attachments and individuality go hand-in-hand, enrich one another, and are not antagonistic. The self is enriched and, as we shall see, ennobled by being social; it is the asocial self that is held back by the *lack* of positive multiple attachments.

The greatest danger to autonomy arises when the social moorings of individuals are severed. The atomization of individuals or the reduction of communities to mobs, which result in the individual's loss of competence and self-identity, has historically generated societal conditions that led to totalitarianism, a grand loss of autonomy. Such atomization preceded the rise of totalitarian movements and governments in Russia after its defeat in the 1905 war with Japan, and in Germany in the 1920s following its defeat in World War I and the ruinous effects of runaway inflation and mass unemployment.[83] Even when atomization is at levels lower than which a totalitarian regime would be "invited," the result is a high level of anomie, alienation, withdrawal, and antisocial behavior, as witnessed in major urban centers over the last decades.[84]

The most common antidotes to mass society, already noted by Tocqueville as a cornerstone of civic society, are the "intermediary bodies" that stand between the individual and the state.[85] It is often overlooked in this context that many of these bodies are not the vaunted voluntary associations, with their meager bonding power (from the March of Dimes to chess clubs), but communities, with their much stronger interpersonal attachments (especially ethnic, racial, and religious ones, as well as residential communities).

The communitarian paradigm, at least as advanced here, recognizes the need to nourish social attachments as part of the effort to maintain social order while ensuring that such attachments will not suppress all autonomous expressions. That is, a good society does not favor the social good over individual choices or vice versa; it favors societal formations that serve the two dual social virtues in careful equilibrium. We shall see that this societal pattern, in turn, requires: (a) a reliance mainly on education, leadership, persuasion, faith, and moral dialogues, rather than the law, for sustaining virtues; (b) defining a core of values that need to be promoted—a substantive core that is richer than those that make procedures meritorious; but (c) not a pervasive ideology or the kinds of religion that leave little room for autonomy.[86]

(The discussion so far has been largely conceptual. Empirical indicators that allow one to establish more clearly whether or not autonomy is properly protected and bounded are introduced, once the paradigm is examined in a specific, historical context, in chapter 3. I should also note that a discussion of the role of socioeconomic factors as both enablers and constrictors of autonomy, while briefly touched upon in chapter 3, is a vast and important subject that requires a separate volume to be properly treated.)

In short, all bodies of thought and belief build on a primary concept. For individualists the cornerstone of a good society is the freestanding person; for social conservatives, it is a pervasive set of social virtues embodied in the society or state. For communitarians, it suffices as a first approximation to argue that a good society requires a balance between autonomy and order. And the order has to be of a special kind: voluntary and limited to core values rather than imposed or pervasive. And autonomy has to be contextuated within a social fabric of bonds and values rather than unbounded. A much closer examination of the relationship between the dual virtues that makes the good society follows in chapter 2.

IMPLICATIONS FOR PRACTICE AND POLICY

As long as the discussion remains at rather high levels of abstraction, many readers may find little to argue with in the preceding exploration. However, when one turns to the policy implications of the paradigm, the differences among individualists, social conservatives, and communitarians stand out rather clearly.

THE FIRST AMENDMENT AS A TEST CASE

An examination of the implications for the right to free speech, as embodied in the First Amendment, is a fine place to start. Civil libertarians (and to a lesser extent, but still strongly, many other individualists) hold that freedom of speech is the most absolute of all our rights, and that it should not be curbed except for the sake of social order, and then if and only if such limitation is shown, under strict scrutiny, to be justified. Alexander Meiklejohn writes:

> [No] one who reads with care the text of the First Amendment can fail to be startled by its absoluteness. The phrase, "Congress shall make no law . . . abridging the freedom of speech," is unqualified. It admits of no exceptions. To say that no laws of a given type shall be made means that no laws of that type shall, under any circumstances, be made.[87]

Hence, limitations on this right through codes that prohibit expressions of hate, bans on pornography and violence in media, and expansions of state secrecy acts and libel laws, are strongly opposed by most individualists. Civil libertarians further argue that the best treatment for problems that arise from free speech is more speech (e.g., about the undesirable social consequences of pornography) rather than reliance on state controls.

Social conservatives, in contrast, are quite willing to introduce censorship, especially when it comes to national security needs and to curbing what they consider immoral and indecent speech. They support legislation to prohibit the sale of pornography, to restrict obscene expression in the media and on the Internet, and to treat the possession of pornography the same as that of illicit drugs.[88] Theodore Baehr, a steering committee member of the Coalition on Revival (a conservative Christian group), heads the Christian Film and Television Commission. He has called for a film code that would impose a legal ban on "lustful kissing" and "dances that suggest or represent sexual actions." His film code declares, "No movie shall be produced that will lower the moral standards of those that see it."[89] Thomas Storck, writing in the *New Oxford Review*, a serious publication whose writers include many thoughtful Catholics and other social conservatives, makes "A Case for Censorship."[90] He points out that he favors more than simply censoring pornography; he would also cover "expressions of erroneous *ideas*."[91] He states:

> Ideas lead to actions, and bad ideas often lead to bad acts, bringing harm to individuals and possible ruin to societies. Just as the state has the right to restrict and direct a person's actions when he is a physical threat to the community, so also in the matter of intellectual or cultural threats, the authorities have duties to protect the community.[92]

The communitarian paradigm advanced here, in line with its predisposition to build a moral rather than a statist order, draws in its quest to curb the abuse of freedom of speech on (a) a specific moral concept, (b) community-based, rather than state-based, mechanisms, and (c) a limited extension of the existing category of punishable speech.

Right Versus Rightness. A communitarian way to deal with vile, hateful speech builds on a distinction between the legal right to speak and the moral rightness of what is spoken. As William A. Galston writes:

> Rights give reasons to others not to interfere coercively with me in the performance of protected acts; however, they do not in themselves give me a sufficient reason to perform these acts. There is a gap between rights and rightness.[93]

While respecting the legal right of individuals to engage in obscene and inflammatory speech, a community is fully entitled, in effect called upon, to inform those who spout venom that it is deeply offended by their speech. Members of the community are well within their rights when they seek to dissociate themselves from people who speak that way.

Those who wonder if such expression of disapproval by a community has an effect should note the de-escalation of the rhetoric of talk-radio hosts, militia leaders, and politicians after they were roundly criticized in the United States following the 1995 bombing in Oklahoma City and in Israel after the assassination of Prime Minister Yitzhak Rabin later that year. Similarly, after Time Warner first rebuffed William J. Bennett's public outcry about the foul rap songs it issued, the media giant fired the executives involved and sold that music division. It has been a long time since Jesse Jackson spoke about New York as "Hymie-town." Even Louis Farrakhan has become more circumspect. In short, community urgings can go a long way to encourage members of the community to express themselves in a civil manner and to make most expressions adhere to some standards of civility and decency.

Community Mechanisms. Beyond the moral voices of community— articulated by intellectuals, the clergy, and individuals expressing themselves anywhere from the watercooler to the back fence—the community has tools that enable it to discourage inappropriate forms of speech. These nongovernmental mechanisms are often ignored, and calls to rely on them more extensively are at best reluctantly embraced by individualist intellectuals and policy makers.

The way the British press dealt with a gruesome law case provides a case in point. In 1995, Britain had a trial that drew nearly as much attention as the O. J. Simpson trial. Rosemary West was charged with the murders of several girls, including her own daughter, in a case that resembled Jeffrey Dahmer's. The British press, including the tabloids, agreed among themselves not to publish certain particularly disconcerting details of the ways the victims were murdered. Specifically, television stations agreed with one another not to show pictures of dismembered victims. They feared that such exposure would "define deviance down"[94] and vulgarize the society, which is one reason that most civilized societies have stopped public hangings.

Such voluntary self-limitation by the American media is far from unknown. When O. J. Simpson tried to sell his videotape containing his versions of the events leading to his trial, 60 percent of radio and television stations, ranging from major networks to the *National Enquirer*, rejected his advertisements.[95] While American television has little trouble showing the gamut of gratuitous violence, network television generally has refrained from showing frontal nudity (excepting on some late-night shows and on cable). Many television stations still beep some obscenities off the air. (However, footage of people relieving themselves in bathrooms is a recent tasteless rage.) And most publications will not carry an openly hateful op-ed piece or one that is deeply offensive—for example, one that argues that African Americans are inferior or that there was no Holocaust. In Congress, if a member engages in speech that is offensive to another member, that person is under pressure to apologize, putting some limits on what is said.

Those who fear that it amounts to censorship to suggest that, in order to curb more hate and foul speech, we should increase our reliance on these informal social mechanisms should note the difference between the government coercively limiting expression and various media outlets freely setting their own limits. First, one recognizes that a particular television station or journal does not have an obligation to air or publish any particular speech. Second, unlike government controls that tend to be fairly total, informal controls always have extensive exceptions. These allow a *Village Voice*, a *Penthouse*, or even a *Soldier of Fortune* to provide a voice for those who feel strongly that they must cross the lines set by the community for appropriate speech and for those who seek to hear them. That is, informal mechanisms ensure that while they protect most of us from speech that has no redeeming merit, they also ensure that even this sort of speech will have some outlets. Still, much is gained when such speech is treated as tolerable but not respectable or even acceptable, versus when it becomes a regular part of daily expressions.

Limited Role for Government. When the absolutist stance of civil libertarians is challenged on the grounds that there is already a category of punishable speech (one cannot shout "Fire!" in a crowded theater), and it is suggested that this category might be expanded for the common good, libertarians often respond that victims of free speech are a "necessary price we pay for a free society." Only after being repeatedly challenged did Nadine Strossen, the president of the ACLU, concede that speech might be somewhat limited, and then only after extreme scrutiny to determine if there is an imminent danger resulting from the speech.[96]

What is the underlying logic that explains existing exceptions to the First Amendment and helps define a line between the exceptions and all other speech? This line is particularly important because libertarians are concerned that, even if it were justifiable to punish some speech on its demerit, it would not be acceptable because banning some speech would soon lead to banning much more. (This kind of argument is often referred to as the danger of a slippery slope.[97])

The answer seems to be that in the case of shouting "Fire!" the form of speech is too closely associated with an action that directly endangers lives to be allowed. Note, though, that nobody claims that every time a person shouts "Fire!" it will cause some people to be trampled in a mad rush to escape. There is only a presumption of a relatively high probability—not certainty.

I suggest that a few other forms of speech we now tolerate actually fall into this category, and hence might be prohibited. Take, for instance, statements like those of G. Gordon Liddy, who informed his audience of how best to shoot federal agents, saying: "Go for a head shot [because] they're going to be wearing bulletproof vests."[98] A ban on such speech does "qualify" on the grounds that it directly facilitates murder. Drawing on the same criterion of proximity, one would ban meetings to exchange tips on how to commit crimes, for instance, or meetings of NAMBLA on how to seduce young children. Such bans should not be the mainstay, but one tool in protecting the moral order, while not intruding unduly into the realm of autonomy.

SPEED LIMITS, SEAT BELTS, AND MOTORCYCLE HELMETS

Public policies that require members of the community to use various safety devices that clearly save numerous lives, enhance social order and curb the autonomy of some but enhance that of many others. These policies have been adamantly opposed by individualists. In effect, the 104th Congress repealed the federal mandate that required states to enact highway safety regulations or lose federal funding. The argument that the states are better suited to tailor these laws to their specific needs (e.g., states with relatively low populations and long distances are said to be more suitable for higher speed limits than others) is empirically ill founded, but not the principal issue at stake here. What is at stake is individualist, especially libertarian, opposition to such restrictions on individual behavior emanating from any level of government.

Strong individualists who have attacked such laws ignore the fact that, by their own criteria, these laws are justified. Individuals who choose to drive without restraining devices do endanger others and impose public costs they do not cover. It has been argued that every act causes some damage to others and some public costs—e.g., the consumption of any good requires production, which uses up scarce resources, causes some pollution, and so on. And that if one is to deny individuals the "right" to choose to drive without a seat belt, one may as well prohibit skydiving, skiing, and many other activities. However, driving without restraints is much more directly linked to causing fatalities and the wounding of others, and imposes much larger public costs, than these other activities. While this cannot be detailed here, the argument could be settled if libertarians would stipulate that if this is empirically verified, they would support public policies that require the use of safety restraints.

For communitarians, limits on speed and requirements to use seat belts and airbags are clearly justified both from individual and community viewpoints because they serve a most elementary foundation of liberty—sustaining life; and of social order—not causing wanton, easily preventable, significant harm to others and the common good. A typical finding is that a small increase in the speed limit from 55 mph to 65 mph on rural interstate highways in Michigan, far short of abolishing the speed limit, resulted in a 27 percent increase in fatalities in 1990 compared to the last year of the 55 mph speed limit on rural interstates.[99] People who lose control of their cars clearly endanger others and draw on scarce public resources to attend to them. Above all, the children of drivers killed unnecessarily are often left to become public charges. In short, there seem to be compelling reasons to favor public policies that promote the use of safety devices and to suggest that they are compatible with the communitarian view of the good society.

TWO

Order *and* Autonomy?

As a first approximation, it sufficed to suggest that a good society requires both a moral order and a bounded autonomy. We can, however, gain a better grip on the specific relationship between these dual virtues. In doing so, we must avoid the trap of thinking that the more order that is imposed on us, the fewer choices we have, and vice versa—that the more liberties we take, the less order there will be. To spell out the actual relationship between order and autonomy three questions need to be addressed: First, is there one specific combination that ensures a good society, or can it be configured from different "mixes" of order and autonomy? Second, what specific effects does an increase in social order have on the level of autonomy and vice versa once we realize that this is not a zero-sum relationship? Finally, what new insights do we gain into the societal condition, especially the ability of a society to rejuvenate itself, once we recognize the unique relationship between order and autonomy?

A DIVERSITY OF COMMUNITARIAN AMALGAS

Communitarian societies do not all exhibit the same combination of order and autonomy. And a communitarian society can add (or subtract) some measures of autonomy or of order, and still maintain its basic pattern.

For example, by several measures, autonomy in Britain is weaker than in the United States. The citizens' (and thus the media's) right to public information is more restricted in Britain than in the United States. Britain, unlike the United States, has an Official Secrets Act, which treats the publication by a newspaper of secret state information as a serious offense, even when national security is not at stake.[1] According to the British Prevention of Terrorism Act, persons suspected of terrorist activities can be detained for two to five days without a hearing, without ever being brought before a judge.[2] In 1992, to deter crime, Britain added surveillance cameras to public spaces, such as squares, streets, sports complexes, churches, and graveyards.[3] In the United States, such surveillance is largely limited to private spaces. A British law enacted in 1995 stipulates that people arrested for a criminal offense will be warned that if they do not answer questions put to them by the police, their silence may be used as evidence if they are brought to trial. Prayers are mandatory in British schools. Still, according to most observers, Britain is a rather free and orderly society, a far from perfect—yet a relatively communitarian—society.

Additional differences among societies that are communitarian to one extent or another can be illuminated by a comparison of sexual conduct in Scandinavian societies, which have a stronger element of autonomy than in Britain. At the same time, Britain has a longer and stronger tradition of protecting autonomy than Germany, where, in turn, Berlin has more tolerance for individual and subgroup differences than small towns in Bavaria. All are rather imperfect communitarian societies at best, but all fall within the communitarian range (though Bavarian towns may be rather close to the social conservative segment).

THE INVERTING SYMBIOTIC RELATIONSHIP

The specific relationship between order and autonomy is different from most other relationships with which we are familiar. We already saw that it is not zero sum, in which the more a society develops order, the less autonomy it has, and vice versa. Nor is the relationship one of zero-plus, in which the factors complement one another, say the ways loans from the World Bank may be combined with reduction of trade barriers by first world nations, making for a larger total amount of aid. The relationship is not one in which the two elements cancel each other out the way bases neutralize acids. We move closer—but not close enough—when we examine symbiotic relationships, in which two actors *enrich* one another rather than merely work well together. For example, plover birds and crocodiles are said to be symbiotically related: The birds stand in the mouths of crocodiles, eating worms and leeches that bother the crocodiles. The rare relationship we observe at the foundation of the communitarian society is a *blending of two basic formations that—up to a point—enhance one another (so that in a society that has more of one, the other grows stronger as a direct result), a symbiotic relationship; but if either element intensifies beyond a given level, it begins to diminish the other: the same two formations become antagonistic.* Lacking a better term, I refer to this unusual relationship as inverting symbiosis.[4] This, I shall show next, is the relationship between ordering and autonomizing formations, the constituent elements of communitarian societies. (One may ask if a society can attain ever higher levels of order *and* autonomy, as long as those are kept in equilibrium. The implication of inverting symbiosis is that at high levels it is impossible to prevent these elements from becoming contradictory.)

To support this observation, it is useful to engage in a mental experiment in which one starts from a very low level of community—e.g., in a recently completed high-rise building—and assumes that some social agents—community organizers, for instance—start to strengthen social bonds and to foster a culture among the new residents. To a point, *both* social order and the individual members' autonomy will be enhanced.[5] As the residents cease to be strangers, come to know one another as people and develop some measure of communal attachments, they will feel less isolated, have a stronger sense of self and a more secure autonomy, and be voluntarily more mindful of their responsibilities, such as parking in the marked spaces and not littering in shared areas.

However, if the newly founded community continuously increases its expectations of its members, a point will be reached at which the two formations will start to undercut one another. Thus, if the ordering formations grow stronger and stronger, not only will the members' autonomy decline, but the communal bonds will fray as social responsibilities turn into imposed duties and opposition to the community will grow, which in turn will undermine the social order. This is what happens in totalitarian regimes: While initial calls for new social responsibilities are often rather warmly received, as these regimes escalate their demands, alienation grows.

In contrast, when autonomizing formations grow stronger and stronger they reach a point at which not only will the service to the shared purposes be denied (as happens when privatizing and reduction of the public sector is pushed to extremes) but the autonomy of millions of individuals who depend (in varying degrees) on the community for their basic needs—from protection to schooling—decreases. In the terms used here, at a particular point, the relation in these communities moved from the mutually enhancing zone to the antagonistic zone.[6] Not only is one unable to eliminate the basic human tension between order and autonomy, reflected in both the old and the new golden rule, but also ignoring the special nature of this relationship leads to considerable misunderstanding.

Moreover, once one recognizes the unusual relationship between social order and autonomy, many arguments can be disentangled by applying the concept of inverting symbiosis. To illustrate and document this point, three examples will be discussed in the following pages: (a) the argument between those who believe that individualism is an American infliction, and those who see it as the heart of the American creed; (b) the debate between those who champion individual rights and those who argue for social responsibilities; (c) arguments between those who seek to slash government regulations and those who argue for a strong regulatory state.

EXHIBIT I: INDIVIDUALISM—CORE VALUE OR MALAISE?

The debate whether individualism is a basic feature of American society or a form of social malaise, whether this is a Lockean nation or one of republican virtue,[7] is recast once it is examined in light of the concept of inverting symbiosis. It leads one to see that *both* notions are excessively centered on one societal element and virtue, and are as misleadingly dichotomous. One realizes that *both* claims are, at best, half right. Actually the American society is a mixture of the two formations, and a society that often seeks at least partial self-correction when it leans too far in one direction or the other, when the relationship between the two elements moves from the mutually enhancing zone to the antagonistic zone.[8] Thus McCarthyism rose rapidly but was also largely discredited, and the 1994 radical Republican "Contract with America," which sought revolutionary changes, generated strong countercurrents.

The fact that both a strong measure of individualization *and* of commitment to the community as a whole are parts of the American experience is reflected in the country's key documents.[9] The Declaration of Independence and the U.S. Constitution contain not only the often cel-

ebrated commitments to individual rights and to liberty, but also statements such as "we mutually pledge to each other our lives, our fortunes
and our sacred honor"; "we have appealed to their [the British] native
justice and magnanimity, and we have conjured them [the British] by
the ties of our common kindred to disavow these usurpations"; and,
"We, the people of the United States, in order to form a more perfect
union. . . [and] promote the general welfare."

Moreover, viewed in sociohistorical context, as such materials should
be, these documents are clearly calls for increased individualism when
communal bonds were very strong (as they were in the early colonies,
in sixteenth-century Calvinist Geneva, or in seventeenth-century
Salem, Massachusetts)[10]—in effect, calls to move from the antagonistic
to the mutually enhancing zone of inverting symbiosis, rather than to a
system based on individualism (or highly autonomistic formations).
This, despite all the important differences (and the fact that they wrote
in different centuries) was also the British sociohistorical context in
which John Locke, Adam Smith (as the author of *The Wealth of Nations*),
and John Stuart Mill (especially in *On Liberty*) wrote. However, when
these philosophical prescriptions are applied to contemporary Western
societies—especially the United States—that are highly individualistic,
they have the opposite effect: They move the society deeper into the
antagonistic zone. (Today these recommendations are much more
applicable to highly collectivistic societies, such as China, where they
would move the society from the antagonistic zone, in which excessive
order constricts autonomy, to the mutually enhancing zone, in which
order and autonomy nourish one another.)

The disregard of context by many individualists is evident in that
they do not cast their arguments in a historical or sociological context,
but rather present them as ahistorical truths. Libertarians, for instance,
do not argue that autonomy must be idealized and championed only
when a secular state is overbearing or a society is dominated by a state-
sponsored religion. Rather, they hold to the same course even when
autonomy is well protected, the state is severely delegitimated and captured by private interests, shared values are thinned and hollowed to the
point of culture wars, and societal strife is increasingly commonplace.

Typically, Milton Friedman, one of the foremost contemporary libertarians,[11] applies the same basic concepts to Communist China and to
the late-twentieth-century United States (and to numerous other societies). In his view, they all need to reduce taxation, slash government
controls, privatize, remove the social safety nets, and so on. Not only does

one size fit all; it is supposed to fit them at all times.[12] More broadly, the quest to maximize liberty, to extend it all one can (as long as others are not harmed) is a universal principle and not one that is historically or socially bound.

From the communitarian vantage point, it is futile to argue that people in general require more liberty or more order, more individual rights or more social responsibilities, more license or more moral duties. The answer is profoundly affected by the sociohistorical context. To promote liberty in a society teetering on the edge of anarchy is like removing the police when rioting, arson, and looting erupt. To promote order in a society teetering on the edge of authoritarianism is like suspending the Bill of Rights in a society that just nullified the election results and shut down the press.

Contemporary communitarian thinking, viewed in this context, is a balancing act, a reaction to excessive individualism. That is, many of the communitarian ideas and ideals have been part of our intellectual heritage for a long time, but they gained a following in recent years because their societal, functional relevance has increased. Indeed, some communitarian elements are found in the works of the ancient Greek philosophers, especially Aristotle (for instance, in his comparison of the person in the communitarian polis with the person in a megalopolis);[13] in the Hebrew and Christian Scriptures; and in the works of many religious and secular thinkers and public figures over the centuries. Saint Francis of Assisi, for instance, has been called a "paradigmatic communitarian."[14]

Even if somewhat of a digression, to further document the point, additional communitarian works are listed next which preceeded the sociohistorical period in which they are most of service. In sociology, communitarians themes are found in the works of Emile Durkheim, Robert Nisbet, Robert E. Park, Talcott Parsons, Ferdinand Tönnies, and William Kornhauser, among others.[15] In social philosophy, Martin Buber, John Dewey, and George Herbert Mead discussed some matters in terms that today would be considered communitarian, without communitarianism as their main position.[16] And there were hundreds of attempts over the last two centuries to build or restore community life, from the Israeli kibbutzim to the Shakers; from New Lanark, Scotland, to New Harmony. These settlements typically entailed a fair measure of reflection on and examination of community life. (Technically, the term "communitarian" seems to have been in use only since the mid-nineteenth century. According to the *Oxford English Dictionary*, the word was first used in 1841 by Barmby, who founded the Universal Communitarian Association. In this and other nineteenth-century usage, communitarian means "a member of a community formed to put into practice communistic or socialistic theories." Just a year later, the first critique of communitarian thought was published. Edward Miall writes, "Your communitarians, or societarians of modern days seem intent on fashioning a new moral world by getting rid of all individuality of feeling." The more common and contemporary usage— "of, pertaining to, or characteristic of a community or communistic system; communitive"—first appeared in *Webster* in 1909.)

In the 1980s a group of political philosophers—Charles Taylor,[17] Michael J. Sandel,[18] and Michael Walzer[19]—challenged individualist liberal opposition to the concept of a common good, although all have been uncomfortable with the label "communitarian."[20] Particularly important works that advanced a communitarian thesis were written by contemporary sociologists, especially Robert Bellah and his associates, and by Philip Selznick[21] and the political scientist Daniel A. Bell.[22] Furthermore, communitarian elements are found in the works of other scholars who are not usually called communitarians. These include, on the liberal side, Robert D. Putnam,[23] Hans Joas,[24] and John Gray;[25] and, on the conservative side, David Willetts[26] and Meinhard Miegel.[27]

Communitarian tracks and traces thus can be found throughout the ages. However, it was only in the 1990s that communitarian thinking became a widely known public philosophy, a social force. This was achieved by expanding the communitarian thesis to include not only the emphasis on the common good and social bonds but also the notion of balance between the communal and the personal,[28] between individual rights and social responsibilities, and the notion of pluralism bounded by a core of shared values.[29] And systematic efforts were made to take the message from academia to wider circles of those who influence opinion, political and community leaders, and the public at large. These efforts allowed communitarian thinking to emerge as an influential public philosophy and, above all, to become something of a social movement. It has served as a corrective to excessive individualism,[30] and produced a value reaffirmation that has become especially acutely needed in societies in which individualism gained too much ground between 1960 and 1990.

Arguments by communitarians in recent years that point to the need for more community in American society are not—as they have been misconstrued—antithetical to autonomy. Tibor Machan, a fierce libertarian on his slow days, argues: "Of course, none of this [communitarian thought] would be awful if it didn't actually mean that we are to enact laws that force people to serve their communities."[31] He continues elsewhere, "Communitarians are interested in diminishing the decision-making power of people as individuals."[32] These statements simply do not follow when applied within the existing disequilibrium. Machan, and others who leveled similar criticisms, are like those who would worry about the breakout of a cold spell when the temperature falls from 98 to 93 degrees. Communitarianism gained its main following when individualism overheated; in this situation, there is little reason to fear collectivism.

EXHIBIT II: STRONG RIGHTS UNDERMINE/PRESUME STRONG RESPONSIBILITIES

The same confusion—and resolution, provided once one brings to bear the concept of inverting symbiosis—is evident in the debate between champions of individual rights (often a legal expression of autonomy) and advocates of personal and social responsibility (chiefly an ordering factor). Several individualists do not merely champion individual rights but actively oppose any notion of social responsibility because, they argue, it might undermine individual freedoms. John Stuart Mill wrote, "But neither one person, nor any number of persons, is warranted in saying to another human creature. . . that he shall not do with his life for his benefit what he chooses to do with it."[33] He eventually concludes "that the sole end for which mankind are warranted, individually or collectively, in interfering with the liberty of action of any of their number, is self-protection."[34] David Held asserts that "the individual is, in essence, sacrosanct, and is free and equal only to the extent that he or she can pursue and attempt to realize, with minimum political impediment, self-chosen ends and personal interests."[35]

Several critics have misinterpreted arguments by the communitarian Mary Ann Glendon, myself, and others who contend that Americans have overemphasized individual rights in recent years,[36] and suggest that these arguments mean that individual rights should be curtailed, if not abolished. Carl Schneider explains their error:

> It is a measure of the fierce grip rights thinking has on America that those who criticize it are commonly taken to desire its complete destruction. Glendon labors hard to show that hers "is not an assault on

specific rights or on the idea of rights in general, but a plea for reevalua-
tion of certain thoughtless, habitual ways of thinking and speaking
about rights."[37]

In contrast, Robert S. Fogarty wonders:

[T]here is virtually no discussion about what happens to groups or individuals outside the "rights" arena when such a moratorium [on rights] is
called. Should gays in the armed services, advocates for the disabled or
right-to-life people all stop their advocacy and get to the back of the bus
because we have to save the family and children?[38]

Fogarty took a communitarian suggestion for a *temporary* moratorium
on the minting of *new* rights, suggested by me, to mean *total* suspensions of *all* rights, thus turning a call for a corrective to the excesses of
the rights industry into a call for a one-sided society.

The generalization that *up to a point* rights and responsibilities are
mutually enhancing can be demonstrated both regarding specific rights
and on a more general level. For instance, the right to free speech presumes that those who are exposed to protected speech—as distinct
from those who exercise it—must be willing to endure what they find
offensive. Without members of the audience assuming this responsibility, the right to free speech is contested at best, and at worst ultimately
stultified.

The fact that rights and responsibilities often require one another, are
corollary, has been overlooked by the majority of Americans who have
claimed their right to obtain numerous government services but stead-
fastly refuse to assume the duty to pay for them.[39] The communitarian
argument here is that greater government services to individuals presume a greater willingness of these individuals to assume the responsibility for paying taxes.[40] Here, again, we are in a zone in which rights and
responsibilities go hand in hand.

More generally, individualists fear that any recalibration of legal
rights will cause a sociological phenomenon referred to as the *slippery
slope*. According to this theory, once a very limited change is made in an
institution or a tradition, it unleashes uncontrollable social forces that
widen and extend the change, leading to the destruction of the institution or the tradition one merely sought to modify.[41] Hence arises the
argument that no changes should be made in the U.S. Constitution.
(The fear of such a slippery slope has been one reason many activists, of

a rather varied political background, opposed having a Constitutional Convention of the states in Philadelphia in 1996.)

This argument is not without merit. Such a slope—the danger of changes spinning out of hand—exists. However, I have shown in a previous publication that one can make sociological "notches" on the slope, format social arrangements that will prevent such sociological avalanches.[42] I provided four specific criteria that guide the decision as to where specifically the balance point lies (see below).

A more profound point must be made: Historically, governments that provided a rich list of legal rights to their citizens were endangered *not* when the community demanded that those who have rights also shoulder their responsibilities, but rather when they *failed* to make such demands. To maintain a strong foundation for a regimen of individual rights, it is necessary to attend to the basic needs of members of the community. For instance, when their safety is not ensured, they tend to call for stronger and stronger police measures, and ultimately for "strong leaders." Providing for basic needs, in turn, requires that the members of the community will discharge their social responsibilities. Otherwise, the society commands neither the resources nor the citizens' loyalties needed to sustain a social order.

Thus, during the first third of the twentieth century, when both the Soviet and the German peoples found that their basic needs were denied, they supported those who replaced democratic governments with tyrannies. Similar trends are evident in other societies. For instance, the rise of right-wing movements in Western Europe and the United States over the last two decades is associated with rising economic frustrations as a result of stagnant wages and rising insecurity. It follows that sociological protection of a regimen of individual rights, of liberty, entails that the basic needs of the members of a community be served. This, in turn, requires that they will live up to their social responsibilities, from paying taxes to serving in neighborhood crime watches, from attending to their children to caring for their elders. No government alone can provide the needed services.

However, if a society legitimizes the minting of ever more individual rights or imposes ever more social responsibilities, there comes a point when these two start to undercut rather than reinforce one another. This is reflected, for instance, when, as a result of bestowing ever more legal rights on a people, individuals move from attempting to resolve conflicts through negotiations, bargaining, and mediation to a high reliance on courts, a phenomenon often referred to as "litigiousness."[43]

Imposing ever more taxes on a people often leads to a tax rebellion, if not a full-blown political one. In short, while individual rights and social responsibilities are mutually enhancing up to a point, they turn antagonistic if the level of either is continuously increased.

The exact point at which mutually enhancing relations turn antagonistic in any of the above-mentioned areas (and in others in which this particular form of relationship exists) is not clear. However, we do know when we have passed from one zone to another. The term "anarchy" is often applied when excessive individualism prevails. The term "collectivism" is often applied (or one of its political forms, such as totalitarianism, authoritarianism, or theocracy) when social duties are excessive. The fact that they are excessive is indicated when large numbers of the members of the society rebel against them, are highly alienated, seek to emigrate, or spend large amounts of resources to evade them.

EXHIBIT III: DEREGULATION

A debate that could greatly benefit from the concepts developed here is the one between those who favor government regulations and those who oppose them. While welfare liberals have conceded in recent years that some regulations may be abandoned, individualists continue to be dogmatic and ideological when they discuss regulations. Indeed, individualists frequently sound as if they would abolish practically all of regulation, given half a chance. Actually, the valid way to look at deregulation drives is to see them as correctives to overregulation in the preceding era. This is especially the case if one looks at developing nations—India, for example—that used to be extremely overregulated, not to mention command-and-control societies. The proper goal, though, is not a deregulated society or economy, drives that lead only to re-regulation as reforms overshoot the mark. (While the champions of deregulation in the 104th Congress actually did not deregulate as much as they promised or intended, their action and rhetoric sufficed to evoke considerable interest in re-regulation, from airlines to meat inspection.)

The communitarian position is compatible with the notion that some regulations—in fact, quite a few—are conducive to both social order and protection of autonomy, while other regulations diminish one element or the other or even both. Most important, regulations, far from being a threat to a free society, can serve, up to a point, to shore up social formulations of the good, but if pushed further, undermine the good society. Regulations are best judged on the basis of their specific merit or within the context in which they are intoduced, rather than embraced or condemned.[44] To review briefly the argument so far:

1: Communitarian societies must maintain an equilibrium between their ordering and autonomizing formations.

2: Such an equilibrium can be found on a low level of both autonomy and order (e.g., in a community that is just beginning to evolve, say in a new residential area), and on a high level (e.g., in a well-developed community, in which affective bonds and shared values are strong but so are the formations that protect autonomy).

3: In either case, the tensed relations between the two basic formations cannot be overcome. However, communitarian societies can enjoy a significant range in which the ordering and the autonomizing formations are mutually enhancing rather than antagonistic.

So far, the discussion has focused on the composition of communitarian societies. It turns next to the ways communitarian societies deal with forces that buffet them: that is, forces which require adaptation within the communitarian pattern if it is to be sustained.

IN A DYNAMIC PERSPECTIVE

Functional theories have been criticized for being static; they have been said to assume that once various societal needs are satisfied, once a society finds its point of equilibrium, it will basically continue as it is, like a well-maintained and -serviced car. This criticism is particularly inapplicable to the kind of functional theory applied here, which contains an inherent, unresolvable contradiction between the two core formations, order and autonomy. The resulting tension is a main source of continuous internal efforts to pull the society off its balance point in one direction or the other, to make it into a high-order, low-autonomy (authoritarian or totalitarian) society or one with the opposite profile (a libertarian society or social anarchy). Moreover, while I will shortly examine the processes that enable communitarian societies to adapt to challenges, I make no assumption that communitarian societies will necessarily activate the needed processes and do so in a timely and effective fashion. Communitarian societies can and do become individualist or socially conservative, or worse. The Weimar Republic is a notorious example.

To put it differently, a society's trends may be compared to the movements of a ball in a bowl: Up to a point, swing the bowl one way, the ball will roll back toward the center (although it will overshoot the center several times until it comes to rest), but push the ball too hard, and it will fly out of the bowl. A society, by analogy, can be pushed out of its pattern. But, unlike a bowl, a society can change its specific formation while sustaining its basic pattern, to try to keep the ball of social change within its confines. This ability is referred to as metastability. Thus, a communitarian society may change the way it orders things (e.g., greater reliance on alternative sentencing and less on prison terms) or extend its measure of autonomy (e.g., from a draft army to voluntary army) or both, but still remain rather communitarian. However, if a society introduces ever more drastic measures to enhance order—for instance abolishing the parliament, disbanding the opposition party, and suppressing religious institutions and voluntary associations (the way Hitler did after he captured the reins of the German government)—the communitarian pattern will break and the society will become basically different (in the case at hand, a highly totalitarian one).

THE CAUSES AND LIMITS OF SOCIETAL SWINGS

All societies are continuously subject to *centrifugal forces* that exacerbate the need to maintain order (if the given societal pattern is to be sustained) and to *centripetal forces* that increase the need to protect autonomy. (I deliberately use neutral terms to characterize the forces; often-used terms such as "disintegrative" and "integrative," or "decomposing" and "composing" are avoided because they suggest that the effect of a given force is always negative or positive, which, as the concept of inverting symbiosis reminds us, is not the case.) Thus, centrifugal forces can make a society more communitarian *if* it was excessively ordered (for example, Poland or Hungary following the collapse of communism in 1990–1991). However, the same force can move an already adequately autonomized society over the edge into an individualistic, if not anarchic, formation. (American society in the 1980s was slipping in this direction; although it stayed within the communitarian pattern, it was not quite far from its edge.) And centripetal forces that affect a highly autonomized society will move it into the communitarian direction; however, if they impact an authoritarian society (say, Chile under Pinochet), they will remove it even further from the communitarian pattern.

Exposure to Western cultures often serves to increase the level of centrifugal forces. This is one reason that the USSR sought to stop its citizens from listening to the BBC, just as India tried to prevent its people from watching CNN. In contrast, exposure to fundamentalism amounts to an increase in the centripetal forces—hence the opposition to it from the relatively democratic governments in Egypt and Algeria, which initially sought to satisfy (at least to some extent) the need for autonomy.

Both kinds of forces are generated not only by *external* random forces, inflicted on society by other societies (from invasions to cultural "pollution") or by the environment (hurricanes, earthquakes, and such), but are also generated *internally*. These forces are often activated within a society because the two basic societal needs for order and autonomy are never completely fulfilled. As a result, there is a perpetual quest by those members and subgroups particularly affected by the "shortfalls" in societal responses to meet the basic needs, to have them more fully served. Thus, intellectuals and students often take the lead in generating centrifugal forces, seeking more autonomy (leading to confrontations with the police in Seoul, Beijing, Santiago, and numerous other capitals). Businesses often act as a centrifugal force, seeking less government regulation and more autonomy in the pursuit of their goals. In contrast, the police and various domestic intelligence agencies such as the NKVD, FBI, and the Mossad, often act as centripetal forces, seeking a tighter order than is in place (even if it is already rather tight).

RESPONSES AND BREAKDOWNS

The image of a bicycle rider is behind much of my discussion: To sustain their communitarian quality, societies need to be pulled *not toward the opposite extreme* of the forces that buffet them, but rather to follow the golden rule, to seek the balanced middle. Given that they are continuously subject to centripetal and centrifugal forces, societies must take special steps to respond to these forces by shoring up the element of their composition that is particularly assaulted, or their basic pattern will first strain, and then break. For example, in reaction to the McCarthy era and later police and FBI excesses in dealing with the counterculture of the 1960s and the anti–Vietnam War movement, the United States enacted several measures to protect autonomy. In 1966, the U.S. Supreme Court curbed the ability of the police to interrogate suspects by establishing the *Miranda* rule. Several cities introduced civilian review boards in their efforts to reduce police misconduct, especially brutality. Troubled by the discovery in the 1970s that the FBI (then under J. Edgar Hoover) had infiltrated various anti–Vietnam War groups and spied on Dr. Martin Luther King Jr., the U.S. Justice Department forbade such covert operations domestically unless the FBI could produce strong evidence of pending or imminent violence or illegal acts.[45] And following the Watergate abuses of power, Congress instituted several limitations on the use of private monies by those in power. In short, the rise of centripetal forces was responded to with new measures to shore up autonomy.

In contrast, after the first assassination of a major Israeli political official—Prime Minister Yitzhak Rabin—in 1995, a nationwide dialogue ensued in Israel that sought to increase the moral censure of hate speech and to move extremists to a common ground. At the same time, several new measures were taken to increase security for the top elected officials, including issuing instructions to the Mossad to keep Jewish fundamentalist groups under closer surveillance. It was hoped that such measures would enhance the social order.

The Canadian Case

To provide an illustration of these concepts, a somewhat more elaborate example follows of the forces at work, responses to them, and the net effects in a communitarian society.

Canadian society is often said to be more communitarian than American society. William Stahl writes that the Canadian Fathers of Confederation "spoke of 'peace, order, and good government,'"[46] which Seymour Martin Lipset and Amy Bunger Pool argue is strikingly different from "life, liberty, and the pursuit of happiness."[47] Lipset and Pool describe the basic contrast: "[T]he respect for law in the northern polity [Canada] is indicative of a society which is more committed to the value of community compared to one like the United States which is more dominated culturally by individualism."[48] One of the national symbols of Canada is a law enforcement officer, the Mountie.[49]

An analysis of responses to statements regarding the balance of order and liberty in society—such as "It is better to live in an orderly society than to allow people so much freedom they can become disruptive"; and, "The idea that everyone has a right to their own opinion is being carried too far these days"—found that significantly more Canadians than Americans agreed with statements that emphasized order.[50] On the whole, the rule of law, social responsibility, and the sense of community were found to be stronger in Canada than in the United States.

Canada's Constitution of 1960 enumerated many rights; however, it seemed not to apply them to the federal and provincial levels of government. The document also "did not explicitly authorize judicial review, and as a result Canadian judges proved to be very self-restrained in its interpretation."[51] In 1982 Canada adopted the Canadian Charter of Rights and Freedoms, which extended these rights. As F. L. Morton puts it, "No such ambiguity [as in the 1960 Constitution] restrains Charter interpretation."[52] Both federal and provincial governments are now bound by the charter.[53]

One result has been a significant increase in the number of court cases. From 1982 to 1985, the number of cases regarding the charter increased from 405 to 548. Most notable was the jump in 1983, a mere one year after passage of the charter, from 405 to 503 cases. Also notable is the steadily increasing rate of "wins" for the individual in suits against the Crown: from 26 percent in 1982 to 32 percent in 1985.[54] The Canadian Supreme Court, which used to wield its power to overrule law with great timidity, has become much more active, with a steadily increasing number of verdicts overturning prior law or custom.[55] Thus, Canada has moved to a more autonomy-minded position, while still within the communitarian zone.

The question of whether the changes may have been overdone has not gone unasked. William Christian of Guelph University writes:

> Slowly, we risk slipping into an American attitude to rights that may clash discordantly with our own political needs and circumstances. We stand now more in danger than at any other time in our history of falling victim to a legal technology and to an ideology which, however much decency and goodness is contained within it (and there is much), is simply too dangerous for us to accept.[56]

He continues by pointing out the potential danger to Canada if the system slides too much toward the American model:

> [W]e are, as Harold Innis warned us, going to have to take active steps to prevent the needless intrusions of Americanisms into the high citadels of our national life, especially our law and constitution. We are a people whose experience and understanding of freedom comes as much from Europe as it does from the United States. If the Charter of Rights and

Freedoms makes us lose sight of this fact for an instant, its proclamation may prove to have been the blackest day in our nation's history.[57]

Canada thus changed its societal pattern to make more room for autonomy. On the question of whether Canada overshot the point of equilibrium in the process (as those who fear Americanization believe) or moved closer to it, the jury is still out.

Other Cases

Societies that do not adequately respond to centripetal or centrifugal forces find that their particular blend of order and autonomy is increasingly challenged. And, if one of the forces is particularly strong—and the response anemic—eventually the basic pattern will break and the society will be transformed into another type. This is not necessarily a loss, because some of the societies become communitarian in the process. For instance, Japan changed under the impact of a Western occupying force after World War II to become a society in which individual rights were recognized and protected (albeit in practice significantly less so than in the West). And toward the end of the twentieth century, several South and Central American societies' authoritarian patterns seem to be breaking, and they, as well as South Africa after the end of apartheid, have been moving toward a communitarian pattern.

When a communitarian society does not respond adequately to the challenging forces, centripetal forces may break it into a totalitarian or authoritarian regime. This is what happened to the Vichy government of France in 1940–1942, under the pressure of German Nazi forces. And centrifugal forces may push a communitarian society in the direction of an individualistic society.

Although both kinds of breakdown are theoretically plausible, it has been largely unnoted that in practice communitarian societies are much more prone to a centripetal breakdown than a centrifugal one. This is documented by the numerous relatively communitarian democratic societies that have broken down to become authoritarian or totalitarian societies, and the almost complete absence of individualistic societies.

While communitarian societies are rather vulnerable to external challenges, especially military invasions, internally they are particularly resilient, stable, and effective. Because they have, without exception, a democratic form of government, communitarian societies benefit from the virtues attributed to this form of government. And communitarian societies provide the social foundation democracy requires by fostering communities, rather than atomized individuals, and by relying largely on voluntary order. Communitarian-democratic societies do not require concentration camps, gulags, and extensive secret police forces, or walled borders and armed guards, for their citizens to abide by their duties and to remain in the country. The basic reason is that a communitarian society is much more adept at understanding its citizens' needs and at responding to them, because autonomy is stronger than in totalitarian and authoritarian regimes. Thus, a totalitarian regime may, as China did during the Great Leap Forward (1957–1958), instruct all the peasants on rural communes to make steel in backyard furnaces because it sought to become a superpower overnight, only to find out many months later that homemade steel was of a very poor quality, and that agriculture suffered greatly, which led to riots.[58] A similar move in a communitarian society would cause opposition much earlier and stop the unrealistic program more quickly.[59] To substantiate this point more fully would require a huge comparative study. I suggest, though, that the higher ability of communitarian societies to respond to internal challenges is a reason to expect that they are more able to maintain their patterns than other types of societies.[60]

IMPLICATIONS FOR PRACTICE AND POLICY

THE LIMITS OF COMMUNITARIAN POLICING AND REGULATION

Numerous measurements help determine the extent to which a given society is communitarian, and these must be watched to ensure that new practices and policies will not push a communitarian society into another pattern. Here, a brief summary of four previously developed criteria[61] that serve to maintain the societal golden rule is provided. While the measurements discussed in chapter 3 are sociological, the criteria discussed here concern the legal framework a society uses to express and ensconce its values. Specifically, the criteria seek to guide public policies that focus on two issues: First, how can the society prevent efforts to increase law and order, when social order has deteriorated, from turning a communitarian society into an authoritarian one? (Often these efforts entail Fourth Amendment issues: considerations of what is thought to be unreasonable, as opposed to reasonable, search and seizure.) Second, how can the society prevent the addition of new regulations (or re-regulation) from turning excessive? Together, the four criteria enable a society to "notch" the slippery slope and protect itself from a tendency to slip from limited adjustments—that reequilibrate a communitarian society—toward excessive ones, which will lead to a society in which the social conservative (or even authoritarian) pattern prevails.

First of all, a communitarian society does not build up its coercive measures (such as its police, jails, and regulation) unless it faces a *clear and present danger*. Societies are often warned that they face grave dangers (for instance, oil is about to be exhausted, a supermeteor is approaching, the ratio of dependent to working population is rising rapidly) and hence should take extraordinary measures to protect themselves. Communitarian societies do not curb autonomy (say, limit travel to save oil) until the danger is proven to be significant and well documented.

Second, when communitarian societies are moved to act to counter a clear and present danger, they ought to start by trying to cope with the dangers *without resorting to autonomy-restricting measures*. For instance, they could encourage people to use solar heaters (for example, by providing subsidies for research that makes these heaters less costly, more efficient, and more attractive) rather than jail people for not doing so. Similarly, communitarian societies would rather increase the tax on cigarettes than prohibit advertising, because banning advertisements impinges on a right most closely associated with protecting autonomy, the First Amendment, while the said taxes have no such effect.

Third, to the extent that autonomy-curbing measures must be introduced, these ought to be *minimally intrusive*. Thus, in attempting to curb driving under the influence of alcohol, communitarian societies rely heavily on moral education and persuasion in campaigns such as "Friends don't let friends drive drunk," and urge people to assume the responsibility of being the designated driver for a particular evening or occasion. Only for those who do not heed such educational messages, communitarians should favor sobriety checkpoints (which individualists often oppose) that are used to remove drunk drivers from the roads. Courts follow the third communitarian guideline when they insist that these checkpoints must be announced ahead of time, managed in ways that minimize traffic jams, and otherwise intrude as little as possible.

Last, communitarian societies work to *minimize* the autonomy-diminishing, often unintended, *side effects* of measures that must be undertaken for the common good. This approach is illustrated when a physician is disaffiliated from a hospital because of major violations of its codes, and this information is recorded in a national data bank. The data bank allows those who seek to retain physicians to check their standing. However, the data should indicate only that the physician has been barred "for cause," rather than provide details of the violation involved, whether it was rape, drug addiction, or gross negligence. (Physicians are disaffiliated only if there is a very strong case against them.) In this way, patients are protected and the social order benefits, while the physician's privacy is not unduly invaded.

These criteria, even when used in conjunction with those discussed in chapter 3, do not provide a precise indication that a society has lost its communitarian pattern. But these guidelines help to make slippage much less likely and thus allow a society to shore up its social order without undermining autonomy.

IMPLICATIONS OF THE FOUR CRITERIA FOR PRIVACY

When one examines the new technologies and techniques that have been developed in recent years which enable the government, private interests, the media, and anyone else so inclined to readily violate one's privacy, a cornerstone of autonomy, the first reaction is horror. Privacy is peeled away as strangers listen in on one's cellular phone calls; employers read their employees' e-mail; medical information provided to one's physician ends up with insurance companies, who sell it to still others. One notes that if reporters can pull up on their home computers former Vice President Dan Quayle's credit record, Dan Rather's expenses for a period of one month, and Vanna White's unlisted phone number, none of our personal records are securely private.[62]

A typical reaction is to demand new laws to protect autonomy. Indeed, various individualists have railed against these new intrusions and demanded that they be curbed. The tenor of these frequent protests is captured in a statement objecting to the creation of a national database for welfare recipients, issued by the American Civil Liberties Union, along with the U.S. Public Interest Research Group and the Electronic Privacy Information Center. It contends that the database would "threaten the civil rights and liberties of every person in the United States by compelling each to participate in an intrusive government system and suffer unwanted and unnecessary invasions of privacy. This truly is an Orwellian nightmare."[63]

A communitarian argues that privacy is an individual right that, like all others, must be viewed in a sociohistorical context and balanced against social needs for order. There follows a series of questions that allow one to examine this issue as if one were the policy maker in charge of these matters within a relatively communitarian society.

Should citizens be required to put out garbage in see-through bags, as Japanese are? Not unless one realizes that transparent bags help ensure that people will separate glass and cans from the rest of their trash. That is, such a requirement encourages people to be mindful of the common good invested in environmental protection without significantly diminishing their privacy.

Fingerprinting those who receive welfare checks makes them feel like criminals, civil libertarians complain. But maintaining the credibility of the public support system, a key component of the social order, requires finding ways to prevent numerous individuals from each collecting several welfare, unemployment, and social security checks. (Moreover, once fingerprinting is widely applied, the stigma will wane. Students already are routinely fingerprinted when they take LSATs.)

Similar questions of balancing the need for maintaining the legitimacy of public assistance with the right to privacy arise when one asks: Does it make sense, in the name of privacy, to allow students to default on their loans and deadbeat fathers to draw a salary from a government agency, just to avoid the use of computer cross-checks?

These issues are even more sharply joined when it comes to safety. Should banks be allowed to hide the movements of large amounts of cash in order to protect customers' privacy, or should they be required to disclose that information in order to hobble drug lords' transactions?

Day-care centers and schools can now find out if security personnel they hire have a record of child abuse, a civil libertarian's nightmare. But few parents would prefer to enroll their child in a facility like the one in Orlando, Florida, where a guard made sexual advances to boys, and the management learned only after the fact that he had been previously convicted of raping a fourteen-year-old. (Such people are entitled to jobs, but must these be ones dealing with children?)

Assuming that one grants that, because of various significant community concerns, one should not condemn as out of hand many of the new surveillance technologies and techniques, even when they infringe to some extent on people's privacy, one must next ask if all these new knowledge-gathering technologies lead to a police state, as civil libertarians claim? As I see it, the shortest way to tyranny runs the other way around: If a communitarian society does not curb violent crime and sexual abuse, or stem epidemics—to undergird social order—an ever-larger number of citizens will demand strong-armed authorities to restore law and order. One should hence allow select use of the new capabilities of cyberspace to help restore a balance between autonomy and order where it has been undermined on the side of unbounded autonomy.

The four criteria suggested as indicators of balance also apply here. Violations of privacy are to be tolerated only when there is a compelling need (e.g., to reduce the spread of contagious deadly disease); if the entailed intrusion is minimized (e.g., measure the temperature of a urine sample for drug tests, rather than observe as it is being produced); if one double-checks that there is no way to serve the same purpose while trimming privacy less (e.g., inform those who seek to check on a future employee that he or she does not check out by a mix of criteria, rather than specify a past crime); and if the side effects are minimized (e.g., if HIV testing is required, it is accompanied with proper counseling).

One is properly distressed when one reads of someone who was denied credit or wrongfully arrested because of mistakes in data banks. But this is not the effect of a violation of privacy; rather, it is the consequence of data poorly collected and sloppily maintained. What is needed are quicker and easier ways to make corrections in the various dossiers rather than a ban on their new and expanded uses. This might be achieved if there were one or more ombudsperson offices on the federal and/or state level to handle complaints and be charged with finding ways to improve and protect the existing information management systems. Better yet, rather than wait until complaints are filed, such offices should proactively test samples of files to ensure that error rates are low and correction expeditious.

THE RIGHT NOT TO SELF-INCRIMINATE

Individualists often argue that the rights of individuals whom the government charges with having committed a crime are trampled. Social conservatives are strongly concerned with the need to restore order even if it means curtailing rights—for instance, limiting the number of appeals allowed those who have been given death sentences. A communitarian seeking equilibrium must ask where, in a given sociohistorical context, the balance point lies. In Japan, for instance, we have seen the answer is that individual rights need to be enhanced. In the United States, we need stronger social responsibilities. But even if one disagrees with this conclusion, which is an empirical matter, one may agree that there is little merit in discussing changes in practices and policies outside of the sociohistorical context in which they are to be introduced. A very brief review of the right not to self-incriminate will highlight the point and lead to a policy recommendation.

The Fifth Amendment defines the right to avoid compulsory self-incrimination. Its historic origins are in "the dark past, when a suspect was brought before the Star Chamber (essentially a torture chamber), [and] was *commanded* to answer questions, even when there was no evidence that he had anything to do with the crime."[64] Judge Harold J. Rothwax adds that in those days, if a person refused to answer he would be jailed, tortured, or banished. Protection in such a coercive context was clearly a basic and essential right. But in contemporary America, people who refuse to testify against themselves are not punished for this refusal per se in any way. The only question debated is whether the jury may take their refusal into account in its deliberation, and whether the judge, in his or her instructions to the jury, should continue to admonish them severely against drawing a conclusion from the fact of refusal. Judges sometimes admonish the jury rather strongly, using words such as: "The defendant is not compelled to testify, and the fact that he does not cannot be used as an inference of guilt and should not prejudice him in any way."[65] Given that about 90 percent of those who come to criminal trial are known to be guilty (that is, would be found so if all the facts where known to the judge or jury),[66] it seems reasonable to correct to some extent the judicial system that frees a large proportion of the guilty. This does not entail repealing the Fifth Amendment, but rather allowing the jury to draw conclusions from the defendant's silence. Note that the Fifth Amendment nowhere refers to a prohibition on drawing conclusions, and that such a notion—like the *Miranda* warning itself—is a rather recent construction. Also, Britain, a rather communitarian society, in the mid-1990s allowed juries to view a claim of the right to avoid self-incrimination as an indication of guilt.

NOTCHING LIBERALIZATION

One may ask whether notching the slippery slope works only to prevent new measures to enhance social order from proceeding beyond what is desired. Can notching also be made to work the other way around, to prevent measures of liberalization from snowballing? The answer is clearly in the affirmative. Various suggestions have been made to end the criminalization of the use of controlled substances. Without going into the question of whether or not such a policy change is in line with communitarian core values, it can be shown that those who promote such ideas differ a great deal in how far down the slope they are willing to go, and how concerned they are about establishing footholds, to be able to prevent a slide.

There are rather few who would simply legalize all drugs. Even David Boaz, who advocates that illegal drugs be treated in the same manner as alcohol and tobacco, poses some limits: He would allow only print but no television advertising, require government warning labels, and prohibit sales to minors.[67] Others carve "notches" according to the nature of the drug. For example, some would legalize marijuana but not other drugs. Still others draw a line between decriminalization and legalization. ("Decriminalization" is taken to mean lessened or no punishments for possession of small amounts and use in the privacy of one's own home, but no change in the level of punishments for sale and import.[68])

In short, notching "the other way around" can be readily conceived: autonomy in some areas can be increased without the changes in policy involved automatically resulting in unbounded license or necessarily diminishing the moral order.

THREE

The Fall and Rise of America

Max Weber, a sociological giant, argued that once a society's moral foundations deteriorate they will continue to crumble. New societies rise out of the ashes of old ones, not through the rejuvenation of decaying ones. This sociological thesis is reflected in several well-known historical studies about the rise and fall of regimes such as the Third Reich, the decline and fall of ancient Rome (or the capitalist West, in Paul Kennedy's account, which should have been written about the Communist East). It is much more difficult to find a magnum opus about the decline and *rise* of well-known societies. In effect, we are mainly aware of cultures that deteriorated without reviving, including those of ancient Greece, Babylon, Egypt, and the Aztecs. The British monarchy—on its last legs when Victoria was crowned in 1837, and reported to have gained much legitimacy by the end of her reign in 1901—is one of the few exceptions, but it's an account that concerns an institution rather than a whole culture, civilization, or society. And even that institution is not faring very well.

My interest here, Max Weber notwithstanding, is which conditions and processes may make possible a regeneration of the moral order in societies that have lost it.

Regeneration refers to a return to a higher level of social order and autonomy, with the two elements being well balanced. I chose the term "regeneration" rather than "reconstruction" or "restoration" to stress that it does not entail a futile attempt to rerun history, which would be normatively unacceptable even if it were sociologically possible.

THE AMERICAN CONDITION: PRELIMINARY NOTES

Terms such as "moral crisis" roll too easily off the tongues of religious leaders, politicians, and other opinion makers. Like other sweeping statements about the "end of ideology" and the "death of the family," those about the decay of the American society are often grossly exaggerated, while containing a kernel of truth. In fact, the situation is much more complex. Moreover, a more careful assessment of the measure and nature of the moral condition of American society is essential for a sound examination of the ways regeneration may come about and the direction in which it will need to evolve.

The following questions need to be specifically addressed:

1: Was there a considerable deterioration of social order between 1960 and 1990?

2: If there was a significant deterioration, was it limited to several social sectors or was it all-encompassing?[1]

3: To what extent did the expansion of autonomy by various liberation movements, such as civil rights and the women's movement, remain within social bounds, or did the quest for more liberties lead to permissiveness, lawlessness, and anomie?

4: Was there a change in the extent to which the social order relies on moral suasion versus coercion?

5: If one sees the period of 1960–1990 as a period of moral decline, at least in some areas, does this societal deterioration continue into the 1990s, or are we observing new beginnings, a *curl back*?

In attempting to answer these questions, I draw on data that are quite familiar (e.g., the decline in voting and the rise of violent crime in the given period) but often contested (e.g., was crime higher or just the fear of crime?) and subject to different interpretations (e.g., is the low level of voting a sign of apathetic withdrawal from the system or one of angry rejection?). My concern is not with the details of the data or with presenting new evidence. Sorting these out would require several volumes larger than this one. My purpose is to document the main points in rather general terms. For example, however one assesses various specific measurements, there is no doubt that violent crime rose very significantly from 1960 to 1990. The same holds for the other data: When strung together they point to some rather clear trends.

One final caveat: In studying a society, one must recall that a whole population, even one much smaller and less varied than the American people, never turns around like a marching band on a football field at the blow of a whistle. Changes are practically always gradual and partial.

BASELINE FIFTIES:
THE OLD REGIME—ORDERLY, BUT HOW MORAL?

Any historical analysis requires a starting point which affects the insights and conclusions that follow. Thus, if one chooses American society in the 1950s as the baseline, that society may seem highly ordered from a vantage point in the 1990s, but it may not seem as orderly if examined from the viewpoint of earlier generations. (The same holds from the comparative sociological perspective: If one compares American society to some Asian societies it may be perceived as less orderly, but if one compares it to Russia of the mid–1990s, it is seen as rather orderly.) Those who argue that the 1950s were atypical[2] may have a case, but a similar case could be made for any period, and the analysis requires some kind of baseline.

The year 1960 is used as a baseline here because the society of the 1950s is often cited as the model of the orderly society we lost, one in which virtues were well in place. "Three decades later, the fifties appear to be an orderly era, one with a minimum of social dissent. . . . In that era of general good will and expanding affluence, few Americans doubted the essential goodness of their society," comments David Halberstam.[3]

J. Ronald Oakley agrees:

It was a time when America still reigned as the strongest nation in the world. . . . It was a time when the Cold War was still seen as an unambiguous battle between good and evil. It was a time when people were proud to be Americans, trusted their leaders, and shared a consensus on basic beliefs and values.[4]

One can argue that the social order of the 1950s was atypical; sustained the "wrong" values; that it was based on social conventions that papered over underlying tensions; and even that the order was based on a considerable measure of coercion (all issues explored below). However, one cannot deny that the occurrence of antisocial behavior in the American society of the 1950s (and that of other Western societies) was much lower than it was by the end of the 1980s.

Core values in the 1950s were relatively widely shared and strongly endorsed;[5] and to these a newly established anti-Communist ideology was added. Most Americans were united in the idea that America was the leader of the free world, and most strongly endorsed fighting a cold war against an "evil empire."[6] Patriotism was high—America had won World War II, saving the free world, and it had the strongest economy in the world. Indeed, the 1950s were thought of as the beginning of the American century.[7]

Members of society had a strong sense of duty to their families, communities, and society. In 1961, when President John F. Kennedy challenged Americans to ask not what their country could do for them, but what they could do for their country, his call was very warmly received. The establishment of the Peace Corps that followed was much more widely supported than AmeriCorps, President Clinton's attempt to introduce national service some thirty years later.

The dominant religion was Christianity and it was more established than in 1990. For instance, prayers in schools were common and rarely questioned.[8] Laws made divorce difficult and costly; abortion was illegal in all states.[9] Families were much more intact. Illegitimacy was relatively low.[10] The cultural pollution proffered by television had barely begun.

In the 1950s, the roles of men and women were relatively clearly delineated, although not all abided by the normative expectations built into these roles. Those who did not were often chastised by their community. Women who did not marry were stigmatized as spinsters; married women who did not produce children were frequently pressured to account for their decision. As one historian of the decade puts it, "[I]t was a supreme sign of personal health and well-being to be engaged in the social act of marriage and family-raising."[11] Promiscuous women were labeled "sluts." By and large, women were supposed to do housekeeping, mothering, and community service, and to be submissive and loving. Men were supposed to be providers (if they were not, they were made to feel guilty) and strong. Douglas T. Miller and Marion Nowak write: "Only by accepting her place as wife, mother, [and] homemaker . . . could woman be content. Man, similarly, must exercise his active and competitive role. The human halves linked together in that basic human wholeness, the natural marital state."[12]

Respect for authority figures (which embodies and helps sustain a society's values), from presidents to priests, from generals to doctors to labor leaders, was high.[13] Few in the 1950s would have dared to ask for a second opinion when ordered by a physician to undergo surgery. At work, alliances between industrial captains and labor bosses were common. The government was rather firmly trusted. The proportion of people who voted was relatively high and alienation was low.

The *extent* to which this order was *based on moral suasion* (versus various forms of coercion) is of particular importance for a communitarian evaluation, but unfortunately this is a subject very rarely studied, and hence very difficult to gauge. It is particularly difficult to establish the depth to which people internalized the core values of the 1950s versus the extent to which many conformed because of social pressure, economic considerations, or fear (for instance, African Americans in the South).[14] On the one hand, most Americans were quite satisfied with their lot and protests were few and far between. Feminist Betty Friedan, who formed the ideology for one of the protest movements that followed, argues that in the 1950s women often appeared satisfied in their traditional roles, which she explains by noting that women "[grew] up no longer knowing that they have. . . desires and capacities" other than those defined by the prevailing social norms of the time.[15] On the other hand, the fact that in the decade that followed, African Americans, youth, women, and liberal men attacked the old regime and stripped it of much legitimacy strongly suggests that these Americans at least did not fully commit themselves to the existing social order, even in the 1950s.

In the 1950s divisiveness was low and a sense of *shared bonds, of community, was relatively high*. American society was even at that time a more heterogeneous one (objectively speaking) and had a stronger sense of being diverse (subjectively speaking) than most European societies. But it did not perceive itself to be deeply divided. Group consciousness along racial or gender lines was relatively low compared to what followed. Ethnic groups stressed that their first loyalty was to American society and not to their country of origin. Groups that were suspected of placing their prime loyalty elsewhere were viewed with disdain, and their leaders were kept out of many public offices, especially the presidency. Communists were suspect because, among other reasons, they were said to toe the line of the Communist capital, Moscow. When John F. Kennedy ran for office, he felt he had to convince Americans that his first loyalty was not to the Pope. Similarly, there were very few activists seeking to speak for a fundamentally different lifestyle—Zen, gay, or any other—although at the margins of society there were small assortments of so-called bohemians, deviants, and rabble-rousers.

Indicators of antisocial behavior, such as violent crime, drug abuse, alcoholism, and other sources of social disorder were relatively low (or relatively concealed, such as gambling, frequenting prostitutes, and the consumption of pornography).

Most Americans felt that they lived in safe and orderly places. In many parts of the country, people could use public spaces without fear; they left their front doors unlocked, their ignition keys in place, and their children playing outside unsupervised. More generally, the majority had the sense that theirs was an orderly and relatively tranquil society.

Relatively low autonomy. American society of the 1950s restricted individual and subgroup choice, although not nearly as much as authoritarian societies (not to mention totalitarian ones). For instance, college students were typically expected to take a fair number of prescribed courses that were considered "good for them" by the faculty, while "electives" were rather limited. The core curricula reflected unabashedly (and often with little self-awareness) the dominant set of values.

The 1950s were called the age of the "silent generation," one in which people were expected to be uncritical and not to challenge authority. Godfrey Hodgson notes that "to dissent from the broad axioms of consensus was to proclaim oneself irresponsible or ignorant."[16] A witch-hunt was raging across the land in which Senator Joseph McCarthy and his investigators pursued perceived Communists and Communist sympathizers, driving people out of work or into exile and even to suicide.[17] Street justice, in which the policeman's nightstick settled many issues on the spot without any hearing or appeal, was common. Law enforcement showed a strong and clear bias along class, racial, and ethnic lines.[18]

In Congress, a small group of Southern senators dominated. They retained their elected offices for many terms, chaired the key committees, and ran roughshod over everyone else in Congress. When Speaker Tom Foley left the House in 1994 after thirty years, he reminisced about the days when he arrived in Congress. He and other new representatives were told by the then speaker, in public and quite openly, that there was one thing that was expected from them: silence.

The autonomy of several social groups was constricted. Women and minorities were treated as second-class citizens. Widespread racial segregation of public schools, transportation, hotels, and restaurants was enforced by law and custom. Various bureaucratic devices were used, especially in the South, to prevents blacks from voting. Powerful stereotypes, traditions, and interpersonal networks effectively kept most women out of political office, high positions in most companies and associations, and influential professions. Sexual partners were expected to be heterosexual, married, and even then limit their sexual conduct to culturally defined behaviors. In short, society was rather orderly (by present-day American standards, not those of, say, Singapore), but life choices, opportunities for self-expression and creativity, and cultural alternatives were limited for many members of the American society (certainly when compared to what was about to come).

THE PENDULUM SWINGS:
1960 TO 1990, MORAL ORDER DETERIORATES,
AUTONOMY EXPANDS, BUT SO DOES ANARCHY

The strong consensus on *core values* of the 1950s was increasingly undermined in the years that followed as some values were contested and others waned but were not replaced by new ones. Americans increasingly doubted the merit of a grand role for their country in the world (especially in the wake of the war in Vietnam). Anti-Communist fervor slowly subsided but was not replaced with any new shared doctrine. The rise of the counterculture in the 1960s further weakened the country's values of hard work and thrift, as well as compliance with most rules of conduct, from dress codes to table manners, from established tastes in music to cuisine.[19]

While the number of those who fully embraced the counterculture was relatively small (although still in the millions) and many who joined it did so only for a transitional period, many other millions of "orderly" Americans embraced, in varying degrees, some of the tenets of the counterculture. The rise of the counterculture in the 1960s was followed in the 1970s, and especially in the 1980s, by a strong endorsement of a different, instrumental brand of individualism.[20] It provided a normative seal of approval to a focus on the self rather than on responsibilities to the community, and saw in self-interest the best base for social order and virtue. Books such as *Looking Out for Number One* and *How to Be Your Own Best Friend*, which assert that "we are accountable only to ourselves for what happens to us in our lives,"[21] became popular. Milton Friedman and Peter Drucker argued that the business of business was business and it therefore had no social obligations.[22]

If the hallmark of the 1950s was a strong sense of obligation, from 1960 to 1990 there was a rising sense of entitlement and a growing tendency to shirk social responsibilities. Americans felt that government should be curtailed and that they should pay less taxes, but at the same time they demanded more government services on numerous fronts.[23]

The role and influence of religion declined. Divorce and abortion were legalized. Prayer was removed from most public schools.

A significant exception to the trend toward individualism was that environmental protection became a shared value. Early in the 1970s, a general consensus emerged in favor of a national environmental policy.[24] By 1990, about three-quarters of Americans consistently considered themselves environmentalists.[25]

In a widely cited article entitled "Defining Deviancy Down" Senator (and sociologist) Daniel Patrick Moynihan pointed out that when there is too much deviance, societies relax their notions of deviance, and allow previously deviant behavior to become "acceptable" or even "normal."[26] For example, Moynihan points out that our most significant response to the decline of the traditional family has been the redefinition of the term "family" such that it came to include a wider variety of households. Similarly, the soaring rate of crime has led to a redefinition of what constitutes an "acceptable level" of criminal activity.[27]

By the 1980s, many Americans paid only lip service to some core values and showed significantly lower commitment to others—marriage, for instance. Contentiousness rose considerably on other issues. Either way, the moral order was either hollowed out or weakened.

Respect for authority declined sharply. The index of people's overall confidence in the leadership of a long list of American institutions has fallen on average from a 1966 baseline (earliest data available) of 100 to 46 in 1990.[28] The list includes the military, Congress, the president, educational institutions, the media, and corporations.

In the process, Americans have become a tribe that savages and consumes its leaders. The average terms of police chiefs, school superintendents, and heads of universities were shortened. Heads of hospitals, the Post Office, the Department of Defense, the CIA, and the FBI were subject to intense criticism.

Above all, Americans came to treat presidents as if they were raw meat. For most of his years in office, Ronald Reagan could do no wrong; but then he retired under a cloud because of the Iran-Contra Affair. Lyndon Johnson was consumed by controversy over the Vietnam War. Richard Nixon had to resign in midterm. Gerald Ford was openly disrespected. And Jimmy Carter was treated as if he were grossly incompetent. The last president to survive two terms without having his legitimacy challenged was Dwight Eisenhower.

Voter turnout declined. Sixty-three percent of eligible voters voted in the 1960 presidential election. In 1988, only 50 percent of Americans voted. Polls found a growing number of Americans (by 1990, the overwhelming majority) were highly dissatisfied with politics, especially at the national level.[29] Running against Washington became a widely used political device, even by those who spend much of their adult life as "insiders" in the nation's capital. Party loyalty declined while the proportion of Americans who see themselves as independent rose from 23 percent in 1960 to 37 percent in 1990.[30]

Alienation rose. Americans have been often asked whether they agree with such pointed statements as "Do you feel that the rich get richer, and the poor get poorer?" and, "Do you feel that the people running the country don't really care what happens to you?" The average response to a battery of such questions stood at 29 percent in 1966, the first year of the poll. It more than doubled by 1990 to 61 percent.[31]

A study that covered ten years of that period found that the percentage of persons in "stable" job conditions (defined as either no job change or only a single change) fell from 67 percent in the 1970s to 52 percent in the 1980s. Meanwhile, the percent of persons in "unstable" job conditions (three or more job changes) doubled from 12 percent to 24 percent.[32] And this was before large-scale downsizing started.

Socioeconomic Conditions and Autonomy, 1960s to 1990s

The focus of my analysis is on what some call "cultural" factors, on values and the ways they are embodied in society (the moral infrastructure), rather than on economic factors. For this reason, I do not examine changes in poverty levels, differential wages, and so on. These factors deserve a major study of their own. I discuss here only briefly the effect of these factors on one cardinal element of the good society, the scope of autonomy.

In the period under study, changes in socioeconomic conditions contributed both to enhancing autonomy—and dependency, and hence the loss of autonomy. The first development occurred as the socioeconomic conditions of the disadvantaged improved, even if their relative condition often did not. The second development was reflected in an increase in the number of those who have become dependent on government support. From 1960 to 1990, the number of persons on welfare increased by a factor of more than five, to 4.2 million by 1990.[33] How many of those who received benefits became more autonomous as their basic needs were met and how many grew psychologically dependent, and thus lost autonomy, or both, is a subject of much ideological debate, but little reliable social scientific evidence.

In broader terms, there are strong data to show that although household income increased in the period at hand, this was due much more to more people working per household than to an increase in real income per worker, especially after 1973. This development had strong autonomy-reducing effects as more and more members of the family felt they were forced to work outside the household and had severely limited time for other purposes, including family, community, and volunteer action.[34] Rising job insecurity added to the sense of constricted autonomy.

Family. The family declined, although it neither "vanished" nor became an "endangered species," as some argued. The proportion of all households that were families (married couples with at least one child) declined from 42 percent in 1960 to 26 percent in 1990.[35] However, more than 60 percent of all children lived with both their biological parents,[36] and more than 70 percent of all children still lived with two parents in 1990.[37]

The rate of divorce doubled between 1960 and 1990, with nearly half of all marriages ending in divorce by 1990.[38] While many of those who remarried divorced a second and third time, still half of all couples stayed married.[39] Both the rate of illegitimacy and its significance are particularly difficult to determine, but it should be noted that it rose sharply, nearly doubling from 21.6 per 1000 births in 1960 to 41.8 in 1989.[40] The percentage of all births to single mothers rose by a factor of five from 1960 to 1990.[41]

Diversity. The percentage of nonwhite and Hispanic Americans more than doubled from 1960 to 1990.[42] The percentage of the population that is foreign born increased from 5.4 percent in 1960 to 7.9 percent in 1990.[43] Men and women, hardly considered distinct social groups in the 1950s, have grown apart. Tension has resulted as the traditional definitions of gender roles were largely cast aside, while no new consensus arose as to what the expected, approved roles were.

Among racial and ethnic groups, an early indication of the rising division and tension came in race-based urban riots that occurred between 1965 and 1967, followed by the U.S. Riot Commission's report, which declared the United States to be two nations, separate and unequal along racial lines.[44] Tensions between Jews and African Americans, once a liberal coalition for social change, rose.[45] African Americans felt threatened by immigrants and resented the special status accorded to them, leading to conflict with Hispanics and Asian Americans.

Tensions among many other ethnic and racial groups seem to have increased in the thirty years under scrutiny. While there is no reliable trend data, according to recent evidence from the early 1990s "one out of every four or five adult Americans is harassed, intimidated, insulted, or assaulted for reasons of prejudice during the course of [each] year."[46]

Indications of a thinning social fabric were not limited to gender, ethnic, and racial relations. The proportion of people who feel that "most people can be trusted" declined from 58 percent in 1960 to 37 percent in 1993.[47] (The importance of trust to a community is expansively investigated by Francis Fukuyama.[48]) Loyalty of corporations to employees declined and so did the loyalty of employees to their corporations,[49] making corporations even less of a community.

Moral suasion versus other means of order. The mix of means used to sustain order changed in complex ways between 1960 and 1990. The picture is complicated because there were several changes in direction during this period, as well as crosscurrents. The following serves only as a preliminary sketch.

The 1960s were marked by a fairly broad-based *reduction in the reliance on coercive means to maintain order without a parallel increase—indeed, with a decrease—in reliance on moral suasion.* Note that this is a relative statement: The reliance on coercive means was never as high in American society as in authoritarian societies, and it was not reduced sharply. Still, "street justice" was cut back following strong advocacy of individual rights and the rise of the civil rights movement. The Civil Rights Voting Act was passed in 1964, numerous African-American mayors and police chiefs were elected, and police abuse of blacks declined (although it far from disappeared). Revulsion at the beating of dissenters during the Democratic Convention in Chicago in 1968 and the shooting of anti-war protesters at Ohio's Kent State University in 1970 made the National Guard and police departments show more restraint. The U.S. Supreme Court, in a 1966 ruling (*Miranda* v *Arizona*) imposed new limits on the police. Sodomy laws were repealed in eighteen states by 1975, and as of 1993, sodomy was legal in twenty-seven states.[50] Abortion, under most circumstances, was removed from the list of acts punishable by the state. Divorce was made easier in the late 1960s and early 1970s by "no-fault" laws. Public support for corporal punishment in schools diminished.[51]

In the 1970s and especially in the 1980s, however, this trend of relying less on coercion reversed direction. Penalties for violating laws were increased, raised some more, and toughened again. The number of incarcerated Americans increased significantly, surpassing those of any industrial nation.[52] The incarceration rate rose per 100,000 from 120 in 1960 to 300 by 1990.[53] Though the Supreme Court overturned all existing death penalty laws in 1972, within ten years thirty-seven states had reinstituted capital punishment.[54] Several states introduced new limitations on abortion and on homosexual activities. The federal Sentencing Reform Act, which took effect in 1987 (it was passed in 1984), ended the federal parole system and sharply increased sentencing generally.[55] Many states also enacted mandatory sentencing laws beginning in the 1980s.

Moral suasion as a foundation of social order also declined in the 1960s as coercion declined, and as first welfare liberal then laissez-faire conservative ideas gained in following. Traditional virtues lost much of their power, and no strong new shared values arose. The notion that one should not be judgmental gained currency;[56] various social and psychological theories that blamed the system for the misconduct of its "victims" caught on, a trend that continued to evolve in the two decades that followed. Permissiveness was much extended, especially in areas such as sexual conduct and lack of achievement in schools. Even etiquette, Miss Manners reports, declined.[57]

As coercion increased again to some extent, moral suasion also changed direction. By the 1970s and especially the 1980s, the so-called cultural issues gained attention. They were put on the national agenda first by groups such as the Moral Majority, followed by the Christian Coalition, conservative elected officials such as Ronald Reagan and Dan Quayle, and then other public figures, ranging from Pat Buchanan to William J. Bennett. However, at least initially, these voices led to intensified divisiveness and intergroup conflict rather than a recommitment to old values or a new core of shared values. Intensive conflicts in school boards over issues such as the teaching of creationism, sex education, book banning, and school prayers all illustrate the contentiousness of the era, leading some to refer to the rise in "culture wars" in America.[58]

Taken *in toto,* the changes in the forces that maintained social order from 1960 to 1990 were paralleled by a sharp increase in *social disorder.* The data about the rise of antisocial behavior are well-known: The crime rate rose from 1,126 incidents reported per 100,000 people in 1960 to 5,820 in 1990. Violent crime rose by 4½ times in that period, and the rate of murder doubled.[59]

In 1990, the percentage of the labor force in the United States that was in federal or state prison was 0.584, almost twice what it had been in 1960 (0.295 percent). If one includes persons on parole, probation, and otherwise under the jurisdiction of the criminal justice system, the number is much higher; over 6 percent of the labor force was entangled in the criminal justice system.[60] Drug abuse, rather confined in 1960, spread considerably in the following decades.[61] (Less is known about changes in the incidence of alcoholism.[62])

While signs of antisocial behavior were on the rise, so was autonomy. The rise in *autonomy* can be seen in minorities gaining most legal rights and quite a few social and political ones. For example, the number of elected African-American officials increased dramatically. Between 1970 and 1990, the number of African Americans elected to education posts had quadrupled; in local political office the number increased by a factor of six; and the number of law enforcement offices more than tripled.[63]

The rise of autonomy for women is widely noted. By 1990, women were legally entitled to the same choices as men , with a few exceptions, such as certain combat duties and entering the Catholic priesthood. Furthermore, gender discrimination and sexual harassment in the workplace became illegal. However, several de facto barriers to women's equality persisted—for instance, the "glass ceiling."

Americans between the ages eighteen and twenty-one gained the right to vote in 1971. The young were anything but a silent generation during the 1960s, leading the counterculture (including the sexual revolution and the movement into drugs). They played a key role in the civil rights movement and in the movement against the war in Vietnam.

THE LINE BETWEEN AUTONOMY AND ANARCHY

To what extent did the increase in autonomy in American society, and in other Western societies between 1960 and 1990, cross over the line that separates bounded autonomy from social anarchy? Before answering this question, the conceptual issues involved in drawing such a distinction must be further explored.

Conceptually, the line between bounded autonomy for individuals and subgroups (a range of legitimate options within an affirmed normative framework) and social anarchy (the absence of order, regulation, and normative guidance) is relatively clear. So is the difference between less strict norms and anomie, between a reformed law and lawlessness. For an example of the difference, one may examine the life of tenured faculty members in university towns in less conservative parts of the country (such as Berkeley, California; Cambridge, Massachusetts; and Palo Alto, California). They lead a rather autonomous life; they are strongly protected from economic and political pressures, but they are subject to the extensive norms of their college communities and even subject to some possible disciplinary acts (for instance, when they mismanage research funds or make hateful speeches) above and beyond those imposed by the law. They lead autonomous, but hardly anarchic lives.

In contrast, outsiders who must traverse parts of the inner cities, in which open drug markets, rampant violence, and economic insecurity prevail, face anarchic conditions in which few mores protect the autonomy of outsiders. Anarchy also prevails in many public spaces, such as parks, plazas, and sidewalks, which people fear to use (especially after dark).

The sexual "liberation" of the 1960s provides another example of the issue involved when autonomy and anarchy are not carefully separated. The movement started as a rebellion against tight mores that limited sexual relations to those between married, heterosexual couples, and then further regulated that relationship (e.g., religious prohibitions on the use of contraceptives even by married couples). Launched from this traditional basis, the sexual liberation movement did expand people's autonomy. However, it eventually led quite a few Americans to a state of normless anarchy which, for example, the Antioch guidelines try to overcome. At the extreme, this lack of moral guidelines led to movies that romanticize incest, such as *Spanking the Monkey*; the campaign by NAMBLA (the North American Man/Boy Love Association) to repeal the age of consent for sex, arguing that sex at age eight is "too late"; and to less extreme developments, such as the spread of hard-core pornography and highly offensive sexually violent material on television and in rap songs.[64]

One indicator that helps to determine whether or not the line between autonomy and social anarchy has been crossed is if the mores are truly endorsed by those involved, or if they are foisted on members of the community. There are several reports that show that many female teenagers feel they are under great pressure to engage in sexual intercourse from both young males and from males significantly older than themselves.[65] And that college women are often subject to date rape. These are indicators of social anarchy, not of autonomy.

Another area in which bounded autonomy has slipped toward anarchy is deregulation. To the extent that deregulation entailed removing meddlesome, costly, redundant, and unnecessary government interventions, the autonomy of private economic actors has been increased. To the extent that new modes of regulation (e.g., indirect regulation), less frequent inspections for those found to be compliant, or professional self-regulation have replaced earlier, tighter government controls, autonomy has advanced. However, to the extent that economic behavior has been left without effective public oversight, antisocial behavior in the private sector followed. This can be seen in the marketing of drugs that are known to be harmful, stonewalling by tobacco companies, and large-scale manipulation of the books by defense contractors, among other examples.

The slippage of bounded autonomy toward anarchy is also evident in the deterioration of the content of television programs for children, in the reemergence of sweatshops, and in the explosion of private funds contributed to politicians in exchange for legislative favors.

By these standards, if one focuses on the elements of society that are relatively intact, one finds that the changes from 1960 to 1990 enhanced the autonomy of many millions of Americans, especially women, minorities, and the young. At the same time, anarchy rose in terms of the waning of sexual mores. The net effect of deregulation and privatization and that of changes in many other sectors is not settled enough at this time to draw a firm conclusion, although it is evident that the absence of laws, or their slack enforcement, has caused pockets of anarchy. When all is said and done, it is difficult to assess clearly how much of the change between 1960 and 1990 enhances autonomy or increases anarchy. A good deal of both is a safe conclusion.

In general, the fact that erosion has been gradual, uneven, and far from complete is rather significant. Regeneration is much more attainable when the foundations are cracked but the building remains standing than after the foundations crumble and the building collapses. And although a regeneration of the moral order, to reiterate, does not require a return to the specific arrangements or values of an earlier era, American society requires a functional alternative to traditional virtue: a blend of voluntary order with well-protected yet bounded autonomy.

A NEW SWING: THE 1990s CURL BACK

Beginning with the 1990s, a regeneration has begun to set in, centripetal forces have increased, and they have begun to push the pendulum back to stave off anarchy and to restore social order. I refer to these new developments as a *curl back*, to stress that after a long movement in one direction, society began to turn the corner and face in the other direction (without, however, retracing its steps), but has not yet moved far enough in the new direction. Moreover, some of the first regenerative measures have been misdirected, and American society remains engaged in a profound moral dialogue regarding the nature of the renewed order. This includes debates about the proper combination of moral suasion and coercive means, and the limits of what is proper versus what is excessive in bringing autonomy back within bounds.

The specific direction of the curl back is still far from clear. Will it lead to the restoration of a traditional, 1950s-style social order? A fundamentalist religious order? A moderate social conservative one? Or regenerative communitarian? Behind these alternative scenarios lies the basic question of *whether curtailing individualism and reestablishing virtues will also cause a significant diminution of autonomy.* This is the core issue for the near-term future of American society, as it is for other societies in similar circumstances.

There were a fair number of signs even before the end of the 1980s that some social groups were seeking to restore a higher level of order but at the time, society at large did not follow their lead. Among the first to react to the decline in social order was a group of blue-collar workers (known as "hard hats") who objected to the counterculture as early as the late 1960s. The Christian right made its first significant organized public-political forays in the 1970s.

The main increase in power of the groups seeking restoration of an earlier order came in the early 1990s. The Christian right rose in membership and influence, as did secular social-conservative groups (such as the Council for National Policy, the John Randolph Club, and the Progress and Freedom Foundation). Together these groups dominated the 1992 GOP platform committee and its national convention. In 1994, the religious right controlled the GOP organization in twenty states and had substantial influence in thirteen more states, and on many school boards.[66] In 1994, the religious right played a major role in the landslide election that resulted in Republican control of the House and Senate, for the first time since 1954, as well as numerous governorships and state assemblies.[67] Democratic political candidates increasingly courted these religious groups and responded to conservative cultural demands. (President Clinton often sought them out, speaking on family values and the importance of faith, and issuing a memo clarifying the right to pray in public schools.) William J. Bennett became a cultural hero. His *Book of Virtues*, which his publisher feared would not sell, became a runaway best-seller.[68]

The communitarian movement rose in this context and contributed to the newly intensified concern with the moral order. It called for a regeneration of virtue, drawing on some traditional values but deeply recasting others and formulating still other new ones, rather than attempting to reconstruct the past. Its platform and leaders argued that strong individual rights (autonomy) presumed strong personal and social responsibilities (moral order) rather than a return to an order based on imposed duties. Communitarians called for a shoring up of the moral, social, and political foundations. Objecting to a liberal notion that the family was dysfunctional, defunct, or unnecessary, but not advocating a return to the traditional family, communitarians have favored a peer marriage in which father and mother have the same rights and responsibilities and both are more dedicated to their children.[69] Communitarians favored relying on moral dialogues, education, and suasion to win people to their ideals, rather than imposing their values by force of law. They showed faith in faith.

As of 1990, communitarian ideas and ideals, as a positive statement rather than mainly as a critical (and largely academic) stance, gained growing public attention. A new publication was launched and a platform was issued, along with several position papers on specific issues.[70] The platform was endorsed by more than one hundred public leaders, not merely academics, including Betty Friedan; Richard John Neuhaus; the first head of the Environmental Protection Agency, William Ruckelshaus; the president of the American Federation of Teachers, Albert Shanker; former Congresswoman Claudine Schneider; and Daniel Kemmis, the mayor of Missoula, Montana. Leaders from a variety of social and political positions embraced several of the communitarian ideas.[71] Soon leaders in other Western societies followed suit.[72]

The movement has had a considerable effect on public dialogue. Discussions of communitarian thinking appeared in all the major papers, magazines, and political journals. The number of articles written on the subject increased seven times between 1990 and 1995.[73] Senator Bill Bradley stated that communitarianism "promises to shape a new political era in much the way progressivism reshaped our nation a century ago."[74] It is the only significant group that provides a "cultural" alternative to the religious right; but the extent of its effect on the direction of the curl back cannot yet be determined.

On numerous social issues, the intensified moral dialogue of the early to mid-1990s moved away from individualist notions toward social conservative or communitarian conceptions. There was a growing agreement among Americans about the importance of families, character education in schools, community bonds, and reciprocity among members of society—and their active participation in providing services to one another, including safety (note, for instance, the increase in community policing and neighborhood-watch patrols). It has been more and more widely recognized that the individualism of earlier decades (referred to as "me-ism" in this curl-back period) had swung too far, and that one must reaffirm John F. Kennedy's often-cited credo: "Ask not what your country can do for you, ask what you can do for your country." Personal responsibility for self and social responsibilities toward others and the community became oft-invoked virtues.

Sexual permissiveness, driven in the 1960s by the mass introduction of the birth control pill and a permissive individualistic ideology, was beginning to be reined in by the rise of sexually transmitted diseases, particularly AIDS, and a new normative thinking that struggled between a return to Victorianism and a linkage of sex to responsible conduct.

While the regeneration of values and institutions had begun, the debate between social conservatives and communitarians about the best direction for regeneration to follow was far from settled. The axis of debate has been along the question of whether moral regeneration must rely on traditional, especially religious, values, or whether it could draw on an inclusive moral dialogue that could include those who are committed to values on secular, humanistic grounds. This debate was paralleled by a discussion of whether the regenerated morality should rely mainly on suasion, or whether it could be rebuilt through legislation concerning social/moral matters, even if millions—even the majority—of the members of society do not endorse these values. Typical were the debates on how to deal with homosexuals, abortion, school prayer, criminals, drug abuse, welfare mothers, violence on television, and teen sex.

As the debates raged, punitive measures reached a new high after 1990. Congress passed a bill mandating life sentences for repeat violent offenders ("three strikes and you're out") in 1994.[75] The number of prisoners and police were further increased.[76] Death sentences were more common and appeals were curbed.

Indicators of antisocial behavior "stabilized" after 1990 or began to recede. The overall rate of crime per 100,000 people fell from 5,820 in 1990 to 5,374 in 1994.[77] Violent crime, including murder, rape, and aggravated assault, has been on a downward trend, as are burglary and car theft.[78] In several major cities, including New York and most cities with populations of over 1 million, murder rates fell back in the early to mid-1990s.[79]

While alienation did not decline, voter turnout has bounced back from its low in 1988, when 50.2 percent of eligible voters went to the polls, to 55.9 percent in 1992. Though participation in off-year congressional elections remains at little over one third, the participation in 1994 was slightly higher than in 1990.

Families may have stabilized, and, according to at least one study, more traditional families may be making a comeback: Since 1990, the number of two-parent families with children has increased (between 1990 and 1995, there were 700,000 more two-parent families, reversing a twenty-year decrease);[80] the divorce rate has begun to fall back from its highs in the 1980s (20.5 in 1994 from 23.0 in 1980);[81] and the rate of teen pregnancy has decreased.[82]

As of the mid-1990s, it seems that the pendulum has begun to swing back toward more social order and some diminution of antisocial behavior and anarchy, while the extent that the new order will be based on moral factors or on state powers, and its effect on autonomy, are still particularly unclear.[83] And there was no indication that in the future American society will resemble, come close to, or even significantly move in the direction of the kind of society individualists envision.

OTHER SOCIETIES

The application of the communitarian paradigm to other societies is in an even more preliminary state then its application to American society. Briefly, societies in Western Europe, especially those in the north, as well as in Canada, Australia, and New Zealand, have followed a similar path to the American one, but on a different level and more slowly. These societies have been on a different plateau because, on many fronts, they started from a higher level of social order, combining much more regulation of social life with stronger moral suasion, and they continued to maintain higher levels even as their social order receded in the period from 1960 to 1990. The direction of their trends, as distinct from their levels, however, were similar to the American path by practically all measures, including the decline in shared values, an increase in diversity, and an increase in antisocial behavior.

One set of data will stand for many others that could be cited. As in the United States, violent crime rose in this period. In West Germany, for example, the rate of all crimes rose by 75 percent between 1972 and 1987;[84] in Britain, the rate of all reported crimes rose by a factor of five between 1960 and 1990.[85] One significant difference: While violent crime rates in Western Europe, Canada, and Australia were somewhat comparable to those of the United States, the homicide rate was substantially higher in the United States.[86] Also, most European countries had lower rates of divorce, single-parent families, and illegitimate births than the United States.[87] And, all European countries except Switzerland had higher political participation, measured by voting rates, than the United States.[88]

In the 1990s, however, these countries were catching up, with increasing speed, according to some data, with the America of the late 1980s, just as American society began its curl back. Moreover, the reaction of these societies to the trends discussed here was also similar, although delayed a bit: They also experienced a rise of social conservative and authoritarian or right-wing groups, and also saw the beginning of a communitarian movement.[89] To reiterate, these very tentative comments just hint at the study of the dynamics of the social order and social construction of autonomy in democratic societies other than the American society. Basically this study remains to be undertaken, with due attention to differences among these countries and not only between them and the United States.

Former Communist societies, especially Russia, experienced a breakdown of order in the early 1990s of great magnitude and on many fronts, swinging from a totalitarian regime and highly coercive order directly to a considerable level of political and social anarchy. Moreover, they even showed some signs of turning authoritarian. Moscow of the early to mid-1990s, with its high crime rate, withdrawal of old laws and anemic enactment and enforcement of new laws, high levels of corruption and self-centered behavior, robber-baron capitalism, rampant alcoholism and drug abuse, constitutes a case study of a society where both order and autonomy are highly deficient.

The notion that former Communist societies could jump from communism to democracy, advanced by several highly influential individualistic economists,[90] and backed up by the International Monetary Fund (IMF), the World Bank, and US AID, failed to take into account the lasting effect of these societies' history and culture and the prerequisites of building a new moral order. As the only nonreligious, nonauthoritarian source of values and design for new social formations, communitarian ideas proved to be of interest to members of these societies, but these societies have only begun to explore their implications.

Several former Communist societies other than the USSR, such as China, Romania, and Bulgaria, have not given up many of the highly coercive means of maintaining order. The Baltic republics, Hungary, Poland, and especially the Czech Republic, which never fully absorbed the totalitarian model, have made greater strides toward finding their own pathway toward some kind of communitarian society.

Japan continues to be a society with strong communitarian elements but also one that is not well balanced internally. Social order is strong: the divorce rate in Japan, at a record high in early 1990s, is still half that of the United States. The illegitimacy rate in Japan hovered at 1.1 percent, compared with the American rate of 30.1 percent, and has remained unchanged since 1960.[91]

At the same time, autonomy is deficient, if measured against a model good society. Japan's tolerance for personal differences, though rising a bit, is still low. The same is true for the rights of women and minority members. While responsibilities are clear and well enforced by the moral voice (and, to a much lesser extent, by the state), the police are barely curbed. If arrested, Japanese must assume that they will be convicted and that they will effectively have no rights. Practically all indictments (98 percent) lead to convictions.[92] Japan provides a case study of a society that must swing in the opposite direction from the West if it is to gain a communitarian balance.

OVERSTEERING

I suggested that societies are like bicycle riders, who constantly need to correct their balance by pulling in the opposite direction the road is inclining. Societies whose steering capabilities are still rather primitive are like inexperienced riders: they often overcorrect, a tendency that is difficult to avoid completely, though its extent can be reduced. To stay with the analogy for a moment, an accomplished rider corrects early, before the bicycle tilts too far in either direction, and corrects gingerly, in small increments, and under most conditions keeps the bicycle on course and on the road. In contrast, inexperienced (or intoxicated) riders slalom wildly and grossly overreact, and they find it difficult to keep on course or even on the road.

In a society that is tilting toward disorder, oversteering is evident when, for instance, decades of large increases in antisocial behavior lead to extreme calls for policies such as the "suspension of the Constitution until the war against crime is won"; when a reaction to the AIDS epidemic is "to quarantine all who have sexually transmitted diseases";[93] or when the realization that several regulations are inane, meddlesome, and redundant leads to indiscriminate slashing of government regulations aimed at protecting the safety of consumers, workers, and the public at large. Over-deregulation is a telling example of oversteering.

The extent of societal oversteering is largely affected by: (a) the magnitude of the centrifugal or centripetal forces that "hit" the society at any given point in time (e.g., a great depression is more taxing for the societal steering than a minor recession); and (b) the availability of assets and techniques that enable the social steering mechanisms (including the intellectual communities, think tanks, social sciences, public minded media, and public discourse) to read correctly the external and internal challenges, and fashion appropriate responses.[94]

All else being equal, the less ideological the response and the more effective the communication lines between those affected and those who do the steering, the less oversteering occurs. Because the polity of communitarian societies, as we have seen, is inevitably democratic, communitarian societies oversteer less often than authoritarian—not to mention totalitarian—societies. (A comparative study of the United States and the USSR suggests that the main strength of the former has been the close links between the society and the polity.[95]) However, because of our limited understanding of societal processes and the ways various responses will work, oversteering even in communitarian societies can at best be minimized, but not avoided.[96]

In conclusion, we have seen that American society is leading the procession of Western societies toward a regeneration of the social order. Whether in the process only anarchy will be reined in, or whether oversteering will cause a diminution of autonomy, is the challenge communitarian societies currently face. Specifically, the regenerative outcomes will reflect which social paradigm will prevail. Social conservatives, spurred on by religious fundamentalists and secular right-wing thinkers, may pull Western societies too far in the direction of imposing social order and undermining autonomy. This, in turn, is likely to lead to a "liberal" correction. Or communitarians, in coalition with moderate social conservatives and moderate individualists, will help the societies involved follow a course that brings them closer to a communitarian equilibrium. This is the "cultural" question for the decade ahead. At the center of that question is how normative directions are fashioned.

IMPLICATIONS FOR PRACTICE AND POLICY

To advance the regeneration of American society requires that the members of the society come together to commit themselves to a core of shared values, and find ways to embody these in the members' daily conduct and in social formations such as the family and the schools. These matters are discussed in the following chapters. There is, though, an overarching contextual matter that is of great importance for the foreseeable future. It concerns the relationship among the centrifugal effects of global economic forces, the responsive policies that have been developed to cope with them, and the social order, especially its moral foundation. Communitarian progress may be severely hobbled unless this issue is addressed.

In this area, too, the United States is leading a parade of Western nations that have committed their public and corporate policies to compete economically on a global level. This is reflected in the reduction of trade barriers; the development of free trade zones (e.g., by the European Community and the North American Free Trade Agreement); international agreements (e.g., GATT); downward pressures on labor costs (to be able to compete with low-wage countries, which provide few benefits to their workers and have low social costs, especially environmental ones); the lowering of public benefits (the welfare state, in the European sense, which provides benefits not merely for the poor but for all members of society—for instance, low-cost college loans); and deregulation and cutting of inspections in matters ranging from the quality of meats to the safety of drugs. Corporations also have reduced their contributions to health care plans, pensions, and other benefits.

Benefits, wages, and job security have also been significantly curtailed by means of a sharply increased reliance on part-time employees. American dependence on "contingent labor" has risen consistently, nearly doubling between 1990 and 1995 (from 1.2 million workers in 1990 to 2.0 million in 1994).[97] All of these measures together, which I shall refer to as the "downsizing society," have resulted in a deep-seated and widespread sense of deprivation, insecurity, anxiety, pessimism, and anger.[98] These resentments have been further exacerbated by technological changes that seem to differ from previous ones in that they cause lasting high levels of unemployment, especially in Europe.

The social effects of these developments have been softened to some extent as second members of the same household (typically women and often mothers) turned to gainful employment, thus enabling the household income to rise since 1973 while that of each worker rose only marginally. But this adaptation had social costs of its own, and it cannot be drawn upon in the future as new socioeconomic pressures arise, unless child labor is to be further increased. (A large number of teenagers already work more than twenty hours a week while still in school.)

Hence, the crowning contextual question for regeneration for the foreseeable future is *how far can a society tolerate public and corporate policies that give free rein to economic interests* and that seek to enhance global competitiveness, *without undermining the moral legitimacy of the social order?*[99]

Champions of individualism argue that, after a transition period, the increased ability to compete will generate many new jobs and a higher standard of living for most (if not all) members of society. If this is the case, the tension between the centrifugal forces of competitiveness and the needs of an orderly, good society will resolve itself. Communitarians, though, need to inquire which policies need to be followed if these individualists' predictions turn out to be excessively optimistic and the indicators of anger and social unrest continue to rise and to find additional expression in rising extremist movements, fundamentalism, xenophobia, and other forms of public resentment and rebellion, all of which threaten the social order.

This is a subject for which there are no ready answers, especially as the moral dialogue about these questions has just begun. Among the options that can be considered and which are communitarian in nature are:

1: *Slowing down the adjustments globalization entails.* This approach entails allowing employees and citizens in general more time to adjust to new policies and socioeconomic conditions. Western Europe, Australia, and New Zealand clearly choose to follow a slower path in these matters than the United States.[100] Removing tariffs, quotas, and other trade barriers and national subsidies gradually rather than rapidly is one such policy.

2: *Community jobs.*[101] American public policies tend to assume that there are jobs for people, and hence training is the way to deal with the unemployed and welfare recipients. However, if jobs are scarce, neither training nor disincentives for those who have grown to depend on welfare will work; at best they will lead some people (at high public cost) to find jobs, replacing others who would have held those jobs otherwise.

Politicians have talked about accelerating economic growth while keeping inflation down, thus creating millions of new jobs, but suitable macroeconomic policies have been elusive. Providing a massive number of public jobs, as was done during the Depression, is costly, while the resulting production is often of limited social merit.[102] Public funds might be allocated (under a workfare program to replace part of welfare, for example) to schools, hospitals, public libraries, environmental protection agencies, and other community institutions, to hire people to carry out work which these institutions would otherwise not have been able to afford. The institutions, in turn, would be required to provide monitoring, transportation, and child care. Boards need to be set up to include community and labor representatives to ensure that the new community jobs will not replace existing jobs.

3: *Work sharing and enhancing job security*. Corporations and workers might agree to reduce overtime, and maybe even to introduce a shorter work week, if this will allow the employment of more people. One must note, though, that work sharing on a significant scale would be possible only if wages were proportional to the time worked (rather than keeping full pay for shorter periods), a position even a few labor unions have come to endorse in Europe.

Agreements that "trade" various desiderata (from the employees' viewpoint—e.g., higher health benefits) with enhanced job security also help soften the transition.

4: *Social basics*. While in Western Europe most political parties agree that the welfare state needs to be scaled back, few seek to dismantle it. In the United States, individualists (including laissez-faire conservatives and libertarians) have sought to roll up the social safety nets altogether, or indirectly destroy them by means testing or partial privatization. One can reduce social costs, public expenditures, and dependency by lowering the safety nets without removing them. Psychological security does not rely so much on the specific level of support available if a person is out of work, disabled, or sick, as on the firm conviction that they and their children will receive some basic help; that they will not be cast into the street, without medical assistance or basic provisions.

A bi- or multipartisan agreement to keep a basic social safety net out of politics, as part of the core of shared values, and to limit the partisan debate to the specifics of what is to be included would significantly curb the rising anxiety in the populace. This would provide an important prerequisite for a good society. Without secure social basics, autonomy is not available to millions of members of the society, a deficiency that, in turn, also undermines the social order.

5: *Voluntary simplicity*. In the longer run, a profound question must be faced: The pursuit of the affluent way of life by 6 billion people (as the underlying goal of global competitiveness) assumes that the earth can sustain a world that is like an American suburb (a direction in which China and India, for instance, have been moving), and that this is a world in which people will generally be content. Both assumptions seem ill founded. After a worldwide sharing of social basics and the enhancement of autonomy that this entails, more consideration will need to be given to sources of satisfaction that are not resource intensive (a search the affluent societies may best lead).

I cannot stress enough that this does not entail that the poor remain in their misery in order to leave enough resources for the affluent societies (and the elites in their societies) to maintain their standard of living. On the contrary, the more the affluent find other satisfactions, the more practical and political it will become to ensure that all members of the world's communities will be able to meet their basic needs.

Of interest in this context are values reflected in the notions of *combining* voluntary simplicity (willingly limiting one's consumption to materials that meet true needs and avoiding "status goods," such as whatever is currently fashionable and the most recent technological devices) with *pursuit of other sources of satisfaction* that are not resource intensive, such as those found in culture, family life, bonding with others, community building, participation, voluntarism, and transcendental projects.

The counterculture of the 1960s championed the rejection of consumerism, often in an extreme form, arguing that if people would consume little, they could drop out of work and find satisfaction in sunsets, cheap wine, and being high on marijuana. These ideas are incompatible with a modern economy (in which work generates not merely consumer goods but also health services, education, science, and art). But a considerable number of suburbanites, city-based young professionals, and campus-based academicians have adopted a much more moderate version of the same basic idea. They have recognized that the acquisition of marginal consumer goods (especially status goods) is a lower source of satisfaction than several other pursuits, which are low in cost: exercise and sports, for instance. And increased involvement in these reduces the need to work overtime, to become career obsessed, and to suffer the attendant psychic and social consequences. Such a change in attitude toward status goods is also associated with an enhanced sense of security (social basics are easier to secure than a consumerist way of life) and a way to break out of the curse of the time squeeze.

People who embrace voluntary simplicity may also be those most willing to share goods with those in need, because such sharing will not threaten their satisfactions. This is the place voluntary simplicity and communitarian thinking most clearly converge.

How can the ideals of voluntary simplicity be shared more widely? What practices can best embody them and which public policies can help promote them? The answer lies in moral dialogues that opinion makers and public leaders can help initiate and nourish, but which they neither control nor command. These dialogues are explored in the next two chapters.

FOUR

Sharing Core Values

The idea that a good society requires social formulations of the good, requires "republican virtue," may seem rather unremarkable until one notes that individualists strenuously oppose such concepts. Social conservatives are inclined to expand the conception of the common good until it becomes pervasive, if not invasive. What is the case for a *core* of shared values? What is the source of such core values, and most importantly, if lost, how can they be regenerated?

A GOOD, NONPERVASIVE CORE

BASIC DEFINITIONS AND THESIS

Moral order—as distinct from all other forms of social order—rests on a core of values that are shared by a society's members and embodied in societal formations ranging from the rituals of marriage to incorporation charters, from the celebration of holidays to the swearing in of elected officials. *Shared* values are values to which most members of the society are committed (albeit not necessarily to the same extent). Shared values differ profoundly from *agreed* positions, which are the results of some procedure, such as negotiated contracts or arbitration, and are reached on practical or tactical grounds—an accommodation by individuals who have different values.

The language here hinders a certain precision of expression. The word "shared," according to the dictionary, can be used both in the case of a group of people who happen to "share" a bus ride although they have precious little in common, and in the case of members of a community that "share" a bus purchased by the community and employed according to the community's tradition and culture (for example, it is never used on Sunday, or children may use it free of charge). In the following discussion, "shared" refers to those social values that are commonly affirmed by a community or society, rather than being the products of a convergent good.

I stressed from the onset that to ensure voluntary compliance, the good society must rely largely on its members' realization that the ways they are expected to conduct themselves are in line with values in which they believe, rather than because they fear public authorities or are driven by economic incentives. I turn now to explore this pivotal point in some detail.

There is a strong tendency to assume that the social order in a free society rests on laws and that these are upheld by inspectors, auditors, the police, courts, and prisons. If the billions of actions that take place in society every day had to be supervised to ensure that they are carried out in line with the mores of the society, half the population would have to serve as enforcers. These guardians, in turn, as Plato already pointed out, would need guardians themselves, who would in turn need enforcers of their own. The ultimate result is closer to a police state than to a good society.

The issue is hardly theoretical. As the moral infrastructure weakened around 1960, American society tried to rely increasingly on police, drug agents, IRS auditors, inspectors, border patrols, and prisons to maintain the social order. The costs have been eating into other social priorities. Education, especially higher education, has been deprived as more prisons are built and police hired. The police force, which is insufficiently supervised, itself becomes a source of corruption, brutality, and racial tensions. And yet order is far from solid. The great difficulties in state-based enforcement of social mores, and the undesirable side effects of such efforts, are most notable in the drive to curb the use of controlled substances. In short, for a good society to maintain order, without drifting in the direction of an authoritarian state, most members, maybe as many as 98 percent, most of the time, must abide *voluntarily* by the mores. Law enforcement then can step in to deal with, at most, the remaining 2 percent.

A core of shared values also *enhances the ability of a society to formulate specific public policies.* The shared values provide criteria for settling differences in a principled rather than an ad hoc or interest-based manner. And these values help mobilize support for public policies, support that is lacking when they are worked out in some other way. Tocqueville observed that "[f]or society to exist and, even more, for society to prosper, it is essential that all the minds of the citizens should always be rallied and held together by some leading ideas."[1] It is reported that one of the main reasons that Estonia's and Latvia's transitions from totalitarian societies toward communitarian ones were much smoother and significantly more extensive than that of the other thirteen former Soviet republics was "the degree of consensus among many politicians and voters. That consensus—which survived five governments in Estonia and four in Latvia—holds that the two countries must press forward with tight budgets [and] free market reforms."[2] Austria, until the mid-1990s, was a sterling case of a high-consensus country. On the other hand, the gridlock in Washington, D.C., in the last decades reflects, among other things, profound value differences.

Some strong individualists argue that, in a liberal state, shared values are not necessary because people who are assumed to have identical or complementary interests will come to agree on public measures that they all consider compatible with their individual formulations of the good. This notion does not square with elementary, readily observable facts. The debates over normative issues, such as whether the state should limit abortion, divorce, and homosexuals in the military; fights over reallocation of wealth (e.g., among workers, top executives, and shareholders); and the strife among communities about where to place undesirable facilities (from incinerators to nuclear plants), all illustrate that there are significant differences of values and interest that are very difficult to reconcile, if there are no shared values upon which to build.

Those individualists who are willing to recognize that the notion that individuals have strongly divergent interests and values argue that these people can draw on procedures, such as voting, to concur on public policies. Critics, such as William A. Galston and Michael J. Sandel, have pointed out that the conception of liberty, both in the presumption that individuals should be free to define the good and in the commitment to procedure, already implies some notion of a common good.[3]

Moderate individualists such as Amy Gutmann and Bruce Ackerman agree that there are additional virtues implied in the very notion of a liberal state (for instance, the need to cultivate the ability to think critically), but they seek to keep the list thin and closely related to the core concept of autonomy. (Critical thinking, for instance, is needed to keep the state at bay and enable citizens to rely on themselves as free agents rather than on the state.)

The sociological facts are that procedural commitments and a thin layer of shared values are often insufficient. Take, for example, the agreement between two groups whose values are incompatible but work together, a pro-life and a pro-choice group that are cooperating on behalf of children in St. Louis.[4] First, such behavior is rather rare. Second, it does reflect a shared profound substantive value: concern for children! The difficulties American society has had in establishing national welfare, a national health policy, and standards for education all illustrate the difficulties that public policy makers and citizens alike encounter when they try to agree on public policies without sharing the values that are to be embodied in them.

Moreover, a consensus reached without the core of shared values is less stable. When the circumstances change, those who endorsed a policy for pragmatic or tactical reasons will be much more likely to withdraw their commitments than when they share a normative commitment to it. This is the basic reason that international agreements are often so much more fragile than national ones. Reliable consensus is based largely on a thick layer of shared values.

Michael Walzer attempts to bridge the differences between individualist and communitarian views by allowing for different definitions of the good for different social areas. He lists such areas as membership; security and welfare; money and commodities; office (bureaucracy); hard work; free time; kinship and love; divine grace; recognition; education; and political power.[5] As a result, a person valued highly in one area is likely not to be valued highly in another. This, sociologists have long argued, is indeed the case, especially in open democratic societies. (In contrast, in caste systems—and, to some extent, in rigid class systems with little room for mobility—those who rank high in economic stature also rank high in political status, public prestige, and so on.) The merit of Walzer's position is that it allows that a community (or a group of communities) may have shared moral criteria without embracing one universal definition of the good (thus avoiding the dangers such a concept entails).

This approach advances the development of "overlapping" conceptions of the good by legitimating pluralism, without necessarily embracing relativism, which accords no special standing to any conception and, at the same time, avoids universalism. One group—for example, a scientific community—could stress the value of telling the truth; another—for instance, a group of social workers—the value of being empathetic to others; while both could agree that truth telling and empathy are positive, substantive values.

Still missing are criteria by which one can account for these values. Communities could meet Walzer's criteria of a plurality of definitions of what is good in different areas by celebrating machismo in one area (say, in gender relations), racism in another, and selfishness in still another (the socioeconomic arena). The question of what the society considers good and how it is to be judged cannot be avoided.

IN A HISTORICAL PERSPECTIVE

Over the last few centuries, several major ideological movements have played down the role of values (or piety) in social life.[6] The rise of secularism, the belief in science and in social engineering (including economic theories), the preoccupation with economic growth, and the rising influence of individualistic philosophies all have minimized the role of moral values in general and of sharing them in particular. Religion—a major source of core values—was believed by the sons and daughters of the Enlightenment to be an anachronistic force. While in the West the main anti-values force was the belief in reason, in large parts of the rest of the world Marxist notions about the predominance of technology and economic forces prevailed. In the post-Depression years and after World War II, and more recently in formerly Communist countries, much public attention has focused on finding ways to gain or maintain the affluent way of life. And, in the last generation, individualistic public philosophies have gained in political importance.[7]

As functional theory leads one to expect, the combination of long- and short-term neglect of shared values led to a thinning of the moral order and to the expected dysfunctional consequences. Another indication of the vacuum left by the thinning of shared values, and the yearning to have that vacuum refilled, is the rise of strong religious fundamentalist movements in many parts of the world, from Indonesia and Algeria to the United States. These movements focus on "cultural factors," on values, and downgrade the concern for and service to other societal needs, especially those of modern economies. The debate about family values versus work outside the home is a case in point.

While the debates with religious groups are openly about shared values, so are numerous other contests that reflect deep differences in secular values, although these differences are not always explicitly recognized as normative ones. Among the issues confronted in this way are the public obligation to children, the scope and nature of our stewardship of the environment, and the extent of our obligations to people of other countries.

It seems clear, from a functional viewpoint, that after a lengthy relative neglect of shared values, many societies entered the 1990s in an intensive phase of *values regeneration,* in which they dedicated much social "energy" to determining which values should be abandoned (e.g., no chastity, even for priests?), which should be reinforced (e.g., mutuality, voluntarism), and which should be reformulated (e.g., moral obligations to welfare recipients). Above all, intensive dialogues are taking place on the question of which values belong in the shared core and which are to be left to individual formulations (for instance, in questions such as whom to hire, fire, or promote, whom to admit to college, and to whom to sell one's house).

It is much less clear at this stage how this intensive phase of regeneration will conclude. Will it lead to the imposition of pervasive fundamentalist religious values on the rest of society, a less extreme version of a development that took place in Iran? Or will the result be heightened normative divisiveness and increased intergroup strife? Or will the quest for regeneration lead to a widely shared and strongly affirmed but limited set of core values, reinforcing the communitarian elements of society?

THE CONTEXT OF THE DEBATE

The same historical context just depicted in terms of societal changes also provides a context for a piece of intellectual history that explains the rise of communitarian thinking and the communitarian social movement. Viewed from this perspective, individualistic attacks on the concept of a core of shared values (or common good) in the seventeenth to the nineteenth century served as a reaction and corrective to previous definitions of the common good that were too pervasive and too restrictive, leaving little room for autonomy.

When individualists employ ideas that served to correct excessive emphasis on social order in earlier centuries to attack the common good in the second half of the twentieth century, in a radically different context, they pull society further away from a point of balance (a point elaborated upon in chapter 2).

To be fair, it is not only individualists who have challenged the concept of a common good. So did various Marxists, champions of conflict theory, and those of *Realpolitik,* who argue that the concept of shared values is advocated by those who seek to deflect attention from basic differences of interest between the classes and the imminent class warfare, and that society is or can be held together by force and economic interests. But none of these arguments suggests that such societies are or can be made to be good societies.

Communitarians maintain that the concept of shared values is pivotal for social thinking. This position has led to a very elaborate, often reported, reviewed, and cited debate between communitarians and liberal individualists.[8] Nothing can be gained by this sociologist reviewing this discussion again. (In this context, there is a huge scholarship that revolves around the writings of John Rawls, neither reviewed nor engaged here.)

I mention briefly only the points that are relevant to the role of shared values in ensuring a good society, which is at issue here. Basically, communitarians have championed the concept of a *common good* and pointed to the limitations of relying only on the good as individually formulated. For reasons already discussed, I agree with those who point out that a good society requires social formulations of the good.

If one grants that such a concept is needed, the question of the *scope* arises: Is that good only procedural? Substantive but thin? Thick? Pervasive? Positions range from that of moderate individualists (especially among individualist liberals) who observe that a thin set of virtues is embodied in their very vision of the liberal state (Gutmann and Ackerman, for instance), to communitarians (such as Galston) who showed that such virtues are thicker. (In his discussion of the virtues that a liberal states requires, Galston identifies a rather extensive list of personal virtues that need to be cultivated, including courage, patriotism, responsibility, tolerance, work ethic, moderation, adaptability, and civic virtues.[9])

I suggest that a good society needs a still richer core of values to frame the community's culture and thus limits, but far from obliterates, pluralism. As for what is to be included in the common good and what is left to particular subcultures, are extensively treated in chapter 7; but let me note here that religious values are a good example of the kind of values that need not be shared by all. In contrast, social conservatives tend to champion a pervasive set of values. For instance, they favor a societal commitment to one religion, often calling for a Christian (or Muslim or Hindu) state; are keen to regulate numerous aspects of personal behavior from sex to consumption of alcohol; and oppose diversifying the curriculum of schools and colleges.

Individualists, to the extent that they recognize the need for a common good, tend to seek to limit its reach to the *public realm but oppose it in the private realm.* The need of all societies to promote shared values is rather evident when it comes to public behavior, that is, to guiding people's behavior toward one another and shared goods and resources, from subways (e.g., tolerating aggressive begging) to parks (e.g., allowing lovemaking in broad daylight), to beaches (e.g., tolerating nudity). Yet when it comes to private behavior—in one's home or car, for instance—even moderate individualists tend to assume that mainly theocracies such as Sudan (or Calvinist Geneva or Puritan Salem) or secular totalitarian societies regulate such conduct.

Actually, the sharp contrast between public and private does not hold empirically, and it is not normatively justifiable.[10] Sociologically, one observes that there are laws in all societies that reflect shared values that guide private conduct. These include what parents may not do to their own children (abuse them sexually, beat them severely), things adults must do for their offspring (immunize them, send them to schools), regulation of the behavior of adults with each other (requiring them to obtain licenses to be married), and so on. Furthermore, even highly liberalized societies regulate the sale and consumption of pharmaceuticals and controlled substances even in the privacy of one's home, and, of course, extensively regulate private relations to objects (property).

From a normative viewpoint, behavior that violates core values—for example, spousal abuse—is immoral whether it occurs in a supermarket or at home, in a plaza or in one's backyard. The same holds for the abuse of children, exploitation of labor, and numerous other behaviors. I join here both with feminists, who pointed to the limited merit of the public/private distinction, such as Carole Pateman, Elizabeth Frazer, and Nicola Lacey,[11] and with communitarians, Galston especially.[12]

As I see it, the important distinction is between behavior that is covered by the society's core values and that which is not, a distinction that cuts across the categories of private and public. Thus, consumers may not "privately" purchase child pornography, surveillance devices, crack cocaine, and many other items. These limitations reflect one or more of our core values. Similarly, people may not marry privately whomever they wish (no polygamy, even for Mormons), must obtain a proper state license, have a blood test taken, and so on. They may, though, speak freely, hug one another, and dress to the hilt, privately and publicly, in liberal states.

The last important point to cull from the debate between liberal individualists and communitarians occupies the rest of this chapter. It concerns the *sources* of values and the ways they are *modified*—two closely related subjects.

SOURCES OF VALUES
AND THE MODES OF RECASTING

CULTURAL, NOT PERSONAL

In a communitarian society (and in quite a few others) *values are handed down from generation to generation rather than invented or negotiated.* This is the profound implication of the phrase that a community has an identity, a history, a culture. David Miller, writing about a national community, elucidates:

> What does it mean for people to have a common national identity, to share their nationality? It is essentially not a matter of the objective characteristics that they possess, but of their shared beliefs: a belief that each belongs together with the rest; that this association is neither transitory nor merely instrumental, but stems from a long history of living together which (it is hoped and expected) will continue into the future.[13]

The starting point, typically, is shared values, not individual choices or formulations of the good.

To the extent that individualists explore directly the source of social values, they tend to suggest or assume that individuals discuss with one another the direction of public policy and other matters about which they must share and reach an understanding.[14] This makes mores like contracts, something that individuals work out rationally.

John Locke employs a heuristic device to highlight this point. He envisions freestanding individuals coming together to choose a social arrangement that, in effect, embodies a set of normative understandings. John Rawls used the heuristic device of a veil of ignorance behind which individuals formulate principles of justice. In his post-1980 work, though, Rawls recognized that his analysis concerns individuals who are situated in a given social context, namely a liberal society, and that these individuals bring to the original position a set of normative commitments.[15] From here on, though, these individuals follow the contract model in his view.

The fact that classical liberals, contemporary classical liberals, libertarians, and laissez-faire conservatives all make individuals their starting point is not accidental; in their paradigms, the individual carries the ultimate moral value, and only autonomous individuals can bestow legitimacy on social arrangements, institutions, elected officials, and so on.

There is no shred of evidence, or any reason to assume, that there ever were true individuals, each with his or her values in hand or at least at heart, roaming the forest on their own, who joined together to deliberate and establish the kind of community that suited their individual purposes and normative predispositions. Nor is there any indication that an aggregate of individuals ever gathered to decide to yield to the community some of their prerogatives, thereby setting up some moral rules and choosing some values members would be expected to follow. To be fair, champions of the individualist paradigm do not claim that mores or social values emerged in this way; they draw on such tales to make their point: Individuals are the ones to make social choices as aggregates of individuals, if not simply on their own (that is, either like lawyers negotiating a deal or like buyers in a supermarket).

On further thought, one soon realizes that, as in the Antioch case, mores and values cannot be worked out on an ad hoc basis at every turn, nor can they draw on prearranged contracts. If a society tried to follow this course, then half the society would be lawyers drafting contracts (or trying to wriggle out of them). It is not an accident that the most individualist society, American society, is also the one that is most litigious. In effect, for a society to function, it must draw on culture and traditions and the shared values they entail. Only these values can provide the normative criteria needed to proceed without constant haggling and to work out differences even when negotiations do take place. Emile Durkheim established this in his well-known observation about the importance of *pre*contractual values and normative commitments that undergird contracts and their observation.

Thomas Spragens Jr. explains that this tradition is itself valuable, and deserves respect:

> To participate in any real-world civil association that has a history is to incur moral obligation. Even if the society in question is seriously flawed, each participant in its ongoing common life is in debt to all sorts of fellow citizens whom he or she has never met and cannot even name. The institutions, the infrastructure, the very existence of a political order that is part of what creates and sustains us—all are received as a patrimony that we did not purchase and that we cannot in any coherent sense be said to deserve.[16]

Note that Spragens's claim is empirical and not merely normative.

The individualists' notion that social order will be negotiated or arranged also ignores the role of shared values (environmental ones, for instance), when the main beneficiaries are future generations. Children pose problems for libertarian theorists, who either assume children to be small individuals with the same rights as others or, much more commonly, ignore them. Obviously, neither future generations nor young children can be at the negotiation table to argue for their interests and conceptions of the good; instead, children are protected by our shared moral commitments that encompass them.

One answer to questions concerning both the content and the processes of regeneration that has been strongly advanced in the mid-1990s (and often championed before) is to restore a civil (or civic) society. Intensified interest in and concern about civility has been evident in social science and philosophical literature, the popular press, and in statements by public leaders.[17] As I indicated earlier, while the term "civility" has been used in different ways, most commonly it has referred to the need to deliberate in a civil manner about the issues the society faces, and to sustain the intermediary bodies that stand between the individual and the state.

Such notions of a civil order reflect, at best, a rather narrow band of values. They speak to some of the conditions necessary for individuals to come to agreement with one another, but take no position on the normative content of such deliberations and negotiations. To put the matter in more colloquial terms, civility ensures good communication but not the ability to tell right from wrong and to abide by the implications of normative determinations. To argue, as I do, that to have a civic society is insufficient, that a virtuous society requires a core of shared values, is not to dismiss civic order. It is a necessary, but far from a sufficient, element of the social order a good society needs.[18]

In 1995, this avoidance of moral substance took what might be considered an almost humorous turn when public leaders repeatedly called for the people to find a "common ground," without any discussion of what this common ground might be. It was like inviting one and all to a meeting without informing them where it will take place. Calls for civility are of service. But, by itself, to be civil is good—but not good enough. As Gertrude Himmelfarb put it, "It is not enough, then, to revitalize civil society. The more urgent, and difficult, task is to remoralize civil society."[19] (For the same reason, teaching values "clarification" or moral reasoning to children is not enough; they require moral education.) In addition to recognizing the virtue of talking civilly, like the virtue of deliberations in general, a regenerating society has to acknowledge the merit of talking civilly about virtues.

An interesting question is whether people in the chess clubs, bowling associations, and even choirs that Putnam extols form only social bonds or also develop commitments to shared values. I suspect that these groups provide some bonding but not much of a moral culture. (True, I have been to chess clubs—and some bowling alleys—in which there was a strong shared culture, but it was an extremely narrow one, limited largely to a few manners. My experience with choirs is much more limited.)

A colleague wondered if the American colonists would not qualify as a bunch of individualists who came together to deliberate and form a society. The same question may be asked about the founding fathers and mothers of any "planned" and anticipated society, from Israel to Communist ones. (The coffeehouses of Switzerland are said to be places Lenin and company spent much time, preparing.) The fact, though, is that none of the individuals came to these meetings as freestanding persons; they came as sons and daughters of particular cultures that deeply affected their deliberations and choices. For instance, the Zionists who shaped the dream of a Jewish state came largely from the secular parts of Jewish culture, and shared a strong rejection of the Diaspora in which they grew up, and drew (especially beginning with the Second Aliya) on socialist ideologies. All these "priors" they brought to the table deeply influenced the core values they shared and the social institutions they designed.

Individuals never write on a blank slate. Community provides them with history, traditions, culture, all deeply imbued with values. In earlier periods, just as in contemporary societies, children (and immigrants) typically found themselves in some kind of community that shared some core values. These values may have been tattered, widely challenged, badly in need of being regenerated, or deeply recast, but there seems to be no record of a morally vacuous starting point.

The fact that cultures have a normative starting point does not mean that individuals do not play a role in sorting out values; "all" that cultures provide individuals is a foundation. Individuals may rebel against their culture, form new cultural elements, or fashion them out of traditional elements combined with new ones; however, the background against which these individuals rebel, and which partially defines the direction and content of their rebellion, is their society's set of values. The new, renewed, or reconstructed culture they develop inevitably builds on given normative elements.

What processes are available to societies to shore up or recast their core of shared values? And which of the available processes are more communitarian? Are the often extolled deliberations such as "deliberative democracy" the answer?

THE LIMITS OF DELIBERATIONS

The literature on deliberations is deeply influenced by the individualist way of thinking, both in academia and among opinion leaders, even in the works and considerations of authors and authorities who otherwise are not particularly individualistic. Individualists argue that a community (or society) may establish its normative guidance of conduct and its policies by assembling an aggregate of individuals to discuss dispassionately the facts of the situation, their logical implications, and the available policy alternatives, and then to choose the most empirically valid and logical course. This idea draws on the Enlightenment notion that reason will free people from the clutches of superstition and ignorance. The process whereby reasoned people exchange views and negotiate a new course is often referred to as "deliberation."[20] The overarching image that prevails in this way of thinking is highly charged with positive, affective, and normative content: the image of a New England town meeting or of an ancient Greek polis.[21] Miriam Galston clearly states:

> Most contemporary legal theorists addressing republican concerns advocate some form of deliberative democracy. The heart of their recommendations for making political life more deliberative is the estab-

lishment of certain procedures in the decision-making process designed to enhance, if not ensure, a rational or reasoned basis for legislative, judicial, and other determinations.[22]

James Kuklinski and his associates put it well: "From Kant to Rawls, intellectuals have unabashedly placed a high premium on deliberative, rational thought and, by implication, rejected emotions and feelings as legitimate (although unavoidable) elements of politics."[23] Jack Knight and James Johnson write, "We view deliberation as an idealized process consisting of fair procedures within which political actors engage in reasoned argument for the purpose of resolving political conflict."[24] Philip Selznick explains, "If deliberation is taken seriously as a guiding principle, it is bound to check populist impulses. Deliberation is an appeal to reason rather than will, including popular will."[25]

Deliberation and civility (or democratic polity) are often closely associated. A civil society is said to be one that deals with its problems in a deliberative manner. Kuklinski and his associates sum up this view:

> In a democratic society, reasonable decisions are preferable to unreasonable ones; considered thought leads to the former, emotions to the latter; therefore deliberation is preferable to visceral reaction as a basis for democratic decision making. The preceding words summarize a normative view that has dominated thinking at least since the Enlightenment. It prescribes that citizens are to approach the subject of politics with temperate consideration and objective analysis, that is, to use their heads when making judgments about public affairs.[26]

The founding fathers, and many others concerned with democratic processes, were deeply concerned about "mobs" being swayed by emotive voices, without regard to reason. More recently, the intensifying clash between Western civilization and that of religious fundamentalists has been depicted as a clash between reason and passion.[27]

There are, however, three powerful, profound reasons that deliberations are elusive. First, participants in communal dialogues are not autonomous agents, stuffed with information and analytic software; they are members of the community who must earn a living, attend to their children, and so on; they study matters of public policy in their rather limited spare time. Moreover, even if each deliberant came equipped with a mind full of information and statistical techniques, the information and analytic capacity required for rational decisions is not available even to a supercomputer, a problem widely recognized by those who study artificial intelligence and decision making. It is common to point out, for example, that so far it has been impossible to decide in a chess game what the best (most rational) move is because the permutations are too numerous. But compared to real life decisions, chess is a very simple choice space. In chess, there are only two players, fully explicit and immutable rules, all the needed information is right in front of the actors, and power relations among the pieces is fixed. In communities and societies, the number of players is large and variable, rules are modified as the action unfolds, information is always insufficient, relative power of those involved and those affected is changeable, and the rules of engagement are in constant flux. As a result, those participating in all social decision making are forced to rely on a much humbler sorting process than the rational decision-making school, at the heart a deliberative model, assumes.[28]

Second, the participants in many society-wide or community "deliberations" are not individuals but subgroups, either outright representatives of such groups or individuals whose thinking and choices largely reflect their membership in various groups and subcommunities. Thus, a dialogue between social conservatives and laissez-faire conservatives on the GOP platform committee regarding what position to take on abortion, or between New Democrats and welfare liberals in the Democratic Party, reflects, to a large extent, group values—not thoughts that have been developed by these individuals.

An understanding of the internal processes of these groups clarifies the dialogues among the groups' representatives or even regular members. These internal processes are affected by many factors, from the competition for power within a given group to efforts to counter centrifugal forces that affect the particular subgroup rather than the community at large. Information about the merits of the case is but one factor influencing the ensuing dialogues.

When I interviewed staff members of the Christian Coalition, asking about the reasons Pat Robertson's speeches, and above all, in-house communications, were so abusive to minorities and women, among others, the staff argued that Robertson had to keep up the hate drums to raise the money his operation required. The same explanation was provided when an ACLU staffer was asked why that organization keeps issuing clearly exaggerated alarms about dangers to our liberties. An example of the latter is a membership-drive letter issued after the 1994 midterm elections, in which the ACLU states:

> A *firestorm* is sweeping across the country that threatens us all. Now that the Radical Right has won political power in Congress and in state legislatures across the country . . . newly empowered extremist groups in nearly every state are fanning the flames of *intolerance* and *bigotry*, igniting fierce *legal battles* and triggering explosive *social conflicts*. . . . *These are your rights that are under fire*.[29]

Third, and most important, the issues communities face are, to a significant extent, normative and not empirical or logical. This fact is often overlooked, or its importance downgraded, under the influence of the rationalistic-deliberative model. To push this point, I suggest that even consideration of many issues that seem technical are often deeply influenced by normative factors. For instance, the question whether or not to put fluoride into a town's water supply brings into play the values of those who oppose government "paternalism";[30] the importation of tomatoes from Mexico evokes values associated with questions such as the extent to which we should absorb real or imaginary health risks for the sake of free trade and fostering better relations with our neighbors; and questions concerning the best way to teach English to immigrant children raises value issues concerning the commitment to one nation. There seem to be no normative-free decisions of any significance.

When it comes to taking a position concerning major policy issues, the sorting out of values is paramount. For example, a consideration of specific environmental measures is deeply affected by the extent to which various members and subgroups within a given community share a commitment to the value of stewardship, our responsibility to leave the environment to our children in no worse condition than we found it. Arguments that if we continue to dump pollutants into the air, lakes, or groundwater we will damage our future carry much less weight with people who are preoccupied with their well-being or have strong value commitments to other causes than with people who have strong environmental values.

Note that, under the influence of individualistic thinking and the libertarian branches of social science, there is a tendency to explain actions driven by values as if they were largely driven by self-interest or, at best, by enlightened self-interest. But this should be considered a libertarian blinder and a pose rather than a reading of the sociological reality of policy making.

If, for example, one takes a policy issue that was hotly debated for decades, and in many countries—the extent to which governments' budget deficits must be reduced—one finds that the issue is often put in terms of economics and self-interest. If the deficit is cut, interest rates will decline, inflation will be avoided, competition with other countries will be made easier. But, from a sheer scientific viewpoint, the level at which deficits cause damage is far from clearly established.[31] Japan, for instance, did rather well in years when its deficit was much higher than that of the United States. Similarly, in the period from 1990 to 1995, countries whose gross national product (GNP) grew much more rapidly than those of the major Western economies, countries often referred to as emerging markets, had significantly higher deficits, rates of inflation, and interest rates than the United States. It hence is quite revealing that the debate about the deficit is often couched in normative terms: Is it "decent" to eat our heritage and rob our children? As President Reagan often argued, a country is like a family; it *should not* spend more than it earns. Many economists are fully aware of the difference between the ways families and nations are financed and are affected by deficits, but this did not detract from the moral force of the way Reagan framed the issue.

I am not arguing that in community-based and national debates about policy issues, information and reason play no role. I am, however, pointing out that they play a much smaller role than is often asserted, both because they are much weaker tools than believed and because a much larger role is placed by another factor: the appeal to values. A fuller study of values talk (and of moral dialogues) will enable one both to better understand the processes of sorting out values and to ask how these may be improved.

THE DANGER OF CULTURE WARS

In contrast to deliberations, the term "culture wars" suggests that the public is divided on which core values ought to guide society and that segments of the public confront one another in ways that are at least counterproductive as they try to grapple with the issues at hand.[32] Culture wars lead to divisiveness, lack of resolution on overdue issues ("gridlock"), intergroup hatred, and tribalism. In recent years, American society's main fault lines have been between the religious right and liberals;[33] in Israel, between secular and religious groups. Earlier, a Kulturkampf raged between the Catholic Church and Otto von Bismarck after he tried to subject the church to German state control.[34] At their worst, culture wars lead to violence (as we witnessed during the bombing of abortion clinics in the United States), and even war.

James Hunter states:

> *Culture wars always precede shooting wars.*. . . Indeed, the last time this country "debated" the issues of human life, personhood, liberty, and the rights of citizenship all together, the result was the bloodiest war ever to take place on this continent, the Civil War.[35]

Given such a sharp contrast between reason and passion, deliberations and culture wars, amicable resolutions and emotional confrontations, I am not surprised that even those who have weak individualistic inclinations tend to favor the deliberative model. As I see it, this discussion, like others cited earlier, suffers from the curse of relying on dichotomies. The indisputable sociological fact is that deliberations of the relatively pure kind favored by individualists are almost impossible to achieve or even to approximate under most circumstances. The examination of actual processes of sorting out values to guide a society, or even a small community, shows that they are rather different from those assumed by the deliberative model.[36] It might be argued that deliberation should still be upheld as the morally superior form, but it is so removed from sociological reality that, as its implied assumptions are routinely and roundly violated, the result is alienation rather than political engagement. Above all, there is virtue in another, more communitarian approach that I refer to as "values talk," the processes through which moral dialogues are advanced.

VALUES TALKS:
THE PROCESSES OF MORAL DIALOGUES

Moral dialogues are communications about value, about the normative standing of one suggested course as compared to another. They have "procedures" all of their own.

One procedure often used in moral dialogues is the *appeal to an overarching value* shared by the various parties to the sorting-out process. Robert Goodin is, in effect, applying this rule when he seeks to pave the road for a community that must sort out a course between the rights of nonsmokers and those of smokers.[37] At first, this may seem to be a typical clash between two values: the rights of one group versus those of another. However, Goodin points out that both groups are committed to the value that one's liberty does not allow one person to violate the "space" of the other. In familiar terms, my right to extend my arm stops when my fist reaches your nose (actually, quite a bit before that). Goodin points out that because nonsmokers in their nonsmoking do not penetrate the space of smokers, while smokers do violate non-smokers' space, nonsmoker rights should take priority. When such arguments, which employ an overarching value to help sort out con-flicts between two or more subordinate level values, are used, we wit-ness one procedure used by communities in sorting out their values, in determining the normative guidance to their policy making and endorsement.

Overarching values are also used to argue that certain specific poli-cies should be rejected or embraced. Members of communities fre-quently argue that a certain measure under consideration is not com-patible with a free society, a self-respecting society, or a caring people. These, as a rule, are not technical arguments; there is often little evi-dence that if the community adopts a given measure, liberty will be seriously endangered, and so on. Actually, the argument is that if the community proceeds in a given manner, such action will be incompati-ble with an important value it seeks to uphold. (For a fine example of such an exercise, see Stephen Carter's book *Integrity*.[38]) I suggest that an empirical examination of successfully completed moral dialogues will show that, often, they draw on such superordinate values to deal with conflicting moral claims.

Another step often taken is to bring a third value into play when two diverge or clash. For instance, those who seek to restore the coalition of the 1960s between African Americans and Jews argue that both groups share a commitment to liberal causes. An attempt to create an interfaith coalition pointed to the shared commitment to religion as the partici-pants struggled to develop a joint statement.[39]

In effect, most of the considerations ethics brings to bear involve the relative merit of various values rather than conflicts between good and evil. Values talk does not occur when members of a community declare their values; for example, labeling oneself "pro-life" or "pro-choice." Values contain an accounting. And those can be examined and chal-lenged, for instance, by such arguments as: These values are inconsis-tent with other values you hold; or these values lead to a normative con-clusion you "could not possibly seek."

Still other relevant procedures entail *values education, persuasion, and leadership* (in which those who do not share in a given value are convinced to embrace it). These are not examined here because they are well-known. It should, though, be noted that they all are open to abuse.

These three procedures share a sociological element; in each, a person is able to change the values or preferences of others. This ability to change other people's values is particularly alien to individualistic thinking and, in effect, threatens individualistic paradigms to the extent that their various advocates have gone a long way to try to deny the significance of values education, persuasion, and leadership. For instance, neoclassical economists (who draw on an individualist paradigm) argue that advertising is informative rather than persuasive[40], systematically skip an examination of the way children are educated and thus the way their values are formed, and ignore the role of leadership in deeply affecting people. This may seem strange until one realizes that libertarians must minimize, if not ignore, this sociological element if they are to maintain their primary focus on autonomy. If people are subject to various forms of value changes that are externally driven, one must deal with the societal formations that cause these changes, rather than assume that the course individuals follow reflects their deliberations and choices. Actually, all these procedures are often applied by communities as they sort out values.

RULES OF ENGAGEMENT FOR VALUES TALK

To protect values talks from deteriorating into culture wars (and to keep them communitarian), rules of engagement can be, and are being, applied. They basically reflect the tenet that one should act on the recognition that the conflicting parties are members of one and the same community; hence, they should fight, as the saying goes, with one hand tied behind their back.

One specific rule is that the contesting parties should not "demonize" one another, that they should refrain from depicting the other side's values as completely negative, as when they are characterized as "satanic,"[41] reflecting the anti-Christ, or treasonous. For instance, after the GOP won the 1994 elections in a landslide, Newt Gingrich, the ebullient new speaker of the House, referred to his side being supported by "God-fearing" Americans faced with an opposition of "Godless" people.[42] (Even academic discussions are reported to have become "too vituperative."[43])

Another rule of moral dialogues is *not to affront the deepest moral commitments of the other groups*. The assumption is that each group is committed to some particular values that are sacrosanct to it, values which must be particularly respected by others; as well as some dark moments in its history upon which members prefer not to dwell. Thus, to confront a German with the horror of the Holocaust whenever one discusses a specific normative difference, or to tell Jews that it did not happen, undermines values talk. Self-restraint in these matters thus enhances the processes that underlie moral dialogues.[44]

Mary Ann Glendon makes a strong case that *using less of the language of rights and more of that of needs, wants, and interests* would make dialogues more conducive to truly shared resolutions. As Glendon puts it, "in its simplest American form, the language of rights is the language of no compromise. The winner takes all and the loser has to get out of town. The conversation is over."[45]

Another important rule is to *leave some issues out of the debate*, both to narrow the area of contest and to be able to draw on existing shared foundations. This is one reason Americans have been careful not to reconvene a constitutional assembly and have made it rather difficult to amend the Constitution.

Liberal individualists stress the importance of keeping ultimate values (especially religious ones) out of deliberations (to keep them "thin" and limited to public matters) to ensure that people will enter them with an open mind.[46] When this valid observation is pushed too far, it leads liberals to join dialogues without strong commitments—only to be reasonable, constructive, and to find a compromise. When they face others who have strong substantive convictions, the result is illustrated by the kind of dialogues President Clinton engaged in during the first two years of his administration. He gave up half of his agenda before the give-and-take started, and was quick to fold much of the rest—all to be reasonable. To call attention to the difference between joining a dialogue with strong positions along with the willingness to listen and respond to others, versus joining it mainly out of a commitment to a good process, I will refer to a "dialogue of convictions" versus a "dialogue of proceduralists." For moral dialogues to take hold, to gain traction so to speak, they must be those of convictions, not of proceduralists.

Additional rules are provided by James Hunter:

First, those who claim the right to dissent should assume the responsibility to debate . . . Second, those who claim the right to criticize should assume the responsibility to comprehend . . . Third, those who claim the right to influence should accept the responsibility not to inflame . . .

Fourth, those who claim the right to participate should accept the responsibility to persuade.[48]

Understanding the ways moral dialogues take place and can be enhanced is of great importance to communitarian societies because such dialogues sustain one of the key elements required for the social order: that these issues be sorted out with limited centrifugal side effects. It is a subject that requires much more study and one that is likely to intensify once both the elusiveness of deliberations and the importance of values talk, as distinct from culture wars, are more widely recognized.

MEGALOGUES

Many who consider the ways people come to share values, to the extent that this subject is considered, tend to view the sorting out of values as a matter in which families or small communities may readily engage, but wonder how a society could possibly come together to affirm a new, renewed, or some other set of values. This question deserves careful attention. The fact that communities engage in moral dialogues, and not only or even primarily during town meetings (which most do not have in the first place), is rather easy to establish.[48] However, critics of communitarians argue that such dialogues cannot take place at the societal level. I argue that *whole societies, even a society whose population counts in the hundreds of millions, do engage in moral dialogues* that lead to changes in the widely shared values. The process occurs by linking millions of local conversations (between couples, in neighborhood bars or pubs, in coffee- or teahouses, around watercoolers at work) into society-wide networks and shared public focal points. The networking takes place during regional and national meetings of many thousands of voluntary associations in which local representatives dialogue; in state, regional, and national party caucuses; in state assemblies and in Congress; and increasingly via electronic links (such as groups that meet on the Internet). Public focal points are national call-in shows, debates on network television, and nationally circulated newspapers and magazines. Several associations—including the Council on Foreign Relations, National Issues Forum, the Public Agenda Foundation, and the League of Women Voters—are explicitly dedicated to nourishing both local values talk and society-wide "megalogue." Many believe that these forums are mainly dedicated to sharing information and clarification of thinking; actually, they play a considerable normative role. (The

Council on Foreign Relations has a strong anti-isolationist slant; the National Issues Forum and the Public Agenda Foundation have a firm progressive, civic slant; and so on.)

National megalogues are often fostered, accelerated, and affected by public events such as hearings (for example, the Clarence Thomas/Anita Hill case focused discussion on what constitutes sexual harassment and the morally proper response to it), trials (the 1925 Scopes trial challenged the teaching of evolution), demonstrations (such events undermined the normative case for the war in Vietnam), marches (protest marches had a major effect in the 1960s in changing the country's view on racial discrimination). While fireside chats and other speeches from what is called the bully pulpit of the presidency play much less of this role than is often attributed to them, especially when one expects that a president could change the direction of a country with a well-honed speech, they do serve to trigger, focus, and nourish nationwide dialogues.

Megalogues are often extensive, disorderly (in the sense that there is no clear pattern to them), have an unclear beginning, and no clear or decisive conclusion. Nevertheless, in societies that are relatively communitarian, megalogues lead to significant changes in core values.

A few brief illustrations will serve. Until 1968, a person was considered dead when the heart and lungs stopped functioning. Movies perpetuate this notion with people listening to a dying person's chest or holding a mirror to the mouth to see if it fogs over. As technology made extension of life that met these criteria rather common, to well beyond the point where a person's chances of regaining a meaningful life were nil, a group of scientists and ethicists came up with a new definition of death: brain death. But community mores continued to demand that doctors do all that could be done for loved ones whose hearts were kept pumping by artificial means. At this point, various scholars primed a society-wide dialogue about the definition of death. The issue was dramatized by the Karen Ann Quinlan case in the 1970s. The ensuing megalogue gradually led to a change in the public perception (and the movies' image) of death. Although the change is still not complete, it was wide enough to establish new social mores.[49] In recent decades, similar dialogues about the deficit, welfare, and the role of the state have occurred, all, like earlier dialogues about women's rights, leading to changes in normative direction.

Until 1970, the preservation of the environment was not considered a shared core value in Western societies (nor in many others). This does not mean that there were not some studies, articles, and individuals who saw great value in it; but the society as a whole paid little systematic heed and protecting the environment was not listed among America's core values.[50] As is often the case, a book, *Silent Spring*, by Rachel Carson, which was very widely read and discussed, triggered a nationwide megalogue. A massive oil spill and the ensuing protests in Santa Barbara, California, and, later in the decade, the Three-Mile Island incident further established the subject on the national normative agenda. Thousands of people gathered in New York City to listen to pro-environment speeches and to pick up garbage along Fifth Avenue. Two hundred thousand people gathered on the Capitol Mall in 1970 to demonstrate concern for the environment on Earth Day.[51] As a result, concern for the environment became a core shared value. (There continue to be disagreements about the level of commitment to this cause, and the best ways to proceed, but not about the basic value. A conservative president, Richard Nixon, founded the Environmental Protection Agency, and during his presidency many environmentalist policies, such as recycling, were introduced.)

The same can be said for values issues raised around the civil rights movement in the United States in the early 1960s, which led to broad-based agreement that legal segregation in the South had to be eliminated; and in the debate about excessive government intervention in the economy, which led, in the early to mid-1990s, to a broad-based agreement that such intervention needed to be curtailed and regulations cut. (Even welfare liberals now call for a lean state.)

Similar megalogues occur in other societies, for instance in the United Kingdom and in Scandinavian countries, where the topics include whether to join the European Community and what change in values this would entail, how to deal with immigrants that seem to threaten the national core values, and the future of the welfare state.

STAGES

Experts on public opinion, especially Daniel Yankelovich, have proposed stages that typically lead to the formation of "public judgment."[52] Stage 1, *consciousness raising*, consists of the formation of a new awareness of an issue. This stage is largely media driven and is often completed swiftly. The public is relatively passive and receptive. Recent examples of consciousness raising include issues of sexual harassment, gay rights, and the HIV crisis.

Working through, Yankelovich's stage 2, involves meeting the challenge of forming a reaction to the issue that surfaced during consciousness raising. Stage 2 generally progresses much more slowly than stage 1; the time frame is dependent on the depth of emotional significance of the issue. Active involvement by the public replaces the passive state of mind. Often, working through entails a struggle among various camps. Such struggles currently include issues of equality within marriage, changes in divorce laws, and ways to deal with illegal immigrants.

The final stage, *resolution*, entails a successful completion of stages 1 and 2. Resolution involves cognitive (clarification of the facts), emotional (amelioration of conflicting feelings), and moral (coming to share normative commitments) facets. The elimination of most legal racial segregation in the United States is an example of an issue that passed all three stages.

Though it is easy to lay out the stages of coming to public judgment, the process itself is difficult. Many obstacles, from the media's desire to remain in stage 1 to objections by experts who feel displaced, must be surmounted.[53]

Not every megalogue, even in the most communitarian of societies, results in a new shared normative direction. Communitarian societies differ from authoritarian societies in that they require a smaller core of shared values (although significantly more than the societies individualists envision). Even when it comes to what the society considers core values, communitarian societies can withstand a few unresolved differences. (Abortion is a case in point.) However, if the net result is that there are no or only a few shared core values, or that many of the values the society views as core are not shared but ignored or contested, then the society is likely to face the danger of a breakdown or transformation to another pattern. The India-Pakistan partition was fueled in part by deep-seated value differences between Muslims and Hindus. In Lebanon during the civil war from 1975 to 1990, irreconcilable differences among various ethnic and religious groups, especially Christian and Muslim, tore the society apart. Canada is being tested to see whether the core values Canadians share (which are widely believed to be rather weak)[54] are stronger than the normative differences between the francophone culture of Québec and the Anglo-Canadian culture of the rest of Canada.

Many societies are now in the midst of an intense megalogue about the specific balance they seek between order and autonomy and the extent to which the social order will be based on values, i.e., if they seek to fall within the communitarian zone and, if they do, what specific position they seek to occupy within that zone. In American society, the dialogue revolves around two axes. The first is the religious and the secular. While the media focuses on specific issues (abortion, prayer in public spaces, laws against homosexual acts), the center of the debate is the question of which core values are going to guide the regeneration of the moral order. Are these going to be traditional Christian values or the secular civic values that are based on what is correctly called secular humanism? And to what extent will the order be voluntary or imposed?

This debate is tied to a second megalogue, one regarding the proper balance between individual rights and social responsibility. Here, as is often the case, core values are discussed in terms of specific issues, such as the proper ways to deal with criminals, the rights of drivers who consume alcohol, and ways to respond to drug use by train engineers. The resolution of these two megalogues will go a long way toward shaping the American culture of the future.

Other Western societies are engaged in similar dialogues, which are often initiated by the religious right debating communitarians and individualists. Note, though, that in Western societies other than the United States, ideas associated with the liberal left still have more influence. Many Asian societies which approach the quest for a communitarian society from the opposite side, starting with strong social order and weak autonomy, have weak traditions and facilities for megalogue, which they seek to develop as they move in a more communitarian direction. Former Communist societies, having dumped their main ideological foundations in short order , facing severe economic and political challenges, find their rather poor megalogue processes overloaded if not overwhelmed.

DIRECTIONS FOR PRACTICE AND POLICY

RULES OF ENGAGEMENT

The rules themselves and their importance have already been discussed. Where these are lacking or have been undermined, moral dialogues must often start with a *conversation about conversations*. Public leaders and opinion makers need to call attention to the ill effects of uncivilized confrontations and the dangers entailed by slipping toward culture wars. Parties engaged in dialogues may be asked to agree to avoid negative advertising during elections campaigns and other occasions in which moral dialogues take place. (The Republicans used to have a so-called Eleventh Commandment: During the primaries, the candidates would not speak ill of each other. This rule was ignored in 1996, although it had been largely honored in several preceding elections.) Legislators and courtrooms often define the proper ways parties must address one another and insist that individuals apologize when they attack others personally or use uncivil language. The media undermines the rules of engagement when it encourages polarization and confrontations, and it helps sustain them when there is room for serious discussion (for example, on *Washington Week in Review*). Above all, rules are sustained to the extent that the public does not merely pay lip service to the rules of engagement but also shows in its behavior (from voting to turning the television dial) that it disapproves of conduct that violates them.

The media, national and local, are often the forum in which small group moral dialogues are linked together to create megalogue. Hence, the importance of legislation that limits the ability of media empires to gain monopoly on media outlets in one town or region, not to mention a whole country. It is also important to maintain some rules that encourage the media—which uses public airways—to set aside time for moral dialogues and not only on early Sunday morning or after midnight. Public access channels on cable television raise numerous problems and in most places seem to have done much less for moral dialogues than expected. However, National Public Radio (NPR) and public television have been major factors in sustaining the needed dialogues. To the extent that they show bias for or against a specific philosophy, it is legitimate to insist that they not take sides. But the wholesale attack on these media—and plans to privatize or commercialize them—damages the forums in which moral dialogues take place.

Fostering public spaces, town meetings, and forums, all enhance the opportunities for moral dialogues. Numerous suggestions to provide citizens with information to enhance these dialogues, often through computerized devices, which provide at the click of a mouse or push of a button the data relevant to a topic, are helpful but much less important than their advocates tend to believe. "Fact checks," which the media instituted more widely after the 1988 election, are of some merit, but they may have also caused considerable harm; the media now tends to find some minor inaccuracies in the statements of all candidates and thus fosters cynicism among the electorate. To reiterate, the issues often are largely normative. Particularly useful are dry runs in schools, in which young people learn the art of dialogue. These include model United Nations, simulated political conventions, and mock trials.

Initiatives (in which petitions are used in states and cities to put specific policy items on the ballot) and referendums have often been criticized as forms of direct democracy.[55] One can, however, argue that they serve a rather different function—and serve it well: They provide institutionalized occasions for moral dialogues on such issues as affirmative action (the California Civil Rights Initiative), treatment of immigrants (Proposition 187), and the proper level of taxation (Proposition 13). Of course ,when many initiatives—sometimes as many as 260—are introduced at the same time, such dialogues are not possible.

Other means to enhance megalogues include citizen commissions (in which citizens are organized to provide suggestions and recommendations to governing bodies; for example, a citizen commission was recently established to participate in the formation of deregulation policy), presidential commissions (like those that have studied pornography, and social security), and the deliberative opinion poll, recently introduced by the University of Texas political scientist James Fishkin, in which citizens contemplate and discuss issues before responding to the questions in a poll.[56]

Much attention is paid to moral dialogues that are focused on laws and elections. However, one should not overlook the fact that moral dialogues that take place in and around places of worship (for instance, African-American churches that stress nonviolence) and within voluntary associations (such as the League of Women Voters), play an important role in shoring up and recasting core values, even though they are often much less focused and dramatic.

VIRTUAL DIALOGUES

The question of whether or not one can have moral dialogues and even elections using electronic devices such as the Internet is important, as such instruments are ever more widely available, and some governments have gone out of their way to make them more so, especially to the poor.

The first question is, Can one form communal bonds in cyberspace? The answer seems to be in the affirmative: there are quite a few accounts of members in server groups, in which the same group of people interact regularly and membership is circumscribed (say, to those interested in starting soup kitchens for the homeless), forming strong bonds and culture. In effect, it turns out that when members of a virtual community criticize one of the members, the responses of that person are rather similar to the same development in a "real" community.[57] It has been feared that virtual communities would further weaken real ones, and hence should be discouraged. In fact, virtual communities enable people who are homebound (because of sickness or disability or because they are raising children) or socially inept, or simply so inclined, to participate in a community. There might be some who turn into computer nerds instead of social butterflies, but there seem many more who otherwise would not have any way to meet the need to participate in a community. (Virtual communities can be further enhanced by rules; for instance, the members must identify themselves.) When all is said and done, virtual is virtuous.

Examination of suggestions for electronic town meetings are of special interest because of their promise and what they tell us about the nature of dialogue and democratic processes. Ross Perot stated during the 1992 presidential campaign that, if elected, he would conduct electronic town meetings, where select experts (and maybe some members of Congress and his administration), would lay out major issues before the American people. Every few weeks, one major issue, such as the budget deficit or the health-care crisis, would be discussed dispassionately for an hour on national television. Then citizens would make their views known by dialing an 800 number, pushing buttons on a gadget, or mailing a postcard. In this way, Perot suggests, electronic town meetings would put the "owners" back in control of their country.

Others have called the idea an attack on constitutional democracy, comparing it to Napoleon Bonaparte's attempt to replace the legislature with frequent plebiscites. Leonard Garment, White House counsel under Richard Nixon, said Perot "would replace a democratic legislature with pseudo-plebiscitarian town hall meetings." Walter Goodman, the resident intellectual of the *New York Times*, wrote that the idea "evokes the scene, so familiar in this century's history, of Big Brother firing up the populace to cow the legislature or co-opt the opposition."[58]

Critics also point out that viewers could be misled during televised presentations by manipulations of the pictures that are presented. And critics fear that most viewers would soon turn to other channels. As a result, voting would not reflect the public's view but the views of the select few who watch public-affairs programs and members of special-interest groups. Finally, critics argue, polls after such shows can be readily manipulated; after all, one can vote as many times as one is willing to dial, click, or otherwise be counted.

Scoff as they may, the idea of technologically enhanced national town hall meetings has been around at least since Buckminster Fuller raised it in the 1940s. It deserves serious examination if only because many citizens feel alienated from national politics as currently practiced, and because there is a need to find new ways to involve them.

Also, there is a big difference between *some* direct democracy *added on* to our representative system and *replacing* Congress with television shows and push buttons. In effect, Perot suggested matching 800 numbers with congressional districts and tallying the results of electronic town meetings accordingly.

Most important, electronic town halls, far from a cure to all that ails democracy, can be arranged in ways that would avoid several of the pitfalls against which critics correctly warn. The list of prerequisites is far from short; it should come as no surprise that democracy is a rather complex composite that cannot be readily duplicated, or even augmented, by technological means. Hence, it is probably best not to think about "teledemocracy" as either "dangerous and antidemocratic" or "bringing the people back in," but to think of it as *a series of models* that range from particularly defective forms of political participation to those that meet several of the essential requirements.

One major principle: It would be *undemocratic* to *replace elected representatives* and legislatures with computerized voting or any other kind of electronic wizardry. One main reason is the Burkean argument that large groups need two (or more) layers of representation, rather than direct representation, in order to work out dialogue-based public policies. In a layered system, the voters grant their elected representatives "mandates"—that is, generalized guidance reflecting what the voters seek: Get us out of Vietnam; focus on domestic issues; do something about competitiveness. The voters best avoid the specifics. For the system to work, citizens must allow their representatives to engage in give-and-take, within the confines of their mandates, to be able to find a public policy shared with other representatives.

To bring teledemocracy a step closer to the real thing, one can follow a model I tested in New Jersey, a model that is both layered and contains mandates. The New Jersey experiment was conducted with the help of the League of Women Voters. Once a year, the League decides which issues should be given priority. We organized the League's members into groups of ten. They conducted their "town meetings" conference-call circuits, in which each group decided which priorities it favored and selected a representative to take its suggestions on to the next level for discussion. Next, we held conference calls of groups of ten *representatives*, who decided among themselves which views and preferences to carry to the third and final level, which decided on the statewide policy. A survey established that the members were highly satisfied with the results. *Every* member got to participate in the decision-making process without leaving her home; and yet the elected representatives were free, within an area indicated by those who elected them, to work out a League-wide consensus.

Such a model *can be applied to a nationwide* audience by drawing on the magical power of exponential curves: the fact that if one continues to layer representatives in the suggested manner, millions of participants can be included. Assume that the country was addressed, on Sunday between 10:00 and 11:00 A.M., by various experts on, say, whether we should cut back the military by 50 percent over five years. Then, the conference buzz would start with groups of eighteen citizens, each having an hour to discuss and vote. By 6:00 P.M. (given seven layers), the whole country (or 110 million adults) could participate in the process! (The New Jersey experiment was conducted before the Internet was available. It would be much easier to carry out using the new technology.)

Sesame Street teaches third-graders about democratic elections in the following manner: You have three dollars to spend. Some people want crayons, others juice. You vote what to buy. If the majority want crayons, you get crayons, and vice versa. Such a simplistic explanation may do for young children, but adults who think of democracy as a voting machine miss an important requirement that is met in town meetings: exposing people to conflicting arguments and making them examine their positions before they vote.

The last thing that a democracy needs is for people to vote their raw feelings, their first impulses, before having a chance to reflect on them and discuss them with others. Hence, it is highly undesirable to expose people to a new idea, policy, or speech and ask them to vote on it immediately, as media polling currently often does. A much more *democratic* model would result if one required at least a day's delay before the vote is taken, enabling people to discuss the matter with their families, neighbors or coworkers, people they carpool with, and so on.

Finally, ballot-box stuffing must be prevented. Even when much less is at stake than national policy, call-in polls have been grossly manipulated. For example, a 1990 *USA Today* poll asked if Donald Trump symbolized what was right or wrong with the United States. Eighty percent of the 6,406 callers indicated that he was great; 19 percent, a skunk.[59] It turned out that 72 percent of the calls came from two phone numbers! In another 1990 run (in this case, the issue was abortion), 21 percent of the callers "voted" at least twice.

This problem can be fixed. People can be required to dial-in their social security number and two other identifying details (their birthday and mother's maiden name, say). Penalties like those now in place for voter fraud could be extended to the electronic ballot box. This would not fully secure the integrity of electronic voting, but—as historians of Chicago and biographers of Lyndon B. Johnson will tell you—neither is regular, nonelectronic voting.

Several of the sharpest critics of teledemocracy focus on the fact that it is highly unrepresentative. They have pointed out that those who are likely to participate in a teledemocratic exchange are those who are more educated or more politically active, or those who feel more passionately about the issue. All this is a problem if one expects electronic town halls to *replace* public opinion polls and the ballot box. It is much less problematic, however, if teledemocracy is *added* to other means of public expression, each of which has its own defects—defects that are to some extent corrected by combining the various means. Public opinion polls play a major role in selecting candidates for office and affect policy between elections. Although the sampling methods used are accurate and result in a representative sample of the public that is much superior to anything that can be hoped for in tele-polling, the results are deeply skewed by the ways the questions are phrased. Even small changes in wording often lead to major changes in what is considered "the public's mind." Moreover, poll takers often allow no time for deliberation or dialogue, and provide no information about the issues to those whom they query.

Last, but not least, those who show up at regular, nonelectronic ballot boxes do not constitute a scientific cross-section of the public. They are more educated, more politically active, and often are more passionate about the issues than those who do not vote. Above all, actual voting allows citizens to have a say only once every *two years*, at most. Present-day government, which directly affects numerous issues, from abortion to unemployment, from school busing to safety of savings, requires ways to read the public mind between elections. In short, adding electronic town halls to public opinion polls will help supplement actual voting, each correcting to some extent the shortcomings of the other way of relating government to the community.

LIMITING PLUTOCRATIC TENDENCIES

When the polity moves in a direction that conflicts with or perverts the normative direction a society (or community) chooses to follow, especially after prolonged dialogues, this becomes a major source of profound alienation. The citizens sense, quite correctly, that they endeavored strenuously to reach and work the democratic levers, but somebody else has a controlling grip on them. Reconnecting the political decision-making bodies to community dialogues is one of the most important items of the communitarian public policy agenda.

The main cause of the disconnect are city councils, state legislatures, and a U.S. Congress (and to a lesser extent, governors and presidents) that respond more to those who can make major campaign contributions rather than to the voters. A great many rationalizations have been spun to argue that dependency on campaign contributions is not anti-democratic. The effects of private money on public life, and what is to be done about it, is a vast and important subject, the kind of subject about which one usually says at this point, "I cannot deal with it here; it deserves a whole book of its own." In this case, however, I must add that I already have written that book.[60] I will not attempt to repeat its argument here but will mention a few highlights.

Basically, one would have to adopt the British model. Election campaigns in Britain are short (four weeks). The amount of money a candidate is allowed to spend on his or her campaign is small and strictly regulated. (An elected official who exceeds the limit is disqualified, and the executive director of the campaign is sent to jail for a year.) Public funds are used to cover the small costs involved in campaigning. Candidates are given a major opportunity to air their views, cost free, on public television.

Less radical changes might be contemplated if the British model was to be applied in the United States and elsewhere. However, there will be no reconciliation between American communities and their elected officials until the role of private money in public life is significantly reduced. In other democracies, the disconnect between elected officials and the society often reflects outright corruption (which is high in Japan and far from trivial in countries such as Italy),[61] in which legislators are bribed or paid fees for political favors or cut in on lucrative deals. Also, stronger civil-service bureaucracies in other democracies, which placate but often ignore the elected officials (as in the British television series *Yes, Minister*), often are allowed to follow their own agenda. In short, each society must work out new bridges between the moral dialogue and the polity to correct its own sources of the disconnect, but none can maintain its communitarian pattern without responding to this challenge.

FIVE

The Moral Voice

BEYOND SHARING: THE NEED TO CONVINCE

Many discussions on values implicitly assume that once people are brought up right, they will be good people, as if they have been equipped with an internal virtue rod that suffices to energize their good behavior. Similarly, good societies are assumed to be inherently stable. Numerous discussions of civil society, for instance, implicitly assume that if a community reaches closure, if it comes to favor a particular line of conduct its members are expected to follow, there is little need for additional action. This seems particularly to be the case with small town meetings. The implied sociological picture is roughly as follows: A community has concluded, after several town meetings, that residents ought to refrain from watering their lawns and washing their cars until there is a substantial rainfall. Most, if not all, members of the community will adhere to this new expression of the community's shared concern for the common good. Similarly, if a community seeks to reaffirm its patriotism, most everyone will fly their flags on the Fourth of July. Such natural compliance is, as a rule, implicitly assumed rather than explicitly stated, precisely because compliance is not considered problematic.

The sociological fact is that values do not fly on their own wings, that more than sharing is required for the values of a society to be realized, to be reflected in behavior, to guide a people's life.[1]

The main difference one finds among societies in this regard is the extent to which they rely on informal social mechanisms and what I shall call the moral voice, versus on the state and its coercive tools of law enforcement. Good societies rely much more heavily on the moral voice than on coercion.

THE MORAL VOICE, INTRODUCED

What is the moral voice? Why is it effective? Why do individualists fear it, and why are social conservatives reluctant to rely on it? The moral voice is a peculiar form of motivation: It encourages people to adhere to values to which they subscribe. It is peculiar because, unlike typical motivations, it is not a quest for physiological or psychological release (like quenching thirst by drinking water) or based on the pleasure principle. The sense of affirmation people have when they abide by values is fundamentally different, as we shall see shortly.

The term "moral voice" is particularly appropriate because people "hear" it. Thus, when a person who affirms a value is tempted to ignore it (for example, to renege on a commitment to a friend), he or she hears a voice that urges him or her to do what is right. True, a small number of people do not hear a moral voice; they are usually referred to as sociopaths. Most individuals, though, hear the voice, albeit at different levels of intensity.[2]

Hearing the voice does not mean that one will always or even regularly heed it, but it always affects behavior. For instance, a person who at first ignores the voice may later repent and engage in compensatory behavior. (For example, people who were induced to tell a lie were subsequently twice as likely to volunteer to carry out a chore than those who did not lie.)[3]

The moral voice has two main sources, which are mutually reinforcing: inner (what the person believes the shared values ought to be, based on education, experience, and internal development) and external (others' encouragement to adhere to shared values). The connection between Freud's ideas about the superego, ego, and the id and the distinction made here between the inner moral voice and that of the community is a subject that deserves separate treatment, because it would require considerable discussion of the meanings of these terms in the Freudian theory.

THE INNER (PERSONAL) MORAL VOICE

The inner moral voice, emanating from the acting self, addressing that self, urges a person to abide by his or her values and to refrain from behavior that violates these values. Most of us need not consult a sociological or psychological study to know what this inner voice is: We have firsthand experience of its call. Typically the voice's call or claim takes the form of statements that contain "I ought to" as distinct from "I would like to."[4]

The inner voice fosters moral behavior by according a special sense of affirmation when a person adheres to his/her values and of disquiet when the person does not adhere to them. I choose my words carefully because the choice of appropriate words in the secular language is rather limited. Our moral vocabulary (in which the moral voice speaks) has been greatly diminished, and the terms used to discuss motivation tend to be reductionist. They reduce moral motivation (such as altruism) to the pleasure principle. To stress that this is not the source of the moral voice, I write about a sense of affirmation rather than satisfaction.[5]

I am hard put to find terms that capture what a person "feels" or "senses" (incorrect terms, because they evoke the pleasure principle) when the person abides by a value in which he or she believes. It is not akin to the satisfaction that results from eating a fine steak or having a "great" sexual experience. The person who gave a large contribution (by his or her standards) to the poor, the parents who ran into a burning building to save their child, the person who fasted to indicate her religious commitment, are not "satisfied" but *ennobled* by what I call, lacking a better term, value affirmation.[6]

Value affirmation affects behavior deeply. Voluntary compliance reflects society members' convictions that rules of behavior which they are expected to follow in their private pursuits, and in directly serving the common good, are values in which they believe. Studies of voting behavior show that the most important factor in determining why a person votes is the extent to which he or she believes that voting is a civic duty, not the length of the lines at the polling place, the weather, or other such utilitarian factors.[7] Studies of people who changed their energy consumption and electricity use show that a major factor was the strength of their commitment to environmental values.[8] Studies of the role of religion and ideology in shaping history are, in effect, also studies of the power of the moral voice. Other studies show that many more people pay much more of their taxes when they believe that the tax burden is fairly shared and the funds are used for legitimate purposes than when they do not believe this is the case.[9] The United States had much less trouble raising tax revenue and maintaining the draft during the war against Nazi Germany and Imperial Japan than it had during the intervention in Vietnam. Recent prohibitions on smoking in numerous public spaces in the United States have encountered little opposition and high compliance because they were introduced after decades of public education and dialogue. Similar measures introduced in France, without such preparation, were largely ignored.

The significance of relying heavily on normative means, a core element of the good society, cannot be exaggerated. This is best highlighted by comparing the reaction of people who comply under three different conditions: when they are coerced, paid, or convinced.[10] The coerced person will tend to be resentful, as inmates in prisons typically are. The paid person will set aside his or her preferred course of action because of the compensation offered, but still would prefer to continue on his or her own course. A person who wanted to see a movie with a date, but was paid enough to stay in the office and work overtime, does so because he or she seeks the money, not because he or she would rather be in the office. Here, too, at least a residue of alienation lingers, especially if the person is made to work overtime repeatedly. However, when a person is convinced of the value of changing course, that person's preference is changed!

To stay with the example of the office worker, if that worker is convinced that the overtime may help stop an epidemic, he or she may be content to skip the movie, and the resulting compliance will engender little alienation. On the contrary, there is a sense of affirmation of values that results in a particular kind of satisfaction, which can be quite intense and ennobling. It is strong enough to compel soldiers to risk their lives for their country, volunteers to serve in the Peace Corps for poor pay in distant countries, parents to endure what otherwise would be considered gross indignities for the sake of their children. This sense of affirmation leads religious people to believe that it is better to give than to receive and to reject notions advanced by neoclassical economists (who, in turn, draw on libertarian notions) that one ought to seek to gain as much as possible and give as little as possible.

Clearly, no society can entirely rely on a single source of motivation to help sustain compliance with the dictates of the social order. Thus, totalitarian societies rely to some extent on incentives (for instance, they have not abolished pay differentials) and attempts at persuasion; and libertarian societies rely to some extent on force. Similarly, communitarian societies cannot and do not rely only on normative means. They still pay their civil servants, command police forces, and so on. However, they rely on normative means much more extensively, and their members are much more committed to maintaining order and much less likely to seek to undermine it than members of other societies. In short, the order of good societies relies significantly more on *the moral voice* than do other types of society.

THE MORAL VOICE OF THE COMMUNITY

While the moral voice is in part an inner voice, in the sense that people hear it addressing them from within ("I believe that I ought to"), in part it is also an expression of the community to which they belong. Indeed, this is the significance of community for the communitarian paradigm, sociology, and philosophy: Communities often have strong moral voices and hence can help maintain a social order that draws significantly on value commitments and is voluntary, rather than bought or forced. Because this role of the community is so pivotal and so widely ignored or contested, the discussion next dwells on this cardinal point.

Communities are often viewed as social webs, in which people are attached to one another by crisscrossing relationships rather than by one-to-one relationships.[11] This is the reason communities are often depicted as "warm and fuzzy" places.[12] In a more popular vein, communities are defined as places in which the postmaster knows your first name or someone wants to hear the answer when they ask you how you are. In a discussion of a movie about a community of diamond dealers, the reviewer captured well this notion of community:

> Everybody knows everybody: first names are the rule and deals are made with a handshake. Sons with nicely coiffed hair follow bearded fathers into the game; competitors study together in synagogue and dance together at weddings.[13]

But this is only one element of what constitutes a community; communities also share sets of values and reaffirm them, encourage their members to abide by these values, and censure the members when they do not. Communities have a moral voice that is external to the ego's own voice, that serves to reinforce the inner voice of the members. While the inner moral voice and that of the community may sing from the same page, there often is at least some difference in the pitch, the words each voice intones, and the exact notes each strikes.

The moral voice is the main way that individuals and groups in a good society encourage one another to adhere to behavior that reflects shared values and to avoid behavior that offends or violates them. The moral voice is often ignored by casual observers (and, to some extent, by social scientists) because it is informal, subtle, and highly incorporated into daily life. It often works through frowns, gentle snide comments (and some that are not so gentle), praise, censure, and approbation.

To determine which values members of a particular community endorse and how firm their moral voice is, one may ask which values they are inclined to speak up for and how strongly. I conducted an informal survey that can also be employed as a self-test. I asked, Would you speak up if: (a) you see a family walking away from a pristine lake, leaving behind soda cans and paper wrappers; (b) you see a pair of lovers carving their initials into the bark of a tree; (c) you see a mother spanking the living daylights out of her child in the supermarket;(d) someone pushes into a line four people ahead of you; (e) you see a couple necking heavily in a public park in broad daylight right next to a group of small children; (f) you see someone you know driving too fast in a low speed zone in your neighborhood (later, you run into the driver in the store); (g) you witness a teenager offering to carry a senior citizen's groceries to the latter's car; (h) you see someone you know is not handicapped pull into a handicapped-only parking space; (i) someone makes a sizable donation (by the standards of their income) to a cause.

If members of a community sense they are rarely called upon to encourage others to abide by the community's shared values, then that community has a rather diluted or weak moral voice. If members speak up at times, the issues they speak up for reflect the values to which they are most committed. If members of a community speak up in most situations on most issues, especially if they speak up strenuously, the community is a moralistic one. Both strong religious communities (for instance, some monasteries) and secular ideological ones (for example, early kibbutzim) are cases in point. They have strong moral voices.

INNER AND COMMUNAL VOICES

Here the deep connection between the two basic elements of the community, social bonds and the moral voice, comes into focus: Persons heed best the moral voice of others they care about, those to whom they are affectively attached—members of their community. (Family is a small community of sorts; it has both an affective web and a set of values.)

A good deal of behavior, even if the society is only partially communitarian, takes place because people believe it is the right way to act and their moral perspectives are validated by others who share these perspectives. Paul Robinson notes about the findings of social science research: "[B]eyond the threat of legal punishment, people obey the law because they fear the disapproval of their social group and because they generally see themselves as moral beings who want to do the right thing as they perceive it."[14]

Try the following mental experiment: Imagine that some stranger at a bus stop mumbles that you are not dressed properly, that you speak too loudly, and that you are badly in need of a bath. Now imagine the same observations being voiced by a person who is a close friend, a loving spouse, or a trusted employee. The second source carries much more weight, because of the affective attachment.

Psychologists may attribute the need for attachment to the way people are first sensitized to moral claims: in their relations to parents. These parents use the attachments that infants fed and cuddled by them develop to encourage children to behave in ways adults deem appropriate. As the child grows older, this relationship is extended to other persons, more remote: members of the extended family, teachers, and community leaders.

The same close powerful connection between affective attachment and moral voice is found among members of groups to which one belongs. (The effect is especially powerful when the groups offer concentrated, multiple, affective attachments.) Numerous studies have shown that the voice of peer groups speaks more persuasively to teenagers than does any other. The particular suasion of peer groups in prisons, the army, factories, street gangs, and militias are all well documented. Normative appeals are well articulated in these strong communities and fade when the social webs of attachments weaken.

It follows that if the moral voice is feeble or absent, if the community disregards the extent to which its members live up to or ignore shared core values, the community's silence becomes a major reason values are disregarded. Edward Banfield's famous study of a village in southern Italy that had no moral voice provides a vivid description of the disconcerting results.[15]

The moral voice of a community is most effective when appealing to the values to which people already subscribe. Thus, if one wonders aloud why a particular atheist did not attend church on Sunday, this will have much less effect than if one addresses the same pointed question to a churchgoing fellow parishioner.

True, moral voices can rise in quasi-communities (say, commuters who regularly share a train ride), even on the Internet,[16] but they are particularly effective when the communal bonds are strong. This is the reason salespeople are quick to call a potential customer by first name, slap the person on the back, tell jokes, and ask about loved ones: They are trying to establish a semblance of intimacy. They are reaching for the kind of closeness community entails, in which people heed one another's expressions of preferences.

It is important to note that affective attachment ensures that the moral voice of the community will be heard but not that it will necessarily be raised on behalf of values of which the reader or the author of these pages approves. The moral voice of a community speaks to and for whatever values the community shares. The ethical standing of the particular values of a particular community, and hence of the content of its moral voice, needs to be evaluated separately from the question of whether or not the values that are underwritten by the community pass ethical muster. (This is the subject of chapter 8.)

To point to the significance moral voices command in ordering social life, in ensuring that people will abide by their communities' values with little or no policing, is not to deny that each individual is ultimately free to pass judgment on whether or not to heed such moral claims. Indeed, to reiterate, it is precisely because such voices are not coercive that the moral voice is much more compatible with individual autonomy than is reliance on policing, which is, on the face of it, coercive.

The preceding thesis has been subject to challenges that are next cited and addressed.

CRITIQUES AND RESPONSES
"Communities Cannot Be Defined"

Several critics have argued that the concept of "community" is of questionable value because it is so ill-defined—that it has no identifiable designation. In "The Myth of Community Studies," Margaret Stacey argues that the solution to this problem is to avoid the term altogether.[17] Colin Bell and Howard Newby argue, "There has never been a theory of community, nor even a satisfactory definition of what community is."[18] In another text, Bell and Newby write, "But what is community? . . . [I]t will be seen that over ninety definitions of community have been analysed and that the one common element in them all was man!"[19]

As I already suggested, community can be defined with reasonable precision. Community is defined by two characteristics: first, a web of affect-laden relationships among a group of individuals, relationships that often crisscross and reinforce one another (rather than merely one-on-one or chainlike individual relationships), and second, a measure of commitment to a set of shared values, norms, and meanings, and a shared history and identity—in short, to a particular culture.[20]

"Communities Are Oppressive, Conformist, and Authoritarian"

Those who long for community, this argument goes, conveniently ignore the darker side of traditional communities. "In the new communitarian appeal to tradition, communities of 'mutual aid and memory,' and the Founders," writes Linda McClain in "Rights and Irresponsibility" in the *Duke Law Journal*, "there is a problematic inattention to the less attractive, unjust features of tradition."[21]

Communities, critics argue, use their moral voice to oppress people, are authoritarian by nature, and push people to conform. According to Will Kymlicka, this oppression can entail the community prescribing roles of subordination, roles that limit people's individual potential and threaten their psychological well-being.[22] Derek Phillips adds:

In their celebration of the ecstasy of belonging, communitarian writers exhibit a frightening forgetfulness about the past. They fail to acknowledge that the quest for community often involves domination for some and subordination for others. In attacking post-Enlightenment liberalism and the politics of rights, communitarian theorists threaten to rob individuals of their most basic protections against abuses of power. In emphasizing the importance of community for people's everyday lives, communitarians fail to see that it is attachment rather than membership that is a general human value.[23]

Amy Gutmann pointedly remarks that communitarians "want us to live in Salem."[24]

Behind many of these criticisms lies an image of old or total communities, which are neither typical to modern society nor necessary for, or even compatible with, a communitarian society. Old communities (traditional villages) were geographically bounded and the only communities of which people were members. In effect, other than escaping into no-man's-land, often bandit territories, individuals had few opportunities for choosing their social attachments. In short, old communities had monopolistic power over their members.

New communities are often limited in scope and reach. Members of one residential community are often also members of other communities—for example, work, ethnic, or religious ones. As a result community members have multiple sources of attachments, and if one threatens to become overwhelming, individuals will tend to draw more on another community for their attachments. Thus, for instance, if a person finds herself under high moral pressure at work to contribute to the United Way, to give blood, to serve at a soup kitchen for the homeless, and these are lines of action she is not keen to follow, she may end up investing more of her affection, time, and energy in other communities. If a person who has recently been divorced is under severe censure by his church community, he may well spend more time in other communal places. This multicommunity membership protects the individuals from both moral oppression and ostracism; it mutes the moral voice to some extent. It thus allows a community to work out a balance between the moral voice (and hence order) and a fair measure of autonomy. However, incongruity among the values of a person's multiple communities may substantially weaken the moral voice. Hence the importance of the next-level moral community, the community of communities, the shared values of the society at large. (If these sociological observations sound rather complex or hedged, it is precisely because they are.)

In short, the moral voice is most powerful when people are members of only one community, but it can be overwhelming in those cases. It is more moderated when individuals are members of several communities, but it still may suffice to undergird a good part of the social order, as long as the various communities share at least some core values.

For the same reason, it is a valid criticism to argue that a total and monolithic community can drive people to conformism, if this means that such a community will push people to sacrifice large parts of their individual differences in order to follow shared values. But total communities are rare in contemporary societies, while multicommunity attachments are much more common. To worry, in this context, about traditionalism is like worrying about the effects of excessive savings in an economy long plagued by debts and deficits and rather reluctant to mend its ways.

Another facet of the same basic criticism is the charge that communities are authoritarian. Derek Phillips, for instance, remarks, "[C]ommunitarian thinking . . . obliterates individual autonomy entirely and dissolves the self into whatever roles are imposed by one's position in society."[25] As Robert Booth Fowler puts it, critics "see talk of community as interfering with the necessary breaking down of dominant forces and cultures."[26] Some critics mean by this that communities are totalistic, a point we have covered. Other critics mean that communities are dominated by power elites or have one group that forces others to abide by the values of those in power.

This criticism has merit, but it is misdirected. Some earlier communities were, and some today are, authoritarian. The well-known line that "the air of the cities frees" captures what the sons and daughters of farmers of traditional villages must have felt when they first moved into cities at the beginning of the industrial era. (Their work conditions and the slums they often inhabited may well not have enhanced their autonomy, but being away from the stricter social codes of their families and villages seems to have given them a sense of freedom, which in some cases spilled over into anarchic behavior.) Totalitarian communities exist in contemporary societies—for instance, in North Korea. However, most contemporary communities, especially in communitarian societies, are typically not authoritarian even when they are territorial, which they often are not. Also the relative ease of mobility means that people often choose which community to join and in which to live. Agnostics will not move into a Hasidic community in Brooklyn, and prejudiced whites will not move into a neighborhood dominated by the Nation of Islam.

Dominance by power elites and other forms of authoritarianism are not basic or inherent features of community but reflections of the way it can be distorted. For communities to be fully or even highly communitarian, they require the authentic commitment of most—if not all—of their members to a set of core values. To attain such a commitment, the values that are being fostered need to be (a) truly accepted by the members and (b) responsive to their underlying needs. The reason is that if some members of the society are excluded from the moral dialogue, or manipulated into abiding by the moral voice, or their true needs ignored, they will eventually react to this lack of responsiveness in an antisocial manner. In short, communities can be distorted by those in power, but then their moral order will be diminished, and they will either have to become more responsive to their members' true needs or transform into some other, noncommunitarian, social pattern.

The Charge of Conservatism

Still others have accused communitarians of not merely overlooking the less attractive features of traditional communities, but of willfully longing to revive these features. According to Michael Taves, the communitarian vision concerns itself mostly with "reclaiming a reliance on traditional values and all that entails with regard to the family, sexual relations, religion and the rejection of secularism."[27] According to Judith Stacey, "centrists" and communitarians have enough in common with Dan Quayle to make people on the left uncomfortable.[28]

These criticisms are off the mark. Early communitarians might be charged with being, in effect, social conservatives, if not authoritarians. However, many contemporary communitarians, especially those who define themselves as responsive communitarians,[29] fully realize and often stress that they do *not* seek to return to traditional communities, with their authoritarian power structure, rigid stratification, and discriminatory practices against minorities and women. Responsive communitarians seek to build communities based on open participation, dialogue, and truly shared values. (Linda McClain, a fair critic of communitarianism, recognizes this feature of the responsive communitarians, writing that some communitarians do "recognize the need for careful evaluation of what was good and bad about [any specific] tradition and the possibility of severing certain features . . . from others."[30]) And R. Bruce Douglass writes, "Unlike conservatives, communitarians are aware that the days when the issues we face as a society could be settled on the basis of the beliefs of a privileged segment of the population have long since passed."[31]

WITHIN HISTORY:
AMERICA LOSES MUCH OF ITS MORAL VOICE

During periods in which the centrifugal forces are strong, especially after they succeed in throwing a good society off balance, the moral voice fades or ceases to be convincing. As a moral voice wanes, more and more people come to view messages from the government or other public authorities (from the Party to religious institutions) as public relations, propaganda, or otherwise as false or insincere. Thus, when Americans were asked in recent years if policies advocated by either political party were advocated for the country's benefit or political posture, the majority viewed most policies advanced as "political"; this indicates that both political parties have lost a good part of their legitimacy and hence of their moral voice.

A major factor in diminishing the moral voice has been ideologies that agitate against the very articulation of a moral voice, especially that of a community. Such ideologies played a major role in America, especially between 1960 and 1990, and are still far from defunct; they have a substantial appeal both in the United States and in other Western societies.[32] These amoral ideologies have often been described and hence are only briefly addressed here. It should be noted that as part of the recent curl back, these ideologies lost some of their appeal. However, unless they are further withdrawn, they will slow a communitarian regeneration.

One such ideology is a strong version of *individualism*, one that objects not merely to state-imposed mores but also to moral tenets endorsed by a community. In some instances, the case is made indirectly or reflects a confusion between government dictates, which are backed up by force and hence basically leave no options to the actor, and the community's suasion, which leaves the ultimate choice to the acting individual. (A communitarian would recognize that the best way to minimize government coercion is to foster rather than dismiss the moral voice.)

The individualist argument often relies on an ambiguity in the use of the word "coercion." The term is used to cover a very wide range of behavior, from imprisonment to psychological pressure. (A more subtle position, but still fundamentally similar, is to treat all attempts at persuasion as seductions.[33]) However, if the term is used in this way, it leads one to overlook that the use of force (or the threat of such use) is what distinguishes the state's coercion from other exercises of power. For instance, a measure of psychological pressure is contained in most, if not all, social relations, and most assuredly in the moral voice of the community. (If everyone behaved in line with their values and those they share with others, at all times, completely voluntarily, there would hardly be a need for the external moral voice.)

Specifically, strong individualists include in their notion of individual rights and negative notions of freedom ("don't mess with me" and the "right" to be left alone) a strong aversion to any suggestions regarding how to conduct oneself. In *On Liberty*, John Stuart Mill argues: "But neither one person, nor any number of persons, is warranted in saying to another human creature . . . that he shall not do with his life for his benefit what he chooses to do with it."[34] At another point Mill writes, "The object of this Essay is to assert one very simple principle, as entitled to govern absolutely the dealings of society with the individual in the way of compulsion and control, whether the means used be physical force in the form of legal penalties, or the moral coercion of public opinion."[35] That is, he sees no principled difference between the coercion of the law and the urging of the moral voice. Steven Kautz argues that individuals must be free not merely from government, but also authority in general, indeed be free from the moral voice of the community. This, he argues, is because liberalism is a theory based on the consent of the individual. It, therefore, must assume that citizens are "not, or not wholly, constituted by their communities."[36] But the little aside reveals the profound confusion between being influenced by community, but still being able to critically examine one's values and options, and being wholly determined by social forces one does not understand or control. The first position, the true communitarian one as I see it, is completely compatible with personal autonomy. Only the second one is not. Moreover, while having allowed for a moment that communitarians are not hypertotalitarians, seeking to control people's minds and hearts, Kautz presumes that they indeed assume total community control. He writes that "[T]he partisans of the idea of community urge liberal democrats to renounce their sober rationalism. They thus invite an immoderate or slavish politics, . . . [one in which individuals] are compelled either to embrace the community thoughtlessly, or to rebel against it thoughtlessly."[37] Thus the gross oversimplification that individuals are either agents free from community influence or slaves leads to a preposterous distortion of the communitarian position. Gertrude Himmelfarb quotes Joycelyn Elders, who, when asked during her term as surgeon general if having children out of wedlock was immoral, responded, "No. Everyone has different moral standards. . . . You can't *impose* your standards on someone else."[38] She ignores the difference between "imposing" and speaking up for mores.

The tendency to overlook the difference between the urgings of the moral voice of the community and coercion by the state is further reflected when individualists label as "censorship" suggestions from moral authorities and public figures that the media refrain from broadcasting gratuitous violence or hard-core pornography. After *Billboard* magazine denounced the rap musician Ice Cube's record album *Death Certificate*, in which he describes Koreans as "Oriental one-penny countin' motherf——ers," Ice Cube remarked: "I'll say the editor of the *Billboard* has a right to give his opinion just like I have a right to my opinion. But when he says. . . think twice before you buy this, that's a form of censorship."[39] Jean Bethke Elshtain, writing from a communitarian perspective, challenges Ice Cube's understanding of censorship. She wonders, "Why censorship? 'Consumer beware' is not censorship, but advocacy."[40]

Another ideology, which undercuts the very existence of the community's moral voice (as distinct from opposing a particular message), has emanated from social science theories that rest on and feed into individualistic assumptions. Their views have seeped into the public culture, especially from neoclassical economics, some branches of psychology, and, more recently, political science and law-and-economics. These theories maintain that people are driven by the pleasure principle: They seek to "maximize" their satisfaction and avoid pain, and are governed by self-interest. Moral concerns are often treated as false masks that, once removed, reveal the quest for pleasure. For example, social scientists in the individualist tradition basically argue that people who act altruistically are actually trying to incur favor with their bosses, community members, or dates, or simply gain more satisfaction from giving than from taking.

The story is told that the philosopher Thomas Hobbes, a seventeenth-century advocate of this denial of the moral dimension, was seen giving a coin to a beggar. When asked why he contributed to a beggar, and whether this was not due to Christ's commandment, he responded that he did so "with the sole intent of relieving his own misery at the sight of the beggar."[41] Those who tried to convince the Hobbeses of the world not to deny the moral voice point out that if this were all that motivated Hobbes, all he needed to do was to walk away and keep his coin to himself.[42]

In effect, the thrust of such arguments is to debunk any claims of special merit for conduct that is virtuous, as well as any social recognition and affirmation it may produce. If moral conduct is but another form of self-serving conduct, it disappears among all the other acts in which people engage to enhance themselves. Viewed in this way, the moral voice is neutralized because, as we have seen, it often calls on people to act against their pleasure in order to do what is right. When the moral voice is muffled, it loses its power to undergird virtuous behavior, to support shared values.

Another mainspring of individualistic ideology is the championing of the quick gains of "pseudo gemeinschaft," a notion that undermines the much more demanding work of rebuilding communal bonds and the moral voice that draws on them. In the early 1960s (and, to some extent, even earlier), this orientation often drew on notions articulated in a very widely read and followed book, *How to Win Friends and Influence People* by Dale Carnegie, a manual that was augmented by training courses and public lectures.[43] Middle-class Americans have been drilled ever since to "stroke" others to advance their purpose and power rather than to antagonize them by expressing moral judgments.

Carnegie's message found a parallel in notions that favored suspending the moral voice that came from the growing influence of psychotherapeutic concepts on the American culture. Thousands of therapists, social workers, and anthropologists, as well as other professionals and civil servants, increasingly endorsed the ideological position that it is inappropriate for them, in their relations with their clients, to foster or even merely transmit the community's values.[44] Every individual is said to have the right to choose his/her own "lifestyle." Most important, people who violated established moral values and engaged in what was called "deviant" behavior before such terms were banished, were to be understood in terms of psychological dynamics (e.g., a person is alcoholic not because he is acting irresponsibly but because he was abused as a child, had a weak father, or suffered some other such early childhood experiences). This came to a head in several widely followed trials. One case, concerning two young men who gunned down their parents in cold blood, was declared a mistrial when the defendants claimed, without supporting evidence, that they were abused as children.

John Leo provides another example:

> When Sol Wachtler, the chief judge of New York State's highest court, was arrested for extortion and threatening to kidnap the fourteen-year-old daughter of his ex-lover, many New Yorkers were under the impression that some crimes may have been committed. Not so, according to John Money, a prominent sexologist and medical psychologist . . . [who]

wrote that Wachtler "was manifesting advanced symptoms of . . . Cler-ambault-Kandinsky Syndrome (CKS) . . . a devastating illness. . . . The law-and-order treatment of people with CKS is the equivalent of mak-ing it a crime to have epileptic spells."[45]

Psychotherapy often emphasizes expressive individualism, which, as Robert Bellah explains, "holds that each person has a unique core of feeling and intuition that should unfold or be expressed if individuality is to be realized."[46] Expressive individualism assumes that the proper focus is on personal psychological well-being rather than social respon-sibility, not to mention commitment to values or raising a moral voice:

> The ideal therapeutic relationship seems to be one in which everything is completely conscious and all parties know how they feel and what they want. Any intrusion of "oughts" or "shoulds" into the relationship is rejected as an intrusion of external and coercive authoritarianism.[47]

Psychologist William Doherty describes his own experiences:

> Like many others, I was trained to avoid "should"-ing my clients, to never inflict the language of "ought" on them. I had been socialized into a therapy profession that by the 1970s had developed the firm conviction that "shoulds" entrap people into living life for someone else. According to this school of thought, the only authentic life is one based on heeding the dictates of "I want."[48]

Ellen Goodman wrote after the custody battle between Woody Allen and Mia Farrow, in which psychotherapists "demurred from making evaluative judgments"[49] in their testimony:

> I rarely side with people who want to put good and evil stickers on every piece of human behavior. . . . But there are times . . . when I wonder whether our adoption of Shrink-ese as a second language, the move from religious phrases of judgment to secular words of acceptance, has-n't also produced a moral lobotomy. In the reluctance, the aversion to being judgmental, are we disabled from making any judgments at all?[50]

In the de-moralized language, people are taught to respond to another person's comments by reading them back to the person ("vali-dating") and to reassure them of their acceptability ("I'm OK, you're

OK") but not be "directive" (as a moral voice would seem to be).

A particular focus of this approach has been the argument that one ought to approve of whatever the other person is doing in order to bolster the other person's self-esteem. Educators and social workers helped to popularize the psychological notions that if one person criticizes the conduct of another, the latter's self-esteem would be diminished, which in turn would further undermine that person's conduct. This is an application of nondirective psychotherapy by nontherapists to all members of the community.

Critics have questioned the evidence that enhanced self-esteem has many of the expected positive consequences.[51] Indeed, there is reason to suggest that the merits of artificially promoting self-esteem have at least been greatly exaggerated. Some critics go so far as to suggest that, in the longer run, approving inappropriate conduct or low performance damages rather than enhances self-esteem. This is the case either because the recipients of false praise see through its inauthenticity or because they would be better off revising their conduct (say, having fewer children while in their teens).[52]

Much of the past debate about these ideologies centered on their effects on cognitive skills, knowledge, and performance at work. However, the main issue here is their effects on moral conduct. Can a community maintain a moral order if its members constantly refrain from chastising friends, children, neighbors, or other members so as not to "hurt" their self-esteem? Dennis Byrne provides an example:

> A friend once took his children to a park where he saw a kid urinate down the slide. . . . [W]hat was my friend supposed to do—let his own kids slide through the pee? Or was my friend supposed to clean it up himself, thereby teaching the little pipsqueak that adults are saps and you can get away with anything? Or was my friend supposed to tell his own kids: "Sorry, the slide is closed today; you're being punished because someone else couldn't restrain his impulses."[53]

The fact that the answer to this question is not self-evident is a strong indicator of the extent to which the moral voice has been muted.

In part, the rush to nonjudgment is a matter of style. Raising one's moral voice does not entail waving a fist, chewing out a person, or attacking a person in order to criticize an act. The moral voice can express judgments without being judgmental, mean-spirited, or self-righteous. That is, to some extent, sensitivity to self-esteem can be reconciled with the moral voice. However, if large numbers of the members of a community suppress their moral voice, the community's ability to respond to centrifugal forces is curtailed and/or reliance on other means to maintain order, especially coercion, increases.

Still another ideology that grew in influence during the same period was the notion of systemic rather than personal victimology. This ideology blames the social system for whatever antisocial conduct in which a person engages. Drug abuse, alcoholism, and violence are said to occur because people are poor or unemployed, have only "dead-end" jobs (jobs that pay low wages, are dull, and do not provide stepping-stones to a meaningful career), or have not been empowered. While social system factors are always important, and sometimes dominate the situation, when they are used to imply that the victims have no choice in the matter, which exempts the actors from moral responsibility for their acts, the notion becomes highly damaging to the moral voice.

One effect of all these ideological developments that have muted the moral voice is evident in a social pattern referred to as "avoidance." M. P. Baumgartner describes avoidance as "the curtailment of interaction with a person whose behavior is offensive."[54] In her study of a suburban community, Baumgartner found that the dominant response to improper behavior is usually "restrained and minimalistic."[55] Baumgartner provides the following example:

> The Shepards were a middle-class family who always got along well with people during their years in Hampton. They were disturbed, however, by the fact that one of their next-door neighbors was prone to exhibitionism. . . . Upon one occasion, for example, he arrived at the Shepards' door completely naked, rang the bell, and told a startled Mrs. Shepard and her children that he just wanted to return some mail of theirs mistakenly delivered to his address. Mrs. Shepard simply took the mail. . . . The man was also observed defecating on his lawn by one of the Shepard girls and her friends. (The girls felt certain that the neighbor waited to be sure he was seen before engaging in this act.) Through all these incidents, the Shepard family continued to be amiable toward the offender.[56]

Lamenting the decline of virtues since the Victorian era in England, Gertrude Himmelfarb observes:

> Moral principles, still more moral judgments, are thought to be at best an intellectual embarrassment, at worst evidence of an illiberal and repres-

sive disposition. It is this reluctance to speak the language of morality, far more than any specific values, that separates us from the Victorians.[57]

Communitarian thinking need not belittle the role of societal and psychological factors on antisocial behavior. It can note, though, that among people in the same socioeconomic conditions and with similar psychological histories, one finds many who conduct themselves in ways that are pro- rather than antisocial. That is, even disadvantaged individuals have some autonomy. Moreover, it is morally untenable to exempt anyone from doing his or her share for the community, for the shared good, from "taking responsibility," even if there are strong limits on what he or she can do and even if much can be done by society to elevate his or her condition. To do otherwise is to declare such people subhuman, because it is a mark of a human being that he or she is a moral agent, capable of making moral choices and commitments.

The point is not to deny that formative experiences or social factors have an effect and that they are beyond the actor's control, or even that they might serve as mitigating circumstances in a court of law or of public opinion. The point is that these factors should not be used as rationalizations which suggest that actors are exempt from doing the best they can, given their history, to live up to shared values. The more a community accepts the notion that the person has no element of autonomy, the less room there is for a moral order.

THERE SHOULD (NOT) BE A LAW

Too Many Laws

To the question of how a society can ensure that millions of members will live up to the prescriptions contained in the values to which they have come to subscribe, the answer that often springs up is the law. Indeed, one obvious sociological function of the law is to prescribe how people are expected to behave (from paying taxes to meeting obligations to children) and to proscribe what people are supposed to refrain from doing (from smoking in defined public spaces to selling, buying, or consuming crack cocaine). Usually, laws also contain penalties to be meted out (and sometimes rewards to be accorded) to those who ignore (or live up to) these normative prescriptions.

When centripetal forces are deficient, people often argue that the society requires more laws, more regulations, stronger sanctions, and more law enforcement resources and powers. Indeed, in all Western societies, one can readily observe that, as social order has deteriorated over the last generation, there has been a constant drumbeat for more and harsher punishments, more police, and more powers for the various public authorities. Although it is difficult to measure the ratio, it seems that many of the recent efforts to strengthen social order in the West have relied much more on the law and much less on reasserting the moral voice.

In contrast, I introduce the principles that for a society to be communitarian, much of the social conduct must be "regulated" by reliance on the moral voice rather than on the law, and *the scope of the law itself must be limited largely to that which is supported by the moral voice.*

Sensitivity to the issue at hand is revealed in suggestions about how to make corporations more socially responsible. While most welfare liberals' suggestions concern legislation, Tony Blair, the leader of the British Labour Party, points to a different approach, in his speech on stakeholders (as distinct from shareholders):

> We cannot by legislation guarantee that a company will behave in a way conducive to trust and long term commitment. But it is surely time to assess how we shift the emphasis in corporate ethos from the company being a mere vehicle for the capital market . . . towards a vision of the company as a community or partnership in which each employee has a stake.[58]

Also, values-based law enforcement in turn has positive feedback effects on the moral voice itself. This observation requires some elaboration.

I cannot stress enough that the moral voice can be made much more compatible with a high level of autonomy—and hence with a good society—than can law enforcement. The main point is that if people ignore the law their wages are garnished, mortgages are foreclosed, and their homes sold out from under them; they are jailed or even executed. (The notion, advanced by some philosophers, that the actor always has a choice, even if he/she has to choose to die, is belied by those who are forced to change course by being restrained, jailed, or forcibly evicted from protest sites [like the Greenpeace people who were removed from nuclear-testing sites by French authorities]—i.e., their choices are curtailed if not preempted.) In contrast, when one disregards the moral voice one can proceed, although some social costs may be attached. That is, the person's basic autonomy is maintained.

Often, when communitarians point to the need to shore up the moral order, they are asked which public policies they will favor in order to achieve this regeneration. What laws, regulations, and administrative changes should be introduced? My answer is that a sizable body of social science research indicates (on the grounds just mentioned) that the best way to change the direction of a society is to have a megalogue about the substance of members' values and the intensity of their commitments to values they affirm. My response has been deemed fuzzy or exhortatory in comparison to the list of specific public policy recommendations typically advanced by other social movements, political parties, and think tanks. For example, Jacob Weisberg opines: "Communitarianism provides a better formula for exhortation than it does a guide to federal action. It doesn't tell you how to fix government—how to balance the budget, fix Medicare, or reform welfare."[59] The *Economist* criticizes: "The problem for politicians seeking inspiration from Mr. Etzioni is that, since he does not believe the state can solve many social problems, he offers few policy proposals."[60]

It is true that megalogues are fuzzy in the sense that one cannot determine a priori with any precision when the process will be completed, which values will prevail, which new public policies will be endorsed, or how to engage in them. In effect, one can only predict that the process often will be disjointed, emotive, repetitive, and meandering. But these are all earmarks of processes that truly engage a mass of people in examining, redefining, and redirecting their values and moral commitments—earmarks of moral dialogues, essential for truly endorsed social change.

All this is not to deny that laws and public policies have a place in societal change, including in moral regeneration, but rather that they are not the main factor. Most important, *the laws and public policies themselves must reflect the change in values* rather than significantly diverge from them. In effect, the more a society relies on the government per se, the more *both* the moral order and autonomy are diminished, the less communitarian the society becomes. The more a society relies on members' convictions that their community has established a legitimate and just order, and the more they conduct themselves voluntarily in line with the order's values because they themselves subscribe to them, the more communitarian the society. To put it more sharply, the communitarian society is not first and foremost one of law-and-order, but one based on shared moral values that the members affirm. It is a society primarily based on virtues and on laws that embody them.

For the same reasons, the main social body is not the state (or even the polity) and the main actors are not citizens, but the body is the society (as a community of communities) and the actors are members in it. Social action, such as that which occurs in and among family members, neighborhoods, voluntary associations, and communities, has priority over political action. I differ here from those who often unwittingly tend to equate social with political action,[61] and society with state.

Alan Wolfe pointed out with great force and much documentation that in both public policy and the social sciences, we tend to focus on the dichotomy of market and state while forgetting society, when in fact both the market and the state are formations that rely on a healthy society to function well: "The secret of success for those political economies that work best often lies in neither politics nor economics," he concludes.[62] In *Whose Keeper*, Wolfe expresses concern that this misplaced emphasis leads to the neglect and degeneration of civic society.[63]

Wolfe chides social scientists who forget about civic society, even when they are critical of either the market or the state:

> Charles Lindblom, for example, wrote a book called *Politics and Markets*, as if politics and markets were the only two choices we have; similarly, a book that attributes the success of Scandinavian social democracy to solidarity calls itself *Politics Against Markets*, as if solidarity were a totally political, and not also a social, concept.[64]

It is toward civic society that Wolfe urges we turn: "There is a need in modern liberal democracies, no matter how committed they may be to either the market or the state (or both), to develop a third way of thinking about moral obligation."[65]

Benjamin Barber's work provides what a lawyer, representing the interests of society, might label Exhibit A:

> If we accept the postulate that humans are social by nature, then we cannot regard citizenship as merely one among many artificial social roles that can be grafted onto man's natural solitariness. It is rather the only legitimate form that man's natural dependency can take.[66]

When the Communitarian Platform was translated into German, the term "member" (of a community) was translated as *burger*.[67] When I noted that "burger," translated back into English means "citizen," I was told that in German there is no word that fully captures the notion of membership. (The word *"mitglieder"* is closer to "dues-payer" than to "member.") This semantic oversight reflects a general tendency to be unaware of the communitarian elements of society.

Conflating citizenship with membership conceals the importance of what Senator Bill Bradley called the third leg of the society (the market and the state are the two others).[68] It overlooks the leg on which the communitarian society particularly leans. Although much attention has been paid in recent years to shoring up the civic society, drawing on Tocqueville, most visibly in the work of Robert Putnam, the shoring up is recommended as a way to make the government work better, rather than to make it work less, and above all, to opportune society more. None of this is to suggest that all, or even most, of the state's missions can or should be turned over to civic society but that the moral voice, if properly nourished, can significantly reduce what both have to carry in the first place.

As a result of the politicization of social thinking, often when discussions turn to social remedies, to the quests to seek remedies for such social ills as racism, poverty, and educational decay, most suggestions that are made concern a change in public policies or law. The notion that parents, neighborhoods, voluntary associations, and other elements of the community can introduce many of the needed remedies on their own is often overlooked, or it is suggested that to achieve such mobilization requires a new public policy or law. (Much follows from the recognition of the importance of mutuality, or reciprocity, as long as this is understood as a social value rather than an exchange. It is highlighted by the way ethnic groups, both for centuries and today, take care "of their own kind," providing them with individualized and rarely abused social services, at little cost to the public. This subject has been extensively discussed in previous work and hence is not further explored here.[69]) It should be noted though that all other things being equal, the more the social order relies on social bonds and moral voices, and the less it relies on the state (and the market), the closer society is to embody the new golden rule. The underlying reason is that the less coercion is employed (and the less relations are utilitarian, those sociologists refer to as "secondary"), the smaller the distance between what members seek of society and what society calls on members to take responsibility for.

Communitarian Law

Given that law cannot be the primary basis of order in a good society, what role does it play? How does it help maintain the communitarian equilibrium between order and autonomy and help to restore that equilibrium when it is undermined?

Volumes have been written about the relationship of the law to societal change.[70] Some argue that it reflects (or ought to reflect) the society's avant-garde; it should lead to societal change. An oft-cited example is an army base commander in the South who simply ordered desegregation as early as 1943.[71] Others, especially from the Marxist left, have maintained that the law serves as a rear guard; that it lags behind societal change, reflects the outgoing regime, is anachronistic. Still others are sure to object that one should not touch this subject without a review of the rich and complex literature on law and society. All I seek to note is that welfare liberals and social conservatives still regularly advocate changing major aspects of society of which they disapprove by enacting laws—whether or not there is the needed moral support for the changes entailed. Therefore I see a compelling reason for communitarians to stress that *law in a good society is first and foremost the continuation of morality by other means.* The law may sometimes lead to societal change to some extent, but if the moral culture (shared values and commitment to them) does not closely follow, the social order will not be voluntarily heeded and the society will be pushed toward the edge of the communitarian pattern—and, ultimately, beyond its limits of tolerance, transforming into an authoritarian society.

The limited ability to rely on introducing social changes through law that is not backed up by values, and the severe distorting effects that results if this is tried, are highlighted by the failure of many prison authorities to prevent inmates from dealing drugs in jails. If authorities cannot enforce a law in prison, when they have the inmates locked up twenty-four hours a day, seven days a week, under constant and close supervision, with next to no autonomy, how can one expect to enforce a law lacking moral backing in a communitarian society?

Prohibition is another well-known case in which laws could not be enforced without the support of a strong moral voice. Recently, it has become fashionable to suggest that Prohibition was effective after all. I cannot, within the confines of this discussion, disprove this claim. I would like, though, to note that if one values highly a voluntary social order, the combination of heightened corruption and police action involved in Prohibition-like acts militate against this approach to social change, even if such acts reduce to some extent the undesired behavior. Above all, note that Prohibition self-destructed.

Laws without a firm moral undergirding, "unbacked" laws, tend to harm the community more than serve it, and tend either not to be enforced or else set aside. Thus, a clever staffer succeeded in sneaking into the 1964 antipoverty legislation the requirement of "maximum feasible participation of the poor," meaning that poor people must be involved in the implementation of the antipoverty laws, despite widespread objection to this idea.[72] In 1967, this provision was revoked by an amendment stipulating that antipoverty funds be funneled through local elected officials.[73] The war against controlled substances is corrupting law enforcement, the lower courts, jail personnel and border guards, and, in many countries, the military and the elected officials. (The "solution" is not necessarily legalization but building up true moral support for the legislation. The Black Muslims, for instance, have shown that, when there is such backing, use of controlled substances can be minimized in one's community.) The fate of new suggestions to draw on state laws—in Iowa and Michigan, for instance—to make divorce more difficult again, and to enforce laws on statutory rape when teenagers engage in sexual activities, all depend on the extent that the needed moral underpinning is first built up, a point all too often ignored by politicians who gain points when they enact laws, even if the laws are poorly enforced.

Does this mean that if a community becomes aware of a serious flaw, say racial segregation, it can never act by mainly relying on the law, without first laying moral foundations (assuming that none or rather weak ones are in place)? If the evil that needs to be overcome is serious enough, combating it may outweigh the undesirable side effects and the low success rate. But these exceptions do not invalidate the rule: Enacting laws bereft of moral underpinning is both an uncommunitarian and ineffectual exercise. While a good society can tolerate a few such unbacked laws, it cannot make them its mainstay. *Leges sine moribus vanae* (laws without morals are in vain).

The Social Conservative Rush to Legislate

Social conservatives, especially religious ones, we saw, tend to disregard the communitarian law against laws. They often show surprisingly limited faith in faith (in education, persuasion, conversion, missionary work, and, above all, in moral dialogues), and seek to impose the values they believe in through laws. Alan Keyes, a social conservative candidate for the 1996 Republican presidential nomination, argued that we legislate morality all the time anyway; why not prohibit abortion, divorce, and other acts he considers immoral? As I see it, the main issue is not whether we legislate morality, but the distance between the values we affirm as an inclusive community and those expressed in law. Governments can enact laws that ban divorce, as they have done in many Catholic countries, but to the extent that people do not truly share the underlying values (as distinct from paying lip service to them), such laws lead to various kinds of antisocial behavior. For example, many men in Italy live with their mistresses and father children out of wedlock, while pretending to uphold the institution of marriage. Similarly, where abortions are banned, those women who do not share the corollary moral convictions, at least not firmly, turn to back-alley abortions as a result. Earlier prohibitions on the use of contraceptives pushed them under the counter, generating the typical distorted consequences of laws not backed by moral commitment, but did not prevent their wide use even among Catholics.[74] The need to lead, accompany, and follow legislation with moral underpinning may be referred to as the values primacy sociological law.

Legal Lag

The opposite also holds: When there are strong mores, they benefit by being expressed in law. The claim, made by Richard Epstein, that if laws were enacted that ensconce moral duties to care for others, those laws would destroy the moral commitment, is unfounded.[75] In effect, such laws further express, articulate, and help enforce moral commitments, when those are in place. For the same reason, the individualistic notions of the law-and-economics school, which seek to base laws on economic considerations and ignore their normative role, are ill founded.

Empirical studies cast some light on this issue. In one, people were asked to evaluate the morality of the conduct of a person who is a competent swimmer and sees another person drowning but does nothing to help. A group of subjects who were told there was a legal requirement of assistance in such situations judged the inaction more severely than a group that was told there was no such legal obligation.[76]

When laws lag significantly, and on a broad front, behind changes in the moral culture, the result is similarly debilitating for a communitarian society. Cynicism was extensive in American society in the early and mid-1990s because elected officials often ignored the moral voice of American society. For instance, the public widely agreed that the flood of private money into the election coffers of politicians should be curbed, but Congress did not act.[77] The overwhelming majority of the public favored gun control, but Congress refused to pass most gun control measures.[78] Corporate welfare was allowed to continue in face of broad-based public opposition.[79] In short, national lawmaking is often out of synch with the core values of most Americans.

In a better-balanced communitarian society, law and morality, at their best, move like a person's two legs: they are never far apart. A case in point, mentioned earlier in this chapter, is the way smoking behavior was changed in the United States as compared to some other countries. In the United States, it was only after twenty-five years of moral dialogue, at the end of which there was wide acceptance of the banning of smoking in public places, that antismoking laws were introduced in a very large number of jurisdictions. These laws encountered rather limited protest and, most important, they were generally followed. In comparison, when similar laws were introduced in France at about the same time without such preparation, the people rebelled.[80]

Note that the main change in the legitimacy of antismoking laws in the United States came when the public learned about the dangers of secondhand smoke. That is, the change was not simply a matter of an increase in the number of those who oppose smoking but a change in the normative standing of smoking. It moved from unwise conduct for an individual, arguably within the discretionary zone of autonomy (behavior the society may wish to discourage but not prohibit), to an act that directly damages others and the common good.

Why, then, enact laws at all in a communitarian society? The main roles the law plays here are twofold. First, we saw, it is expressive of the community's values. Second, communitarian law helps maintain the social order by dealing with those who disregard the moral voice. In a perfect communitarian society, their number is small, but one cannot expect it to be zero. Because some people either have no inner moral voice or only a rather weak one, and/or such people are immune to the moral voice of the community, they will try to circumvent the mores if not to violate them outright. If society fails to deal with these violators, people who abide by the society's norms and laws will question the authority of and commitment to the moral order, which will, therefore, slowly decline as more people become violators.

Many liberals often ignore this point when they do not take into account that *some* criminals cannot be reached by the moral voice and must be incarcerated, and often kept in jail for rather long periods. This issue is particularly evident when one deals with psychopaths and with sex offenders, the latter having a very high recidivism rate.[81] The pro-portion of basically incorrigible criminals, though, is small. Social con-servatives are mistaken to the extent that they assume that public authorities can be used to restore social order. What is needed is moral regeneration and *some* law enforcement. Although the relationship can-not be measured in precise terms, the suggestion that the moral order must carry 70 percent or more of the burden and law enforcement 30 percent or less may help express the basic idea. Both are necessary but not in equal proportion.

Note that the suggested proportions include those who are deterred by the law and not only those directly restrained by its agents. The lat-ter need to be kept at a much lower proportion, probably below 2 per-cent. When a larger proportion of the citizenry is not deterred, there is a sense of lawlessness that adds to the damage to the social order caused by the illegal behavior itself. For instance, the sense that "nobody pays taxes," not only shortchanges the treasuries of countries where it is common, such as Italy and France, but also contributes to the sense of a damaged moral order (especially when it comes to public duties as dis-tinct from those to family and friends). The same holds for drug laws in many Western countries, especially the United States.

To underscore this interaction between law enforcement and the moral order, it might be useful to examine a new trend prevalent in the United States: to define driving while under the influence of alcohol as morally unacceptable. This characterization has been gradually catch-ing on (although it has not run its full course by the mid-1990s) due to the influence of Mothers Against Drunk Driving (and Students Against Drunk Driving), the media, and campaigns aimed at changing the moral vocabulary (by drawing on slogans such as "friends don't let friends drive drunk" and showing increased appreciation of designated drivers rather than offering them "one for the road"). These efforts need to be augmented by sobriety checkpoints, but laws allowing their deployment have been more difficult to introduce than antismoking laws (only thirty-seven states have such checkpoints), and are more rarely applied, because the relevant change in the moral culture has not yet matured. (The public seems more outraged about drunken drivers than about smokers, but less willing to put up with checkpoints than with antismoking regulations. The reasons the legitimacy of check-points is lagging are not clear, but they do seem to reflect a stronger opposition to this form of police action than to regulations that are enforced typically by restaurant owners, office managers, and fellow citizens.) In short, the law mops up after moral changes have carried out the main sweep; and it does play a key role in shoring up the moral order or in avoiding slippage by dealing with those who do not heed the moral voice.

A COMPARATIVE PERSPECTIVE

The question might be asked, given the preceding discussion of the role of law, Why are societies that rely on the law for social order more than American society considered *more* rather than *less* communitarian?[82] Indeed, there is a very long list of specific behaviors that are controlled by law in these societies which many Americans would find it difficult to believe could come under legal jurisdiction or government regulation. In France, the curriculum of all public schools is controlled in fine detail by one central government agency in Paris. In Germany, government cars, equipped with electronic gear, snoop around private residences to see if the owners have paid the bill for television service, which is government-owned. (Television sets emit electronic signals unless the bill for service is paid.) Prayers are mandated in British public schools. Crucifixes are displayed in many German public schools. There are strict codes concerning what television programs for children must include in many Western societies. Separation of state and church is unknown in Scandinavia, where the Lutheran Church is financed by taxpayer revenues and where the state appoints bishops.

The reason it makes sense to consider these countries basically communitarian, despite their relatively heavy reliance on law, is that many of their laws do *reflect* their moral values rather than *deviate* from them. That is, for the purposes at hand, a law is not a law is not a law. Laws that are truly coercive conflict with the values of a people, the way Soviet laws that prohibited religious practices did. Such laws diminish the communitarian nature of the social order (although, to reiterate, all societies have at least some such measures). When, however, most laws follow closely in the footsteps of the moral values of a community or society, such laws are much less coercive—and relying on them is closer to moral suasion. This closeness should be reflected empirically in a much lower ratio of people who violate such morally backed laws. In short—while as a first-order approximation of the communitarian paradigm one may state that the less a society relies on laws and the more it relies on values to ensure social order, the more communitarian that society—a fuller statement includes the proposition that a communitarian society must rely largely on laws backed by moral values and little on laws that are morally bare.

IMPLICATIONS FOR PRACTICE AND POLICY FOR BUILDING COMMUNITIES

NOURISH COMMUNITIES

Public policies can nourish communities by ensuring that the state does not take over activities that provide opportunities for communities to act. The point individualists make about the ill effects of the government's excessive intervention in the marketplace applies to communities as well. In many societies, especially in Western Europe, in which the welfare state has taken over many missions communities undertook in earlier ages, communities have weakened. Hence, some functions must be returned to communities if they are to be regenerated. In Denmark, this is being tried by allowing communities to decide how to spend their educational budgets (within state guidelines) rather than following the Danish tradition according to which central authorities tightly controlled local schools. In the United States, a decline in government services has led to a significant increase in community activities. For instance, in New York City, following the reduction in government services, the number of organized community groups increased from 3,500 in 1977 to 8,000 in 1995.[83]

Among the missions the government relinquished to various communities, in whole or in part, and other communities might consider taking over are: fire fighting (75.2 percent of fire fighters in the United States in 1994 were volunteers);[84] public safety (via crime watch, neighborhood anticrime and antidrug patrols); mutual aid (in which volunteers work as emergency medical technicians and staff welcome wagons); creation of credit cooperatives, block parties, local chamber music, jazz groups; development of parks; and support for schools.[85]

In most cases communities cover only part of the missions rather than replacing the state or the private sector. However, such increases in community activation suffice to reduce public costs (and the alienation high public costs generate). Also, community services (whether they are completely voluntary or draw in part on donations or on public funds) are more tailored to individual needs, more humane, and less subject to false claims. Moreover, community activation strengthens the web of interpersonal bonds that are one of the two core elements of communities. These bonds, in turn, have been shown to lead to longer, healthier, and happier lives.[86] Hence, fostering community actions that have specific goals, from cleaning a park to supervising children's trips to and from schools, has the beneficial side effect of enhancing bonding among the members of the community.[87]

While communities can take over only a part of the functions of the government,[88] and while such takeover is particularly difficult for poor communities, most communities grow stronger and more able to serve their members the more they do so. As in sports, the communitarian muscle is built up through practice, a point often stressed by those who combine study of these matters with community training and action, such as Ernesto Cortes Jr., Benjamin Barber, Harry Boyte, and John W. Gardner.[89]

Legal Protection

Although there are some laws on the books to protect communitarian activities, some additional ones are called for. All fifty-one U.S. jurisdictions have Good Samaritan laws that protect physicians who come to the aid of the injured in an emergency situation. As of 1983, thirty-eight states had Good Samaritan laws that granted immunity from civil liability to all would-be rescuers.[90] In five states, there is a duty to rescue, meaning that someone who fails to render reasonable assistance could receive a citation from police or face some other form of legal sanction.[91] Such laws are common in Europe. These laws cover situations such as calling for help when one sees a person being attacked or a stranded motorist. The use of torts (which impose a liability) for social hosts who serve alcohol to guests who are already intoxicated and are about to drive, has been suggested, after careful analysis, by Robert M. Ackerman.[92]

For the same reasons, Congress or state legislatures should enact the medical volunteer act, which extends federal tort claim coverage to any health-care professional who provides free medical services to people in need. Additional legal protection seems to be needed for those who organize block parties and other social events.[93] This need is highlighted by a recent regrettable development: Several hospitals have ceased to offer free X-ray screening of Halloween candy, for fear of liability if they fail to detect something.[94]

Subsidies for Civic and Faith-Based Groups

Senator Dan Coats champions a whole battery of bills that aim to help jump-start community efforts to take over missions now carried out by various levels of government. The bills include grants to community organizations that confront crime in cooperation with the police; vouchers women can "cash" at private and religious maternity group homes; and requirements for the Department of Housing and Urban Development (HUD) to transfer ownership of unoccupied single-family housing units to local governments, after which the local governments would be required to offer these properties for sale to local community development corporations. Coats also favors a $500 tax credit for donations to charitable organizations, including religious ones, whose primary purpose is the prevention or alleviation of poverty; and demonstration grants, to help communities of faith to reach out to both welfare recipients and nonviolent criminal offenders.[95]

There are here two policy ideas that need to be treated separately. The first concerns whether the government, giving nominal grants, can reactivate communities. As I see it, such grants have a limited but positive symbolic effect. The second concerns the effects on the separation of church and state if government grants are accorded to religious organizations. The experience of providing public funds to hospitals run by religious orders suggests that these dangers have been grossly overstated. In 1994, Lutheran social ministries received 54 percent of their income from government sources; Catholic charities received 62 percent, and Jewish federations 59 percent.[96] In contrast, European societies and many others, from Israel to Argentina, in which the relation between the state and a particular religion are much closer, may need to move in the opposite direction if communitarian activities are to be enhanced.

Community Devolution

Communities can be overloaded and, especially when they are weak or lacking in resources, require outside support, either from more endowed communities or from the society of which they are members. But such allocations can be made in ways that strengthen communities rather than undermine them. This is achieved when public funds are provided to voluntary associations and to other community bodies rather than devolved to state governments.

In recent years in the United States, Britain, and quite a few other countries, it has been argued that if missions and funds were moved from the central government to the states (or their equivalent) the society would become more communitarian. In effect, what is necessary is a much more complex understanding that includes the recognition that some missions are best left in the hands of the federal government (bank controls, for instance); some may indeed be best turned over to states; while still others, quite a few, in fact, are best devolved to communities. These last missions cannot be handed over to communities without state-based guidelines and accountability, if massive abuses are to be avoided.[97] The discussion here focuses on the undesirability of turning over numerous federal missions to the states, the most recent policy fashion, and suggests instead that communities should more often be the beneficiaries of devolution.

By practically any measure, the typical state government in the United States is even less responsive to its citizens than the federal government. One major reason is that state legislatures are much less accountable to the public than Congress, and many are even more corrupt.

The problem starts with the fact that most state assembly members serve only part-time. The standard length of a legislative session in New Mexico and Montana is 90 days every two years. Washington's legislature meets an average of 82.5 days per year, while Nevada's legislators are only paid for 60 days every two years. For Wyoming, it is only an average of 30 days per year.

State legislators are legally entitled to work at other paying jobs, and practically all do, including in jobs that entail representing industries that the state governments are supposed to regulate. State legislatures rely even more than Congress on "voice votes," which means that an estimate is made as to whether the nays or yeas sounded more numerous, without recording individual votes. In Florida, for instance, an estimated 93 percent of all votes were disposed of in this manner. In many state legislatures, no written records of votes are kept. Both practices enable legislators to vote for special interests while claiming that they voted for the common good.

Members of Congress often dash from one bell to another (voting more than 1,000 times a year) armed with rather limited knowledge of what they are voting about. But Congressional members can rely on huge staffs to help determine their positions. In the states, legislators vote about as often as in Congress but typically are backed up by only minuscule staffs or none at all.

Nepotism, cronyism, and outright corruption are far from unknown in Washington, D.C., but they are distressingly rampant in the states. When the Maryland assembly allocates scholarships, many are allotted to politicians' children and the children of friends and supporters. Arizona legislators have been indicted for accepting cash bribes to support a gambling bill. Florida legislators have been charged with accepting numerous gifts and junkets from lobbyists. In South Carolina, when the FBI set up a sting operation in which they offered bribes in exchange for legislative favors, so many legislators showed up that they practically caused a traffic jam. The governor of Rhode Island was fined $30,000 for steering state contracts to friends and business associates.

A comparison of federal and state administration agencies is revealing. The FBI is so squeaky-clean, few people would even think of offering a bribe to an agent; but few need to think twice about greasing the palms of cops in many parts of the country. Medicare (100 percent federal) shines in comparison to Medicaid (partly state-run). The Internal Revenue Service (IRS), which is not beyond reproach, is a paragon of virtue when compared to state tax agencies. Red tape is worse in many states than in federal government.

True, the states are closer to the people, at least in the narrow sense that most citizens have to travel fewer miles to reach their state capital than to Washington, D.C. However, those who do make the voyage find it is no pilgrimage. Indeed, the people of New York City hardly feel that Albany is much more understanding than Washington, D.C.; the citizens of Los Angeles and San Francisco do not feel particularly appreciated in Sacramento; and so on. After all, state-centered devolution is simply moving missions and funds from one level of government to another, with little if any net reduction in government.

The solution is not to keep all the public's business that is currently bottled up in the federal government corked in. Some additional privatization is possible. And state assemblies may be reformed to become much more transparent and accountable, and limits on lobbies and campaign contributions may be enacted. But above all, missions and funds need to be devolved to the community level, where people can see what is being done and actively participate. More public programs can be run as are many of our public schools, our best hospitals, and numerous colleges now: by community boards, subject to public guidelines and accountability. This is the way community-development corporations run economic projects (e.g., launching a supermarket in a low-income area). It is also the way early HIV intervention programs are run by Community and Migrant Health Centers, which are funded, but not managed, by the Department of Health and Human Services (HHS). The largest program funded in this way is Head Start.

A number of highly successful community programs were killed by previous administrations that favored state block grants. The abandoned programs include neighborhood self-help development programs funded by HUD and community anticrime programs in which the U.S. Department of Justice paid only for community organizers. The rest of the work, such as crime watches and marking property with identifiers (often the owner's social security number), was done by community members themselves. These programs should be expanded. Other programs could be delegated to communities working within federal guidelines. Local nonprofits are well suited to generate community service jobs for those on welfare who are not able to find work in the private sector.[98] Programs to curb teen pregnancy must be part of local schools, preferably as part of full-service health clinics. Community policing is a good idea if the community is truly involved. Voluntary recycling is a community's, not a state's, job. Increased parental involvement in education is best done neighborhood by neighborhood. And so are many other social missions.

Local Institutions as Community Foci

Local institutions, especially public schools, but also post offices and libraries and hospitals, often serve as places communities use to establish their identity, to conduct meetings and public performances. Tendencies to consolidate local institutions into regional ones on grounds of efficiency cannot be avoided, but before such mergers take place, the full costs should be taken into account, including the damage to the social fabric of the local communities that are affected. This makes many, albeit not all, of these consolidations unattractive even from a sheer accounting viewpoint.

Protecting Public Spaces

Public spaces such as plazas, sidewalks, parks, and playgrounds are places where members of communities interact, bond, form, and raise their moral voice. For these places to serve as community spaces they must be kept safe, and they cannot be allowed to be taken over by drug dealers, aggressive panhandlers, gangs, or any other group. This requires providing alternative ways to serve special groups while opposing, in court, the ACLU army of lawyers who tend to put the rights of a few citizens over those of all others and above the community's needs. Homeless people need both to not be allowed to monopolize a park and to be offered shelter. (If they refuse to use the shelters, assuming these shelters are safe and clean, they can be denied the takeover of parks.) Drugs dealers and gangs should be offered rehabilitation programs but be subject to updated loitering laws that are not discriminatory.[99] The introduction of surveillance cameras into what is, after all, a public space, also helps. One way or another, public spaces must be kept available for the community, without ignoring the requirements of groups with special needs.

Community Courts

Community courts can serve as alternatives to the official justice system in providing restitution and rehabilitation. In Manhattan, for example, the Times Square district has been conducting a three-year pilot Midtown Community Court. The court targets street drug users, prostitutes, unlicensed vendors, aggressive panhandlers, subway turnstile jumpers, peddlers of counterfeit goods, shoplifters, vandals, and other low-level criminals who undermine the community's ability to enjoy public spaces. The court can require defendants to enroll in drug and alcohol treatment programs, seek employment counseling, and perform community service. Someone brought to the court for vandalism, for instance, will often be sentenced to clean up the graffiti on walls of buildings in the community.

Community Policing

Returning police officers to patrolling the neighborhoods, out of their cars, and shifting them from a response mode to a proactive one have brought police closer to the community. However, for community policing to be truly successful, it is often necessary for the composition of the police force to be changed, so that it includes more people who speak the language of the neighborhood, and to change the attitude of the police toward people of cultures and social backgrounds different from their own. Most important, the community needs to be continually involved in setting priorities for the deployment of the police if the hoped-for benefits are to be reaped.[100] Community policing, too, can be rather thin or fairly thick.

Community Design

Several town planners have suggested new ways to design neighborhoods to foster community. Basically, they argue that workplaces have been located at a distance from residences because they used to involve smokestacks. Now that most businesses use computers, workplaces (and shopping) should be within walking distance of home. This would allow for narrow streets, wide sidewalks, and porches facing the walkways, and much less use of cars, all measures that encourage community. Some towns have actually been built following these ideas. Although this particular kind of design may not provide the pattern for a more communitarian design, there is strong evidence that the way developments, neighborhoods, and whole towns are laid out affects the extent to which they form communities. The use of barriers, checkpoints, and gates are all loathsome and should be tolerated only as long as other tools of public policy and community endeavor are insufficient to protect life and limb, as they often are in major parts of American cities.

GRADUATED RESPONSE

The extent to which a community can and should provide rehabilitation services for drug addicts, alcoholics, and criminals has long been a bone of contention between welfare liberals and social conservatives. The former, we saw, tend to stress rehabilitation (and prevention); the latter, punitive measures. A third approach, suggested by Mark Kleiman, is to establish a graduated response so that those who are caught the first time will be given maximum opportunity for rehabilitation—although they might be jailed if they refuse to enroll in or drop out of a rehabilitation program. Those who commit a second offense would be given stiffer sentences but still considerable rehabilitation, and so on—until, at some point, offenders are denied additional rehabilitation at public cost. The same might be said about alternative sentencing to community service: First-time nonviolent offenders might be given such opportunities much more readily than repeat and/or violent offenders.

ALTERNATIVE DISPUTE
RESOLUTION (ADR) TECHNIQUES

Much has been written about the merit of ADR techniques. They are clearly much less costly and tend to leave all parties more reconciled than courts, in which there is a winner and a loser. In that sense, ADR techniques are profoundly communitarian. However, it is less often noted that ADR tends to favor the stronger party because the third parties involved are often keen to find a peaceful or acceptable resolution rather than a just one. In divorce cases, mediation tends to favor men. Brokers use mediation to make it almost impossible for clients who are being inappropriately served to win their case. To the extent that these ADR techniques are used, they should be voluntary in two ways: People should be allowed to appeal the result in court as long as they notify the court of the result of the mediation (as is the case in claims against physicians in Maryland), or they should be provided ADR as one option but not the only channel.

MAKING LAWYERS (MORE) OFFICERS OF THE COURT

I posed a hypothetical case to several legal authorities: Eight women charge that a physician sexually molested them while he had them connected to a wire that he claimed would endanger them if they moved. The defense argues that the women fabricated the whole thing, conspiring to extort money from the physician. No evidence of any kind is presented to support this argument. Assume that the lawyer made up the whole defense: should this be allowed?

All those who were approached responded that lawyers' only obligations are to their clients. George E. Bushnell Jr., at the time the president of the American Bar Association, put it starkly:

> While your report of the sexual molestation defense on its face is irresponsible, I cannot agree that the rights of the defendant should in any way be changed or modified. Rather it is my judgment, and conviction, that *only* through full protection of defendants' rights is the total community best served. For it is only by emphasizing the rights of the least of us that the rights of all of us, the rights of the total community, are preserved.[101]

Floyd Abrams, an eminent lawyer, noted that in our current climate we should not be surprised when lawyers state things that have "nothing to do with truth" because we should know that they will say anything that might help a client.[102] It's like sitting down to play poker; one should expect the other side to bluff.

But courts are not a game. The moral order is undermined when the fate of one's life, liberty, and property are decided according to who can play the game better (or with more chips). Justice is not served by both sides playing the court for all they can get. Are there ways to maintain our adversarial system but also to encourage lawyers to live up to their responsibilities as officers of the court—that is, of the community?

There are already several rules on the books, in the law itself and in the ethics code of the profession, that curb lawyers in the community's interest. For example, if a lawyer knows that her client is about to commit perjury, the lawyer is supposed to stop the client or to alert the court.[103] Similarly, the U.S. Supreme Court ruled that lawyers may not elicit what they know to be a false answer from their clients. Also, there are now some limitations on what aspects of the sexual history of a rape victim the defense may bring up. Why not consider strengthening these rules in the interest of justice and the community?

Among the policy ideas that deserve consideration are prohibiting lawyers from entering a plea of "not guilty" for clients whom they know would be found guilty if the facts known to the lawyers were available to the judge or jury; and, similarly, prohibiting lawyers from challenging the other side's veracity when they know it is telling the truth.

It might be most productive to encourage judges to become a bit more active. Warnings to lawyers that they are neglecting their duties during a trial, reprimands after a trial is over, or notes written into the verdict would go a long way to correct the system.

Policy implications of the relationship between law and moral order. The relevant policy ideas have been woven into the preceding discussion. They are merely summarized next.

1: Intensive moral dialogue and public education best *precede* significant changes in the law if there is no or only insufficient support for the suggested changes.

2: Moral dialogues can be expected to be *prolonged, messy, and costly.*

3: Such dialogues are likely to follow Yankelovich's stages, moving from *consciousness-raising,* to *working through,* to *resolution.* The difficulty of gaining a broad-based supportive moral voice for the anticipated changes in the law is less if the relevant parts of the public are already in stage 2 (let alone 3), but is much greater if stage 1 has barely been entered. To legislate in stage 1 is particularly uncommunitarian.

4: *The moral voice per se does not suffice to control most behaviors,* including such private behaviors as parents dealing with their children and sexual conduct. Some law enforcement is needed even in the most communitarian society. (This is a fact Israeli kibbutzim discovered when, much to their dismay, they had to call in the police to deal with incidents of murder among their members. They had no police of their own.)

5: Suggestions to change the law are in themselves part of the moral dialogue. Initiatives that seek to introduce a new law or to modify existing ones help focus and often sharpen the moral dialogue. Laws also serve to express values, not just to deter or remedy behavior that violates the society's code. Hence, it is essential that *the provisions of the law will not merely reflect economic considerations of losses and benefits but also the community's values.*

6: An important illustration of reliance on the moral voice versus other approaches is found in discussions of how to deal with the shortage of organ donations, a shortage that costs thousands of people their lives each year and sharply reduces the quality of life for many others. Some individualists call for paying donors, others for continuing to rely on their goodwill. Strong social conservatives would pass laws mandating organ donations. Communitarians would seek to advance mores establishing that such donations are expected as part of one's moral duty; instead of asking people if they would donate their organs, people who check into hospitals (or members of their families) would be reminded of the mores and allowed to refuse (i.e., check out rather than check in) by simply checking a form. Similarly, rather than mandating HIV testing and disclosure, hospitals and physicians (who screen the blood of patients anyway) should ask those at risk to consent to have their blood work include a test for HIV. If positive, such findings are best accompanied with counseling and the expression of a moral expectation that the person disclose the finding to previous and prospective contacts.

SIX

====

The Implications of Human Nature

THE DEBATE ABOUT HUMAN NATURE (AND ITS AVOIDANCE)

One's assumptions about human nature set an important context for the endeavor to build and sustain a good society. For instance, if one assumes that human nature is inherently benign, somewhat in the Rousseauean vein, it would lead one to oppose societal agendas that interfere with the unfolding of the good nature of people. If one assumes that human nature is naturally evil or sinful, in line with St. Augustine's approach, strong societal institutions, often a forceful government, may be needed to keep it in check. If one assumes that people are, by nature, half beast, half godly, the question arises under what conditions will the better half be best developed, an Aristotelian issue. Reference is deliberately made to assumptions, rather than facts, about human nature because it is widely agreed that these facts are rather difficult to establish. The assumptions nevertheless deserve attention, for they have profound effects on our thinking, paradigms, and public policies.

I refer to universal human nature to stress that I deal strictly with those features all human beings are assumed to share, formed by the biological needs people share with animals (for example, for sustenance) and the result of universal "socialization" experiences (for instance, infants' need to be attended to by adults, which is a basis of the need for human attachments). The approach followed here is thus in direct opposition to those who focus on finding and drawing conclusions from human nature's *particulars*, such as differences in genetic composition.[1] To put it in a different language, I join those who recognize that we are all God's children; it is mainly racists who believe there are superior and inferior people, whose condition is determined by immutable factors.

A brief discussion of two key assumptions that have been made in the past about universal human nature follows; it provides a context for the assumptions that are most appropriate for the communitarian paradigm. I cannot stress enough that it is not my purpose to review the age-old, rich, and complex debate about human nature.[2] My limited goal is to outline a position that I suggest undergirds communitarian thinking about the good society—or least ought to nourish it.

THE SANGUINE VIEW

The notion that human nature is essentially benign and can be perfected is at the heart of the Enlightenment worldview. Individualists often champion this sanguine view. They believe in progress; they hold that reason, science, and engineering (including, for some, social engineering) can lead human beings to ever higher levels of sociability, if not perfection.

Two major sets of public policies, often promoted in many societies, reflect this optimistic vision. One is associated with individualists, who assume that numerous social ills are largely due to government interventions that have led to perverted behavior. Ergo, if these interventions were to be removed, and people were freed to confront the natural forces of competition (or the marketplace), their antisocial conduct would cease and their pro-social behavior would emerge, reflecting their underlying benign nature.

This view, in recent years, has been often evoked in discussions of welfare policies that are said to cause "dependency." Weaning people from welfare dependency is expected to return them to the good behavior their nature inclines them to follow. Some individualists argue that even crimes of passion, rape, and murder reflect the wrong constellation of incentives; that criminals are not different in nature from the butcher, baker, or candlestick maker; they are inherently good, at least rational and socially benign, by nature.[3]

The sanguine assumptions about universal human nature are not merely ontological; they are also employed to draw normative conclusions. This is highlighted by the fact that this view of universal nature, which is dominant in neoclassical economics, leads to the normative notion of consumer *sovereignty*. Neoclassical economists often argue that individual choices are not to be tampered with (they should not be "disputed," as the Nobel laureates Gary Becker and George Stigler put it)[4] and that, in aggregate, they should guide the economy.

Simple theories of democracy also build on the notion of an informed citizenry whose members are able and entitled to make up their own minds individually as to what they prefer, and the aggregate of such preferences ought to guide the polity. And the notion that individual rights should take precedence over the common good draws, in part, on basically the same sanguine concept of human nature.

The second version of the sanguine view is usually associated with welfare liberal ideology. These liberals tend to assume that antisocial behavior is largely caused by factors external to the person but locate these factors in a different place than do libertarians. Welfare liberals see the sources of personal misconduct in disadvantaged socioeconomic conditions, past and current discrimination, or abusive parents, rather than in antisocial inclinations of the person, who is good by nature. Hence, liberals argue that, given the proper conditions (a "good" or "meaningful" job, well paid and part of a career track), hope, education (e.g., Head Start), nutrition (e.g., prenatal care), job training, and some psychotherapy, "deviants" will drop their antisocial behavior and become good members of society.

Liberal educators who subscribe to the sanguine view of human nature maintain that children naturally take to learning like ducks to water; and that educators, rather than deflecting them, should serve as resources on which children may draw in their natural development. John Stuart Mill already allowed that "human nature is not a machine to be built after a model, and set to do exactly the work prescribed for it, but a tree, which requires to grow and develop *itself* on all sides."[5] As Gertrude Himmelfarb points out, the problem with such free development is that Mill "looked to liberty as a means of achieving the highest reaches of the human spirit; he did not take seriously enough the possibility that men would also be free to explore the depths of depravity."[6]

In a discussion of young children, Ivan Illich contends that, in an ideal world:

> [T]he educational path of each student would be his own to follow, and only in retrospect would it take on the features of a recognizable program. The wise student would periodically seek professional advice: assistance to set a new goal, insight into difficulties encountered, choice between possible methods. Even now, most persons would admit that the important services their teachers have rendered them are such advice or counsel, given at a chance meeting or in a tutorial.[7]

John Holt writes:

> We teachers can be seen as travel agents. When we go to a travel agent, he does not tell us where to go. He finds out first what we are looking for. . . . Given some idea of what we are looking for, he makes some suggestions. . . . He does not have to take the trip with us. Least of all does he have to give a little quiz when we get back to make sure we went where we said we would go or got out of the trip what we hoped to get.[8]

During debates about which steps to take to combat drug abuse, welfare liberals typically argue that the focus should be on rehabilitation and not on punishment. The underlying assumption is that people can be cured rather than that they are perverted by nature.

Above all, optimism is reflected in the idea of progress, in the Age of Reason notion that if we, as individuals and as a society, put our minds to it, we can improve our destiny. We are not governed by fate, luck, stars, chaos, or random walks, as much less optimistic paradigms assume. Science can banish disease; statesmen and stateswomen can resolve conflicts; policy analysts can fashion effective social programs. The past is dark but the future is bright. We are empowered and the world is our oyster, for us to crack open and to enjoy. We are the sun around which the world revolves.

THE DOUR VIEW

Social conservatives, especially authoritarians, take a much dimmer view of human nature. They view people as essentially brutish, impulsive, irrational, or sinful.[9] Virtue requires indoctrination (assertive inculcation of values) and policing.

Although religions vary greatly, several major Western religions view people as fundamentally sinful, and as having succumbed to evil although not fully conquered by it. Catholicism has expressed this idea under the doctrine of original sin (we share in the sin of Adam and Eve) at least since Augustine.[10] Protestant denominations have been heavily influenced by the thought of Martin Luther and John Calvin. For Luther, a diet of *sola scriptura* and *sola fide* ("scripture alone" and "faith alone") is needed to save a soul driven to sin by a corrupted body.[11] Calvin's teachings have been summarized in the acronym TULIP: total depravity; unconditional predestination and reprobation; limitation of redemption to the elect; irresistibility of divine grace; perseverance in grace is assured to the elect.[12] Baptist and evangelical faiths often see humans as immersed in "total depravity."[13] Judaism views humanity as prone to "lose its way" because of the evil inclination, the *yetzer ha-ra*,[14] while the *yetzer ha-tov*, the inclination to goodness, has less prominence.

While all these religious groups favor religious indoctrination at home, in places of worship, and in schools, there is no assumption that it will turn individuals into virtuous people. On the contrary, the common assumption is that people will continue to sin—their nature being weak and at least to some extent corrupt.

Although social conservatives may deny that they hold a dour view of human nature, it is reflected in their strong support for punitive measures. This has been manifest in recent years, as these groups gained in political ascendancy, in the reduction of support for rehabilitative and preventive programs for criminals and in an increase in support for longer jails sentences, fewer opportunities for parole, more death penalties, and harsher prison terms. (Alabama even brought back the chain gang and restored forced labor for inmates.) The widespread approval by Americans of the caning Singapore meted out to a young American charged with rather minor violations and the fact that 38 percent of Americans still favor spanking as a form of discipline in schools[15] reflects a belief that at least some young people are rather difficult to civilize and that educating them requires severe punishments. The sense that society must "keep the lid on" a dangerous bubbling human nature is a telling image of this view of human nature and the external and imposed sources of social order.

Far from believing in progress, those who subscribe to dour paradigms often presume historical deterioration, a past that was more virtuous than the present. In *After Virtue*, Alasdair MacIntyre, a renowned

scholar and leading social thinker, far from a rabid extremist or ideo-
logue, laments "the new dark ages which are already upon us."[16] Some
even write romantically (hence the label sometimes used to distinguish
these groups from the believers in reason and progress, the Romantics
or neoromantics) about premodern ages. Still others view history as the
turning of wheels, with cycles of ups and downs repeating one another,
but cast all endeavors to reach ever higher plateaus, not to mention nir-
vana, as Sisyphean, futile, and naive.[17]

While there is no necessary connection, by and large the dour school
tends to view social entities that are more encompassing than the individual, as the seat of virtue. Service to the nation or fatherland, mother
church, or the Party is perceived as paramount. Virtue lies in doing
one's duty, and in keeping human nature in check, under trying conditions. Russell Kirk wrote that "man must put a control upon his will and
his appetite, for conservatives know man to be governed more by emo-
tion than reason. Tradition and sound prejudice provide checks upon
man's anarchic impulse."[18]

When all is said and done, dour paradigms assume that if individuals
are left to follow their natural inclinations they will destroy society and
most likely one another. Strong institutions, the state included, are a
precondition of peace and civility, of social order.

HUMAN NATURE AS AN ETERNAL STRUGGLE

A third view is compatible with the communitarian paradigm, especially with what has been called "responsive" communitarianism. This
communitarian paradigm presumes no superiority of community over
the individual (or of the common good over individual rights) but, as
developed here, argues for a social world in which order, best voluntary,
is balanced with autonomy, the new golden rule.

The view of human nature that is most compatible with communitarian thinking is a *dynamic (developmental)* view. It holds that people are
indeed born basically savage, as the social conservatives would have it,
but can become much more virtuous, although never as virtuous as
individualists or welfare liberals envision.

Most important, the extent of human virtue depends on three conditions: first, on the *internalization*—rather than merely or mainly reinforcement—of values, on making them an integral part of self; second,
on the evolution or development of *social formations* needed to undergird the given values; and, third, on *reducing the inevitable contradiction*

between full order and full autonomy by making the main social formation more responsive to human nature.

STARTING GATE: BARBARIAN AT BIRTH

My starting point is the observation that infants are born physically human, but are psychologically, socially, and morally animal-like. Although people have a *potential* to become virtuous, they have no innate or built-in values. Indeed, even such elementary human features as walking erect and being able to communicate using symbols, an essential foundation of a rich language and culture, are learned rather than innate.

A telling case is the account of a thirteen-year-old girl found in Temple City, California. Her parents kept her in the back of the house and fed her, but did little more for her. When found, she was basically like an animal, growling and aggressive, snarling and scratching, unable to speak, and bereft of any culture or values.[19] Douglas Candland offers portraits of four children who were raised outside of culture, presumably by animals.[20] Peter, discovered near Hameln, Germany, in 1724, showed "few signs of socialization or civility," was "[a]lways alert and suspicious . . . [,] sat on his haunches or waited on all-fours," and "did not care for cooked foods but readily ate raw vegetables and grass . . . captured birds, dismembered them, and ate the pieces."[21] When Parisians went to see Victor (also known as the Savage of Aveyron), they saw

> a degraded human being, human only in shape; a dirty, scarred, inarticulate creature who trotted and grunted like the beasts of the fields, ate with apparent pleasure the most filthy refuse, was apparently incapable of attention or even elementary perceptions such as heat or cold, and spent his time apathetically rocking himself backwards and forwards like the animals at the zoo.[22]

Dr. Jean-Marc-Gaspard Itard attempted to civilize Victor, but failed.[23]

If one imagines a forest full of such creatures in a state of nature, one realizes how far that world is from the one depicted in the individualistic liberal fairy tale. If ever a paradigmatic argument should be settled by now, it is the question of initial nature of the self. The communitarian observation that *the me needs the we to be* is clearly the only one compatible with social science findings and observations. The normative implications of this ontological observation are subject to legitimate, different interpretations; however, that humans are social or that they are animal-like is incontestable. Infants are born only with a human potential, one that is not self-realizing. They must be made human.

THE PIVOTAL ROLE OF INTERNALIZATION

Once one fully takes into account that infants are the true barbarians at the gate, the importance of sharing the community's values with them becomes clear. The question then arises which social agents are available to trasmit values to the newest and youngest members of society.

In this context, the role of internalization stands out—or at least it should. Internalization refers to the processes through which children incorporate values into their evolving inner self, until these values become their own, become an integral part of their selves, help shape their preferences. This is not the only way to gain compliance to social values. Values are *also* part of one's social environment. Children and adults sometimes comply—that is, adhere to what values call for—out of exterior motives, out of fear of punishment or the yen for rewards. However, one observes significant differences between complying behavior that reflects internalization and complying behavior that is a response to environmental pressures. If compliance reflects social pressure, people will abide as long as the penalties or rewards exceed what they would gain if they ignored them and violated the mores—or only as long as their behavior is visible and they cannot conceal it. Moreover, as long as values are external, the maximum incentive is to seem compliant but do what one pleases, conduct that allows one to avoid punishment or collect rewards and still, for example, smoke on the sly, malinger, and abuse one's children. That is, a person can arrange to be considered an upright son or daughter, model student, altar boy or girl, and, later, citizen—while in fact engaging in one form of antisocial behavior or another.

Equally important, even when external compliance works well, when it generates full compliance rather than deceptive conformity, its costs are high because of the required measure of supervision and policing and the steady stream of rewards and punishments. And such compliance without internalization generates alienation, because the person is made to stay a course he or she does not truly seek to follow. Alienation, in turn, especially when high, has various ill consequences, from fostering psychosomatic illness to rebellion. In contrast, if values are truly internalized, compliance is high, its costs are low, and it engenders a positive sense of affirmation. In turn, people are ennobled when they live up to their values, which further sustain their commitments.

One need not accept the traditional assumptions about how internalization is achieved—something along the lines that from being nursed by the mother, the child develops an attachment that the mother utilizes in teaching acceptable behavior, and gradually the infant "generalizes" and incorporates what it is taught.[24] However, we need to understand under what conditions internalization occurs, and which ones make it fail, in order to foster internalization of shared core values and thus make society more communitarian. One thing is clear: Internalization occurs in close, affect-laden relationships, often referred to as bonding. And these relationships are one of the two defining elements of communities.

The discussion so far has focused on the first and most important acquisition of values, by children, the new members of society, during their formative years. However, internalization occurs throughout life. The most common avenues are peer relationships in school, at work, and among neighbors in a community. The more bonded the members of a group, all other things being equal, the more a new member is likely to internalize the values of the group of which he or she is a member. (This is most evident when a person who has grown up in one community truly accepts the values of another that he or she joins.)

The term "peer pressure" is particularly unfortunate in this context and reflects an unwitting individualistic bias. It implies that whatever peers foster is experienced by ego as an external—and a negative—force, as pressure. Such peer pressure does take place, but to focus exclusively on pressures is to ignore that peers can help one another to reach higher levels of accomplishment, delight, complement, and enrich one another. The term "peer (mutual) fostering" should find its place right next to "peer pressure."

Beyond parents and peers, internalization occurs also in bonding relationships with leaders who are parental figures. The conditions under which these occur and their implications would take the discussion too far afield to be followed here. However, the very fact that such internalization occurs on a large scale (for instance, when, in 1995, tens of thousands of men joined the Promise Keepers, a religious movement[25]) points to one more way this important functional need of a moral order, and thus a communitarian society, may be satisfied.

REINFORCING SOCIAL FORMATIONS:
THE MORAL INFRASTRUCTURE

Although I cannot stress enough the importance of internalization, I fully agree with those (especially Dennis Wrong in one of the most influential articles ever published in social science, "The Oversocialized Conception of Man in Modern Sociology") who argue that internalization alone cannot carry the burden of even a highly voluntary social order.[26] The incontestable sociological fact is that even if the agents and processes of socialization are maximally effective, there are still significant limits on the extent to which people incorporate their communities' values into their selves. Much follows from this observation about universal human nature.

One fundamental reason the ability to foster internalization is limited is that there is an unavoidable contradiction between the needs of social order and the need for individual and subgroup autonomy. In part, the need for autonomy reflects the animal base of universal human nature. Whether one thinks of this base as a set of specific needs (for food, shelter, and sexual release) or as a pool of generalized libidinal energy, it is far from fully malleable and absorbable into pro-social roles and the values they embody. In Freud's terms, sublimation is often far from fully successful, leaving an unsocialized "residue" that is sizable, surely larger than the sanguine concepts of human nature assume. Thus, a church may, for thousands of years, insist that its priests should be celibate, but thousands of them—despite the fact that they are a chosen lot (not a random sample of humanity), carefully trained, have their own peer groups and leaders, and a strong culture and internalization processes—will circumvent the rule in one way or another, answering the call of their nature.

The quest for frequent gratification of needs is another element of human nature. Our physiology sees no reason for prolonged self-denial. (Hence the great difficulties people have in losing weight and keeping it off. About 95 percent regain what they have lost within five years.[27]) Because social order often requires some self-denial, some deferment of gratification, and some mobilization of individual and subgroup resources for service to societal needs, its demands conflict with this underlying biological predisposition.

Other sources of limitations on internalization are oddly built into the internalization process itself. The agents of internalization cannot be made completely compatible, consistent with one another, under the best of circumstances. And often the circumstances are far from ideal. Dysfunctional marriages and broken ones, conflicts between parents and schools and between various peer groups—all put limits on the success of internalization. The net result of all these factors is a tension between the culture that internalization introduces and the forces that seek to extinguish its effects, to regress the person to a less socialized level.

While the discussion so far has been based almost exclusively on social science findings and the discussion of their paradigmatic and normative implications, it should be noted here that, on this particular issue, one has a direct personal experience and need not rely on other observations. Most individuals "hear voices": one voice reflects an urge to proceed with behavior that a person would enjoy (the pleasure principle) and another suggests what the person "senses" is the moral way to act (a reflection of values internalization). Simple sentences such as "I would like to sleep more, but I ought to go to work" and "I would like to buy a new car, but I promised myself to save these funds for the kids' college education" reflect the tension between the pleasure principle and the moral voice. (Social scientists will correctly point out that even the pleasure principle reflects one's culture, but it is much closer to our animal base than our normative commitments. These, as a rule, agitate against the calls of nature, typically calling to defer gratification, to frustrate sexual urges, to fast, and so on.) Probably most telling is the fact that those individuals who do not hear the second, inner-moral voice— psychopaths—are very likely to engage in severe antisocial behavior and, after the fact, not even to sense remorse. And those who hear only a weak moral voice are much more likely to engage in antisocial behavior than those who hear a stronger one. The communitarian person is thus one who is continuously conflicted between the calls of nature (as modulated by society's culture) and the moral voice, a person "doomed" to a struggle between a lower and a higher (a debased and a nobler) self.

This model of the self has been depicted by others, and the ways they treat it serve to highlight the way it is approached here. The philosopher Harry Frankfurt explains that what distinguishes humanity is not that we can will or choose: "[We] share these things with the members of certain other species, some of whom even appear to engage in deliberation and make decisions based upon prior thought."[28] What makes us distinctive is that we can *evaluate* our choices and desires through what

Frankfurt terms "second-order desires," which are essentially desires about what to desire (or will): "No animal other than man . . . appears to have the capacity for reflective self-evaluation that is manifested in the formation of second-order desires."[29] An example of a second-order desire would be the experience of the person who enjoys and desires chocolate, but, for the sake of health, *desires not to desire* chocolate. The tension between the first- and second-order desires parallels the tensions we have already discussed between the animal base and the effects of socialization.[30]

Charles Taylor further explains the origins of this "congenial tension." He explains that the self is essentially "dialogical": formed in conversation with certain interlocutors. "This is the sense in which one cannot be a self on one's own. I am a self only in relation to certain interlocutors. . . . A self exists only in what I call 'webs of interlocution.'"[31] This interlocution, a dialogue, is how we learn what relational terms such as "anger, love, anxiety, [and] the aspiration to wholeness" mean for us.[32] Though it seems as if this would not allow much room for independence, Taylor explains: "Even as the most independent adult, there are moments when I cannot clarify what I feel until I talk about it with certain special partner(s), who know me, or have wisdom, or with whom I have an affinity."[33] Thus, as our conversations change, so will our conception of ourselves, which makes these affective "webs of interlocution" deeply important.

Both Frankfurt's and Taylor's positions speak volumes about the nature of the internally divided self and how it is fashioned. However, neither focuses on the implications of this quality of the self for the moral order. In this sense, their analysis is more generic: The "other" voice may indeed reflect nonnormative considerations—for instance, the voice of the more cultured pleasures versus those that are more natural (e.g., a preference for gourmet versus unprocessed food). The subcategory of second-order voices under discussion here contains those that reflect internalized values, and we call attention to the fact that even those who are well brought up tend to degrade in the continuous face-off with the first-order voices.

In this sense, the conception presented here is close to one that is incorporated into many religions, which draws on their centuries of social observations and experiences: a struggle between evil and goodness, between Satan and God, within the human soul.

THE EXTENT OF INTRACTABILITY
AND ITS IMPLICATIONS

If one takes the eternal struggle between the lower and higher selves (or, more accurately, subselves) as a starting point, the next order of questions is: What is the extent of the gap? How far from one another are the behaviors prescribed by these two voices? How much of a struggle is involved in trying to reconcile the two? A good part of the answer lies in the extent to which one finds universal human nature malleable versus intractable. If one finds it to be highly malleable, one moves closer to the sanguine position. Thus, even if one assumes that people are not born virtuous but assumes that one can rather readily make them into people of good character, then the social world that individualists envision is conceivable. If one finds human nature highly intractable, one moves closer to the dour, and hence the social conservative or even authoritarian position. The more one sees human nature as setting strict limits on the beneficial effects of internalization, the more one must rely on indoctrination, and, above all, policing.

The communitarian position lies in the middle of this continuum of views: It suggests that the effects of internalization can be extensive but also that internalization is a far-from-sufficient basis for a moral order. Human beings require considerable secondary (that is, postchildhood) internalization as well as reinforcement of moral commitments.

Human Nature as Constraint: The Limits of Ethical Heroism

Human nature poses constraints on societal endeavors not by making it impossible to form or follow a normative course that contradicts human nature, but by exacting high costs if such a course is followed. The term "heroic" has been used in ethics to describe very strenuous claims.[34] Thus, to argue that people in affluent societies should fast one day a week, each week, and donate the food they save to the hungry, is heroic. The concept does not mean that a community cannot foster heroic values, only that this should be done only after special consideration. This point deserves some elaboration.

Given that human nature is rather intractable, as evident in the fact that even the most effective character education and moral infrastructure cannot expunge antisocial urges (such as aggression and inappropriate sexual inclinations), the range of values that a society, especially a communitarian society, can effectively sustain, without subjecting its members to heroic efforts, is significantly constrained.

One of the defining qualities of totalitarian societies is that they tend to assume that they can—in varying degrees, to be sure—ride roughshod over human nature as they seek to impose values their elites favor. Hence their limited ability to win true affirmation of their values by their citizens, and their heavy reliance on propaganda and, above all, coercion.

True, to some extent the totalitarian use of force reflects other factors—for instance, the confrontation between those who gained power and those classes or groups who oppose them (what the Communists called "reactionaries" and "kulaks"). But these groups are often rather quickly weakened, if not slaughtered, or driven out by totalitarian regimes. The main persistent resistance comes from a large body of members of the society who find that the imposed demands violate not only their values but also their nature. Typical are attempts to suppress autonomy that take the following forms: limits on the number of children a family can have; denial of the right to express one's ethnicity and/or religious differences; and sharp limitations on geographic mobility, and on satisfaction of transcendental needs.[35]

Totalitarian societies are not the only ones that underestimate the constraints set by human nature when they fashion their policies. For instance, numerous religious orders and secular communes have tried to embrace the vows of poverty, but most have found that they cannot sustain a high level of asceticism, even when they allowed many of those who originally joined to leave, and thus were left with a select few, who were theoretically more able to abide by a strict regime.

All this is *not* to suggest that a community or society should set aside shared values that it affirms just to suit human nature. The evidence does, though, suggest that members of communities and policy makers must *take into account* whether practices and policies they promote are compatible with or conflict with human nature. To "take into account" means that they should not attempt to fly in the face of human nature unless there are strongly compelling moral reasons and unless alternative avenues to advance these values cannot be found.

The moral matrix that results is illustrated by the kind of issues one faces when one joins the argument about whether to distribute clean needles to drug addicts or condoms to teenagers. Those who oppose such moves tend to take the moral high ground by arguing that such distributions entice individuals to become or remain addicts, or to engage in premature sex, and signal that the community legitimates such behavior. Instead, abstinence is recommended. However, the more one recognizes that, in a communitarian society (as distinct from, for example, Saudi Arabia), the ability to curb the addiction of derelicts, or the sexual urges of teenagers is limited, the more one faces the moral question: What is the scope of a community's obligations to those who cannot restrain themselves? That is, not all the *moral* arguments are on the side of abstinence. Moreover, policies can be crafted that strongly condemn drug addiction and chastise teenagers who engage in sex—and still allow for protecting the lives of those who violate the call to abstinence. Among sex educators, one such approach is known as abstinence-plus.[36] It strenuously urges youngsters, on normative and practical grounds, to defer sex—but also teaches them how to make it safer, if they fail.

Good societies, precisely because they need to base their order largely on voluntary commitments and to preserve a relatively high level of autonomy, are particularly limited in the extent to which they can foster "heroic" moral agendas, those that put heavy demands on their members—"heavy" because of their incompatibility with human nature.

One frequently runs into a liberal cliché, used by well–meaning people who wonder, with much understandable anguish, why the "richest of nations" cannot use its assets to take care of the poor and sick, especially children, in other countries or even our own society. While, of course, people can be inspired to make considerable sacrifices under special conditions, including the sacrifice of life itself, most of the time people do not live up to the demands of heroic calls. To blame it all on the lack of leadership, the consumerist culture, or the media is to disregard universal human nature, including one's own.

Human Nature as a Resource

At the same time, human nature can serve as a resource that communities and societies can and do draw upon in advancing their normative agendas. It would be a grave error to view human nature merely as a hindrance to normative endeavors. Most important for communitarian agendas is the need for human attachment, for affective bonding, which is satisfied most readily in families, peer groups, voluntary associations, and various kinds of (not necessarily residential) communities. Because these are also the social formations that foster internalization and sustain the moral voice, as a society nourishes these formations, it also fosters the internalization of values. Thus, one can build on a basic human need to foster moral obligations, which themselves may not come naturally.

Volumes have been written on this subject, dealing with various other aspects of human nature—for instance, with the need for transcendental means and connection to ultimate values. All that I can do here is to flag the significant connection between these notions and the communitarian paradigm.

It might seem at first that the argument advanced here has become contradictory. On one hand, it has been suggested that human nature limits the normative courses that can be followed and, on the other, that people can be lifted to a higher level of moral conduct by drawing on their human nature. This seeming contradiction is resolved when one applies, one more time, the principle of inverting symbiosis, when one notes that a society can garner ennobling benefits by drawing on human nature until the limits of its malleability are reached; if one lays claims beyond these limits, the psychic, social, and economic costs of the normative endeavors will rise, although progress is far from impossible.

Social Formations and the Inner Struggle

Given that human nature is not very malleable but is far from intractable, what determines the final results in the communitarian development from the predominance of the lower self to a strong, higher self? The answer lies largely in the particular social formations the society brings to bear. Social formations differ significantly to the extent and in the specific ways they help the inner struggle between the selves to help make people nobler than they would be otherwise. These formations can be reformatted both to make internalization stronger and to provide reinforcement where internalization is insufficient. They draw on both external value inducements (the moral voice of the community) and on incentives and punishment (utilitarian and coercive) to "reinforce" the inclinations one's conscience is supposed to carry.

Numerous holidays and rituals are a case in point. They have served throughout human history to nourish and sustain people's commitments to their values. Christmas and Easter, Passover and Yom Kippur, May First celebrations, Ramadan, Independence Day celebrations, and memorial days all have such an effect: They take people away from their daily ("secularizing") experiences, which tend to diminish their normative commitments, and reconnect them to the sacred or its civic equivalent.[37] Even family meals can serve such societal needs.[38]

Some holidays and rituals may, at first, seem to serve the opposite purpose, giving free rein to the pleasure principle; among them are

Mardi Gras and New Year's Eve, Oktoberfest, and maybe Purim. However, these are carefully circumscribed occasions—Ash Wednesday closes Mardi Gras—which serve to relieve some of the tensions that result from the stress on compliance during all the other days of the year. Only in societies whose values are being hollowed or lost do these "tension release" holidays and rituals become paramount while values-affirming holidays and rituals deteriorate, as has been the case with Memorial Day, the Fourth of July, and wedding rituals in the period from 1960 to 1990 in the United States.

The media is another major social formation that affects the extent to which internalization is enforced versus undermined, and the means of enforcement. The media effects in this area are much more complex and varied than has been suggested by some of its harshest critics, who blame the media for having played a major role in debasing values.[39] While the media clearly has some negative effects, it also provides the forum for nationwide moral dialogues, allowing people to become morally aroused and mobilize (for instance, when they see footage of police dogs attacking civil rights marchers or of starving children in Africa); for presidential "fireside" exhortations; and so on. Last, but not least, the ownership and control of the media is far from monolithic, allowing much more autonomy for individuals and subgroups than its extreme critics have argued.

Although all social formations affect the level of internalization and reinforcement, they differ greatly in their composition. Some, to which I refer as the "moral infrastructure," are more dedicated to fostering internalization and reinforcement via the moral voice—as it is heard in the family and places of worship, for instance—while other social formations affect reinforcement mainly by other means (various kinds of policing). A good society is particularly dependent on its moral infrastructure.

The Moral Infrastructure

The moral infrastructure draws on four social formations: families, schools, communities, and the community of communities.

The four core elements of the moral infrastructure are arranged like Chinese nesting boxes, one within the other, and in a sociological progression. Infants are born into *families* that have been entrusted through human history with beginning the process of planting values, launching the moral self. *Schools* (in relatively complex and late societies—there were none in earlier societies, in the sense of special formations set aside for educational purposes) join the process as children grow older, adding to the self (or "character"), or trying to remedy character neglect, that occurred in the launching families.

"Graduates" of families and schools, even if properly educated, still require the bonding and fostering of *communities*, the social basis of the moral voice. (The communities, in turn, draw on various formations such as voluntary associations, places of worship, public spaces—from plazas to playgrounds—and peer groups.) Finally, internalization and the fostering of the moral voice draw on *a community of communities* (the society at large) to extend the moral commitments of their members to more encompassing social entities than their own communities. (This element is the subject of the next chapter.)

One can use the four elements as a checklist to help determine the state of the moral infrastructure of a given society. It is rather evident that even in a country with a thriving economy and at peace, if the moral infrastructure decays, antisocial behavior will rise. And to the extent that these elements have corroded, they need shoring up— although a regenerative social movement may look to functional alternatives rather than attempt to construct traditional formations.

The question that has been raised in recent years, especially as the concern about the moral infrastructure of Western societies has intensified in the early 1990s is, What are the functional alternatives? Granted that there is a need for a stronger moral infrastructure in many societies, can one change the specific social formations, for example the family, and still enable them to serve their social functions? (Note that while functional needs can be served in alternative ways, the various ways are never equivalent. Hence, one must ask not merely if there are alternatives but about their relative societal performance, especially with regard to internalization and reinforcement of values.)

Here lies a great difference between the communitarian position and that of various religious social conservative groups. Both recognize the need to regenerate a moral infrastructure, but conservatives seek to return to the traditional ways of doing so and the communitarians are suggesting new ways. (Sanguine libertarians see little need for old *or* new social formations in this area, unless they are desired and fashioned by freely contracting individuals. They often view marriage as a contract, while actually it reflects a moral commitment that is open-ended. Couples do not agree with one another that "as long as you cook dinner, I will take out the garbage," and so on, but "in sickness and in health. . . .")

Individualists who object to most if not all forms of regeneration of the family (and other parts of the moral infrastructure), especially if these reflect moral suasion or public policy rather than the "free" choices by individuals, point out that often in the past these elements did not encompass many members of the society (for instance, family breakups, due to death, were rather common[40]).

As I see it, to state that a good society flourishes if certain elements of the moral infrastructure (for example, the family) are in place and well tended is not to imply that historically *all* members of a given society were encompassed in the particular social formation (for instance, the two-parent family). However, even if only the majority was so served, such formations may still have had the expected beneficial effects, although most likely in proportion to their scope. Hence, showing that a given formation was less universal than some believed does not by itself disprove its sociological functionality.

Second, to point to the contributions of these formations is not to deny that they may have had some distorting effects of their own, or that for every thousand members of society who were served by a given formation (e.g., youngsters in schools that benefit from character education programs) there were not a few who did not need it and were even set back by it. Hence, the fact that some children are abused by their parents and need to be removed from the home is not an argument against having homes, nor is the fact that some people are better off divorced by itself a compelling argument for disposable marriages.

The discussion next turns briefly to the moral infrastructure, which has been discussed more extensively elsewhere.[41] The communitarian analysis, at least as practiced here, involves a keen awareness that values need to be embodied; that is, for values to guide behavior, a society needs to evolve social and personal formations that undergird the society's values. For example, political leaders and ministers can talk about the value of families in speeches and in sermons, respectively, but such talk by itself commands little force until the society deals with difficult questions such as: how it can enable parents to dedicate more of their time to their children when the parents feel they need two full-time jobs to make ends meet; how to revalue parenting without turning women into second-class citizens; and so on. The same holds for all other values. Embody or perish is the communitarian motto behind much of what follows.[42]

Embodiment refers to the need for shared values to be internalized by the members and for these values to be integrated into the societal formations that help shape behavior. Without such embodiment, values often have rather limited societal effects and tend to fade. Embodiment often proceeds collectively—for instance, when a nation declares a day of mourning for a person who died and who exemplified the nation's values. Citizens are expected to participate in a moment of silence, lower flags to half mast, pray in places of worship, and so on, as ways of recommitting themselves to the values at issue. At other times, the society encourages its members to embody shared values in their individual behavior, from conserving water to using public transportation to voluntarily recycling garbage.

The Communitarian Family: Peer Marriage

Although there are considerable disagreements about the extent to which the family was available in earlier periods and in other societies, there is considerable agreement that the traditional family declined in the West, especially in American society between 1960 and 1990. The question, therefore, is whether or not some other social formation can provide the moral education the family provided in the past. Various alternative formations have been tried—for instance, Israeli and Cuban communal children's houses. These are so removed from the contemporary sociological reality of most Americans and are so costly, they are not further discussed here. The most widely used alternative under discussion in the West is child care by hired individuals or in specialized child-care institutions.

Given that most members of society cannot afford nannies (who are integrated into the family and the continuity of whose presence and, hence, bonding with children, is relatively assured), and that grandparents often are in different locations or otherwise unable or unwilling to act as significant moral agents, one cardinal question for those who examine functional alternatives to the traditional family is whether child-care personnel can act as satisfactory functional alternatives to the parents in terms of the role of moral agent. The crux of the issue is the early formative years, especially the first two years of life. And the issue is not custodial care or even learning but the internalization of values. The question might be asked, Are values acquired that early? I have argued elsewhere, in detail, that the basic foundation of character is the capacity for self-control and empathy. The foundations for these are laid in the first years of life. If I am correct in arguing that without these psychological foundations, the values of a good society cannot be properly installed, the importance of the formative years for later internalization of values becomes clear.

There is no conclusive answer to this question. One notes, though, that there is considerable data that cast serious doubt on the ability of child-care personnel (especially when they are poorly paid and trained and there is frequent turnover, as is the case in most American child-care centers) to do the job.[43] Other Western societies have answered the question indirectly by accepting the very large public expense of providing full pay to all parents who seek to spend the first year of their child's life at home, and have forced employers to keep the jobs parents held available for them for at least an additional year, often more.

It may seem that the question of whether a single-parent family can substitute for the two-parent family is a distinct question, but actually the two issues are closely related. Most single parents must earn a living and often work outside the household, which makes the question of child care even more acute for them than it is for families with two parents who both work outside the household.

Communitarians join those who see a need for bonding with parents in these first formative years, but they have sought an alternative formation to both the single parent and the traditional family. Communitarians have concluded that the most effective answer—using as criteria moral education of the children as well as socioeconomic costs as well as fairness to both genders—is a two-parent family in which both fathers and mothers have the same rights and the same responsibilities, a *peer marriage*.[44]

Those who argue that both parents often do not choose to work outside the household, but are pressured to do so to make ends meet, have a valid argument. However, this is an argument in favor of public policies that enable parents to be more parental but not against the need to dedicate more time, be more involved, and make a greater investment in parenting. Last, but not least, given the same economic conditions, values affect people's choice of whether to dedicate more of their time and resources to their children, or to expand their stock of consumer goods or move more rapidly up the socioeconomic ladder.

In short, while there are many ways to assess alternative family structures and alternative arrangements for child care, especially child care for infants, from the viewpoint of internalization and reinforcement, a peer marriage in a society in which parents are provided with the socioeconomic conditions that enable them to dedicate more of themselves to parenting seems preferable to other formations.

Implications for Pro-Family Practices and Policies

If one accepts the preceding analysis, one comes to the question, Which public policies would shore up parenting, and do so in line with the communitarian approach?

Most immediately, the president, in consultation with Congress, various voluntary associations active in this area, and academicians, should appoint a *science court*. Such a court would be composed of a panel of top experts, ideally experts who have not previously taken a position on the issues to be examined. The court would examine the existing evidence from conflicting studies in an effort to accelerate the research process, with an eye toward closure. (Such efforts are often undertaken by the National Academy of Science.) The court would review all the available evidence on the effects of bringing up infants largely in child-care centers as compared to in their homes, paying special attention to their character and moral development rather than merely, or firstly, to their cognitive skills. The findings of this court would help guide the public dialogue and public policies. The following discussion presumes that the court would find that, in most cases, deep and extensive involvement of a parent is necessary for proper bonding; that such bonding is essential for the initial transmission of values and their internalization by infants; and that two parents are, on average, more able to discharge this social responsibility than one parent.

Such a judgment would legitimate several categories of policies:

1: *Nonlegal policies to strengthen families* rely on studies which show that couples who stay together have conflicts about as often as those that break up, but they manage their conflicts in a more constructive manner.[45] *Conflict resolution* should be taught in all schools for this and other purposes. Premarital counseling should be available to couples intending to marry, to help them determine beforehand if they have at least faced the basic questions with which they will have to deal, such as whether or not children are planned and how to control finances.[46] (Although some couples currently receive premarital counseling, most couples need it.) Activities that *strengthen marriage* (such as marriage encounters and renewal of vows), provided by places of worship and by voluntary associations, are supportive of families, as is marriage counseling.

2: *Socioeconomic policies* that aim to encourage parents to act as parents and make it easier for them to do so should be adopted. These

include child allowances; paid family leave for one year and requirements to keep a job for a parent for two additional years; proportional
fringe benefits for individuals who work part-time; re-zoning to make
work at home easier; and flex time. Introduction and enforcement of
"deadbeat dad" laws, which collect child support from parents who
abandon their children, are of particular significance, because such laws
bring in revenue (in contrast to several of the other changes suggested,
which are very costly and hence are unlikely to be introduced in the
foreseeable future).

3: *Measures to enhance the recognition of the family* include ceremonial
occasions on the national level (the White House used to have a celebration of families of special achievement in the East Wing) and on the
local and personal level (celebrations of anniversaries and renewal of
vows). Supervows, whereby couples agree, in a prenuptial agreement,
to abide by a higher standard of commitment than the law requires, are
another tool.[47] And the existing megalogue should continue to stress the
importance of parents' dedication to their children.

4: *Changes in law* should come only after proper megalogues reestablish the value of the family and support changes in law. Among the
changes that might be considered are delays in divorces, to allow for a
cooling-off period; and a children-first principle, according to which
assets will be set aside for children (rather than merely divvied up
between the parents) in cases of divorce. Restoration of some form of
fault divorce seems less attractive.[48]

PUBLIC SCHOOLS AS CHARACTER-BUILDING AGENTS

Schools are the second building block of the moral infrastructure. As
few people object to private schools (many of which are religious)
engaging in moral education, this examination focuses on the public
schools in which 89 percent of the children in the United States are
enrolled.[49] (In many other industrialized countries, the percentage of
children in state schools is even higher.)

From a communitarian viewpoint, while schools were pivotal for
character education in earlier periods, public schools play an even larger
role in the contemporary sociohistorical context, in which families less
often serve this functional need. Moreover, a regenerative agenda must
take into account that families are only indirectly affected by public pol-

icy, but public schools can be much more directly mobilized to respond to societal needs.

An examination of the schools of the early 1990s has found them to be rather reluctant to explicitly and systematically engage in character education, for several reasons: because they are often overloaded with other missions and face budgetary pressures; because the public demands that the schools focus on cognitive learning; because many individualists and social conservatives strongly oppose moral education in public schools; and because the schools have had no clear notion of how to proceed in this area. Since the early 1990s, as the need for character education has become more evident, scores of new curricula have evolved and have been adopted by an increasing number of schools. Still, most public schools have no articulated program of character education but engage in it unwittingly, unsystematically, with little accountability.

Most powerful are noncurricular elements—the experiences schools generate. A telling tale serves to underscore the point. In April 1968, Jane Elliott, a teacher in Riceville, Iowa, decided that a conventional discussion of the plight of black Americans shortly after the assassination of Martin Luther King Jr. was not appropriate.[50] Instead, she decided to teach discrimination to her third graders by giving them a firsthand experience. Her students, Elliott felt, understood discrimination in a neutral, distant sense—what she termed "sympathetic indifference"— but they did not comprehend its true impact.

Elliott divided her class into two groups, the blue-eyed and the brown-eyed students. "Today," she said one Friday, "the blue-eyed people will be on the bottom and the brown-eyed people on the top." Elliott continued: "What I mean is that brown-eyed people are better than blue-eyed people. They are cleaner than blue-eyed people. They are more civilized than blue-eyed people. And they are smarter than blue-eyed people." In addition, she gave various privileges to the brown-eyed students during recess and in the classroom that were denied the blue-eyed ones.

The effects were swift and severe. "Long before noon, I was sick," Elliott recalls.

> I wished I had never started it. . . . By the lunch hour, there was no need to think before identifying a child as blue- or brown-eyed. I could tell simply by looking at them. The brown-eyed children were happy, alert, having the times of their lives. . . . The blue-eyed children were miserable.[51]

In short, the children had learned through *experience* what discrimination is like. It left a deep and lasting impression. In 1984, Elliott's class had a reunion. Many members of the class vividly remembered Discrimination Day and reported that it changed their life's course. Students reported that their career choices were influenced by the discrimination experience. Several chose, as a result, to join the Peace Corps or work in other cultures overseas.

From a communitarian viewpoint, to draw on public schools as developers of character (for a stronger higher self) it is most important that they focus on development of personality capabilities that enable people to act civilly and morally. First among these capabilities is the ability to control one's impulses. The underlying assumption is that aggressive and other antisocial impulses cannot be extinguished; a mature person needs to learn to recognize urges—anger, for instance— and acquire ways to curb them or channel them toward socially constructive outlets. Second, a well-formed person must have what Adam Smith called "sympathy": roughly, the ability to put oneself in the other person's shoes, what we would refer to as empathy.[52] Without this quality, there is little likelihood that children will develop charity, fairness, respect for other people, or the other virtues. When a person possesses these twin capacities, the psychological foundations for abiding by internalized values are in place.

Once schools are restructured in ways that enhance personality development, the question of which specific values are to be taught recedes in importance but still needs answering. It should be noted that, from a sociological viewpoint, the debate over whether or not public schools should engage in moral education is off the mark. It disregards the fact that there is no way for a school to avoid affecting the moral values of its pupils. Much teaching material cannot be morally cleansed, made neutral, even if this were desired. In history classes, whether the pupils are taught that George Washington never told a lie or that this story is a myth, a moral lesson is imparted. If one depicts Native Americans as a bunch of savages or as victims, one imparts a normative lesson. Lessons about the Civil War, Vietnam, and, in fact, most if not all liberal arts are deeply imbued with values. There is no way to teach history, geography, English literature, not to mention social studies and civics, in a value-neutral fashion. And even if this could somehow be achieved, it would send a strong moral message: that being "objective" and thus detached or relativistic about these matters is the morally superior way to be. There is no values-free education. Schools differ only in that some are self-aware, frank, and accountable about the values they transmit, while others are confused, are unaware of their normative agenda, or deliberately disregard the values of the communities of which they are part as they promote values the teachers favor. And communitarians maintain that one can identify a broad-based set of values that communities do share.[53]

CHARACTER BUILDING: PRACTICES AND POLICIES

We need to look at the school as a community and one that reaches its members best (when the acquisition and reinforcement of values are concerned) through bonding. From this viewpoint, it is important that all the *experiences* the school generates will be evaluated to check whether the character messages they send support or undermine the development of self-discipline and empathy. These experiences include all extracurricular activities, especially sports; and the bases on which grades, promotion (from class to class), and graduation are awarded; the ways small and major infractions of the schools rules are handled and the ways these rules are set and reset; and the ways behavior in corridors, playgrounds, parking lots, and cafeterias is conducted. If these experiences are not supportive of the character agenda, they need to be realigned to support it.

Peer mediators should be trained and introduced throughout the schools. Conflict resolution should be taught and exercised via role playing and other techniques. Grades, promotion, and graduation should be tied to achievement and not enhancement of self-esteem or some other status considerations.

Infractions are best viewed as educational opportunities rather than ignored or treated only with punitive measures. Pupils may be involved, as junior partners, in evolving the rules and their enforcement, but schools cannot be run as democracies. The role of adult authority should be openly acknowledged. Special pains should be taken to explain rules and avoid capricious ones. The fact that the school stands in for the parents and that educators and pupils are not in adversarial relations should limit the legal remedies available to students.[54] Thus, they should not be entitled to a court hearing before they are suspended or expelled or to cross-examine the faculty (that is, not all the rules of due process should apply in school), but after they leave school, they should be entitled to turn to the courts.

The school should be able to rule on conduct within its confines, including searches for guns, and to require that students wear uniforms. Lockers should carry a notation that they are school property and subject to examination.

Sports need to enhance respect for the rules and referees, rather than stress winning by most any means. Competitive teams are best deemphasized in favor of activities that involve all pupils. Because of the importance of sports for character development, they should be considered part of the regular curriculum rather than treated as something that can be cut because it is "extra."

Civic education should include opportunities to practice civic skills, just as other items of the school curricula include practice sessions (from labs to the use of computers). Community service can be used for civic practice, but voluntary is preferable to mandatory service.

Schools will be better able to develop character if they are in session for more hours during school days, more days a week, and more months a year. Such "community schools" will have a more intensive and comprehensive involvement with the students and they will be able to better protect them from the streets, empty homes, and television, and enrich their educational—and not just learning—experiences.

Parental involvement in school is helpful to character development. This must be achieved without sham and manipulation, and there must be an open and clear demarcation of those professional matters on which the school will have the final say (for example, methods of teaching English) and those matters on which the parents will (for instance, the right to opt-out their children from a sex education program as long as the parents first attend a briefing about the program).

Public schools should focus on values shared by the community rather than on those that divide it. Narratives can play an effective role in building commitments to shared values. Students in public schools should learn about the important historical role of religion but not be taught to follow any particular religion. Students should be free to express their religious commitments as long as their values are not foisted on others—for instance, in private clubs, albeit on school premises—and their expressions do not disrupt the education of their fellow students. Sex education should not be taught as a technical subject but one that is replete with values ranging from respect for others to socially responsible conduct.[55]

THE COMMUNITY AS MORAL AGENT

Human nature is such that even if children grow up in strong families—families dedicated to children and their moral education—and graduate from strong and dedicated schools, they still are not sufficiently equipped for a communitarian society. This is a point often ignored by those who assume that once people have acquired virtue, are habituated, they will be guided by their inner moral compass. The very concept of a conscience is one of an inner gyroscope.

The incontestable fact about human nature is that the good and virtuous character of those who have acquired it tends to degrade. If left to their own devices, going through the routine of life, individuals gradually lose much of their commitment to values—unless these are continuously reinforced. A major sociological function of the community, as a building block of the moral infrastructure, is to reinforce the character of individuals. We have seen how this is achieved by the moral voice, built into a web of informal affect-laden relationships, which are a constitutive element of communities. In general, the weaker the community—because the population turnover is high, there are few shared core values, heterogeneity is very high, or some other reasons—the thinner the social web and the slacker the moral voice.

More specifically, one can fruitfully examine each element of the web of social relations that make a community, asking whether they reinforce, neglect, or undermine the moral infrastructure.

The significance of voluntary associations in this context has often been highlighted as protecting individuals from the state (a protection they would not have if they faced the state as isolated or "atomized" individuals), and as intermediating bodies that aggregate, transmit, and underwrite individual signals to the state. In terms of the moral infrastructure, the very same voluntary associations often fulfill a rather different additional function: They serve as social spaces in which members of communities reinforce their social webs and articulate their moral voice. That is, they often constitute subcommunities within more encompassing communities. Thus, the members of a local chapter of the Masons, Elks, or Lions care about one another and reinforce each others' particular brand of conservative views. Similarly, the members of the New York City Reforms Clubs, Americans for Democratic Action, and local chapters of the ACLU reinforce one another's particular brand of liberal views.

Churches, synagogues, and mosques serve, in this sense, as voluntary associations. They differ, though, in one respect: While they, too, often nourish the affective attachment, they make much more room for the moral voice than many other voluntary associations do. Indeed, when places of worship devote a large proportion of their resources and social space to social activities (from square dances to bingo games), they are neglecting their role in the moral infrastructure.

Communitarians correctly focused on the condition of the public space as a place communities happen (as distinct from private cars and private homes). Even though one may have friends over for a visit or join them in a carpool, these are mainly activities of small friendship groups (what Robert Putnam calls "bowling alone");[56] communities need more encompassing webs, and those are formed and reinforced in public gathering places—from school stadiums to parks, from plazas to promenades. To the extent that these have become unsafe, communities lose one of their major sources of reinforcement; recapturing them for community use is hence a major element of community regeneration.

If, in addition to strong families and schools that build character, a society has communities whose social web is intact and whose moral voice is clearly articulate, it will go a long way toward providing the sociological prerequisite for a social order based largely on moral commitments.

LAYERED LOYALTIES

Many discussions of community and of the moral infrastructure stop at this point, having explored the moral agency of family, school, and community. However, social and moral communities are not freestanding; they are often parts of more encompassing social entities. This is the case because members of any one community, especially a modern one, have memberships and bonds in other communities; because the values held by one community affect the moral voices of the others; because the reach of one's moral commitments ranges beyond the membership of one's own community (for instance, our humanitarian concerns about hunger or civil wars in other societies); and because unless communities are bound socially and morally into more encompassing entities they may war with one another.

SEVEN

Pluralism Within Unity

ORDER AND AUTONOMY AMONG COMMUNITIES

If no systematic attention is paid to ensuring that communities will relate to one another in a manner that is respectful of both order and autonomy, then there will only be communitarian islands in a noncommunitarian sea in which hostility and strife are likely to erupt if not to prevail. While some communitarians have focused on the internal structures and dynamics of individual communities, the paradigm advanced here also concerns itself with the relations among communities.

To put it differently, good societies need to find and maintain a balance between social order and autonomy, not merely in the lives of their individual members, but also in the relations between the society at large (at the end of the twentieth century, this is still often a national society) and its member communities and subgroups, and among societies. Such a balance, I will show, aside from undergirding domestic peace, also enables each member community to honor its particular traditions and subculture, and to advance its interests and needs while still working with other communities to sustain a core of shared values.

Building and sustaining a community of communities is a particularly difficult challenge for communitarians, who seek to nourish communities, because the stronger the communities, the less they are inclined to see themselves as, and to act as, members of a more encompassing whole.

After a few drinks at a summer cocktail party on Martha's Vineyard, several people who own summerhouses there and who enjoy the island a great deal suggested, in a light vein, that the island secede from the United States to protect its beauty and its "real" community against ravaging hordes of tourists. Several offered, in a semijocular manner, that the first step should be to drown the ferries and put oil drums on the runways of the one local airport.

The members of many communities would like to pull up the drawbridges, post guards at the gates, and limit their moral concern mainly to members of their own community. This community self-centeredness is also reflected in the numerous reports of communities which insist that risky projects be placed in other communities, even if the projects would bring them new services and jobs. The opposed projects include garbage incinerators, low-income housing, prisons, drug rehabilitation centers, and nuclear storage facilities.[1]

More extreme versions of community self-centeredness are a factor in intergroup violence. Although the second half of the twentieth century has been free of world wars, it has been rampant with intercommunity strife. Aside from the well-known civil wars along ethnic, racial, and clan lines in Lebanon, in the former Soviet Union, and the former Yugoslavia, there were also armed conflicts in Somalia, Afghanistan, Rwanda, Liberia, Ethiopia, Sri Lanka, Northern Ireland, India, and Liberia, among others. Some societies broke up; the Czech Republic and Slovakia, for instance, have gone their separate ways. Even long-established democratic, basically communitarian societies exhibit some intercommunity strains. Canada is grappling with a strong separatist movement in Quebec. The United Kingdom faces a separatist movement in Scotland (and, to a lesser extent, in Wales), where two-thirds of the people prefer to consider themselves Scottish rather than British, and extremist organizations advocate violence as a means to independence.[2]

While many Americans seem to believe that this is largely a foreign problem, the intergroup tensions in the United States have also been far from trivial. No fully systematic data are available from before 1990, when Congress added the reporting of hate crimes to the Uniform Crime Reports, but available evidence indicates a rise in interracial and interethnic violence since 1980.[3] According to 1992 testimony, "one out of every four or five adult Americans is harassed, intimidated, insulted, or assaulted for reasons of prejudice during the course of [each] year."[4] Aside from conflicts between African Americans and whites, intergroup tension has spread to other ethnic communities in recent years: Conflicts between Cambodians and Latinos in Long Beach, California, resulted in the deaths of 10 people and the wounding of more than 100 between 1989 and 1992.[5] The 1992 riots in Los Angeles reflect violent divisions in that city along racial lines, especially among blacks, Hispanics, and Korean Americans. Arthur Schlesinger Jr. warns that "ethnic and racial conflict will now replace the conflict of ideologies as the explosive issue of our times."[6]

The challenge to the communitarian paradigm is to point to ways in which the bonds of a more encompassing community can be maintained without suppressing the member communities. In many ways, the sociological formation required is similar to what is needed in the relations between an individual and a single community: autonomy that is bounded rather than unfettered. And just as individual rights must be balanced with a commitment to a shared core of values, so the commitment to one's community (or communities) must be balanced with commitments to the more encompassing society.

This communitarian way of thinking is rather different from individualist thinking that seeks to deal with the same fundamental issue by making everyone a member of a universal state, with the same basic rights and duties, but without a particular commitment to one community or another. (This notion is reflected in the position of those who argue that we should have a color-blind society, or that we should treat people only as individuals and not as members of groups.[7]) Even if this would be a desirable state, it is not practical to disregard people's community affiliation and commitment to the values of their community. In short, we cannot help but be concerned about the relationships of the constituent communities to one another and to the encompassing whole.

MELTING POT, RAINBOW, OR MOSAIC?

In exploring the relationships among racial and ethnic American communities, we often grope for an image. Some envision a *melting pot*,[8] in which all groups are assimilated into one homogeneous amalgam. The melting-pot metaphor became popular at the beginning of the century, when the United States absorbed large numbers of Eastern and Southern Europeans. As Roberto Suro writes, "The melting pot is the oldest and most familiar model used to describe what happens to immigrants once in the United States. It is most potently symbolized by those who changed their names at Ellis Island so that they would fit better into the new society."[9] Mark Helprin expresses this notion forcefully—maybe too forcefully—when he opposes the division of Americans into groups and asks that they be treated as individuals rather than as members of this or that group:

> The contemporary passion to classify and divide Americans is a portent of fascism red and black. Where the communal approach rules . . . blood flows and no one is treated fairly. We, on the other hand, have fought many times for the sake of being appreciated not as classes of people but as individual souls.[10]

Time, in a special issue on the subject, provided a cover picture of the "new face of America": a computer composite that amalgamates the various racial features of the groups that make up America into one, new American face.[11] The sweet and beautiful face depicted is that of a person whose color is light milk chocolate, with dark (but not raven) hair that is straight, and eyes that are slanted but just a wee bit—the product of a genetic melting pot.

Others see a *rainbow* as a metaphor for American society, in which various people of different colors are arranged next to one another.[12] Jesse Jackson introduced this image during his 1984 presidential campaign. Others refer to American society as a "multiracial society."[13] *Time* reports that "American culture used to be depicted as a Eurocentric melting-pot into which other cultures were stirred and absorbed. . . . Today it seems more like a street fair, with various booths, food and people, all mixing on the common sidewalks."[14]

As I see it, the image of a mosaic,[15] if properly understood, best serves the search for an intercommunity construction of bounded autonomy suitable to a communitarian society. The mosaic is enriched by a variety of elements of different shapes and colors, but it is held together by a frame and glue. The mosaic symbolizes a society in which various communities maintain their cultural particulars (ranging from religious commitments and language to cuisine and dance), proud and knowledgeable about their specific traditions. At the same time, these distinct communities recognize that they are integral parts of a more encompassing whole. Moreover, they have a firm commit-ment to the shared framework. "We came on different ships, but we now ride in the same boat," to draw on a popular saying. Roberto Suro observed correctly that "[i]mmigrants do not blend into a uniform national type, but neither do they retain fixed and distinct ethnic iden-tities forever."[16]

Furthermore, there are important differences within each group. Some are more "framework" minded; others are more particularistic. It is often implied that Latinos, or African Americans or some other group, have a monolithic view on this issue, but this notion is hardly the case. For instance, when immigrants were asked if it would be better for the United States if immigrants were encouraged to blend into Ameri-can culture, 59 percent of immigrants answered in the affirmative, while only 27 percent said it would be better for them to maintain their own culture.[17]

HIGH HETEROGENEITY, WEAK SOCIETAL INTEGRATION

The more heterogeneous a society, the greater the challenge of keeping intergroup autonomy bounded within an overarching society, as one community, to sustain the golden rule. The heterogeneity of American society is greater than that of most democracies. In the United States, whites account for 77 percent of the population; by contrast, in most European countries the dominant ethnic group accounts for 90 percent or more (in Germany 95 percent); and in Japan, the figure is 99 per-cent.[18] And the heterogeneity of the United States is rising steadily. The African-American, Native American, and Asian portion of the popula-tion (Hispanics, according to the Census Bureau, may be of different races) rose from 11.4 percent in 1960 to 19.7 percent in 1990.[19] The high and rising level of heterogeneity is reflected in the fact that numerous public schools must accommodate children who speak mainly one lan-guage other than English. The number of people in the United States who speak a language other than English at home rose more than 40 percent in the 1980s, to 32 million in 1990.[20] More than 2.5 million stu-dents were enrolled in language assistance (bilingual and other) pro-grams in 1992, more than ten times the number in 1972.[21] Reference has already been made to indications of intergroup tensions and strife. (A factor that, to some extent, mitigates these centrifugal tendencies is that

as heterogeneity has risen, so has a powerful mechanism of social integration: intergroup marriages.)

The social mechanisms that societies draw upon to cope with heterogeneity, and to counter the centrifugal forces that all societies experience, are less powerful in American society than they are in many
other Western societies. American society does not draw on a nationwide educational curriculum, through which a shared set of core values
is transmitted from one generation to another generation, to all the
new members of society. The media largely lacks a normative binding
content and is increasingly locally controlled. There are only a few
opportunities like that which the settling of the West provided, in which
people from different backgrounds intermingled. Participation in
AmeriCorps, the Clinton administration's voluntary national service
program, has been tiny (just over 25,000), and the experience has not
built nearly as many bonds as one might have hoped. The result of relatively high centrifugal forces and no strong integrative force is a society
in which various racial and ethnic communities continue to pull away
from one another.

Another indication that the American community of communities is
fraying is the tendency of various segments of the society to calculate
how much they receive from whatever is allocated by the national
whole, and how much they contribute (taxes, services, and the like).
This is typically followed by demands to equalize what one receives
with what one gives, as if each community were a fully autonomous
entity and had no shared concerns or inclination to contribute to the
weaker segments of society, or to the common good.

What is lost or missing is reminiscent of what's lacking for a married
couple who are preoccupied with ensuring that each partner pays half
of all costs and do half of all chores. Such an orientation leads to frequent arguments about the equal worth of tasks, overtime, and so on.
While clearly there is room for such concerns, marriages—and other
communal bonds—are better sustained when the sides allow for some
latitude, follow what is known as the 75 percent/75 percent rule,
according to which each side agrees, out of interest in preserving the
shared bond, to give more than is required without forgoing its rights to
seek redress if the pattern is seriously out of kilter. (A case could be
made that a 60 percent/60 percent rule would leave less room for
exploitation of the party more committed to the bond.) The same rule
applies to relations among communities: the more they demand to
receive their exact share, the stronger the centrifugal forces.

To sum up the thesis advanced so far: In America, we can see ethnic and racial tensions rising against the background of a society that has increasing intergroup objective differences (heterogeneity), and people who are increasingly mobilized along group lines in a society whose nation-building mechanisms are far from strong.

Other societies face the same basic problem: how to sustain society-wide integrity—a key element of social order—without suppressing subgroup autonomy. Many Western societies are somewhat less challenged in this area than American society, but still face a rising problem. For instance, the diversity of France, Germany, Britain, and Belgium, although not nearly as great as the United States', is increasing, reflected in tensions with North African, Turkish, and other ethnic minorities. Still other societies were never as integrated as the United States used to be—for instance, the former USSR; the former Yugoslavia; and many former European colonies, especially in Africa, where the national borders were drawn arbitrarily, encompassing rather divergent ethnic communities. Several societies have not made sufficient room for the autonomy of member communities and show signs of the resulting tension. The place of the Korean community in Japan is a case in point. The problems faced by Turkey and Iraq in their relations with the Kurds are others. While the details differ significantly, there seem to be few societies that can avoid dealing with the relations among the member communities and with the society at large. The balance of the discussion, which follows, focuses on this issue within the American context, but its conclusions apply to other societies as well.

COPING WITH RISING DIVERSITY

One way of dealing with group centrifugalism is *assimilation* (melting pot), in which people of different identities give up their subcultures and particular group loyalties to become undifferentiated members of the overarching community. This is what the USSR tried to achieve in its dealing with the members of several minorities, especially the Jews, and how mainland China has attempted to deal with the Tibetans. Both countries combined strong acculturation efforts with forceful suppression of cultural differences. In American society, those who favor assimilation have largely sought to rely on acculturation, although occasionally pressures that border on the coercive have been applied. Children have been prohibited from speaking their native language, even in play-grounds,[22] and laws have been enacted in several states requiring that all ballots, street signs, and official transactions will be only in English.[23] Quebec enacted laws that prohibit the use of English on street signs and in menus.[24]

In terms of the paradigm developed here, assimilationist ideologies and policies are a case of strong oversteering. There is no compelling sociological reason to assimilate Americans into one indistinguishable blend, to apply, as James Bryce put it, the great American solvent that removes all traces of previous color and to strip Americans of their various ethnic or racial hyphens.[25] There is no need for Greek Americans, Polish Americans, African Americans, or any other groups to see themselves as plain Americans without any particular distinction, history, or subculture. Similarly, Americans can, if they so choose, maintain their separate religions, from Greek Orthodox to Buddhist, and their subcultures (including distinct tastes in music, dance, and cuisine), without constituting a threat to the American whole.

Indeed, this society's culture is richer for having an introduction to jazz and classical music; the jig and the polka; Cajun and soul food; and so on. Nor is there any evidence that American society would suffer if we were to learn more about each other's backgrounds and traditions—know the teachings of the Qur'an, learn about Asian philosophy, or study the traditions of Native Americans—and if each community would proudly recall its particular heritage and nourish its interest in its country of origin.

True, as Arthur Schlesinger Jr. put it, one of the great virtues of America is that it defines people individually and according to where they are headed (to science? politics?) rather than where they came from (an aristocratic family? a peasant background?).[26] But this does not mean that Americans need to jettison their interest in and knowledge of their particular past or communal attachments in order to be regarded according to their contemporary contributions or to maintain their loyalty to the encompassing community of communities.

The sociological challenge is to develop societal formations that leave considerable room for the enriching particulars of autonomous subcultures and communities while sustaining the core of shared values. (The relationship of American society to still more encompassing communities, such as North America, the Western Hemisphere, or the human family, is a subject not explored here. Suffice it to say that these more encompassing societies so far have not developed sufficient communitarian elements to create viable communities, as much as one may regret this fact.)

The concept of a *community of communities* (or diversity within unity) captures the image of a mosaic held together by a solid frame. "E pluribus unum" may not be equal to the task; it implies that the many will turn into one, leaving no room for pluralism as a permanent feature of a diverse yet united society.[27]

DIVERSITY AND THE NEED FOR A FRAMEWORK

The discussion so far has dealt with two competing images of society, that of assimilation and that of the community of communities. A third view favors recognition of differences with little attention to the shared framework. Those who embrace this orientation speak of "diversity" without any qualifiers or additions. To the extent they discuss a shared framework at all, they reject it. The voices of unqualified diversity tend to view the existing framework as one that reflects traditional white, male, or European-American values. These advocates of diversity tend to ignore the question of whether diversity needs to know any bounds, let alone what the content of such bonds might be.

When I served as the president of the American Sociological Association, I dedicated the program of the 1995 annual meeting of the association to the community of communities. A special plenary session was organized on the future of race, ethnic, and gender relations in the American society. Three of the speakers were leaders of the African-American, Hispanic, and Asian-American communities, respectively. They were especially challenged to discuss how they envisioned relations among racial and ethnic groups in America in the year 2020. All three speakers chose to stress past injustices, and two out of the three suggested that there may have to be a civil war before justice might be done for their respective group. All three avoided the question of the nature of a shared framework that would keep social order, albeit a recast one. It is a question that remains unanswered for American society and many others. Israelis, for instance, struggle with the same question whenever they are asked about the future of relations between Jewish- and Arab-Israeli citizens.

Still more extreme versions of unqualified diversity hold that there is no society at all, only various groups confronting one another or one group that dominates the others.[28] Such views seriously undercut the legitimacy of the framework, the community of communities. The position followed here is based on the observation that societies whose frameworks weaken are subject to tensions, if not civil wars, that diminish both order and autonomy, developments that are incompatible with a good society. In contrast, the question of whether the existing framework can be recast does not threaten the foundations of the communitarian society because it recognizes the basic functional need to have a framework.

THE FRAMEWORK: THIN OR THICK? PROCEDURAL OR SUBSTANTIAL?

The discussion of which social formations need to be shared by all versus which may remain particularistic often focuses on the question of which values need to be shared by all. Other terms are used, but sociologically speaking they address the same issues: Does the nation need one core creed? An identity all of its own? A unitary culture? Or, as it is traditionally put, is there such a thing as a unique American character?[29] Seymour M. Lipset is one of those who answers this last question in the affirmative, and he provides a detailed analysis, backed up with cross-national public opinion data, to show the "exceptionalism" of the American society, its distinct set of values.[30]

Such discussions of the normative content of the framework, however, skip a question that must be addressed first: Should the framework contain shared values at all? As we have seen, individualists maintain that social formulations of the good endanger individual rights. Melinda Fine represents this view well when she calls for a curriculum that would teach youngsters to define America not as a unified society, in which cultural, racial, and ethnic differences exist but are secondary, but as a "diverse and pluralistic society," period.[31] No shared bonds and values here. Democracy is then explicitly characterized as "being about establishing the *processes* whereby these conflicts [resulting from diversity] can be played out."[32] In contrast, we saw, communitarians hold that unless there are some shared *substantive* core values, a "thicker" framework, which most people in a community find compelling, social order cannot sustain itself.

To point to the importance of shared substantive values, however, is not to suggest that they form a strict and rigid creed, a canon immutably handed down from one generation to the next. On the contrary, historical experience shows that the substantive normative content of the framework continually adapts to changing balances within the society and to changes within the world environment while maintaining its own continuity.[33] Examples come handily from American constitutional history. For instance, the value of privacy, which is now deeply ensconced in American constitutional lore, is not even mentioned in the original text of the Constitution. The notion that some Americans are not to be recognized as full-fledged persons[34] has long been cast aside, as have the notions that women have no right to vote and that only those who own property can run for office. In effect, much of what the Supreme Court does is reinterpret the constitutional tradition, while it seeks to maintain it.

If one grants the need for a thick shared framework, albeit one that may be recast, what are its key elements?

CORE ELEMENT I: DEMOCRACY AS A VALUE (NOT ONLY A PROCEDURE)

Individualists view democracy as a mechanism; communitarians, as a core value that must be shared. The basic reason is that if democracy is viewed merely as an arrangement or procedure, it may be abandoned when it comes into significant conflict with a major interest group or the values of one of the major contesting subgroups. Democracy, in this sense, is akin to a contract, the compliance with which is ultimately based on precontractual commitments to abide by contracts (as the fear of enforcement by itself often does not suffice to hold parties to contracts, the parties will find ways to circumvent or violate contracts when strong inducements arise).[35] Similarly, democracy holds best if it has the rank of a substantive value rather than only an instrumental standing.

This is far from a theoretical issue. The debate with fundamentalists is precisely on this matter: Will their values take priority when they conflict with those the majority favors or those embodied in the Constitution? We have already seen that the notion that religious values may govern in private matters and that democratic decision will govern in public matters works only up to a point, as the debates about abortion, divorce, and sodomy laws illustrate. And the community suspects that those who have a strong religious commitment will heed it even when they are in public office. This came up when John F. Kennedy, in order to run for president, had to convince the voters that his obligations to the Pope would not take precedence over the interests of the country.

The strong role that normative commitment to democracy plays was highlighted during the budget fights in mid-1995. First, by a margin of only six votes, the House voted to prevent cuts to environmental programs; but then the House reversed itself, and major cuts were approved.[36] The second vote would have gone the other way if a single House member had voted the other way or merely abstained.[37] However, as far as I could determine, no one—not even die-hard environmentalists—argued that it was improper for such a slim majority to decide such a critical matter. Democratic rule is held in high regard even in a society that has come to cast much else in deep doubt. In short, a normative commitment to democracy, despite its flaws, as the best system there is and one that must be continuously perfected, is an essential shared element, part of the framework of a community of communities.

CORE ELEMENT II:
THE CONSTITUTION AND ITS BILL OF RIGHTS

Another major element of the American framework (and that of many, albeit not all, democratic societies) is the Constitution and its Bill of Rights. The Constitution embodies core values that guide the American polity and society. It is the embodiment of shared conceptions of the ways liberties will remain ordered, of the measures that serve to ensure individual and minority rights and maintain a civic society.

It is less often noted that the Constitution provides a significant source of guidance for the relationships among the communities that constitute the society, and the relationships of those communities with the society at large. It does so by drawing a line between the decisions local (and nongeographic) communities may make (even if the decisions greatly differ from one particular community to another) and those that are framed by the overarching society (which are not subject to variation by member communities). This is expressed in terms of those numerous matters on which the majority may rule and those in which the majority does not govern but where minority and individual rights are guaranteed. For instance, no majority (local or otherwise) can vote to allow individuals to be sold as slaves, be denied the right to vote, to speak freely, and so on. On the other hand, the majority is entrusted with deciding the level of taxes that will be exacted, the allocation of these funds among various competing demands, and numerous other matters.

Although the line between legitimate majority decisions and the areas from which the majority is excluded does not *necessarily* parallel the line between community particulars and the societal commonweal (the pieces and the frame of the mosaic), it often does. Most policies concerning education, transportation, and the like are set locally, and numerous other policies are formulated by the fifty states . The policies local and state governments pursue often reflect values particular communities seek to uphold. This is the reason antidrug policies are stricter in Houston, Texas, than in New York City; immigrants are treated more harshly in Southern Californian communities than in Maine; and so on. In each of these communities, local or state majorities set their particular course. However, all these communities must act within the values embodied in the Constitution. This prevents communities from following their particular values in those specified areas where the society at large has agreed shared values take precedence. Foremost among these values are various freedoms—such as freedom of speech, association, and assembly—that prevent communities from banning speakers whose views a given community finds offensive, outlawing troubling books, or discriminating against a given racial or ethnic group. Here the Constitution—speaking for the shared values of the community of communities, the society at large—upholds core values in the form of limits on local policies. (In the same manner, the Constitution also limits what the national majority can do, often by protecting societal values against values favored by a particular group. For instance, during the civil rights era, the Supreme Court consistently overturned Southern states' attempts to retain segregation, despite majority opinion in many of those states. More recently, a law prohibiting flag burning was struck down by the Supreme Court, despite the fact that 66 percent of Americans support an amendment to the U.S. Constitution protecting the flag.[38])

While the division between community autonomy and societal order is at the core of the American democracy, the specific lines between the legitimate domain of specific communities and that of the community of communities are continually contested and redrawn—at the margins. Two recent U.S. Supreme Court decisions illustrate the point at hand. These decisions are often discussed in terms of separation of church and state, but this is only one facet of a broader issue: What are the issues that a community is entitled to decide on its own, and when must it yield to society at large, the community of communities?

In a 1990 case, the question arose whether the Native American Church was entitled to use peyote during its religious ceremonies as its tradition commands, or whether it had to abide by the national laws prohibiting the use of controlled substances. (This is somewhat akin to asking whether wine could be legally used in the Sacrament or Kiddush during Prohibition.) The Supreme Court upheld the state court ruling prohibiting the use of peyote, and one cannot help wondering if it correctly drew the line between the common and the particular in this case (*Employment Division* v. *Smith*, 1990). Indeed, the decision was superseded in 1993, when Congress passed the Religious Freedom Restoration Act.

Another relevant case concerns the Santeria, a group primarily based in Florida, Southern California, and New York City, which practices the sacrifice of live animals as part of its religious ceremonies. The group hauled the town of Hialeah, Florida, to court in 1989, challenging a city ordinance that prohibited animal sacrifice. The Supreme Court ruled that the state must have a compelling interest to restrict any religious practice, and indicated that in this case no compelling interest had been established (see *Church of Lacombe* v. *Hialeah*, 1993). Thus, in this case, the community's values were allowed to take priority over a national normative stance toward animals.

If, however, a group of African immigrants were to practice female circumcision in an American town, one would expect public health authorities and social work agencies to stop the practice. Furthermore, the courts would be likely to uphold this action on the ground that female circumcision offends basic values of the American society as a whole against child abuse.

The purpose of citing these cases is to highlight that there are ongoing societal moral dialogues, or megalogues, couched in legal terms, regarding the proper place to draw the line between the societal set of values and the particular ones, those of the community of communities and those of the constituting communities. Indeed, the fact that these lines can be redrawn reflects the adaptive nature of the American system. However, it does not cast into doubt the basic setup: Frames are recast, but society is not frameless.

CORE ELEMENT III: LAYERED LOYALTIES

To maintain the proper equilibrium between the particular constituting communities and the overarching framing community, *layered loyalty* must be fostered. This entails nurturing a split loyalty, divided between commitment to one's immediate community and to the more encompassing community, and according priority to the overarching one on key select matters. This functional need is best served when members of any one community view themselves as a part of an immediate community as well as of more encompassing wholes (containing communities other than one's own).

The fact that such layered commitments can be developed is well supported by American history. Into the 1890s, many Americans saw themselves primarily as members of local communities. (When asked, "Who are you?," a typical answer was, say, "A Virginian.") After the 1890s, many Americans developed the sense of being a member of a two-layered community. Today the answer to, "Where are you from?" especially if asked overseas, is typically: "An American (from Virginia)." Symptomatic of the change is that the Supreme Court up to the 1890s referred to the United States in the plural (using the verb "are"), but referred to the United States in the singular ("is") from then on.[39] And, only as of 1866, with the enactment of the Fourteenth Amendment, was citizenship in one state fully recognized in all others.

It seems that by 1960 Americans came to view themselves first as "Americans" rather than first and foremost as citizens of a state or a region. However, between 1960 and 1990, a growing number of Americans have started to see themselves as belonging to one "tribe" or another, and their loyalty to the encompassing community of communities has been diminished. Many immigrants from Spanish-speaking countries refused to seek American citizenship even when they lived in the country for many years. Some African Americans endorsed the view of themselves as a separate nation. Black separatism was strongly advanced by Malcolm X:

> We only want an equal chance on this earth, but to have an equal chance we must have the same thing the white man himself needed before he could get his nation started. ... *We must have some land of our own!* ... How else can twenty million Black people who now constitute a nation in our own right, *a nation within a nation*, expect to survive ... ?[40]

All this reinforces the sociological observation that layered loyalties need to be constantly nourished if a communitarian society is to be sustained.

CORE ELEMENT IV:
NEUTRALITY, TOLERANCE, OR RESPECT

For the community of communities to be sustained, members of the constituting communities need to combine their appreciation of and commitment to their own particular traditions, cultures, and values with respect for those of others. And this must be achieved without the fear that paying this respect will be interpreted as indicating that they embrace others' values as their own or endorse them morally.[41]

Individualists often do not face this issue because they shy away from judgments about what is a social virtue. It is consistent with their position to be "neutral" about such matters—say, about the difference between homosexuality and heterosexuality. David Boaz of the Cato Institute, for example, has denounced social conservatives for attacking homosexual rights, and has supported extending health benefits to homosexual partners when they are extended to spouses of heterosexuals.[42]

Strong social conservatives, and above all fundamentalists, tend to uphold a unitary set of values and to condemn people whose values are different, from gays to Jews, from Catholics to Zen Buddhists. Pat Robertson argues that:

> You say, "You're supposed to be nice to the Episcopalians and the Presbyterians and the Methodists and this, that and the other thing"—nonsense. I don't have to be nice to the spirit of anti-Christ. I can love the people who hold false opinions, but I don't have to be nice to them.[43]

The orientation of most strong social conservatives to diversity is fairly characterized as intolerant.

James Hunter argues that our goal should be tolerance, which does not mean accepting all views as equally valid as one's own, but rather learning to live peacefully beside those one disagrees with.[44] The term "tolerance," however, implies considerable distancing. It implies that one will put up with such views out of good manners or for the well-being of society, but actually judges them to be lower in moral standing than one's own mores. In contrast, respecting subcultures other than one's own, so long as there are particulars at issue rather than mores and values that concern the "framework" (the core of shared values), seems more communitarian. Respect means that while these are not values I hold, I have no normative objections to others holding them. Thus, I am not a Buddhist, but I respect Buddhism; I am not a devotee of jazz, but (unlike many religious fundamentalists and Communists) I respect those who are.

There is no sociological evidence or reason to expect that commitment to one's own culture is antithetical to knowing and respecting those of others. Moreover, focusing on one's own to the exclusion of other cultures hinders crosscultural communications and understanding, and thus the community of communities. A typical example is a schoolteacher chiding Asian-American children for not making eye contact, which she considers part of being forthcoming, while in the given subculture staring into someone's face is considered impolite. American core values, culture, and integrity would not be undermined, but its pluralism would be rewarded if all members of the society had a higher degree of understanding and appreciation of other cultures. Such understanding and appreciation, of course, would also help make Americans better able to deal with other parts of the world.

CORE ELEMENT V: LIMITING IDENTITY POLITICS

The centrifugal effects of demographic and subcultural group differences are exacerbated in a political culture that stresses differences and downplays commonalities. One particularly common form this has taken is defining people as if they had only one social status, as if they were members of only one community rather than multiple and overlapping and interlaced communities.

This is evident when people are encouraged to view themselves mainly, if not exclusively, as black or white, men or women, and so on. This monolithic orientation plays down the fact that each person has multiple statuses—that is, someone may be black but share with some whites the condition of being, say, a woman, and, with still others, being a working-class person, and so on. And it plays down the fact that all are members of one society. This orientation, reflected in "identity politics,"[45] is reinforced when group differences are depicted as total and other groups are depicted as the enemy. Instead, group differences must be seen as differences among members of the same community that can and need to be worked out while maintaining the community, even if it needs to be deeply recast in the process.

Lewis Lapham laments:

Were I to believe what I read in the papers, I would find it easy to think that I no longer can identify myself simply as an American. The noun

apparently means nothing unless it is dressed up with at least one mod-
ifying adjective. As a plain American I have neither voice nor authentic
proofs of existence. I acquire presence only as an old American, a female
American, a white American, a rich American, a black American, a gay
American, a poor American, a Native American, a dead American.[46]

At a 1995 conference on race, one participant, who is both African-
American and Puerto Rican, said, "It's all black, white, black, white. If I
were only to listen to the media, only half of me exists."[47]

Janet Saltzman Chafetz points out that by not recognizing the differences *within* groups, people are able to make statistical claims about the
differences *between* various groups and "a mythologized, dominant
group of 'white, heterosexual males.'"[48] She adds, "By continually
focusing on average differences between statistical groups, or 'typical'
descriptions of individuals within different categories, policymakers
and the media perpetuate the harmful notion that our nation is composed of homogenous groups with the same interests and social deter-
minants."[49]

Against this conception of stressing differences along mono-status
lines, the communitarian perception is that all self-definitions—and definitions *by* others and *of* others—that reduce individuals to one standing
endanger the community of communities. Being informed and loyal
members of one group or another is not at issue. What is at issue is the
exclusionary orientation and the attempt to monopolize one standing
to drown out all others.[50]

It is rather evident that, in many societies between the 1960s and
1990s, identity politics has risen sharply, especially along racial, ethnic,
and gender lines (while class identity politics has, in effect, often been
muted for numerous reasons, including the fact that the other lines of
division crosscut and hence blur class lines). However, it is much less
clear to what extent the mass of the members of the various groups,
defined by identity leaders, indeed follow their group leaders, and,
above all, their claim for primary—if not exclusive—loyalty, the type
that is detrimental to communitarian society.

Even though the data that reflect directly on this issue are scant, one
can gain some insight into the issue from the reluctance of most members of the various groups to accept the designated label and identify
with "their" group. Thus, many "Latinos" do not see themselves as
belonging to one group, but as belonging to a variety of ethnic groups
(such as Cuban American, Mexican American, Puerto Rican), and

within each such group, views on numerous issues vary a great deal.[51] Similarly, when it comes to "Asian" Americans, most see themselves predominantly as Korean American or Filipino or Japanese American and only sometimes as Asian Americans, and the perceived differences between the labels are considerable within each group.[52]

When it comes to political views, Puerto Ricans, Cubans, and Mexicans do not share the same political views, even though they fall within the so-called Latino community. According to recent surveys, over 60 percent of Puerto Ricans and Mexican Americans identify themselves as Democrats, while 65 percent of Cubans say they are Republicans. On the topic of abortion, the majority of Cubans identify themselves as prochoice, but the majority of Mexican Americans and Puerto Ricans are prolife. Furthermore, their views diverge from the usual rhetoric of their leaders. An overwhelming majority of the respondents think there is too much immigration, while Latino leaders often advocate fewer restrictions on immigration.[53]

California's Proposition 187 demonstrates similar discrepancies. During the 1994 campaign, the press billed the measure as a right-wing nativist effort to combat immigration. An analysis of the votes, however, reveals that the proposal passed with the support of one-quarter of all Latino voters and nearly half of the African-American and Asian voters in the state.[54]

In their political views, different minority groups have shown as much, and sometimes more, division within their own ranks than from other ethnic groups.[55] Conservative African Americans are now coming into their own, with such leaders as Alan Keyes, Shelby Steele, Thomas Sowell, and Michael L. Williams. And anyone who thinks that all women form a unified front need only think of the conservative Phyllis Schlafly and the feminist Catharine MacKinnon to realize how diverse their views are.

But, argue the leaders of various groups, drumming up hostility along mono-status lines and setting up confrontations is an effective way to mobilize one's group, raise funds, keep the troops loyal, and achieve a measure of block voting. The secret, though, for community of communities politics to work, is for the constituting groups to realize that they must fight for their causes with one hand tied behind their back. They must realize that if they go all out and try to maximize their group's share, to the disregard of the shared bonds, they will endanger these bonds. For instance, if each group demanded all the subsidies, federal loans, and tax exemptions it could squeeze out of the politicians, the resulting deficit would destroy the economy. Ergo, to sustain a communitarian society, identity politics need to be replaced by the admittedly more complex politics that allow a group to advance its particular needs while recognizing that its members have other affiliations and loyalties, to a more encompassing community and to other groups that are part of that society.[56] In effect, the more individuals are active in multiple and crosscutting groups—for example, a national professional association and a local ethnic group—the more likely the communitarian nature of society will persist. The more individuals are monopolized by any one group, the less communitarian a society will be.

CORE ELEMENT VI: SOCIETY-WIDE DIALOGUES

We have already seen (in chapter 5) the importance of keeping dialogues civil and preventing moral dialogues from turning into culture wars. All that remains to be noted here, on the list of the elements needed to develop and sustain a community of communities, is that this thesis applies to dialogues among communities and not merely within communities.

CORE ELEMENT VII: RECONCILIATION

One of the least studied processes that form and nourish communitarian societies is that of reconciliation. The little we know about reconciliation largely concerns relations between individuals rather than between groups. Reconciliation should not be confused with mediation, conflict resolution, or negotiation: Each of these is closely tied to the separate interests of the parties, and therefore focuses on instrumental processes such as splitting the difference and bargaining. Reconciliation deals with affective elements, such as resentment and hate and associated psychological states.

Nicholas Tavuchis identifies four stages of reconciliation: the call for apology, the apology proper, forgiveness, and finally genuine reconciliation.[57] Before any apology is made, it must be clear that the apologizing group is deemed worthy by the offended group[58] and that the offended group is ready to be apologized to. (Apologies that follow hot on the footsteps of a major offense may be much less effective than those that occur after a period of cooling off, while minor aggravations might be treated on the spot, so to speak.)

The act of apology itself is subject to several requirements. It must be a public one and clearly documented "for the record." Secret or private apologies cannot as a rule substitute for official, public apologies between groups. For example, it became known in the 1980s that the CIA had conducted damaging experiments on unwilling Canadian subjects during the late 1950s. Though CIA officials were quick to say that they personally regretted these activities, they refused to offer a public apology on behalf of the U.S. Government, and, though called for, none was ever made.[59]

Examples of properly constructed apologies include those Japan made for its role in World War II in the United Nations General Assembly.[60] They helped advance the reconciliation between Japan and her Asian neighbors. Another example is Southern Baptists' apology to African Americans for having condoned racism for much of their history.[61] Still another case in point is the official (and much belated) apology of the United States to Japanese Americans who were interned during World War II, which was made in 1988. The apology was followed by a cash payment to the survivors, not so much for the sake of compensation but as a token of sincerity. As such, it was much appreciated.[62]

The apology must clearly acknowledge the injustice that was inflicted. In a book on racial reconciliation, Harlon Dalton stresses, in addition to the need to be open about differences, to put all "our 'priors' on the table."[63] In an account of a reconciliation between Jews and Germans, another author argues, "Genuine transformations occur only if . . . Jews and Germans together confront injurious memory and become vulnerable in each other's presence."[64] Tavuchis points out that this need for openness is one explanation for what frustrated many people in the United States about Richard Nixon: Even though he publicly said that he was regretful, he continually refused to acknowledge what he was sorry about, making it difficult to move on to forgiveness.[65]

Forgiveness cannot be granted too easily without suggesting that the original wrong was excusable. Nor can forgiveness be so all-encompassing so as to lead to forgetting. This has led many Jews, for example, to be rather cautious about even the most sincere apologies by Germany.

The last stage is described as one of transformation. In describing the gradual reconciliation occurring between Jews and Germans, Bjorn Krondorfer writes:

As I envision it, reconciliation is a ritual practice or experience that strives toward transformation. It liberates . . . [both parties] from the stalemate of current discursive practices and encourages them to seek new ways of relating to each other without neglecting the history and memory . . . [66]

Examples of partial and fuller reconciliation play a much larger role in community building than is typically noted. Reference was already made to the beginnings of reconciliation between blacks and whites, and between Jews and Germans. Other examples include the reconciliation between the South and the North in the generations that followed the Civil War; and the reconciliation between Germany and France that followed three major wars, leading them to become the mainstays of the European Community.

A CORE LANGUAGE?

Many societies debate whether languages belong in the shared framework—that is, whether all members of the society are expected to communicate in one and the same language, or if several could coexist. It is an issue that was contested in Belgium, Switzerland, Canada, and Israel and is still debated within American society. In all these societies, in one stage or another, the issue has been discussed in highly emotive terms. In the United States, some ultraconservative groups have used the commitment to English as a code phrase for nativism and anti-immigrant sentiments.[67] Some of these groups have been associated with a movement to keep immigrants out and to keep America white and Aryan. Others merely demand that street signs, ballots, and government documents be issued only in English and that English be the official language of the country.[68] Some on the left have used the existence of racist pro-English groups as proof that to favor English as a core language is to seek to rob immigrants of their culture. Rosalie Pedalino Porter notes, "Most critics of [English-language amendments] . . . attack the legislation as nationalistic, xenophobic, racist, and bigoted."[69]

However, if stripped of such emotive overtones, several facts stand out. First, most immigrants are keen to learn English.[70] Most of those most directly affected do not view learning English as an attack on their culture, or something forced upon them. On the contrary, for reasons ranging from utilitarianism (English is useful) to identification with the community of communities, most immigrants seek to acquire the language of the land. When California passed an English-language proposition in 1986, it received support from 73 percent of the voters, many of them immigrants.[71] Porter notes that no lawsuits have challenged the law, and that "no discriminatory effects have yet been found in states where English-language legislation has been approved."[72]

One also notes that there is no inherent contradiction between learning English and maintaining one's own culture. Most societies have discovered that having one shared language that all members of society command enhances the cohesion and functioning of the society. Indeed, much business is conducted worldwide—from air traffic control to banking—in English. Other issues often tied to the question of whether or not we should foster one shared tongue, from the proper treatment of illegal immigrants to the scope of opportunities for bilingual education, deserve full airing. However, this is best achieved if they are not commingled with the question, In which language are Americans going to address one another in their daily pursuits?

The notion of a community of communities in general, and that of layered loyalties in particular, suggests that command of English should be promoted as the language of the community of communities, while other languages should be learned for several reasons, including maintaining the subcultures and the constituting communities.

IMPLICATIONS FOR PRACTICE AND POLICY

General policy guidelines that follow from the preceding discussion hardly need to be pointed out: A society that is straining due to group centrifugalism needs to *promote formations and processes that shore up societal bonds and shared values.* The purpose is not to abolish differences, to "assimilate," but to reinforce the framework that keeps the pieces together.

The Display of Symbols. Among these are opportunities in which symbols of society-wide unity are displayed in an affirmative context. Laying wreaths on the tombs of unknown soldiers, flying flags at half-mast when a national hero passes away, and Fourth of July parades are cases in point. Between 1960 and 1990, there was a tendency to turn such symbols into sources of confrontation (Should President Reagan go to Germany to lay a wreath on the graves of fallen SS soldiers in Kolmeshöhe cemetery in Bitburg? Should gay people be allowed to march in a St. Patrick's Day parade in New York City?) or to shy away from deploying them and retreat from such societal symbolic activity into private pursuits (for instance, by turning the Fourth of July into backyard barbeques).

Regeneration requires restoring shared symbolic activities and enhancing commitment to them. (Such a development is already occurring on the family level when it comes to marriage ceremonies, which were played down in the 1960s and are treated much more ceremonially again.)

Media Policies. The public media, which includes such elements as C-Span, National Public Radio, and public television, *is* an important arena for *unity-building* as well as for megalogues. One may argue whether such media should be supported by the taxpayers or largely dependent on contributions from individuals and foundations. There is, however, little doubt that such media contributes to society-building, a purpose it could not serve as well if it were commercialized.

There is room for discussion on how to ensure that public media will not "tilt" in favor of one set of values against others. (Public media was often charged with exhibiting a liberal bias.) Indeed, such a debate is productive because it highlights the search for shared values and a shared arena.

Educational Policies. Centripetal forces are enhanced to the extent that it is possible to develop *some* elements of a *shared, society-wide curriculum for public schools*, especially if the curriculum contains teachings that reflect the core of shared values and not only the diversity of cultures. Recent attempts to move in this direction have raised sharp objections on the grounds that the resulting materials reflect left-liberal views and stress diversity rather than unity. This issue rose when the National Educations Standards and Improvement Council issued suggested guidelines for American and world history curriculum in 1994,[73] as part of an attempt by the federal government to formulate some teaching standards under the Goals 2000 Act. Rather than abandon all such attempts, the lessons of these dry runs might be that other bodies than the federal government best serve this need. The goal should be a limited shared curriculum, since a broad national curricula is neither possible nor desirable, in light of the position articulated here, a curriculum that combines considerable approval for pluralism as long as a framework is maintained. This would mean, for instance, that agreement might be reached that all public schools will dedicate some time to the teaching of civics, American history, and American literature. And that these will be taught in ways that are respectful of basic American institutions and history without glossing over the darker periods and troubling events.

Two examples will stand for all the others that could be given. First, respect for the presidency can be taught while the fact that not all presidents were outstanding leaders is acknowledged. And second, children can be taught to respect the founding fathers and the documents they crafted, while recognizing that some of them owned slaves and that the Constitution contained some clauses we today no longer accept. This line contrasts with teaching civics or American history as texts to "prove" that American history is nothing but one form of exploitation followed by another, as Ronald Takaki urges.[74]

The same issue must be faced in individual colleges. If they are to follow the community-of-communities model, they need to provide some "core" courses, required of all students, and not merely offered as "electives," to ensure that the framework and not only the particulars are transmitted from generation to generation. And the content of the core courses needs to cover some shared elements and not be merely a patchwork of different ethnic, racial, and gender-based narratives. The underlying principle that needs to guide schools and colleges is that it is necessary that those who graduate will have some shared heroes, respect some shared symbols, and relate to some shared narratives, all reflecting the core of shared values.

National Service Policy. National service has been often recommended as a way for individuals who are members of different communities to meet one another as individuals and learn to form cross-community bonds. National service can take other forms than serving in armed forces or taking the coercive form of a draft. It can rely on voluntary participation in bodies such as the Peace Corps, AmeriCorps, or Vista.

Several "catches" must be noted, factors that, if left unattended, will greatly diminish the centripetal contributions of the national service. One is that if volunteers are part-timers who reside at home and/or serve only within their communities (as is the case for some Ameri-Corps members), the opportunity to bond across communities will be limited. Another is that just combining individuals from very varied backgrounds in one national service unit will not automatically ensure that they will form positive, affective bonds.

Last, but not least, for national service to be effective, it must reach at least one out of every ten members of each age cohort so that this person can transmit his or her new social insights to the others. This would require increasing the number of Americans who serve in the Peace Corps or in AmeriCorps, which has barely topped 25,000, fifteen times or more. Although these corps had considerable symbolic value, and some of their graduates played important roles enhancing the bonding of the diversifying society, their total centripetal effect was commensurate with their relative size: rather small.

Bicultural Educational Policies. Should immigrant children be taught in their native language or in English? To the extent that the question concerns a transition period, a year or two commencing with the arrival of the children in the United States, and the purpose of the policy is to ease the transition, the issue is largely an empirical one: Do pupils do better in the long run if they are immediately immersed in English or if they are allowed to continue to learn at least some subjects, such as science and math, in the their own language, so that they do not fall too far behind? Is this more of an issue for older than for younger pupils? And so on.

To the extent that the policy advocated is that there will be a parallel teaching system, which will allow youngsters to keep learning in their cultural context, from kindergarten through the twelfth grade, and the goal of the policy is the preservation of their immigrant cultural heritage, such policies violate the communitarian model outlined here. They do not allow the framework and "glue," the shared elements, to take hold, and they edge young people toward ethnocentrism.

The policy most compatible with the community-of-communities model is to avoid bicultural educational systems, and to mainstream students from the start or after a transition period. Such mainstreaming should be combined with teaching all students about the importance and cultural contributions of various traditions, and enabling students to participate in classes, clubs, extracurricular activities, Sunday schools, and other activities that will enable them to also maintain their knowledge and commitment to their subcultures, if they so choose.

Promoting English. We saw the importance of a core language. The best way to promote it is not to pass laws that declare it as the official tongue or to remove all street signs in other languages, but to ensure that there are enough opportunities to learn English. Given an environment in which resources are particularly scarce, teaching English is an ideal activity for volunteers, because the skills involved are not as high as those required for providing medical assistance, for instance, and, for old-timers, getting to know immigrants as people helps community building.

Residential Policies. Housing provides a particularly challenging exercise in applying communitarian concepts to particular policies. The difficulties involved are highlighted in a discussion of the relatively "easy" subject of housing on the campus. The much larger question, of housing in general, is touched upon briefly.

The question of which policies colleges should follow when they assign incoming students to residences (assuming that the college provides or controls such facilities) does not rank among the great policy issues of the day and has received rather little attention in the debate about the rising diversity and how to deal with it. Actually, the question is important because bonds formed in residences are psychologically more consequential than most of the changes in textbooks that are so widely debated. Moreover, an examination of the policy alternatives provides a fine exercise in thinking through the implications of the three grand approaches to group centrifugalism. A melting pot approach, followed at least nominally by many colleges, requires assigning students to share rooms disregarding their social background, so that a white from a small town in the South may room with an African American from the inner city, and a gay man with a Christian Fundamentalist. Many colleges that officially follow such policies in effect follow a policy closer to the communitarian one by (a) allowing students to relocate and thus regroup themselves with people more like themselves, and/or (b) allowing groups such as Jews, Asian Americans, gay people, and others to have their own dorms or floors of dorms. Colleges that allow students to choose residences from day one on the basis of their social group affiliation follow the diversity model.

An approach that reflects the community-of-communities model allows students, from the outset, to choose residences in line with their social preferences, but also involves them in activities that bring students from different backgrounds together either in one-on-one situations or in group activities. Participation in campus-wide activities, from sports to volunteering, can also help foster cross-group bonds. It must be assumed that these activities will not automatically be centripetal; students need coaching and guidance, at least initially, or they will tend to self-segregate even in these activities.

General Housing Policies. Defining communitarian housing policies is much more difficult than defining most other such public policies. This is one area in which the appointment of a high-powered commission is called for; such a commission could help articulate policies that would reflect the communitarian model advanced here. Existing policy seems rather unsatisfactory. Strong individualists tend to favor allowing each family work out its own residential arrangements, without interference from the government. This would lead to racially and ethnically segregated neighborhoods, and because attendance at public schools is closely associated with residence, to schools segregated along racial and ethnic lines. Oddly, there are both social conservatives and ethnic and racial tribalists who favor such segregation.[75]

Melting pot advocates helped pass laws that prohibit the deliberate perpetuation of housing segregation by using laws, regulations, restricting covenants, and other means. For instance, the Fair Housing Act of 1968 prohibits discrimination in housing on the basis of race and several other characteristics. Courts have interpreted the act to prohibit, for example, real estate agents from "steering" clients of different races to particular neighborhoods, as well as "blockbusting," or using the prospect of an influx of minorities to scare white homeowners into selling their land for less than market value.[76] "Tester" couples, who have nearly identical attributes but are of different races, are used to check whether real estate agents and rental companies act in a color-blind manner, clearly a melting pot notion.[77]

A communitarian policy that builds on our model would allow people of the same cultural background to choose to live in a neighborhood that contains people who share their subculture (and not merely their culture) and would not actively use the government powers, from the police to housing loans, to mix neighborhoods. It would, however, prohibit using legal means—i.e., the state—to enforce restrictive covenants or other segregation *laws*. The rationale would be that living with people with whom one shares a subculture, an identity, a history, a community, is an important source of identity and psychological support, and fosters bonding and the articulation of the moral voice. At the same time, steps would be taken so that communal bonds will not be used for economic and power advantages (for instance, by advertising job openings widely), and that members of different residential communities would learn to know one another as people in other contexts, especially at work.

Busing for the purposes of racial integration does not fit into this model because it breaks communal bonds and undermines communal institutions. (Busing often takes children to schools outside of their community.) But creating magnet schools that draw youngsters from several neighborhoods; cross-neighborhood assemblies, sports and debating teams; and other such measures may suffice to keep the community of communities intact. To reiterate, this is one of the least studied issues from a communitarian viewpoint and one in which much additional dialogue is most needed.

EIGHT

The Final Arbiters of Community's Values

VALUES ARE NOT BROCCOLI: THE NEED FOR ACCOUNTABILITY

Those who seek a good society are fairly challenged to explain the ways core values are accounted for: What justifies commitment to them? Another way of posing the same basic challenge, often formed when educators debate which (if any) values are to be taught in public schools, is to ask: *Whose* values should be taught? The question is often rhetorical; it suggests that it is impossible to account for values in a way that is widely shared, that all values are particularistic to one community or another, and hence, teaching values in *public* schools—those that belong to and speak for the society at large—must be avoided. However, for reasons already discussed, the good society requires sharing core values, and their selection needs to be justified.

The need for accountability profoundly distinguishes moral-social values from expressions of tastes and emotions (or mere preferences). The latter require no justification. When President George Bush stated

217

that he disliked broccoli, no sensible person would have asked him to justify his choice. Values, however, combine the kind of affect that true emotions evoke (without such cathartic involvement, values tend to become little more than icons for lip service), with an intellectual account. "I maintain that the war against Hitler was just, *because* . . . ," "Liberty should take precedence over equality, *because* . . . ," and so on.

Individualists can try to avoid this challenge by arguing that there should be no society-based formulation of the good. Actually, individualists, too, face the same fundamental question. They are called upon to justify making liberty, individual choice, critical reasoning, and/or various procedures their core virtues.[1] One can, though, readily acknowledge that providing normative accounts is much easier for an individualist because in cultures like ours, in which individual liberty is highly regarded, the individualist normative position has a strong appeal, at face value. It sounds so self-evident, at least to many members of Western societies, that libertarians and liberals can evoke the value of freedom with little or no further accounting, or rest on statements such as that what they favor is something "that every rational man is presumed to want."[2] (As I see it, such statements are the philosophical equivalent of name-calling, because they strongly imply that if you do not agree with my position, you are irrational.)

The combined commitment to autonomy and social order requires more elaborate justification. I proceed by suggesting that several accounts provided by communitarians and other scholars have merit but are not fully satisfactory. Moreover, in the past most of these responses have been considered as alternative approaches that compete with one another. I argue in the following pages that by combining these responses into a series of normative criteria, and by crowning the resulting construction with a criterion communitarians have not typically employed, a strong normative edifice can be erected.

THE FIRST CRITERION: COMMUNITY AS ARBITER

Several communitarians argue or imply that the particular values a community upholds, rather than some universal virtues, are legitimate because they are an integral part of that community, its history, identity, and culture. In part, this position is based upon an ontological observation that there are no universal values and that, empirically speaking, people derive their values from their particular communities. Daniel A. Bell, for example, writes:

> [H]igher goods are not somehow invented by individuals, but rather they're . . . located within the social world which happens to have provided one's framework. . . . It's a moral orientation which is learned by virtue of having been socialized in a particular time and place.[3]

Communitarians further argue that universal concepts of rights that are abstract from any culture have no anchoring in the commitments, loyalties, and solidarities of any community.

Critics argue that communitarians turn these ontological observations into a normative criterion; that they are inclined to view the *fact* that a community affirms a core of values as a determination that these affirmations are *justified*. Indeed, Sandel comes close to this position in statements such as: "the story of my life is always embedded in the story of those communities from which I derive my identity. . . . [T]hese stories make a *moral difference*, not only a psychological one."[4]

Sandel himself notes that communities may subscribe to "bad" values (or promote "bad" character) but he does not avail himself of extra-community criteria to distinguish communities that affirm "bad" versus "good" values.[5] Instead, he argues that the alternative approach to fostering community values, the individualistic one of fostering none, is worse.

Sandel notes in particular two dangerous problems which stem from a politics that tries to be neutral with regard to the common good. First, more extreme voices try to fill the vacuum: "Where political discourse lacks moral resonance, the yearning for a public life of larger meaning finds undesirable expression. . . . Fundamentalists rush in where liberals fear to tread."[6] Second, the politics of neutrality allow our civic virtues to degenerate: "The procedural republic . . . cannot secure the liberty it promises because it cannot inspire the moral and civic engagement self-government requires."[7]

Sandel's observations are valid, as far as I am concerned; the question remains whether we are limited to either relying solely on the community to determine the legitimacy of the values it endorses, or else refraining from communal formulations of the good altogether.

Others are more explicit than Sandel in their assumptions about the primacy of community in matters concerning value judgments. Writes Michael J. Perry:

> [T]he truth (or falsity) of any belief is always relative to a web of beliefs. A belief can be true relative to one or more webs, and not true, even false, relative to one or more others. If one or more beliefs necessary to support a claim-belief are not a part of the web of beliefs of a community, then the claim-belief is not true insofar as that community is concerned. . . . "[T]ruth" and "falsity" are relative to webs of beliefs.[8]

Such statements lead critics to argue that communitarians maintain that the values a community embraces are virtuous because the community embraces them. As I see it, while it is evident that the fact that a community affirms a given value does not provide sufficient normative accountability, it does indicate that such a value has passed one test. This can be shown by examining two processes through which communities come to affirm a value (as distinct from merely handing a value down from generation to generation), processes to which communitarians implicitly refer: The first concerns democratic political structures, the second the building of social consensus. (Amy Gutmann makes a similar distinction between "political relativism" and "cultural relativism."[9])

INTERNAL DEMOCRACY (A POLITICAL PROCESS)

According to a widely held approach, if the values that a community embraces have been reached through a democratic process, these values command the legitimation of this "flawed but the best there is" political process. That is, if a community must choose a course on issues that evoke values—issues such as abortion, affirmative action, or even if and how to curtail a deficit—and that community proceeds by deliberating properly about these issues and then subjects the conclusions of these deliberations to a vote in which all members of the community are free to participate, then the final outcome of these democratic processes would be morally superior to conclusions arrived at in some other manner.

Critics characterize such an approach as dangerous. Nadine Strossen, the president of the ACLU, depicts communities as a congenital threat to minorities.[10] And Ira Glasser, the executive director of the ACLU, pointed the finger more directly: "Communitarians really means majoritarians."[11] And as Peter Singer, among others, points out, any moral theory that relies on definition by a majority leads to unacceptable conclusions: "Consider, for example, where it leaves moral reform-ers: they must be speaking falsely as long as their views remain those of a minority in a society, but should they be able to persuade a majority that their false claims are true, then these views will indeed be true!"[12]

As I see it, we judge the conclusions a community reaches democratically to be morally superior to those reached by a community that has been swayed by a demagogue, a traveling preacher, a small elite, or some other undemocratic method. For instance, when the state of Oregon introduced the Oregon Health Care Plan, a health-care rationing policy that raised numerous normative issues, the policy was partially justified on the ground that it had been first discussed in numerous town meetings and approved by the elected legislature. At the same time, few find this normative test quite sufficient.

The reason the democratic test is insufficient lies, in part, in the particular form of democracy envisioned. A community that relies on majorities to establish what is right—I agree with the libertarians here—may violate individual and minority rights, or simply impose the normative judgments of 51 percent of the members of the community on all the others.[13]

In short, majority support for a community to follow a course of action that reflects a particular set of values does not necessarily make the action normatively compelling; additional criteria are needed.

CONSENSUS BUILDING (A SOCIAL PROCESS)

Communitarians point to another community-based process that lends accountability to the normative conclusions of the community: consensus building. Sandel implies such a response to the criticisms of simple majoritarianism: "The answer to that majoritarian threat is to try to appeal to a richer conception of democracy than just adding up votes."[14] Benjamin Barber favors a "true" or "creative" consensus that "arises out of common talk, common decision, and common work . . . is premised on citizens' active and perennial participation in the transformation of conflict through the creation of common consciousness and political judgment."[15]

One key version of consensus building is "Navajo democracy," in which dialogues continue until all members of a tribe embrace a given position. Navajo democracy was practiced by several counterculture communes, usually rather small groups. It turned out to be a tortuous process that worked only if the moral agenda was quite limited and the social bonds and normative preexisting understandings (understandings that were in place upon entering the dialogue) were strong; even then, it required substantial investments of time and commitment.

People who are willing to embrace a kind of consensus building that is less demanding, one that continues only until there is broad agreement, face challenges similar to those posed to the champions of democracy, above all the charge of majoritarianism. The main difference is that the criteria for resolution are less clear here. If there is no voting, when has the process of consensus building been properly completed? And if there is a vote at its conclusion, what is considered satisfactory? A strong majority of, say, 66 percent? 80 percent? or 99 percent? And on what grounds?

In short, consensus building does not provide a much more satisfactory base than majoritarian democracy, even though it, too, lends some justification to values embraced when compared to values imposed by a religious or ideological minority or small elite.

COMMUNITY-BASED RELATIVISM AND PARTICULARISM

Whatever the process—democratic, consensus building, tribal councils, or some other—as long as the outcome is community based, we face what might be called community-based relativism (as distinct from individual-based relativism). This form of relativism finds favor among some communitarians on the ground that if one recognizes universal formulations of the good, these would entail passing judgment on the values of the communities of others. Thus, the same communitarian who may argue that a community ought to raise its moral voice to encourage its members to abide by values shared by the community (rather than leaving it to each individual to follow his or her own formulation of the good) may oppose the application of the same position across communities, even within the same society. Thus, for example, a communitarian may hold that it is morally justified for a religious community to raise its moral voice to encourage its members to abide by its tenets, but not to foist such notions on other communities that are committed to other religious values or to secular civic values.

Liberal communitarians are particularly attentive to concerns that a diversity of cultures—rather than one set of values (typically Western values or those derided as those of "dead, white, European males")—will all be respected. The same communitarians are less attentive to the criticism that this approach leaves no secure moral foundation on which one can rely to criticize a community—for instance, one that allows covenants that prohibit the sale of a house to people of a different race, ethnicity, or sexual orientation, or that bans books such as *Lady Chatterley's Lover* and *The Catcher in the Rye*. Those who rely only on intra-community valuations have no ground to stand on when they are asked questions such as if we should chastise (relying on our moral voice) a community whose country club excludes women, Catholics, or Jews; or a private university that prohibits interracial dating, as Bob Jones University in South Carolina did until 1983. There is not even a sound basis on which Americans may morally censure a Southern town that embraces the values of the Ku Klux Klan; white South Africans—an Afrikaner village that drives out blacks; and Germans—the Nazis at the height of their popularity in some German town.[16]

Critics have a field day with such community-based relativism. Derek Phillips writes:

[For many] communitarian thinkers today, the only sources and measures of judgments about morality are those of a given society. There can be, then, no detached, independent standards by which the morality sanctioned by a particular society can be evaluated.[17]

Stephen Holmes observes that:

Shared self-conceptions or aspirations or allegiances are not . . . intrinsically admirable. Conversely, immoral behavior is not defined by any lack of social dimension. . . . [T]he personal identity of a racist or religious bigot is certainly 'socially constituted' without being in any way morally laudable.[18]

And Ronald Beiner notes that:

In some measure, certain communitarian writers brought these difficulties upon themselves. Walzer and MacIntyre, for instance, tended to argue that the inadequacy of liberal morality stems from its universalism, and this seemed to imply that one ought to embrace particularism as a counter-morality.[19]

Some liberal communitarians respond that they are not relativists but particularists. That is, they argue that while there are multiple social definitions of the good any one community may embrace (or different communities might affirm), not all must be considered legitimate merely because a community has embraced them. Some are beyond the pale. As I see it, for reasons that will become clear shortly, this is a significant step in the right direction. However, we are still missing criteria for defining which are moral positions to be excluded versus included, criteria which themselves need to be justified.

THE SECOND CRITERION

SOCIETAL VALUES AS MORAL FRAMEWORKS

If one accepts that communities cannot serve as the ultimate arbiters of their values, it does not follow that one must replace intra-community normative procedures, processes, and criteria with universal rights that individuals bear and which effectively serve to make communities morally irrelevant. Communitarians can *contextualize the community by framing the values it affirms within a higher order of legitimacy.* That is, a community's particular normative commitments will take precedence so long as they do not violate another set of normative criteria, to which the said commitments are *additionally* accountable. For instance, a community's values may be judged as legitimate if they are supported by majority voting or because they carry the imprint of consensus-building within the given community—but only as long as they do not violate the next order of normative criteria.

We have already visited one major such contextualizing framework, namely the Constitution, which acts as a depository of societal values. Viewed in this way (as we saw in chapter 7), the Constitution provides limits on the values communities can embrace, provisions that safeguard individuals not merely from the national government but also from communities of which they are members. (The application of the Constitution, especially the Bill of Rights, to communities, it must be recognized, has not always been accepted. Up to the Civil War, and to some extent even later, it was thought that the Constitution only applied to the federal government.) These safeguards, we saw, define some areas in which community-based processes cannot legitimately make rules. No American community, for example, can legitimately deny any person who is of age the right to vote (unless they violate specific guidelines, such as—in certain states—having been convicted of a felony), or deny a group the right to assemble because its moral values trouble the rest of the community, and so on. By the same token, the

Constitution also defines numerous other matters that are legitimately subject only to the first communitarian accountability principle. Thus, communities may decide what to charge for water, the level of real estate taxes, the direction of the traffic, and so on.

I cannot stress enough the difference between the concept of *framing*, whether by a constitution or by overarching social values ensconced in some other way, as compared to normative *preempting*. To frame a set of values means that the values that are being framed have a higher standing than (or "trump") others, as long as their reach remains within given normative boundaries, that within this context the particular values are sufficiently accounted for. By contrast, preemption occurs when one set of "universal" laws or values replaces other, often local, laws, customs, and traditions. This distinction is, in part, reflected in such legal and institutional concepts as the difference between Roman law and case law, the unitary state and federalism, and universalism and subsidiarity. (The layered communitarian position, previously introduced, is a normative expression of the framed, and not the preemptive, conception applied to the issues raised by diversity.)

Other societies (including Canadian society and numerous others in Western and Northern Europe) draw on constitutional documents in a similar manner or—like Britain, for example—have a set of framing laws, even if these laws are not formally ensconced in a constitution. Recently, in Britain, there has been a growing demand for a written constitution because the British "bill of rights" is simply an act of Parliament. Legally, it could be repealed if the Parliament so desired.[20] But so far, it has remained intact for hundreds of years. It reminds one of terms of tenure granted by universities, which are accorded at "the pleasure of the trustees," but are secured, under most conditions, against the trustees and all others by long moral and legal tradition. When colleagues in Britain raised responsive communitarian ideas in their country, they encountered critics who argued that in Britain one cannot recalibrate individual rights because—lacking a constitution—British rights are not protected "as they are in the United States." Actually, societal framing values in Britain are "absorbed as part of [the] common culture"[21] and seem rather strong, as if there were a constitution already in place. Although there are differences between unwritten and written constitutions, it is a serious error to treat an unwritten one as if it is congenitally weak. Indeed, an unwritten constitution can be more robust.[22] In any case, both kinds of constitutions reflect a higher order of shared values beyond those of any single community: the society-wide values.

In addition, societies typically affirm framing societal values that are not directly included in their constitutions or constitution-like laws, but are nevertheless incorporated into either long-established legal tradition (for instance, case law), or otherwise widely held as shared societal values. For example, in the United States, there are the vague notions of fairness and equality of opportunity (as distinct from equality of result).[23]

A strong argument for a two-layered criterion is provided by William A. Galston. He argues that a liberal state cannot be completely neutral regarding the values that particular member communities affirm, and cannot build its moral order simply around the attributes needed for citizenship in the liberal state, as individualists have argued.[24]

I should note that I am applying Galston's argument the other way round than he made it. Galston argues with individualists who would use the state power to override a community's values to ensure the capacity of the members to develop and maintain their capacity to be critical and to reason. Galston argues for *less* intervention and more tolerance for community values, which he calls "diversity," and for communities to be the arbiter of the particular values involved. For instance, Galston argues that the state should not force the Amish to give their children a standard public education, which conflicts with their religious views.[25]

I apply the implications of Galston's argument to the dialogue with community-based relativist communitarians who would *generally* yield to the community, so I can show that there *are* some values that call for overriding the normative commitments of member communities of a given society. Galston's basic argument is that the state reflects a society organized to embody a distinct set of values which require more than "minimalist" interventions.[26] Specifically, he lists protection of human life, "no free exercise for Aztecs."[27] He would also weigh in against communities whose values lead them to impede the physical growth and maturation of children (for instance, binding their skulls). And he would interfere with communities that do not allow individuals to develop the understanding needed to participate in society, economy, and polity. One way or the other, the point is that the state must override communities when they violate these "shared liberal purposes," but otherwise particular community values take precedence.

From a practical viewpoint, the two-layered approach, the conception of community as a normative arbiter contextualized by a set of shared societal values, the framed conception, is rather satisfactory. In most situations, normative positions that pass the tests of both the community and the constitution will stand up under further normative scrutiny. This very statement, however, points to the existence of—and, indeed, the need for—a still higher framing criterion. Without it, we have no way of determining whether or not the outcome of the two-layered approach is legitimate.

This is evident in several ways. First, the need for additional normative criteria stands out when one examines cultures that are rather different from one's own. For instance, we judge beheading an adulterous princess and amputating the right hand of a thief as morally troubling, even if the values implied have been affirmed by Saudi communities and are in line with its constitution.[28]

Second, we continually scrutinize that which is stated in the U.S. Constitution (for instance, its lack of explicit reference to women) and various rulings of the U.S. Supreme Court. That is, we are clearly applying some higher criterion when we argue that the Constitution should be amended (for example, to include a requirement for a balanced federal budget or the Equal Rights Amendment) or question whether or not the Supreme Court was morally "wrong" when it ruled that sodomy could be outlawed (*Bowers* v. *Hardwick*, 1986).

Two approaches have been proposed for making supra-societal, cross-cultural judgments: dialogues and global framing. Much has been written about each. They are briefly reviewed here because they add to the normative accounting scheme I am trying to construct.

A THIRD CRITERION:
CROSS-SOCIETAL MORAL DIALOGUES

The search for accountability has led several scholars to argue that the conclusions of *properly constructed dialogues* are moral. This approach deserves special attention because it is intimately connected to the notion of community—as we saw, dialogues often build on and help build communities—and also because this criterion cuts across the others reviewed so far, given that dialogues occur both in and among communities, a point whose importance I spell out shortly.

In exploring this approach, I find it useful to distinguish between "procedural dialogue" and "dialogue of conviction." These are ideal types that few completely embrace; however, various scholars come closer to one or the other. The works of Jürgen Habermas and Bruce

Ackerman, for instance, are closer to the proceduralist ideal than to each other. (As I turn to discuss one aspect of these rich works, which I find helps significantly in addressing the question of accountability, I note that the main body of the scholarship of Habermas and Ackerman is not reviewed here and that by borrowing an element but leaving its context behind, the element is modified.)

PROCEDURAL DIALOGUES

A rather elaborate and somewhat obtuse model of a dialogue-based normative accounting is found in the writings of Habermas. According to Habermas, "normative rightness" can be salvaged from the post-modern world of deconstruction and abject relativism. It arises out of what he calls "inter-subjective discourse" (as opposed to individual reflection). He notes, "Ultimately, there is only one criterion by which beliefs can be judged valid, and that is that they are based on agreement reached by argumentation."[29] (Habermas here is referring to values needed in the public context rather than in private ethics.[30])

Habermas spells out the conditions a dialogue about normative rightness must meet to qualify. The rules, paraphrased, are roughly: Everyone must be allowed to participate; all assertions are subject to questioning; people can assert whatever they believe in, as long as what they assert is really what they believe in; and force is not employed to undermine the first three conditions.[31] That is, he points to a *procedural* rather than to a *substantive* normative criterion. It is presumed that if a group follows such a procedure, it will not come up with what could be claimed as "wrong" values.

Ackerman develops a discursive model of his own. His starting point is "the problem of liberal politics"—namely, that people have moral disagreements, yet still need to find some means of peaceful coexistence.[32] He views dialogues as the only pragmatic solution, the "supreme pragmatic imperative" of politics, the primary obligation of citizenship.[33] To conduct proper dialogues, we must follow the rule of "conversational restraint": "We should simply say nothing at all about [our moral disagreements] . . . and put the moral ideals that divide us off the conversational agenda of the liberal state."[34] (Like Habermas, Ackerman refers to the limited layer of choices we must make in the public realm, not to moral choices we might render as members of society or a community.)

The conversational restraint does not limit what one may propose, but only the sort of arguments one may advance in defense of one's proposal.[35] Thus, I may propose prayer in public school, so long as I do not defend this policy on the grounds of a belief in God which you might not share. I would have to give some other reason, for example, that school prayer has some practical benefits—say, that it enhances the mental health of the students. Ackerman realizes that "conversational restraint will prove extremely frustrating—for it will prevent each of us from justifying our political actions by appealing to many of the things we hold to be among the deepest and most revealing truths"; nevertheless, we "must try to repress [our] desire to say many things which [we] believe are true"[36] to enable a dialogue among people who hold to a plurality of formulations of the good.

Psychologists and sociologists have pointed to different processes that enable a community to chart a course, although these are not based on deliberations but draw on ongoing processes (which differ from the former as rivers differ from canals), and that encompass much of social life and not merely the political. George Herbert Mead, for instance, sees the very concept of the self and the concepts one applies in thinking, whether political or otherwise, as arising out of dialogues. Dennis Wrong argues that mores arise out of interaction, arise out of an "ongoing social life."[37] Mark Gould writes that these social science notions suggest that "[h]abitual actions become [moral] expectations insofar as they create felt obligations."[38] Still other social scientists view mores as handed down from generation to generation, from older members to newborn or newly admitted ones, who in turn may change the mores before they hand them down to the next generation. Note that these and numerous other social scientists who follow a similar line of thinking are mainly interested in the source of mores and their dynamics rather than in assessing the moral standing of the outcomes of these processes, whether the outcomes are merely political, broadly social, or inter- and intra-personal. But the ways one may assess these outcomes is the question before the house.

DIALOGUES OF CONVICTIONS

As I see it, dialogues about the course a community might follow as a community, about mores its moral voice should speak for, which are justifiable, are as a rule among at least partially *articulated moral positions*. Dialogues about affirmative action, foreign aid, sex education in public school, or most other topics do not start with a normative tabula rasa, merely from "let's sit down and talk this out, and see where we come out" (as long as we follow Robert's Rules of Moral Dialogues). They are launched among individuals and subgroups who bring their values to all dialogues that are not highly limited and technical in nature (and often even to these). And, we have seen earlier, the distinction between private and public is much less useful than has often been implied in general and especially when it comes to moral dialogues. We cannot bracket our deepest convictions any more than we can leave them at home when we attend a town meeting. I grant that this fact makes for more difficult dialogues, but it cannot be wished away or ruled out.

One may ask, What is the normative significance of the sociological observation that most dialogues are value laden? Political theorists may argue that they are concerned with what is right or best—not what is common. However, I have already explored the implications of trying to repress human nature. People are *unable* to separate values and facts the way the ideal of deliberation and reason requires. To urge that people ought to have this faculty fosters frustration and rejection rather than deliberative democracy.

Moreover, a good society needs dialogues about the common good. These, in turn, require that the values that various participants bring to the dialogue will be engaged. Therefore, substantive dialogues, those of convictions, are not only common but essential for a good society. They are the processes through which a community formulates and reformulates its shared values.

For example, over the last few decades, there has been a worldwide dialogue about the extent to which "we" (that is, all nations, and in a sense the people of the world) ought to respect the environment. Of course, the dialogue is affected by numerous nonnormative considerations, such as expressions of economic interests or power considerations. However, there is no need to rehash the debate between *Realpolitik* and idealism to note that one factor involved is public opinion in countries other than one's own. And it, in turn, is affected by what people consider morally appropriate. Thus, one reason most nations try to avoid being perceived as environmentally irresponsible is that they do not wish to be considered to be acting illegitimately in the eyes of other nations. This is reflected in a rising worldwide consensus on specific environmental matters such as whaling, the ivory trade, acid rain, hazardous waste, and ozone depletion.[39]

A case in point was the worldwide condemnation of the United States following the 1992 Earth Summit in Rio de Janeiro, a rather atypical summit that built on worldwide evolving consensus (as it served to amplify it) rather than trying wantonly to assume or declare one. As a result, when the United States forced a weakening of the climate-control treaty, and refused to sign the biodiversity treaty, it drew heavy criticism from all over the world, even from allies such as Germany and Japan.[40]

Sharing of values that emerged out of moral dialogues has a higher moral standing than sharing that reflects values fostered by one group or another, or that results from the educational work of the state. Still, even dialogues of conviction do not provide the ultimate normative accounting criterion that is needed. What is still missing is a way to determine if the values a community embraces, left as the dialogues advance, are virtuous by some criterion other than that they are the outcome of a dialogue. Historians are sure to find that dialogues took place in nations that "justified" genocide on the grounds that those subjected to it were inferior or not fully human (at a fascist conference during the Nazi era), or that claimed to provide a normative account for an invasion (of Ethiopia by Mussolini's Italy or of Czechoslovakia by Communists) on the grounds that in this way some alleged historical wrong would be corrected. True, one can always fault the ways a dialogue was conducted, for instance, by arguing that it was not truly open, if one seeks to reject its conclusions. However, this puts too much onus on the process and tends to render our judgments tautological. Additional moral grounding seems still necessary.

FOURTH CRITERION: GLOBAL COMMUNITY?

At first blush, it may seem that one can provide a crowning criterion on the global level by applying to societies the same framing criterion we apply to communities within a society. If the values of a society will not violate a worldwide set of values, closure seems to be reachable. This approach, however, runs into several difficulties.

CROSS-CULTURAL RELATIVISM

Even among those who accept that community-based values need to be tested against society-wide ones, and that both ought to reflect moral dialogues, there are those who object to applying these criteria across cultures. I refer to cultures rather than national societies, because many who are ready to evaluate another society that has a similar culture—for instance, Americans willing to evaluate the values reflected in the public policies of other Western societies—object to doing so to other cultures, such as Asian or Latin or African ones. These might be referred to as cultural (as distinct from community) relativists.[41]

Cross-cultural judgments are opposed on the grounds that there are no worldwide or other overarching moral truths, and that such judgments tend to lead Westerners to view their values as superior to those of others and to treat other people, races, and cultures as inferior. Indeed, such an orientation was widely held in the West. Much of anthropology has been dedicated to broadening the horizons of those who thought that "we" were scientific and modern while "they" were primitive and, by showing such Westerners that other cultures were different but not inferior. As a result, as Carolyn Fluehr-Lobban writes, anthropologists "have been unwilling to pass judgment on such forms of culturally based homicide as the killing of infants or the aged. Some have withheld judgment on acts of communal violence, such as clashes between Hindus and Muslims in India or Tutsis and Hutus in Rwanda."[42] James Q. Wilson observes, "The adoption of cultural relativism . . . made the word 'barbarian' not only pejorative but meaningless. . . . [Anthropologists] could discuss, dispassionately if not quite acceptingly, cannibalism and infanticide."[43]

Some feminists have argued against "outside" criticism of female circumcision, the mutilation of young women's genitals to reduce their sexual pleasures and render them more faithful to their future husbands (who are not themselves particularly known for fidelity).[44]

Daniel A. Bell notes that "voices in East Asia object to the very idea of human rights even as an end goal on the ground that the concept of 'human rights' is a Western invention incompatible with East Asian traditions."[45] Others claim that the West should not chastise Asian societies for their violation of human rights just the way China, for example, should not censure American society for its neglect of filial duties.[46] Even the Muslim tradition of amputating a thief's hand is beyond cross-cultural challenge, according to this view.[47] Bell does allow, though, that those who are morally outraged by this and other such practices often can find *intra*-cultural grounds for their objections. For instance, Islam lays several conditions that must be met before one can morally justify the amputation, which in practice are almost never met. The stress on the need to find such intra-cultural grounds is in part tactical, perceived as a more effective way to appeal to virtues across cultures;[48]

but it also reflects the great reluctance to form cross-cultural judgments.

The problems of cross-cultural judgments were highlighted at a 1993 meeting of Asian leaders in Bangkok whose purpose was to formulate an Asian stance on human rights. According to one report, "What surprised many observers . . . was the bold opposition to universal human rights . . . made on the grounds that human rights as such do not accord with 'Asian values.'"[49] Asian intellectuals justify this opposition on the grounds that Western notions of human rights are founded on the idea of personal autonomy, which is either alien to Asian culture or, at least, not fundamental.[50]

In *Thick and Thin*, Walzer argues that while there are some minimal values that appear in all cultures, the list is "neither objective nor unexpressive [of a particular culture]. It is reiteratively particularist and locally significant, intimately bound up with the . . . moralities created . . . in specific times and places."[51] The word "universal" is simply an adjective that happens to modify some particular cultural values, when in fact they occur in all particular cultures.[52] For this reason, Walzer concludes that "[a] given society is just if its substantive life is lived . . . in a way faithful to the shared understandings of the members."[53] As Stephen Mulhall and Adam Swift put it: "It cannot be doubted that there is a significant relativistic strand in Walzer's position."[54] Ronald Beiner observes that, in Walzer's view, "the only standard of critical judgment is the internal standard of whether a concrete community remains true to the traditions, practices, and shared understandings that compose its communal identity." Beiner adds, "What is absent here is any independent, external standard that sheds light on whether identity-constituting communities confer worth upon their members beyond the bare fact of possessing something shared."[55] As a colleague put it, when all is said and done, Walzer's thin (globalism) is based on the thick (communities). Several other communitarians have taken positions similar to Walzer's.

As I see it, such relativism fails when one notes that it matters little where values originated; the question is whether or not they can be justified. Indeed, some argue that the so-called Western ideals originated in Africa—in Egypt, to be specific. If this were to be found historically valid, would this fact enhance the moral standing of, say, individual rights and our "right" to lay moral claims on African societies? Only Egypt? North African? Asian too? Values cannot be that geographically contingent.

EMPIRICAL AND MORAL GLOBALISTS

In recent years, as cultural relativists found it increasingly difficult to sustain their position, some recognized a few global values to which they agree that the values of whole cultures, not just those of communities within a given culture, may be held accountable. The positions of these global minimalists range from the largely empirical to the normative.

On the side of the empirical global minimalists, two anthropologists report:

> No culture tolerates indiscriminate lying, stealing, or violence within the in-group. The essential universality of the incest taboo is well-known. No culture places a value upon suffering as an end in itself. . . . We know of no culture . . . where the fact of death is not ceremonialized.[56]

And Alison Dundes Renteln points out that all cultures limit the number of deaths that may be inflicted in what they consider legitimate acts of revenge.[57] Beyond listing some elementary values, such as condemnation of murder, torture, and rape, empirical minimalists have pointed to the existence of the same categories in many different languages, even if they are given a rather different content.[58] Rhoda Howard observed that even relativists agree that "[t]he *concept* of human rights is universal, but the *content* (what, substantively, are or ought to be rights) varies among different societies."[59]

Others, especially Robert Wright and James Q. Wilson, note the existence of a universal moral sense.[60] Those who believe that this moral source is based on the existence of moral genes—for instance, one for altruism[61]—find a complete answer: To the extent that the gene is universal, they leave relativism behind, and to the extent that it is particularistic, it is a given fact that no moral voice can change, at least until genetic engineering is much more developed. Such notions of the biological source of values are not further explored here because it would take the discussion far afield.[62]

The argument that universal socialization experiences ensure a moral sense in all people, the result of the sociological fact that all infants require others to care for them, and that in the process we acquire certain universal features, seems rather compelling.[63] But the question remains, How much normative content can such a process carry, and is it ennobling or regressive? What is the moral standing of such social science findings?

Some have drawn normative conclusions from data about global uniformities, arguing that we can hold people of different cultures to values that all cultures share, because these values are shared by all societies, a global application of the consensus test. A typical statement is one made about the old golden rule. Marcus Singer writes, "The nearly universal acceptance of the Golden Rule and its promulgation by persons of considerable intelligence, though otherwise of different outlook, would therefore provide some evidence for the claim that it is a fundamental ethical truth."[64] Singer is cautious and very much on the mark: Global endorsement does provides *some* normative accounting. Surely we note that a moral ideal all people respect has a much stronger standing than one that is affirmed by one people or culture or even a handful. Something, though, is still clearly missing: If all societies, for instance, subscribe to a prejudice that helps them justify treating women (or some other group, such as immigrants or the disabled) as second-class human beings, would this globalism justify the said prejudice? Moreover, when one compares these global values to core values, and the elaborate arguments in their support, found in many religious or secular ethical conceptions, such as that of the Old and New Testaments; and in works such as those of Aristotle, Confucius, or Immanuel Kant, the paucity of the empirical list and ethics that build on it stands out.

To the extent that normative globalists rely on empirical observation, their criterion is both rather thin and not well grounded because the data are tricky. The criterion is thin because it embraces only a few values, such as condemning murder, theft, and rape. And even here we are on unsure grounds. The deliberate taking of a life—considered as offending the most global value—is often legitimated in one way or another: betrayal of religion, violation of select laws (hence death sentences) even with respect to members of one's own tribe. (Outsiders are often fair game in numerous societies.)

HUMAN RIGHTS

Recognition of rights of all humans represents an attempt to move beyond a thin and empirical grounded global list of values and find a set of worldwide moral foundations that could undergird judgments of the values of various particular societies. Specifically, "thicker" globalists draw on the Universal Declaration of Human Rights, an evolving body of international law, the United Nations Charter and General Assembly resolutions, and the resolutions of various international conferences, such as those on the environment and on women. Among those who uphold this approach is George Weigel (who also draws on a conception of human nature), whose list of global values is limited to basic civil rights and political freedoms.[65] Rhoda Howard adds basic economic rights to Weigel's list.[66] Others extend the list much further.[67]

The trouble with this approach is that the United Nations Charter, international law, and various declarations—in which the globalists find the values they seek to build on—are not widely affirmed. This is largely the case because of the ways these documents have been formulated. Typically, they are neither the reflection of a truly democratic process in the international bodies or in the countries represented in them, nor do they reflect the result of a worldwide moral dialogue. Indeed, it often seems that various pronouncements of international bodies are tolerated by many nations precisely because it is known that these resolutions have little legal, political, or normative standing. (This is evident when their legitimacy is compared to resolutions of the evolving European Parliament, which itself has much less standing than national legislatures.) Such resolutions would command much more respect if they reflected the work of a properly representative world parliament or a global tribunal.

The weaknesses of global claims for human rights cannot be overcome in a definitive way merely by redrafting the United Nations Charter, or by changing the voting patterns in the General Assembly, or by other such institutional reforms. Before we can expect to see global mores that have the compelling power of those of various societies, the citizens of the world will have to engage in worldwide moral dialogues. Technological developments have made such global megalogues possible. Indeed, there has been some progress in this direction, especially in matters concerning individual rights, the treatment of children, and above all the environment. The somewhat increasing role and legitimation of the International War Crimes Tribunal, especially evident concerning the recent Bosnia conflict, is also encouraging. But a worldwide community of communities, one that has core values that crown the edifice of normative accountability, is largely a gleam in the eyes of a small number of visionaries.

CROSS-SOCIETAL MORAL VOICE

To help nourish global moral dialogues, communitarians need to favor moving in the opposite direction from the one cultural relativists have followed. Communitarians need to support the raising of moral voices cross-culturally, especially when they truly reflect the people of a society that is raising them. This is necessary in order to advance the articulation of a core—rather than a thin list—of globally shared values. A relativist or a pluralist may agree that a person in one culture may approach the members of a different culture and try to share with them his or her values. In this view, however, such a person would not be making such claims in terms of values that the other culture was committed to—unless, of course, the other culture *happens* to subscribe to the same values. Thus, to use Walzer's example, a visitor to India may try to convince a town that the caste system is "wrong," but could not lay this claim in terms of a universal value to which the other culture is held accountable.[68]

I deliberately refer to laying moral claims. Expressions of appreciation of moral progress of societies other than one's own, and censure of those that violate one's values, should not be confused with acts of nations that see themselves as called upon to impose their values by sending in the marines, special forces, or the foreign legion, by erecting blockades or enforcing boycotts, or otherwise applying military or economic power. Such coercive measures do not build a moral community and are justified only under special circumstances (e.g., if we were to face another Nazi regime) discussed in the literature on just wars and other writings on international ethics. One also notes that while only powerful nations can employ military or economic power to push values, even the smallest of nations can exercise the moral voice, as demonstrated at various points by Costa Rica, Mexico, the Scandinavian countries, Switzerland, and Israel.[69]

To call on all people to respect the same set of core values does not entail arguing that all have to follow the same path of economic development, enjoy the same music, or have the same table manners. Indeed, international bodies err when they allow each member nation to add its normative wish list to those of others, ending up with scores upon scores of resolutions covering practically every conceivable topic. The long road to a world of shared values will be shortened somewhat if the laying of moral claims across nations would be focused on a limited set of core values.

Cross-cultural moral voices, however, cannot avoid addressing political development for countries whose order is coercive rather than largely based on moral grounds. Because of the close connection between the democratic form of government and communitarian core virtues, calling for a democratic form of government (broadly conceived, not merely one supported by free and open elections) is a pivotal and necessary part of cross-national moral dialogues.

The same must be said about the moral call to provide socioeconomic basics to all members of all communities. No argument for cross-cultural relativism has carried more weight than the suggestion that the West is already economically developed and hence can "afford" political freedoms, but other countries must defer political development until they are economically developed. The former prime minister of Singapore, Lee Kuan Yew, argues that:

> As prime minister of Singapore, my first task was to lift my country out of the degradation that poverty, ignorance, and disease had wrought. Since it was dire poverty that made for such low priority given to human life, all other things became secondary.[70]

Julius Ihonvbere simply concludes that "for countries that have known no peace, stability or progress since their contact with the forces of Western imperialism, civil and political rights have no meaning."[71]

The ethical question that is being raised, to put it succinctly, is whether overcoming wanton death, plagues, and hunger trumps political rights such as freedom of speech and the right to vote. The question is often treated as if it were merely rhetorical, because the answer seems self-evident—if only because people who are starving and ill are often in no position to exercise their political rights. However, this way of approaching the subject constitutes a rather poor framing of the debate.

First of all, there is precious little evidence that developing totalitarian states are inclined to indicate a level of GNP per capita that, once it is reached, would mean they would be willing to tolerate the development of political freedoms. The per capita GNP of Singapore exceeded $12,000 in 1990.[72] The United States passed the $12,000 mark only in 1980.[73] Seymour M. Lipset may well be right that economic development makes political development easier;[74] however, this neither suggests that it is ethically justified to defer political development until ever higher levels of economic development are reached, nor that because democratization at lower economic levels is "more" difficult, it should be deferred.

Second, the people of countries that are politically underdeveloped are denied more than the "luxuries" of democracies, of which freedom of speech is frequently given as an example. Many people in countries that are not free are tortured, sold as slaves, subject to wanton execution. A strong case can hence be made that a basic respect for political human rights ought to be as "basic" as—or even more "basic" than—creature comforts.

Third, as Rhoda Howard points out, without political development there is no assurance that the benefits of economic development will be widely shared. And we must worry that economic development will be carried out without huge undue suffering caused by thinking that is capricious or rigidly ideological.[75]

Fourth, the notion that economic development cannot be launched within a democratic framework in Asian countries is belied by the economic development of India, for example. One can recognize that there is more than one pathway to economic development; however, these different pathways can be limited to those compatible with democratic government.

Last but not least, some Asians point with horror to the social disorganization of the West, blaming it on the democratic nature of these societies. Kishore Mahbubani comments: "[F]reedom does not only solve problems; it can also cause them." He points to "massive social decay" in the United States and writes, "Many a society shudders at the prospects of this happening on its shores."[76] Some Islamic intellectuals share this view. Writes Mohamed Elhachmi Hamdi, "On certain moral questions . . . Western democracy appears . . . to be running amok. It is hard to see why lax Western mores that weaken or destroy the family . . . should be exported to the rest of the world."[77]

Actually, social order was intact in the West, say, in the 1950s, long after basic democratic institutions were well established, even if some segment of the population still had to fight to ensure that they would be encompassed. And recent social disorganization, which reflects the decline of moral values and the moral infrastructure, may well be corrected within the political framework of Western societies.[78]

Rather than muting the cross-cultural moral voice, as the cultural relativists do, all societies should respect the right of others to lay moral claims on them just as they are entitled to lay claims on other societies. Thus, the West should realize that it is well within its legitimate, world-community-building role when it criticizes China for its violation of human rights. And China should be viewed as equally legitimate when it criticizes American society for its neglect of filial duties.

Cross-cultural moral dialogues build on substantive global values, values that lay a claim on all and are not particular to any one community or society. Thus, as I see it, individual rights do not reflect a Western value (even if historically they arose in the West), but a value that lays claims on all people. Moreover, far from being deterred or chastened by some third world protests when the West applies this value to other cultures, I see in the furor that such claims generate a recognition of the validity of these claims. And for that same reason, the fact that, when Asians call on the West, for example, to enhance our respect for the elderly, the guilty responses are an indication that a shared value has been tapped. If one instead chastised Asians for using little sticks instead of forks, they would hardly be perturbed. Similarly, if Muslims would call on the West to embrace their divorce laws, most people would ignore such normative appeals or laugh them out of court. Not all cross-cultural claims are heard, and it is rather evident which gain our attention.

Aside from defensive reactions, there are other signs that many cross-cultural moral voices do not fall on deaf ears. After ignoring human rights issues for decades, Asian countries recently reported that "human rights were no longer dismissed as a tool of foreign oppression but were promoted as a means of asserting Asian distinctiveness."[79] China seems to have reformed some of its most grievous orphanages and labor camps under pressure from Amnesty International and other moral voices.[80] And the Singaporean diplomat Bilahari Kausikan writes,

> Human rights have become a legitimate issue in interstate relations. How a country treats its citizens is no longer a matter for its own exclusive determination. . . . There is an emerging global culture of human rights.[81]

Recognizing the need to raise moral voices globally does not mean that one legitimates berating other people cross-culturally, any more than one is called upon to berate other members of one's own community. The moral voice is most compelling when it is firm but not screeching, judging but not judgmental, critical, if need be, but not self-righteous.

One can also acknowledge quite readily that those who champion global values themselves sometimes do not fully heed their call; but this observation does not invalidate the standing of these values. And one might readily concur that there are universal values other than those for which a given party speaks, values that the societies that are being chastised on some other matter do follow quite admirably, providing a shining example for the rest of the world to follow. Japan, for example, may do more for beauty of design and landscape than any Western society.

None of these observations, however, undermines the merit of bringing strong substantive values to the nascent worldwide dialogue; on the contrary, these observations themselves are a reflection of such values. At the same time, one must recognize that until worldwide moral dialogues are much more advanced, and a much stronger global core of shared values evolves, global values cannot serve as a satisfactory frame for societal values.

COMPELLING MORAL CAUSES

Even if and when there is worldwide consensus about value, we are not done. We reject the idea behind the refrain that "50 million Frenchmen can't be wrong," arguing that national consensus *can* err. Similarly, one can state with considerable assurance that 5 billion people can be wrong. Not so long ago there was an almost worldwide consensus that women could be treated as second-class citizens; this fact hardly legitimated that position. The normative accounting scheme is still not complete.

To review briefly the line of argument followed so far: In search of a principled way to determine which values are properly accounted for, I join with those who hold that if a community (by democratic process or other forms of consensus building) reaches closure, the values endorsed or implied have been imbued with a measure of legitimacy, but not sufficient accountability. I further argue that if these values also comport with the societal values (often ensconced in the constitution or other such laws), this fact enhances the standing of the chosen values, but even these two criteria applied together are insufficient. The same, for reasons provided, holds for the fact that a given set of values are the results of properly constructed moral dialogues and/or the product of a global consensus building. In searching for the final touchstone, I draw on the observation that *certain concepts present themselves to us as morally compelling in and of themselves.*[82] For example, when one points out that we have higher obligations to our own children than to the children of others, this moral claim speaks for itself, effectively and directly. One does not sense that a reason is needed; nor does one demand some consequentialist explanation or sociological analysis: Such moral concepts have the kind of special standing the founding fathers referred to as "self-evident." Our moral sense informs us that "of course, we do."[83] Indeed, I have not found a single person who maintains, believes, or argues that we have the same moral obligations to all children that we have to our own.

The best way I can further elucidate the notion of compelling moral concepts is to report about an experiment I conducted in several countries with more than 300 groups of rather different social, intellectual, and political backgrounds or persuasions. In each case, I asked the group to pretend that it was a public school committee that must decide which values to teach in the third grade next year. First I pointed out that it is impossible to formulate a value-free or neutral curriculum about most matters. Next I asked the various audiences if one should teach that truth-telling is superior to lying or vice versa under all but limited conditions (such as when someone is dying from cancer and asks if there is any hope left). Without exception the groups looked puzzled. They wondered, Where was the question I led them to anticipate? Was there something I meant to ask and did not? Why, the answer was so self-evident!

Furthermore, none of the groups I queried engaged in any kind of argumentation, such as "one must note that if one tells a lie, soon others will do the same, and then we shall find ourselves in a world of liars, a world we do not wish to live in, therefore, we must not lie." Group members did not require such a utilitarian, consequentialist explanation. They found the answer staring them in the face, or more accurately, speaking directly to them. (Some added the argument just given as an afterthought, to explain the moral judgment they had already articulated and pronounced.)

There is, of course, a huge literature about both the use of primary concepts (which all paradigms require) in general and deontological concepts (which I build on here) in particular, though not all theories that start with a list of virtues are deontological. To properly proceed, I would have to engage in an extensive review of this literature and then justify the reason I choose to follow one course rather than another, especially as I follow a position that communitarians often have not followed. As I see it, however, such a review of the literature has been done frequently; there is little I can add to it. Although I am aware, of course, of the controversial nature of the position I follow, and of the ambiguities it entails, for the reasons I have discussed, I see no other position that is more compelling and which, pragmatically speaking, enables one to construct a more sound communitarian paradigm.

Furthermore, my training is sociological, while the debate has taken place largely in political theory and philosophy. All I can do is point out what I am building on. I am building on the notion that one may start a moral paradigm by identifying the virtues that serve as its foundations. This is particularly acceptable to the neofunctionalist approach applied here because functionalism is much less concerned with *origins* and focuses instead on the constellations, processes, and structures that enable given societal traits or virtues to be sustained and recast.

The point has also been made that the concepts used here are expansive; that, as David Anderson wrote to me, they are not like green beans and oranges, but rather like vegetables and fruits. Note, however, that this book opens with my attempt to point to the specific concepts of order and autonomy I am using. Indeed the conception of order as largely voluntary is a rather unique one; while it may not be everyone's cup of tea, surely it is a rather specific brew. Likewise, the conception of autonomy that includes not only negative and positive liberties but also individual and subgroup expression, and which must be socially bounded, may be rejected by those who hold to a much more narrowly constructed concept, but it is hardly unspecific.

Such statements about moral causes that present themselves to us as compelling are similar to what religious authorities speak of as *revelation*. This does not mean that we cannot *reason* about these matters. The fact that some cause initially appears to one as powerful does not obviate the need to examine it closely. However, here reason follows and buttresses revelation, and not the other way around. (That is, primary concepts are like other values, which we define as containing an element of accountability, and not merely a statement of preference. It should be noted, however, that reason plays a rather different role here.) Charles Taylor emphasizes this dual nature of morals, arguing that "our moral reactions . . . have two facets, as it were. On one side, they are almost like instincts . . . ; on the other, they seem to involve claims . . . about the nature and status of human beings."[84] Naturalists and emotivists, Taylor argues, want to forget about the second half;[85] but it would be equally a mistake to forget about the first half. We must keep in mind that rational explanations of moral value are attempts to, as

Taylor puts it, "articulate" the moral sense but are not its essence.[86]

There is another major difference between the position followed here and emotivism.[87] Emotivism treats all values like the taste of broccoli, favored or rejected because ego feels so. In the approach advanced here, only the primary concepts are accounted for by relying first on their moral force (and second that these concepts have been buttressed by critical review of the kind to which social order and autonomy were subjected at the opening of our discussion); all other concepts are derived from, and explicable in terms of, these primary concepts.

The difference between the present approach and emotivism stands out when one compares the basic virtues affirmed here to the extensive list of virtues a person or a community should uphold according to other approaches. For instance, the list of such virtues provided by Michael Josephson contains six "pillars": trustworthiness, respect, responsibility, fairness, caring, and citizenship.[88] William J. Bennett lists ten virtues[89]; Colin Greer and Herbert Kohl have a list of sixteen.[90] All these virtues are all treated as concepts of equal standing, and they are not derived from or accounted for by any basic concept. (The virtues on Galston's list are instrumentally justified in that they are needed to maintain a liberal state, the primary concept. Galston's approach hence methodologically parallels the one followed here, except that he focuses on personal virtues, such as courage, loyalty, tolerance, and moderation, while I focus on societal ones.[91])

THE BASIC VIRTUES

LIKE LIFE AND HEALTH

The basic social virtues are a voluntary moral order and a strong measure of bounded individual and subgroup autonomy, held in careful equilibrium, the new golden rule. Although in preceding chapters I provided instrumental justifications for the merit of social formations that embody these virtues, such sociological explanations are secondary. The needs for voluntary order and for well-protected opportunities for individuals to express themselves speak compellingly for themselves. (The virtue of subgroup autonomy is less immediately compelling, and is indeed largely derived from other values.)

The normative standing of moral order and autonomy (and for minimizing their antagonism) for the communitarian paradigm is similar to the normative standing of life and health in medical sciences. Theoretically, one could ask, "Why treat these as virtues? Could one not find virtue in death and illness and build sciences that embody these values? Some kind of Satanic science?" It is, though, far from accidental and rather telling that very few if any would grant such a possibility serious consideration.[92] Life and health are compelling virtues that speak to us unmistakably when compared to their opposites. One can augment their normative standing by various secondary and instrumental accounts—for instance, that a dead person can neither exercise moral responsibility nor be a bearer of rights, or that illness limits our autonomy—however, we correctly judge these arguments to be secondary. Life and health are compelling in and of themselves. (This observation is not belied by the fact that there are some limiting conditions under which one may find virtue in sacrificing life or health, say, for a just war, or in an experiment to test new drugs for the sake of others. Given that we recognize multiple virtues, which cannot be all fully adhered to at the same time, we must work out conflicts among them, and even sacrifice a measure of some for the sake of the other.)

As I see it, moral order and autonomy, the twin virtues, crown the communitarian normative account; they provide the final, substantive normative criterion this account requires. A mental experiment might help here. (The main purpose of the experiment is not to show the validity of the dual primary concepts, which is self-evident. The purpose is to show the need for an additional layer of normative accountability, one that provides the final anchoring for the whole enterprise.) Assume there is a country called Intabad, in which several communities allow very young girls to be married off to old men, provided that the men pay a fee to the girls' fathers. There is nothing in the values of these communities and in Intabad's constitution to prohibit such marriages, nor are they on the cross-national taboo list. While several international conferences condemned such marriages, these pronouncements were largely ignored by the world's communities. Moral dialogues on the subject have not been initiated in earnest. What is the normative standing of such marriages? If we adhere only to the criteria evoked so far, without adding the crowning basic virtues, there is no firm, shared basis on which to fault these marriages. However, if we examine them in light of the basic virtues, their troubling status becomes clear. We note that because the girls are, in effect, sold, their basic autonomy is being violated, and we judge such marriages as immoral.

Now let's visit another imaginary country, Libertat. Here we find hosts who encourage already intoxicated guests to "have one for the road." We further establish that the suburban communities of these hosts are "nonjudgmental" about such behavior, nor does it violate any law of Libertat. The subject has not been addressed by whatever moral dialogues Libertat has. And the "global village" is otherwise preoccupied. We still would consider such behavior troubling, if not out of concern for the drivers, then at least out of concern for the safety of others on the road—in other words, out of concern for the social order. We judge such behavior on the part of hosts to be morally irresponsible.

These mental experiments are limited in that they deal by necessity with one issue at a time. A society may be quite virtuous even if it fails to embody the basic virtues in a single or a limited number of areas, so long as the virtues otherwise prevail. And, as we saw, societies may differ in the relative weight they accord to the twin virtues and still maintain their overall communitarian pattern. However, societies that violate these virtues on a broad front are authoritarian or anarchic, and their values fail by a major principle of communitarian normative accounting; they are not virtuous.

The fact that not all people in authoritarian or totalitarian societies are aware of the special standing of the communitarian virtues is not surprising, given that they are subject to strong, misleading propaganda and systematic miseducation efforts, as well as various distorting forms of coercion. (Nevertheless, in recent years, as communication technologies have improved, the proportion of the members of these societies that appreciate the communitarian virtues seems to have grown heftily. This was one factor in bringing about the collapse of many of those regimes.)

Among democratic societies, one wonders about millions of individuals, who in the pursuit of ever more consumer goods and mind-altering substances (alcohol and television included), help maintain a society in which the worship of consumer goods shortchanges both basic virtues. There are indications that many of these individuals, in their deeper, inner selves, realize that the consumerism they help uphold has little virtue, but they are either unaware of the social alternatives or so addicted to their current lifestyle that they require help to break out of it. These people, and others who are caught in some religious fanaticism or feel secure in a police state, are people who have not yet been properly engaged in communitarian dialogues, dialogues that will help them listen to their muffled inner voices, which speak for a society in which both moral order and autonomy are well nourished and balanced. These are the people that the communitarian movement has yet to reach.

THE MORAL VOICE REVISITED: VIRTUOUS VERSUS ERRANT

The moral voice, I have suggested, is a crucial element of the communitarian social order. If one examines this concept in light of the normative accounting scheme here introduced, one finds that this voice is relativistic because it is raised to speak for the particular values a given community affirms. The Mafia claims that its members ought to be loyal to their community by not "ratting" to the police; the Boy Scouts show loyalty to theirs by being ready to serve others. Most social scientists view both groups as having a commanding moral voice, speaking for their "values." The values themselves are not judged.

However, once normative accounting is introduced and virtues are recognized, differences among moral voices stand out. Those that speak for values that fail the various tests (including the ultimate one, of speaking for the basic dual virtues) are *errant voices*. They may sound like true moral voices, but they deceive us. Those of the Mafia, for instance, do so if only because they violate the framing values of the encompassing society. Voices speaking for values that are fully accounted for, especially when they reflect the basic virtues, are *virtuous voices*. This is a distinction that makes no sense to true relativists and most social scientists, but is essential for the communitarian paradigm. Without it, there is no final exit from the maze of relativism. All communities have moral voices, but because they speak for values we judge differently, we must separate moral voices that support community values we find deficient from those that enhance values we deem to meet all our normative criteria.

PARTICULARISM AND UNIVERSALISM

Building on universal moral criteria, which apply to all people and lay claims on all of them, has been associated with an individualistic, and not a communitarian, position. At the core of the main schools of individualism is the notion that all human beings have the same basic individual rights—a universal principle not contextualized by any community or culture. This position is powerfully captured in Kant's version of the old golden rule, the categorical imperative: "Act in such a way that you treat humanity, whether in your own person or in the person of another, always at the same time as an end and never simply as a means."[93] In contrast, the communitarian position is usually supposed to be associated with the common good of specific communities, and hence based on particularistic rather than universal values. Communitarians would see the merit of Joseph de Maistre's statement that "[i]n my lifetime I have seen Frenchmen, Italians, [and] Russians. . . . But as for 'man,' I declare that I have never in my life met him."[94] However, as I have tried to show in the preceding discussion, it is not only possible but highly necessary *to combine some universal principles with particularistic ones to form a full communitarian normative account.* Like many other dichotomies, that between universalism and particularism stands in the way of developing a solid paradigm, and recognizing the merit of combination moves us forward. One can both recognize the universal power of the basic dual virtues and the moral standing of communities to render different, particularistic, judgments on all matters that do not offend "higher," contextualizing principles.

The fact that the universal and particularistic considerations clash at some points does not invalidate the approach; on the contrary, it is compatible with the neofunctionalist notion that the virtuous society is not one that is all cut from one moral cloth but one in which there is a continuous tension between two forces, and that it approximates best the good society when these two forces are kept in a carefully crafted, continuously challenged, but ultimately restored balance.

Many scholars on both sides of the debate have in effect moved in the suggested direction. Individualists have contextualized some of their claims—for instance, by suggesting that they presume a liberal society. And responsive or new communitarians have written about the standings of individual rights (unlike many early communitarians, who often stressed only communities, and who should be considered collectivists).

Furthermore, one should be wary of those communitarians who base individual rights only on community needs. Contextualizing rights in this way provides an insufficient foundation to autonomy because it will remain without normative accounting if community needs—for instance, the need for rapid economic development—can be shown to conflict with autonomy.

To view both autonomy and social order as "basic" or primary in their own right, and to recognize the inherent conflict between them, indicate one's ultimate commitment to both virtues. True, *both* virtues are socially and culturally contextualized, but not in their basic standing. We saw, for instance, that whether those who are morally active need to throw their weight on the side of shoring up autonomy *or* social order is contingent on the direction in which the society has been disequilibrated. But this takes nothing away from the observation that a good society is building on a balanced combination of both virtues.

Closely related is another dualism best maintained because we lose considerable sociological and psychological insight if we ignore one of the two elements, or claim that one element is derived from the other and hence has a secondary standing. I refer to the role of compassion and the sense of obligation. As Hans Joas has put it, "a Kantian understanding of 'duty' without compassion would be insufficient and condemn us to being cold moralizers. . . . On the other hand, I also agree that compassion alone makes us merely sentimental if it remains a passing experience and does not become the emotional basis for a deeper attachment and the formation of a stabilized value-orientation."[95]

SOCIAL VERSUS PERSONAL VIRTUES

The question may arise, What makes the twin virtues I build on communitarian? Indeed, it might be pointed out that the idea that certain moral concepts are compelling in and of themselves is a personal idea, not applicable to a community, and surely not to a complex and often large entity such as a society or a "global village." Thus, an individualist might quite willingly accept that each person will individually find some values compelling and suggest that whatever agreed (as distinct from shared) values we have arise from these individual conceptions of the good. From this viewpoint, the fact that many different people all find some of the same important values compelling merely serves to ease the processes of aggregation of individual formulations of the good.

In contrast to this individualist perspective, the virtues I point to as compelling concern characteristics of social formations—and are neither individual nor simply aggregated attributes. An individual person can contribute to the moral order, but order is a system attribute. (One can speak of a just person and a just society, but these are hardly the same.) And an individual can enjoy and celebrate autonomy, but it exists only as a social construction.[96]

Moral order and autonomy also provide the communitarian paradigm with a source from which other *social* values that good societies uphold (corollary and secondary values, to be discussed shortly) may be derived, or may be reached via moral dialogues, which are a social formation themselves. These dialogues can help a community uncover shared commitments hidden by variations in wording or interpretation, or help it work out differences concerning implications and applications of values that are already shared.

The importance of moral dialogues in this context cannot be overestimated. If all the members of all communities were born with or automatically realized the compelling qualities of moral order and autonomy, differences among the members of any one community and among those of different communities would be limited to questions of interpretation, priorities, and practical considerations. This is hardly the case. The compelling nature of the basic communitarian virtues can be hidden under the influence of historical and cultural factors and economic duress. Often, only after people are exposed to these virtues through continued dialogue do they realize their compelling nature.

ULTIMATE VERSUS EXPEDIENT

The notion that we have ultimate values (in the sense that they are not instrumental or steppingstones to some other, higher values) is sometimes challenged on the ground that even highly principled people, when they come under pressure, may yield. "Everyone has a price" is a vulgar, colloquial way of expressing this notion. First, this observation is not compatible with empirical evidence: Jews have jumped into the fire and perished rather than eat pork; villagers have been hanged by Nazis when they refused to bring forward refugees they were hiding; and many government officials (especially in the executive branch) are quite unbribable.

Second, even if under some rather extreme circumstances a person will bend, and commitments he or she experienced as absolute give way to calculated and expedient considerations, this does not mean that up to that point those values were not being absolutely held. A Jew who will not eat pork but does so when his life is directly threatened has not given up his commitment to his religious beliefs just because he cannot live up to them in some extreme, "limit" situation.[97] Communitarian societies facing severe challenges—a civil war, an invasion—may declare an emergency state and suspend parts of their constitutions or other normative commitments that undergird autonomy and moral order. However, so long as they fully restore these when the emergency recedes, such suspensions are not indications that the dual virtues are not cardinal to communitarian societies. Exceptions do not make the rule.

COROLLARY AND SECONDARY VALUES

Are moral order and autonomy the only communitarian virtues? In particular, communitarians are often asked, What is the standing of social justice and equality? First of all, the communitarian virtues also include the concept of an equilibrium between autonomy and social order, the basis of the new golden rule, the recognition of the virtue of reducing the inevitable tension between order and autonomy by relying extensively on a moral (and hence ultimately voluntary) basis for social order rather than on a coercive one, and by bounding autonomy.

Second, several important virtues find their place as corollaries of the basic communitarian virtues. That is, *the respect for these virtues lends support to other virtues*. For instance, a measure of social justice is required both to sustain moral order and to advance autonomy for all the members of the community. A strongly hierarchical society—one in which one class, a few elites, or a state bureaucracy monopolizes much of the power and many of the resources—will be unable to evolve communitarian responses to the basic societal functional needs. To put it differently, a high degree of inequality is incompatible with a good society. However, how much equality and of what kind (only political? also economic? still others?) a good society requires, and at what point advancing this virtue begins to undermine the basic virtues (to evoke for the last time the principle of inverting symbiosis) are questions open to much debate, a debate communitarians are deeply engaged in but have not yet advanced to a firm conclusion.[98] There is a world of difference between seeking to reduce sharp inequality, which a good society requires for the reasons just cited, and favoring the advancement of equality on a broad front. The difference is captured in the debate between, on the one hand, those who seek to ensure that everyone's basic socioeconomic needs are provided for and that sharp differences in assets and income are curbed (for example, by a progressive income tax and inheritance taxes), and, on the other hand, those who argue that all assets belong to the people and consumption should be equalized, as the kibbutzim tried to do. The same issue is reflected when it comes to affirmative action in the debate between those who seek equality of opportunity and all it entails, and those who favor equality of results across the board.

It should, though, be acknowledged that by not making equality a basic virtue, and above all, by not treating autonomy as if it had only a secondary derivative standing, communitarian thinking is in principle less equality-minded than Communist and other forms of nondemocratic socialism. Even though they use a somewhat different terminology, this basic point has been made very well indeed by Elizabeth Frazer and Nicola Lacey, who write:

> To say that justice is the first virtue of social institutions and that the state's primary role is to do justice between individuals, is very different from emphasizing the maintenance of a shared public culture, the values of benevolence and solidarity, and concepts of public duty. Yet these all form a necessary backdrop for the living of worthwhile lives in society.[99]

Avoiding armed conflicts among communities or societies, *promoting peace*, is a virtue closely associated with the communitarian paradigm, as highlighted in the discussion of the community of communities. And, there is a profound linkage between *some feminist values* and communitarian thinking, as both ways of thinking recognize the importance of particular social formations for the embodiment of virtues, a subject that cannot be further explored here. The virtue of *stewardship toward the earth*, the commitment to the environment as a common good, is profoundly communitarian, on the face of it.[100] (Oddly, environmentalists often draw on mainly utilitarian, instrumental, and consequentialist argumentation.)

Still other normative issues are left open-ended, in the sense that the basic virtues of the communitarian society do not suggest a particular stand regarding these values. For instance, unlike communism, fascism, and religious fundamentalism, all of which abhorred jazz, the communitarian paradigm does not point to a moral stand on jazz that I can discern. The same holds for numerous other issues. To the extent that a community-wide position is needed on these issues, this is an area in which moral dialogues find their legitimate place.

MUST ONE BE RELIGIOUS TO BE COMMUNITARIAN?

During the Enlightenment, there were those who saw human progress as entailing a movement away from religion (and myth) to reason (and science) as the source of accountability for virtue. And followers of

Nietzsche maintained that "God is dead" and hence that man is free to fashion his own values. By contrast, there were always some who doubted that reason alone could account for values, and who argued for the primacy of religious commitments. This age-old issue has been rekindled recently in numerous societies. In non-Western societies, it takes the form of fundamentalism, especially of the Muslim variety, which rejects modernity and its values on religious grounds.[101] The West experiences its own fundamentalism, in the form of the extreme segments of the religious right.

A large number of social conservatives and authoritarians argue that only religious values are truly legitimate and that a regeneration of morality requires at least a spiritual, most likely a religious, revival. Charles Colson states rather starkly, "A secular state cannot cultivate virtue."[102] Pat Robertson argues that "no society in recorded history has ever survived without a strong moral consensus and there has never been a moral consensus that was not founded upon religious truth."[103] And in a recent discussion regarding the role of religion in politics, Richard John Neuhaus expressed concern that a public life stripped of religion "is the most dangerous of all places."[104] When *Commentary* asked more than seventy-two leading conservatives—including Robert Bork, Charles Murray, Dinesh D'Souza, and Michael Novak—to comment on the problems facing the American society, the dominant theme sounded by the contributors was the need for revitalization of religious belief in America.[105]

Several critics maintained that the communitarian paradigm is unsound because it is not based on a commitment to God, or does not draw directly on the scriptures. For example, Michael Joyce writes that responsive communities such as those proposed by communitarians "are not based on the moral and spiritual values that animate real communities . . . but are, rather, secularized, homogenized, sterile substitutes."[106] Joshua Abramowitz wonders about communitarianism without religion: "But—since religion has been largely rejected—where will this morality, both individual and communal, come from? What will create it? What will shape it?"[107]

Must a person be religious to be virtuous? As this is an oft-treated subject, I merely relate its main points to the communitarian position as I see it. Empirically, one readily notes many individuals, communities, and whole societies that have been rather devout but nonetheless have conducted themselves in ways that few would consider moral. The torturing and burning of people during the Inquisition comes to mind when one thinks about the numerous atrocities committed throughout history in the name of religion. Most of the groups that, in recent years, have thrown bombs at buses in Egypt and Israel and at abortion clinics in the United States, and that have blown up buildings and airplanes full of innocent civilians, have been religious fanatics. And so on and on.

Robert Wuthnow, in a 1992 comprehensive study of religion and secular behavior, has shown that in many areas there is little behavioral difference between weekly churchgoers and the population at large. For example, churchgoers are only slightly more likely to have spent five hours or more a week in volunteer activities (29 percent of churchgoers to 24 percent of the general population), and slightly less likely to have given money to beggars (40 percent to 41 percent).[108] Attitudes toward money are only marginally affected (for example, 51 percent of churchgoers think that money is the root of all evil, but 72 percent also feel that having money gives them a good feeling about themselves; these numbers are 46 percent and 76 percent, respectively, for the general population).[109] And religion only slightly rearranges peoples' ranking of personal values (both churchgoers and the general population place family and moral standards at the top, hobbies and making money at the bottom).[110] Wuthnow concludes,

> On issue after issue, we . . . see that religious teachings make some difference . . . but not a strong difference or one that could readily be anticipated from knowledge of these teachings themselves. Religious leaders want the churches to play a heroic role in our society. . . . In reality, religious faith prompts few people in any of these directions.[111]

In short, being religious does not guarantee virtue.

The same holds for those who subscribe to secular ethics. Embracing Kant provides no assurance that the followers will not war with one another, have compassion or deal fairly, or abide by the golden rule (old or new). And some who are true believers in various secular ideologies of the left and right are as dangerous as religious fanatics.

In sum, whether a system of beliefs is based on the concept of a supreme being or is secular seems not to determine how virtuous its followers are. The specific content of the values (for instance, do they respect the rights of others?) and the nature of the commitment (for example, how deep or pervasive is it?) seem much more consequential. Good societies require people who can balance their religious *or* secular ethical commitments with respect for autonomy, especially the rights of

others; who are willing to engage in moral dialogues rather than promote state-enforced morality; and who limit the scope of their shared
formulations of the good to core values.

Moreover, the line that separates secular and religious values is much
less sharply drawn than is often suggested. Secularists often draw on
religious concepts, frequently without even noting their source. For
instance, when environmentalists speak of our stewardship of the
earth, our obligation not to leave it to our children in worse condition
that when it was bequeathed to us, they apply—often unknowingly—a
concept rich in religious tradition and overtones. Similarly, when champions of conflict-resolution speak of the value of reconciliation, they
apply a religious concept in a civic, largely secular, culture.

The same holds the other way around: Religious authorities regularly draw on secular values and observations to make their case, to
legitimate their normative positions for the general populace. For
instance, they point to social science studies that show that being religious is good for one's mental health.

As I see it, one can come to a communitarian position from religious
values and from secular sources (including ethics, social philosophy,
political theory, and social science). Most important, the main fault line
does not separate those whose commitment to core values is a matter
of religious considerations from those whose reasons are secular;
instead, it separates those who are truly committed to a core of shared
values from those who have lost theirs, have not affirmed any new ones,
or deny the very existence of virtues, or worship self-interest, cynicism,
or postmodern or old-fashioned nihilism. It is hence hardly surprising
that people who are committed to carefully balanced voluntary moral
order and bounded autonomy include both people of strong religious
conviction (including Mary Ann Glendon, who represented the Vatican
during the United Nations World Conference on Women in China in
1995; Bryce Christensen from the Rockford Institute; and Bruce Christensen from Brigham Young University); and people who are strongly
committed to secular ethics (such as William D. Ruckelshaus; Henry
Cisneros; and Daniel Kemmis, the mayor of Missoula, Montana).

Regeneration of values is rare and very challenging. Societies whose
values commitments and moral infrastructure have deteriorated tend
to lapse further much more often than they shore up and recast their
moral foundations. The communitarian endeavor requires a broad
coalition rather than a situation in which those on the side of regeneration condemn one another, because some do not recognize the impor-

tance and role of religion, and others deny the possibility of secular recommitment to virtues. At best, if both religious and secular advocates of the return to virtue will join their endeavors, their commitments may suffice to carry the day.

IN CONCLUSION

At the end of the day, when all the commitments are clarified and normative issues are thoroughly dialogued, I—like all actors ultimately responsible for their conduct—must judge whether or not the values advanced by various communities and societies (whether or not I am an active member or an outside observer) square with those I find compelling. I am subject to a communitarian obligation to listen intently to others who subscribe to different values and to try to follow their reasoning. At the same time, as a participant in moral dialogues, I am free—indeed, called upon—to make the case for my normative commitments.

I may find that differences between my position and those of others are limited to questions of applying shared principles, or concern levels of commitments, or are at the margin rather than at the heart of the matter. Thus, I share the sense of stewardship toward the earth with many environmentalists (and many more who do not view themselves as environmentalist but still have a moral commitment to the protection of the environment). I may, however, differ from these others in the importance I attach to wetlands, how far I am willing to go to protect spotted owls, or the urgency I attach to keeping the earth cool. Such differences, within a community of beliefs, are not at issue here. The question arises when the differences are deeper, especially if they concern core values, and I am still in the minority, even of just one—Should I yield? It is here that the difference between consensus (a term I avoid except when describing the positions of others) and affirming one's values comes into relief.

True, to reiterate, as a communitarian I have a strong moral obligation to check and double-check, and review one more time, whether or not I am holding on to an erroneous principle or misapplying one, and whether I am sticking to my position out of inappropriate motives such as pride, desire to seem consistent, or partisanship. However, if I cannot, in good conscience, find such explanations, I must assume that it is the others who need to be swayed. When all is said and done, if the community's moral course deeply offends my ultimate values, I must refuse, rebel, object, try to join with like-minded others to change the course, act as a conscientious objector, demonstrate peacefully, and even engage in civil disobedience (but not resort to violence[112]).

In short, a person should hold on to the values he or she finds most compelling, seeking to be joined by the community but steadfast even if others initially or ultimately do not approve. The community provides one with a normative foundation, a starting point, culture and tradition, fellowship, and place for moral dialogue, but is not the ultimate moral arbitrator. The members are. This is the ultimate reason that the communitarian paradigm entails a profound commitment to moral order that is basically voluntary, and to a social order that is well balanced with socially secured autonomy—the new golden rule.

Notes

PREFACE

1. *The Antioch College Sexual Offense Policy* (Yellow Springs, Ohio: Antioch College, 1992).

2. Jane Gross, "Combating Rape on Campus in a Class on Sexual Consent," *New York Times*, 25 September 1993. Gross quotes a speech given by the Antioch administrator Karen Hall to freshmen in the workshops.

3. *Sexual Offense Policy*, 3, 6–8.

4. Gerald Dworkin, *The Theory and Practice of Autonomy* (New York: Cambridge University Press, 1988), 62–81.

5. For another profound reason not to "value choice," see William A. Galston, "Two Concepts of Liberalism," *Ethics* 105, no. 3 (1995): 523.

6. Noel Epstein, "America's Minority Reports," *Washington Post*, 5 October 1980, Book World.

7. Alan Ehrenhalt in his fine-grained description of the "Lost City" provides a compelling account of life in select communities in the 1950s where members did forgo some options to enable themselves to have an affectionate and orderly existence. Alan Ehrenhalt, *The Lost City: Discovering the Forgotten Virtues of Community in the Chicago of the 1950s* (New York: BasicBooks, 1995).

8. Elizabeth Kolbert, "Politics: In Iowa; G.O.P. Candidates Struggle to Stand Out in Blur of Ads," *New York Times*, 20 January 1996.

9. For example, see "Communitarian Conceits," *Economist* 334, no. 7906 (1995): 16–17; "Down with Rights" *Economist* 334, no. 7906 (1995): 59; and "The Politics of Restoration," *Economist* 333, no. 7895 (1994/1995): 33–36.

10. Morton Gabriel White, *Pragmatism and the American Mind* (New York: Oxford University Press, 1973).

I . THE ELEMENTS OF A GOOD SOCIETY

1. Alasdair MacIntyre, *After Virtue* (Notre Dame, Ind.: University of Notre Dame Press, 1984), 263.

2. Charles Taylor, *Philosophical Arguments* (Cambridge, Mass.: Harvard University Press, 1995), 182.

3. *The Responsive Communitarian Platform: Rights and Responsibilities* (Washington, D.C.: Communitarian Network, 1991); Linda C. McClain, "Rights and Irresponsibility," *Duke Law Journal* 43, no. 5 (1994): 989–1088; Amitai Etzioni, *The Spirit of Community: Rights, Responsibilities, and the Communitarian Agenda* (New York: Crown, 1993); Amitai Etzioni, ed., *New Communitarian Thinking: Persons, Virtues, Institutions, and Communities* (Charlottesville, Va.: University Press of Virginia, 1995): 18–24.

4. Michael Walzer "The Communitarian Critique of Liberalism," *Political Theory* 18, no. 1 (February 1990): 10; Michael J. Sandel, *Liberalism and the Limits of Justice* (Cambridge: Cambridge University Press, 1982); Charles Taylor, *Sources of the Self* (Cambridge, Mass.: Harvard University Press, 1989).

5. Bernard Barber, "Structural-Functional Analysis: Some Problems and Misunderstandings," *American Sociological Review* 21, no. 2 (1956): 133; and Don Martindale, "Limits of and Alternatives to Functionalism in Sociology," in *Functionalism in the Social Sciences: The Strength and Limits of Functionalism in Anthropology, Economics, Political Science, and Sociology*, ed. Don Martindale (Philadelphia: American Academy of Political and Social Science, 1965), 127, 140.

6. Amitai Etzioni, "The Need for a New Paradigm," *Responsive Community* 5, no. 1 (1995): 91–92. Cf. Walzer, "Communitarian Critique," 6; Philip Selznick, *The Moral Commonwealth* (Berkeley, Cal.: University of California Press, 1992), xi, 371–86, 477, and chapter 16; and Philip Selznick, "Foundations of Communitarian Liberalism," *Responsive Community* 4, no. 4 (Fall 1994): 16.

7. William A. Donohue, *The Politics of the American Civil Liberties Union* (New Brunswick, N.J.: Transaction, 1985), 3–6.

8. Theodore Lowi writes, "[T]he single defining attribute of liberalism is individualism. Liberalism embraces the individual as the purpose of society and the state. Liberalism defines the individual *in opposition to the collectivity*." Theodore J. Lowi, *The End of the Republican Era* (Norman, Okla.: University of Oklahoma Press, 1995), 11.

9. Mill's position on many issues changes through his various writings. Gertrude Himmelfarb accurately portrays the ways in which his thought changes. In our terms, he tends to be a strong libertarian in *On Liberty* and is more of a social conservative in *Utilitarianism*. Gertrude Himmelfarb, *On Liberty and Liberalism* (New York: Alfred A. Knopf, 1974).

10. John Kenneth Galbraith, *The Good Society: The Humane Agenda* (Boston: Houghton Mifflin, 1996); Jacob Weisberg, *In Defense of Government: The Fall and Rise of Public Trust* (New York: Scribner, 1996).

11. Steven Mulhall and Adam Swift note that the term "liberal" refers to a whole package of different beliefs. Mulhall and Swift, *Liberals and Communitarians* (Cambridge: Blackwell, 1992), viii.

12. James K. Glassman, "Truly Liberal," *Washington Post*, 28 November 1995. Virginia I. Postrel, an editor of *Reason*, writes, "[L]ibertarian (read: real liberal)." Virginia I. Postrel, "Bloc Busters," *Reason* 27, no. 9 (February 1996): 4–5.

13. Michael Oakeshott, *Rationalism in Politics and Other Essays* (Indianapolis: Liberty Press, 1991), 439–40.

14. Paul Gottfried, *In Search of a Liberal Essence* (forthcoming), 1.

15. This is explained succinctly by Matthew Dallek, "The Conservative 1960s," *Atlantic Monthly* 176, no. 6 (December 1995): 130. "In the late 1950s and early 1960s conservatives were widely dismissed as 'kooks' and 'crackpots' with no hope of winning political power. In 1950 the literary critic Lionel Trilling spoke for a generation of scholars and journalists when he wrote that 'in the United States at this time liberalism is not only the dominant but even the sole intellectual tradition.'"

16. "Canada's most distinguished conservative intellectual, George Grant, emphasized in his *Lament for a Nation* that 'Americans who call themselves "Conservatives" have the right to that title only in a particular sense. In fact, they are old-fashioned liberals.'" Seymour Martin Lipset, *American Exceptionalism* (New York: W. W. Norton, 1996), 36.

17. E. J. Dionne Jr., *They Only Look Dead: Why Progressives Will Dominate the Next Political Era* (New York: Simon & Schuster, 1996), 158. See also David Frum, *Dead Right* (New York: BasicBooks, 1994).

18. MacIntyre, *After Virtue*. For a spirited defense of MacIntyre, see Ronald Beiner, *What's the Matter with Liberalism* (Berkeley, Cal.: University of California Press, 1992), 61–64.

19. For a presentation of social conservatism by a syndicated columnist, see Charles Krauthammer, "A Social Conservative Credo," *Public Interest* 121 (Fall 1995): 15–22.

20. Alasdair MacIntyre, letter in *Responsive Community* 1, no. 3 (Summer 1991): 91–92.

21. Selznick, *Moral Commonwealth*, especially xi, xii, 386; Dana Milbank, "Republicans Split on the Role of Government in Aiding Poor after Social Programs Are Cut," *Wall Street Journal*, 29 December 1995.

22. These measurements provide first approximations. More sophisticated measurements must take into account that not all the funds raised through taxes enhance social order, nor do all civil servants serve the social order, and so on. Still, statistically, the thicker—or heavier—the social order, the higher these measurements are going to be. For a very encompassing discussion of the problem of order from a sociological viewpoint, see Dennis H. Wrong, *The Problem of Order* (New York: Free Press, 1994).

23. For further exposition of this point, see Amitai Etzioni, *The Moral Dimension: Toward a New Economics* (New York: Free Press, 1988).

24. Jeremy Bentham, *An Introduction to the Principles of Morals and Legislation* (New York: Doubleday, Doran, 1935), 8.

25. Thatcher goes on to say, "There are individual men and women, and there are families. And no government can do anything except through people, and people must look to themselves first. It's our duty to look after ourselves and then to look after our neighbor." Margaret Thatcher, *The Downing Street Years* (New York: HarperCollins, 1993), 626.

26. James K. Glassman, "A Messenger, Not a President," *The Washington Post*, 13 February 1996.

27. John Emerich Edward Dalberg-Acton, *Essays on Freedom and Power*, ed. Gertrude Himmelfarb (Glencoe, Ill.: Free Press, 1949), 51.

28. Robert P. George, as quoted by Paul Starobin, "Right Fight," *National Journal* 27, no. 49 (1995): 3022.

29. John Locke wrote: "The only way whereby any one divests himself of his natural liberty, and puts on the bonds of civil society, is by agreeing with other men to join and unite into a community." John Locke, *Two Treatises of Government*, ed. Thomas I. Cook (New York: Hafner, 1956), 168–69, 170.

30. Robert Nozick, *Anarchy, State, and Utopia* (New York: BasicBooks, 1974), 32–33. Nozick is said to have changed his position in later writing not discussed here.

31. Ronald Dworkin, "Liberalism," in *Public and Private Morality*, ed. Stuart Hampshire (Cambridge: Cambridge University Press, 1978), 127. Note that those who adhere to the libertarian paradigm, like those of all other persuasions, differ in the extent to which they have a single focus, and even the same scholar changes over time. Rawls's and Dworkin's later books lean a bit closer toward recognition of a communitarian social order than their earlier works. Mill is less mono focused in *Autobiography* than in *On Liberty*.

32. John Rawls, *A Theory of Justice* (Cambridge, Mass.: Belknap Press, 1971), 448. Rawls argues, "[F]rom the standpoint of the original position, it is rational for the parties to suppose that they do want a larger share, since in any case they are not compelled to accept more if they do not wish to, nor does a person suffer from a greater liberty." Rawls, *Theory of Justice*, 143.

33. Shlomo Avineri and Avner de-Shalit, ed., *Communitarianism and Individualism* (New York: Oxford University Press, 1992); Daniel A. Bell, *Commu-*

nitarianism and Its Critics, (Oxford: Clarendon Press, 1993); Markate Daly, *Communitarianism: A New Public Ethics* (Belmont, Cal.: Wadsworth Publishing, 1994); C. F. Delaney, ed., *The Liberalism-Communitarianism Debate: Liberty and Community Values* (Lanham, Md.: Rowman & Littlefield, 1994); Will Kymlicka, "Liberalism and Communitarianism," *Canadian Journal of Philosophy* 18, no. 2 (June 1988): 181–204; Mulhall and Swift, *Liberals and Communitarians*; Michael J. Sandel, *Liberalism and Its Critics* (New York: New York University Press, 1984); Charles Taylor, "Cross-Purposes: The Liberal-Communitarian Debate," in *Liberalism and the Moral Life*, ed. Nancy Rosenblum (Cambridge, Mass.: Harvard University Press, 1989).

34. Selznick, *Moral Commonwealth*, 526.

35. Michael Kramer, "The People Choose," *Time*, 27 May 1996, 56.

36. Amitai Etzioni, *The Active Society: A Theory of Societal and Political Processes* (New York: Free Press, 1968), 356.

37. For example, Andrew Peyton Thomas suggests the re-creation of a frankpledge for crime prevention. His policy suggestion would give each household a $250 yearly tax credit for participating in community crime control. In return, participants have the sole duty to report crimes in progress to police. This system would be voluntary. Andrew Peyton Thomas, "The Case for an American 'Frankpledge,'" *Weekly Standard*, 27 November 1995, 28–29.

38. The term "civic" is to be preferred to "civil" if one discusses social formations. Ronald Beiner writes, "In Rousseauian vocabulary, 'civil' corresponds to the world of the 'bourgeois,' whereas 'civic' corresponds to the world of 'citoyen.'" Ronald Beiner, letter to the author, 13 November 1995. For a more detailed discussion, see George Armstrong Kelly, "Who Needs a Theory of Citizenship?," in *Theorizing Citizenship*, ed. Ronald Beiner (Albany, N.Y.: State University of New York Press, 1995).

39. William A. Galston, *Liberal Purposes* (Cambridge: Cambridge University Press, 1991). See also Michael J. Sandel, *Democracy's Discontent: America in Search of a Public Philosophy* (Cambridge, Mass.: Belknap Press, 1996).

40. Beiner, *What's the Matter with Liberalism*, 51–52.

41. Rodney Barker, *Politics, Peoples and Government: Themes in British Political Thought since the Nineteenth Century* (New York: St. Martin's, 1994), 23.

42. Joseph Marie comte de Maistre, *The Works of Joseph de Maistre*, trans. Jack Lively (New York: Macmillan, 1965); Joseph Marie comte de Maistre, *St. Petersburg Dialogues*, trans. Richard A. LeBrun (Montreal: McGill-Queen's University Press, 1993).

43. The Institute for Cultural Conservatism, *Cultural Conservatism: Toward a New National Agenda* (Washington, D.C.: Free Congress Research and Education Foundation, 1987), 133–35.

44. Ibid., 134.

45. Ibid., 134–35.

46. Robert P. George, *Making Men Moral: Civil Liberties and Public Morality* (Oxford: Clarendon Press, 1993), 44.

47. MacIntyre, *After Virtue*, 68.

48. Ibid., 69. Emphasis added.

49. Ibid., 263.

50. George F. Will, "The Francis Boyer Lecture" (paper presented at a meeting convened by the American Enterprise Institute, Washington, D.C., 6 December 1995), 32.

51. For an analysis of the conservative impetus behind early anti-Communist efforts, see Richard Fried, *Nightmare in Red* (New York: Oxford University Press, 1990), 47.

52. The militia movement is not without its ideologues. See, for instance, Andrew MacDonald, *The Turner Diaries* (Washington, D.C.: National Alliance, 1980).

53. Quoted in David Cantor, *The Religious Right: The Assault on Tolerance and Pluralism in America* (New York: Anti-Defamation League, 1994), 6.

54. Ibid., 97. Ralph Reed states that "'What Christians have got to do is to take back this country, one precinct at a time, one neighborhood at a time and one state at a time. . . . I honestly believe that in my lifetime we will see a country once again governed by Christians . . . and Christian values.'" Ibid., 5. See also William R. Goodman Jr., and James J. H. Price, *Jerry Falwell: An Unauthorized Profile* (Lynchburg, Va.: Paris & Associates, 1981), 14.

55. Harvey Cox, "The Warring Visions of the Religious Right," *Atlantic Monthly* 276, no. 5 (November 1995): 66. See also H. Wayne House and Thomas D. Ice, *Dominion Theology, Blessing or Curse? An Analysis of Christian Reconstructionism* (Portland, Ore.: Multnomah, 1988).

56. Cantor, *Religious Right*, 97. See also F. LaGard Smith, *ACLU: The Devil's Advocate* (Colorado Springs, Colo.: Marcon, 1996), 231. Others who clearly cross the line that separates even strong social conservatives from fundamentalists are those who are willing to set aside the democratic form of government and, if necessary, use force to sustain virtues. Randall Terry, founder of Operation Rescue, says, "Our goal is a Christian nation. We have a biblical duty, we are called by God, to conquer this country. We don't want equal time. We don't want pluralism" (Cantor, *Religous Right*, 4). R. J. Rushdoony is said to favor "the abolition of democracy and [to advocate] a theocracy based on his understanding of the Hebrew Bible's strictures," including the possible imposition of the death penalty for "adulterers, homosexuals, blasphemers, incorrigible juvenile delinquents, and propagators of false doctrines, among others" (ibid., 80).

57. The need for a core of shared values and the moral voice is discussed in chapters 4 and 5; the differences between the moral voice and the law, and between laws that are backed by the moral voice versus those that are not are discussed in chapter 5, and the relationship between core values and others is explored in chapters 7 and 8.

58. John Gray critiques the idea of harm as a litmus test for liberty. "A liberal ideology should contain a Principle of Liberty (or an account of rights)

which gives guidance to practice by specifying the contours of legitimate restraint of liberty. No such principle has been stated by any liberal theorist," John Gray, *Liberalisms: Essays in Political Philosophy* (New York: Routledge, 1989), 261.

59. Nozick, *Anarchy, State, and Utopia.*

60. Please see a sampling of issues of *Reason, Regulation* and, to a lesser extent, *Policy Review.*

61. William Tucker, "Why We Should Decriminalize Crime," *Weekly Standard*, 27 November 1995, 33.

62. Donohue, *Politics of the ACLU*, 6, 10–13; William Gerber, *American Liberalism* (Boston: Twayne, 1975), 123.

63. "ACLU Briefing Paper: Freedom of Expression," from the ACLU World Wide Web site at [http://www.aclu.org].

64. "ACLU Briefing Paper: Guardian of Liberty—ACLU," from the ACLU World Wide Web site at [http://www.aclu.org].

65. Ira Glasser, "Making Constitutional Rights Work," in *Our Endangered Rights: The ACLU Report on Civil Liberties Today*, ed. Norman Dorsen (New York: Pantheon, 1984), 8–9.

66. Smith, *ACLU*, 15.

67. This is still the position of the ACLU according to its policy book. See policy no. 270. The book is unpublished and not readily available. See also Donohue, *Politics*, 263. William A. Donohue, *Twilight of Liberty: The Legacy of the ACLU* (New Brunswick, N.J.: Transaction, 1994), 273.

68. Nat Hentoff, "The Teacher from NAMBLA," *Village Voice*, 16 November 1993.

69. Richard Allen Epstein, *Takings: Private Property and the Power of Eminent Domain* (Cambridge, Mass.: Harvard University Press, 1985); Donald G. Hagman and Dean J. Misczynski, eds., *Windfalls for Wipeouts: Land Value Capture and Compensation* (Chicago: American Society of Planning Officials, 1978).

70. George J. Stigler, *The Citizen and the State: Essays on Regulation* (Chicago: University of Chicago Press, 1975), 9–10.

71. Isaiah Berlin, "Two Concepts of Liberty," *Four Essays on Liberty* (New York: Oxford University Press, 1969), 122.

72. Ibid., 131.

73. Karl von Wolferen, *The Enigma of Japanese Power: People and Politics in a Stateless Nation* (New York: Alfred A. Knopf, 1989), 176, 236, 245.

74. Leo Srole, "Measurement and Classification in Socio-Psychiatric Epidemiology; Midtown Manhattan Study (1954) and Midtown Manhattan Restudy (1974)," *Journal of Health and Social Behavior* 16, no. 4 (1975): 347–64.

75. For articles on the effects of isolation on inmates and juveniles, please see Sheilagh Hodgins and Gilles Cote, "The Mental Health of Penitentiary Inmates in Isolation," *Canadian Journal of Criminology* 33, no. 2 (1991): 175–82; and Jeff Mitchell and Christopher Varley, "Isolation and

Restraint in Juvenile Corrections Facilities," *Journal of the American Academy of Child and Adolescent Psychology* 29, no. 2 (1990): 251–55.

76. Sandel, *Liberalism and the Limits of Justice*, 179.

77. Ibid.

78. Taylor, "Cross-Purposes," 159.

79. Taylor, *Sources of the Self*, 500–501.

80. Taylor, "Cross-Purposes," 170. Some feminists have also responded to liberalism with a notion of the "social self." Marilyn Friedman, "Autonomy in Social Context," in *Freedom, Equality, and Social Change: Problems in Social Philosophy Today*, ed. James Sterba and Creighton Peden (Lewiston, N.Y.: E. Mellen, 1989).

81. Michael A. Mosher, "Boundary Revisions: The Deconstruction of Moral Personality in Rawls, Nozick, Sandel, and Parfit," *Political Studies* 39, no. 2 (1991): 296.

82. On this point, see Benjamin Zablocki, *Alienation and Charisma* (New York: Free Press, 1980), chapter 6.

83. Erich Fromm, *Escape from Freedom* (New York: Holt, Rinehart and Winston, 1941); William Kornhauser, *The Politics of Mass Society* (Glencoe, Ill.: Free Press, 1959).

84. Kornhauser, *The Politics of Mass Society*.

85. Peter L. Berger and Richard John Neuhaus, *To Empower People: The Role of Mediating Structures in Public Policy* (Washington, D.C.: American Enterprise Institute for Public Policy Research, 1977). Berger and Neuhaus use mediating structures as a variation of intermediary bodies.

86. One may ask whether order and autonomy are substantive values or merely formal vessels that lack specific normative content: Order for what? Autonomy to realize which values? As I see it, these are ultimate values, a concept explored herein, rather than procedural or instrumental values. Social order has a normative standing all its own, as life does, preceding whatever specific format it takes and other values that benefit from it. For additional discussion, see Wrong, *The Problem of Order*. The same holds for autonomy. Indeed, without the assumption of autonomy, all other virtues lack standing because they presume a measure of free will, i.e., of autonomy as well as socially structured opportunities to exercise it.

87. Alexander Meiklejohn, *Free Speech and Its Relation to Self-Government* (Port Washington, N.Y.: Kennikat Press, 1948), 17.

88. Gary L. Bauer, *Our Hopes, Our Dreams* (Colorado Springs, Colo.: Focus on the Family Publishing, 1996), 137–41.

89. Robert Boston, *Why the Religious Right Is Wrong* (Buffalo: Prometheus Books, 1993), 189.

90. Thomas Storck, "A Case for Censorship," *New Oxford Review* (May 1996): 23.

91. Ibid.

92. Ibid., 23–24.

93. William A. Galston, "Rights Do Not Equal Rightness," *Responsive Community* 1, no. 4 (Fall 1991): 8.

94. Daniel Patrick Moynihan, "Defining Deviancy Down," *American Scholar* 62, no. 1 (1993): 17–30.

95. Brooke Gladstone, "O. J. Simpson Struggling to Buy Ad Time for Videotape," *Morning Edition*, National Public Radio, 12 February 1996.

96. Such positions are not the extreme views of an outlier group, but are more or less standard fare for those who subscribe to the individualist paradigm. See National Public Television, *Freedom Speaks*, 12 January 1996.

97. Douglas N. Walton, *Slippery Slope Arguments* (New York: Oxford University Press, 1992).

98. G. Gordon Liddy, *G. Gordon Liddy Show*, WJFK-FM, 26 August 1994.

99. The U.S. Department of Transportation also reports that of the forty states that increased the speed limit on rural interstates, seventeen experienced an increase of greater than 50 percent in fatalities on rural interstates. All but six of the forty states experienced some increase. U.S. Department of Transportation, *Effects of the 65 mph Speed Limit Through 1990* (Washington D.C.: GPO, 1992), 16.

2. ORDER *AND* AUTONOMY

1. David Feldman, *Civil Liberties and Human Rights in England and Wales* (Oxford: Clarendon Press, 1993), 668–73.

2. Under the United Kingdom Prevention of Terrorism Act of 1984, a person can be held for forty-eight hours without a hearing, then the Secretary of State can review the case and order the person held for another five days. Ibid., 225.

3. Steve Coll, "Britain's Omnipresent Private Eyes," *Washington Post*, 8 August 1994.

4. A colleague suggested a similarity between my notion of inverting symbiosis and Gregory Bateson's schismogenesis. See Gregory Bateson, *Naven* (Stanford, Cal.: Stanford University Press, 1958), 175.

5. Daniel A. Bell refers to this possibility with respect to China in "A Communitarian Critique of Authoritarianism," *Society* 32, no. 5 (July / August 1995): 39–43.

6. Note that this relationship is different from relationships that are depicted as dialectic, and from those of a declining marginal utility, as well as those that are curvilinear.

7. For an example of the argument that America is a Lockean nation, see especially Louis Hartz, *The Liberal Tradition in America: An Interpretation of American Political Thought since the Revolution* (New York: Harcourt, Brace, 1955). In response to Hartz, see, among others, J.G.A. Pocock, *The Machiavellian Moment: Florentine Political Thought and the Atlantic Political Tradition*

(Princeton, N.J.: Princeton University Press, 1975); Isaac Kramnick, *Republicanism and Bourgeois Radicalism: Political Ideology in Late Eighteenth Century England and America* (Ithaca, N.Y.: Cornell University Press, 1990); and Rogers M. Smith, "Beyond Tocqueville, Myrdal, and Hartz: The Multiple Traditions in America," *American Political Science Review* 87, no. 3 (September 1993): 549–66.

On the other side, Robert Bellah explains that "in Alexis de Tocqueville's *Democracy in America,* individualism was treated as a destructive tendency that needed firm restraint if American democracy was to flourish." Robert N. Bellah, "Individualism, Community, and Ethics in the United States and Japan," *Moral Education* 4 (1995): 1–2.

8. For a study of the American society from this viewpoint, see Bruce Ackerman, *We the People* (Cambridge, Mass.: Belknap, 1991).

9. This is well documented in ibid. See also Sandel, *Democracy's Discontent.*

10. Paul Boyer and Stephen Nissenbaum, *Salem Possessed: The Social Origins of Witchcraft* (Cambridge, Mass.: Harvard University Press, 1994). For a dramatic presentation of oppressive community bonds during the early history of the United States, see Arthur Miller's *The Crucible* (New York: Penguin, 1995).

11. Personal communication with David Boaz, vice president of the Cato Institute.

12. Milton and Rose Friedman, *Free to Choose: A Personal Statement* (New York: Harcourt Brace Jovanovich, 1980).

13. Ronald Beiner, *What's the Matter with Liberalism?* (Berkeley, Cal.: University of California Press, 1992), 4–5; Italo Calvino, *Invisible Cities,* trans. William Weaver (New York: Harcourt Brace Jovanovich, 1978).

14. Alan Jacobs, "Auden's Local Culture," *Hudson Review* 47, no. 4 (Winter 1995): 543.

15. Emile Durkheim, *The Elementary Forms of the Religious Life,* (1915; reprint, New York: Collier, 1961); Robert Nisbet, *Community and Power* (New York: Oxford University Press, 1962; formerly, *The Quest for Community: A Study in the Ethics of Order and Freedom* [New York: Oxford University Press, 1953]); Robert Nisbet, *The Social Philosophers: Community and Conflict in Western Thought* (New York: Crowell, 1973); Robert Nisbet, "The Concept of Community: A Reexamination," *Sociological Review* 38, no. 4 (August 1973): 397–416; Robert Nisbet, *The Social Bond* (New York: Alfred A. Knopf, 1977); Robert E. Park and Ernest W. Burgess, *Introduction to the Science of Sociology* (Chicago: University of Chicago Press, 1924); Talcott Parsons, *The Social System* (Glencoe, Ill.: Free Press, 1951); Talcott Parsons and Edward A. Shils, *Toward a General Theory of Action: Theoretical Foundations for the Social Sciences* (Cambridge, Mass.: Harvard University Press, 1951); Ferdinand Tönnies, *Community and Society,* trans. Charles P. Loomis (East Lansing, Mich.: Michigan State University Press, 1957); Ferdinand Tönnies, *Com-*

munity and Association, trans. Charles P. Loomis (London: Routledge & Paul, 1955).

16. Martin Buber, *I and Thou*, trans. Ronald Gregory Smith (New York: Charles Scribner and Sons, 1970); Martin Buber, *Paths in Utopia* (Boston: Beacon Press, 1958). For a comprehensive analysis of John Dewey and his thought, see Alan Ryan, *John Dewey and the High Tide of American Liberalism* (New York: W. W. Norton, 1995). George Herbert Mead, *Mind, Self, and Society* (Chicago: University of Chicago Press, 1934).

17. Charles Taylor, *Sources of the Self: The Making of the Modern Identity* (Cambridge, Mass.: Harvard University Press, 1989).

18. Michael J. Sandel, *Liberalism and the Limits of Justice* (Cambridge: Cambridge University Press, 1982).

19. Michael Walzer, *Spheres of Justice: A Defense of Pluralism and Equality* (New York: BasicBooks, 1983).

20. "First, a word of caution. Those typically put forward as communitarian critics of liberal political theory—Alasdair MacIntyre, Michael Sandel, Charles Taylor, and Michael Walzer—have yet to identify themselves with the 'communitarian movement,'" Daniel A. Bell, *Communitarianism and Its Critics* (Oxford: Clarendon Press, 1993), 4. MacIntyre explicitly repudiated the label in "The Spectre of Communitarianism," *Radical Philosophy* 70 (March/April 1995): 35. Walzer places his work within a context of the "periodic communitarian correction" required by liberalism but considers his basic position liberal. Michael Walzer, "Communitarian Critique of Liberalism," *Political Theory* 18, no. 1 (February 1990): 6–23. The term "communitarian" does not even appear in the index of Sandel's most recent book, *Democracy's Discontent*.

21. Philip Selznick, *The Moral Commonwealth: Social Theory and the Promise of Community* (Berkeley, Cal.: University of California Press, 1992); see also Philip Selznick, "The Demands of Community," *Center Magazine* 20, no. 1 (January/February 1987): 33–54; Philip Selznick, "Dworkin's Unfinished Task," *California Law Review* 77, no. 3 (May 1989): 505–13.

22. Bell, *Communitarianism and Its Critics*.

23. Robert D. Putnam, *Making Democracy Work: Civic Traditions in Modern Italy* (Princeton, N.J.: Princeton University Press, 1993).

24. Hans Joas, *Pragmatism and Social Theory* (Chicago: University of Chicago Press, 1993).

25. John Gray, *Post-liberalism: Studies in Political Thought* (New York: Routledge, 1993).

26. David Willetts, *Modern Conservatism* (London: Penguin, 1992).

27. Meinhard Miegel and Stephanie Wahl, *Das Ende des Individualismus: Die Multur des Westens zerstoert sich selbst* (Munich: Verlag Bonn Aktuell, 1993).

28. Etzioni, *Spirit of Community*; *The Responsive Communitarian Platform: Rights and Responsibilities* (Washington, D.C.: Communitarian Network); *Responsive Community Quarterly: Rights and Responsibilities*.

29. See note 28.

30. Stephen Holmes sees communitarianism as "the form of antiliberalism currently most popular in the United States." Stephen Holmes, *The Anatomy of Antiliberalism*, (Cambridge, Mass.: Harvard University Press, 1993), 8. Attesting to the influence of communitarianism, see *Politics Monitor* 1, no. 1 (November 1992): 11, which promulgates, "There is nothing, so to say, like the power of an idea whose time has come. And if you can measure the force of communitarian thought by the effect it has on people, then this new kid on the block of political theory might just be coming into its own." Communitarianism has also exerted considerable influence internationally. In *Newsweek International*, Michael Elliot remarks of communitarianism, "If any idea is 'hot' in the Euroleft today it is this. Tony Blair can hardly speak for five minutes without talking about the need to rediscover a sense of community." Michael Elliot, "What's Left?," *Newsweek International*, 10 October 1994, 13.

31. Tibor Machan, "The Communitarian Manifesto," *Register*, 12 May 1991.

32. Tibor Machan, "The Individual and the Community," *Freeman* (September 1991): 328.

33. John Stuart Mill, *On Liberty*, ed. David Spitz (New York: W. W. Norton, 1975), 71.

34. Ibid., 10–11.

35. David Held, *Political Theory and the Modern State: Essays on State, Power, and Democracy* (Cambridge: Polity Press, 1989), 164.

36. For example, Richard E. Morgan, *Disabling America: the "Rights Industry" in Our Time* (New York: BasicBooks, 1984). Also see Mary Ann Glendon, *Rights Talk* (New York: Free Press, 1991), and Etzioni, *Spirit of Community*.

37. Carl S. Schneider, "Talking about Rights," *Hastings Center Report* 22, no. 3 (May/June 1993): 43. Schneider's article cites Glendon, *Rights Talk*, 15.

38. Robert S. Fogarty, "All Together Now," *Nation*, 6 December 1993: 699.

39. Lloyd A. Free and Hadley Cantril, *The Political Beliefs of Americans: A Study of Public Opinion* (New Brunswick, N.J.: Rutgers University Press, 1967).

40. Savings from cutting fraud and abuse are rather small, a statement that I cannot document in the context of this book but which is well supported by even a cursory examination of numerous recent drives to cut fraud and abuse in the government.

41. Frederick Schauer, "Slippery Slopes," *Harvard Law Review* 99 (December 1985): 361.

42. See Etzioni, *Spirit of Community*, 177–90.

43. Mary Ann Glendon expertly develops this point in *Rights Talk*.

44. Another example of inverting symbiosis is the relations between men and women. Notions that treat autonomy and bonding as if they are antithetical are too simplistic. Several feminist scholars and family therapists view the relations between the sexes as needing correction after ages in

which a very high level of bonding was expected in the family, a level that included a subordination of women's identities and interests. However, after decades of correction, the sexes may have moved too far toward independence, and the question of a higher level of bonding—albeit in much more egalitarian terms—is being faced. See, for instance, Francesca M. Cancian, *Love in America: Gender and Self-Development* (New York: Cambridge University Press, 1987); Lillian B. Rubin, *Intimate Strangers: Men and Women Together* (New York: Harper & Row, 1983); Deborah Anna Luepnitz, *The Family Interpreted: Feminist Theory in Clinical Practice* (New York: BasicBooks, 1988); Carol Gilligan, *In a Different Voice: Psychological Theory and Women's Development* (Cambridge, Mass.: Harvard University Press, 1982); and Nancy Chodorow, *The Reproduction of Mothering: Psychoanalysis and the Sociology of Gender* (Berkeley, Cal.: University of California Press, 1978).

45. These limits were thought to have allowed domestic militias to flourish without being subject to the same scrutiny as terrorists from overseas. Thus, there have been moves to weaken these curbs after the Oklahoma City bombing. For further analysis, please see David G. Savage, "Rule Changes Limit FBI's Infiltration of Extremists," *Los Angeles Times,* 22 April 1995.

46. William A. Stahl, *"May We Have Dominion": Civil Religion and the Legitimation of Canadian Confederation* (Regina, Sask.: Luther College, University of Regina, 1986), 4.

47. Seymour Martin Lipset and Amy Bunger Pool, "Balancing the Individual and the Community: Canada versus the United States," *Responsive Community* 6, no. 3 (Summer 1996): 38.

48. Seymour Martin Lipset and Amy Bunger Pool, "Rights and Responsibilities: Comparing Issues of Crime and Law in the Communitarian Culture of Canada and the Individualistic Culture of the United States," unpublished, 1.

49. Lipset and Pool, "Balancing," 42.

50. Ibid., 43.

51. F. L. Morton, "The Political Impact of the Canadian Charter of Rights and Freedoms," *Canadian Journal of Political Science* 20, no. 1 (March 1987): 32.

52. Ibid., 32.

53. There is, however, an exception in section 33, which allows the legislature to pass a law struck down by the Supreme Court "notwithstanding" the court's determination that the law violated the Charter.

54. Morton, "Political Impact," 35–36.

55. "In the five cases where the Crown relied on pre-Charter precedents to support its case, the Supreme Court explicitly overruled three of its previous decisions and found in favour of the individual litigant," ibid., 36.

56. William Christian, review of *The U.S. Bill of Rights and the Canadian Charter of Rights and Freedoms,* edited by William R. McKercher, *Canadian Journal of Political Science* 17, no. 2 (June 1984): 427.

57. Ibid.

58. Yuan-Li Wu, *The Steel Industry in Communist China* (New York: Praeger, 1965).

59. See Zbigniew Brzezinski and Samuel P. Huntington, *Political Power: USA/USSR* (New York: Viking, 1964).

60. For further discussion of responsiveness, please see Amitai Etzioni, "The Responsive Community: A Communitarian Perspective," American Sociological Association Presidential Address, published in *American Sociological Review* 61 (February 1996): 1–11; and Amitai Etzioni, *The Active Society* (New York: Free Press, 1968), 76ff.

61. The four criteria for balancing have been called our most original contribution to this discussion. Daniel A. Bell "Together Again?," review of *The Spirit of Community* by Amitai Etzioni, *Times Literary Supplement*, 11 November 1994, 5–6. For additional discussion of these criteria, see Etzioni, *Spirit of Community*, 177–90.

62. Jeffrey Rothfeder, "What Happened to Privacy?," *New York Times*, 13 April 1993.

63. Letter from the American Civil Liberties Union, United States Public Interest Research Group, and Electronic Privacy Information Center to Congress on 15 November 1995, with regard to the new databases required by a welfare reform bill. Full text can be found at [http://epic.org].

64. Harold J. Rothwax, *Guilty: The Collapse of Criminal Justice* (New York: Random House, 1996), 191. Emphasis in the original.

65. Ibid., 193. This was the instruction requested by Carter's attorney in *Carter v. Kentucky.*

66. Ibid., 130.

67. David Boaz, "The Legalization of Drugs: Decriminalization," speech for the Drug Policy Forum on 27 April 1988, *Vital Speeches of the Day* 54, no. 21 (15 August 1988): 656–58.

68. Elliott Currie, "Toward a Policy on Drugs: Decriminalization? Legalization?," *Dissent* 40, no. 1 (Winter 1993): 65–71.

3. THE FALL AND RISE OF AMERICA

1. Everett Carll Ladd, "The Numbers Are Far Too Often Wrong," *The Public Perspective* 6, no. 4 (June/July 1995): 1–3. Also, Everett C. Ladd, "The Myth of Moral Decline," *Responsive Community* 4, no. 1 (Winter 1993/1994): 52–68.

2. Stephanie Coontz, *The Way We Never Were: American Families and the Nostalgia Trap* (New York: BasicBooks, 1992); Michael Elliott, *The Day Before Yesterday: Reconsidering America's Past, Rediscovering the Present* (New York: Simon & Schuster, 1996).

3. David Halberstam, *The Fifties* (New York: Villard Books, 1993), x. See also Alan Ehrenhalt, *The Lost City: Discovering the Forgotten Virtues of Community in the Chicago of the 1950s* (New York: BasicBooks, 1995).

4. J. Ronald Oakley, *God's Country: America in the Fifties* (New York: Dembner Books, 1986), 434–35.

5. Robin M. Williams Jr., *American Society: A Sociological Interpretation* (New York: Alfred A. Knopf, 1951). Williams outlines American values in fourteen "value systems" to which Americans generally adhere. See also Ralph H. Gabriel, *American Values: Continuity and Change* (Westport, Conn.: Greenwood Press, 1974), 148–211.

6. The term itself was popularized much later by President Reagan.

7. Halberstam, *Fifties*, 116–20. The term "American Century" was first used by Henry Luce, who, to quote Halberstam, envisioned "an all-powerful America spreading democracy and riches across the globe" (ibid., 207). See also Ronald Steel, *Walter Lippmann and the American Century* (New York: Vintage Books, 1981).

8. Seventy-nine percent of Americans approved of religious observances in public schools in a 1962 poll. *The Gallup Poll: Public Opinion 1935–1971, vol. III* (New York: Random House, 1972), 1779. See also Oakley, *God's Country*, 320–21.

9. Mary Ann Glendon, *Abortion and Divorce in Western Law* (Cambridge, Mass.: Harvard University Press, 1987), 10–11, 63–64.

10. Illegitimate births were approximately 5.3 percent of all births in 1960, calculated from data in George Thomas Kurian, *Datapedia of the United States 1790–2000* (Lanham, Md.: Bernan Press, 1994), 37, 40. The rate of illegitimacy is a complex statistic because many of the births are to couples in common-law marriages.

11. Douglas T. Miller and Marion Nowak, *The Fifties: The Way We Really Were* (Garden City, N.Y.: Doubleday, 1977), 147.

12. Ibid., 153–54.

13. Ehrenhalt, *Lost City*, 8–32.

14. For some comments on these points, see David Riesman, *The Lonely Crowd: A Study of the Changing American Character* (New Haven, Conn.: Yale University Press, 1950) and William Hollingsworth Whyte, *The Organization Man* (New York: Simon & Schuster, 1956).

15. Betty Friedan, *The Feminine Mystique* (New York: W. W. Norton, 1963), 68. See also pp. 15–32.

16. Godfrey Hodgson, *America in Our Time* (Garden City, N.Y.: Doubleday, 1976), 72.

17. Richard M. Fried, *Nightmare in Red: The McCarthy Era in Perspective* (New York: Oxford University Press, 1990).

18. Homer Hawkins and Richard Thomas, "White Policing Black Populations: A History of Race and Social Control in America," in *Out of Order?*, eds. Ellis Cashmore and Eugene McLaughlin (New York: Routledge, 1991),

65–86; Pamela Irving Jackson, *Minority Group Threat, Crime, and Policing: Social Context and Social Control* (New York: Praeger, 1989).

19. Daniel Yankelovich Inc., *The Changing Values on Campus: Political and Personal Attitudes of Today's College Students* (New York: Washington Square Press, 1972); Morris Dickstein, *Gates of Eden: American Culture in the Sixties* (New York: BasicBooks, 1977).

20. For a discussion of the two kinds of individualism, expressive and instrumental, see Robert N. Bellah, Richard Madsen, William M. Sullivan, Ann Swidler, and Steven M. Tipton, *Habits of the Heart: Individualism and Commitment in American Life* (Berkeley, Cal.: University of California Press, 1985). Regarding the level of individualism, on page viii, the authors state: "We are concerned that this individualism may have grown cancerous—that it may be destroying those social integuments that Tocqueville saw as moderating its more destructive potentialities, that it may be threatening the survival of freedom itself."

21. Mildred Newman and Bernard Berkowitz, *How to Be Your Own Best Friend: A Conversation with Two Psychoanalysts* (New York: Random House, 1971), 7; Robert J. Ringer, *Looking Out for Number One* (Beverly Hills, Cal.: Los Angeles Book Corp., 1977).

22. Milton Friedman with the assistance of Rose D. Friedman, *Capitalism and Freedom* (Chicago: University of Chicago Press, 1962, 1982), 133–36; and Peter F. Drucker, *Management: Tasks, Responsibilities, Practices* (New York: Harper & Row, 1985), 343–45.

23. Lloyd A. Free and Hadley Cantril, *The Political Beliefs of Americans: A Study of Public Opinion* (New Brunswick, N.J.: Rutgers University Press, 1967). See especially table III-2 on p. 32.

24. Richard G. Niemi, John Mueller, and Tom W. Smith, *Trends in Public Opinion: A Compendium of Survey Data* (New York: Greenwood Press: 1989), 79. Since 1973, those thinking we spend too little on the environment have heavily outnumbered those thinking we spend too much.

25. *The Gallup Poll Monthly* (April 1991): 6.

26. Daniel Patrick Moynihan, "Defining Deviancy Down," *American Scholar* 62 (Winter 1993): 17.

27. Moynihan, "Defining Deviancy," 23–24, 27–29.

28. *Harris Poll* 11 (1 March, 1993). See also the *Gallup Poll Monthly* (April 1993): 24.

29. For example, R. W. Apple Jr., "Poll Shows Disenchantment with Politicians and Politics," *New York Times*, 12 August 1995.

30. Bruce E. Keith, David B. Magleby, Candice J. Nelson, Elizabeth Orr, Mark C. Westlye, and Raymond E. Wolfinger, *The Myth of the Independent Voter* (Berkeley, Cal.: University of California Press, 1992), 18.

31. Humphrey Taylor, *Harris Poll* 1 (4 January 1993): 3.

32. G. Pascal Zachary, "Sharp Decline in Job Stability Is Found in a New Study, Contradicting Prior Data," *Wall Street Journal*, 6 June 1995.

33. Kurian, *Datapedia*, 132. As a percentage of the total population, this represents a fourfold increase.

34. Juliet B. Schor, *The Overworked American: The Unexpected Decline of Leisure* (New York: BasicBooks, 1991).

35. U.S. Department of Commerce, *Household and Family Characteristics: March 1993* (Washington, D.C.: GPO, 1994), fig. 1; U.S. Department of Commerce, *Statistical Abstract of the United States* (Washington, D.C.: GPO, 1975), tables 51, 56.

36. Calculated from statistics in Wade F. Horn, *Father Facts* (Lancaster, Pa.: National Fatherhood Initiative, 1995), 2, 10.

37. Ibid., 2.

38. Kurian, *Datapedia*; and U.S. National Center for Health Statistics, *Vital Statistics of the United States* (Washington, D.C.: GPO, 1993).

39. David Popenoe, "American Family Decline, 1960–1990: A Review and Appraisal," *Journal of Marriage and the Family* 55, no.3 (August 1993): 532.

40. Kurian, *Datapedia*, 40.

41. U.S. National Center for Health Statistics, "The Advance Report: Final Natality Statistics," *Monthly Vital Statistics Report* 44, no. 3, supplement (September 21, 1995).

42. Kurian, *Datapedia*, 16–17.

43. "The Immigration Story," *Public Perspective* 6, no. 5 (August/September 1995): 13.

44. *Report of the National Advisory Commission on Civil Disorders* (New York: Bantam, 1968), v.

45. Jonathan Kaufman, *Broken Alliance: The Turbulent Times Between Blacks and Jews in America* (New York: Scribner, 1988); Michael Lerner and Cornel West, *Jews and Blacks: Let the Healing Begin* (New York: Putnam, 1995); Paul Berman, ed., *Blacks and Jews: Alliances and Arguments* (New York: Delacorte, 1994).

46. U.S. Commission on Civil Rights, *Racial and Ethnic Tension in American Communities: Poverty, Inequality, and Discrimination—A National Perspective* (Washington, D.C.: GPO, 1992), 71. From the testimony of Howard Ehrlich, director of research at the National Institute Against Prejudice and Violence.

47. Seymour M. Lipset, "Malaise and Resiliency in America," *Journal of Democracy* 6, no. 3 (July 1995): 7.

48. Francis Fukuyama, *Trust: The Social Virtues and the Creation of Prosperity* (New York: Free Press, 1995).

49. N. R. Kleinfield, "The Company as Family, No More," *New York Times*, 4 March 1996.

50. Hayden Curry, Denis Clifford, and Robin Leonard, *A Legal Guide for Lesbian and Gay Couples* (Berkeley, Cal.: Nolo Press, 1994).

51. "Solutions? One Response to Lack of Discipline—Spanking—Has Lost Favor," *Public Perspective* (October/November 1995): 32. Approval fell from 62 percent in 1958 to 38 percent in 1994.

52. Michael Wolff, Peter Rutten, and Albert F. Bayers III, *Where We Stand* (New York: Bantam, 1992), 296.

53. Alfred Blumstein, "Prisons," in *Crime*, ed. James Q. Wilson and Joan Petersilia (San Francisco: Institute for Contemporary Studies Press, 1995), 388, fig. 17.1.

54. Lee Epstein and Joseph F. Kobylka, *The Supreme Court and Legal Change: Abortion and the Death Penalty* (Chapel Hill, N.C.: University of North Carolina Press, 1992), 6–7.

55. Brian Forst, "Prosecution and Sentencing," in *Crime*, ed. Wilson and Petersilia, 377.

56. For discussion and references, see chapter 5.

57. Judith Martin, "Who Killed Modern Manners?," *Responsive Community* 6, no.2 (Spring 1996): 50–57.

58. James Davison Hunter, *Culture Wars: The Struggle to Define America* (New York: BasicBooks, 1991). See also Todd Gitlin, *The Twilight of Common Dream: Why America Is Wracked by Culture Wars* (New York: Metropolitan Books, 1995).

59. U.S. Department of Justice, *Uniform Crime Reports for the United States: 1993* (Washington, D.C.: GPO, 1993), table 1; and U.S. Department of Commerce, *Historical Statistics of the United States: Colonial Times to 1970, Part 1* (Washington, D.C.: GPO, 1975), H 952–61. The violent crime rate was 160 in 1960, and 732 in 1990; the rate of murder was 4.7 in 1960 and 9.4 in 1990.

60. Calculated from Kurian, *Datapedia*, 74, 164; and Richard B. Freeman, "The Labor Market," in *Crime*, ed. Wilson and Petersilia, 172.

61. Deborah M. Barnes, "Drugs: Running the Numbers," *Science* 240, no. 4860 (24 June 1988): 1729–31.

62. In 1960, the per capita consumption was 2.04 gallons. In 1990 it was 2.76 gallons, an increase of about 35 percent. Kenneth J. Meier, *The Politics of Sin: Drugs, Alcohol, and Public Policy* (Armonk, N.Y.: M.E. Sharpe, 1994), 166.

63. Alfred N. Garwood, ed., *Black Americans: A Statistical Sourcebook* (Boulder, Colo.: Numbers & Concepts, 1991), 162.

64. For example, "Pop That Pussy" and "A F**k is a F**k" by 2 Live Crew, and "Ain't No Fun (If the Homies Can't Have None)" by Snoop Doggy Dog.

65. Studies find that two-thirds of pregnant teens are impregnated by men over the age of twenty. (State of California, Department of Health Service, Vital Statistics Section, 1993.)

66. Steven V. Roberts, "Onward Christian Soldiers," *U.S. News & World Report*, 6 June 1994, 43.

67. People for the American Way, "60 Percent of Religious Right-Aligned Candidates Victorious," press release issued 11 November 1994.

68. William J. Bennett, ed., *The Book of Virtues: A Treasury of Great Moral Stories* (New York: Simon & Schuster, 1993); see also Ben J. Wattenberg, *Values Matter Most: How Republicans or Democrats or a Third Party Can Win and Renew the American Way of Life* (New York: Free Press, 1995).

69. The Communitarian Network, *The Responsive Communitarian Platform: Rights and Responsibilities* (Washington D.C.: Communitarian Network, 1991), 5–7; Jean Bethke Elshtain, Enola Aird, Amitai Etzioni, William Galston, Mary Ann Glendon, Martha Minow, and Alice Rossi, *A Communitarian Position Paper on the Family* (Washington, D.C.: Communitarian Network, 1993). Also, William Galston, "A Liberal-Democratic Case for the Two-Parent Family," *Responsive Community* 1, no. 1 (Winter 1990/1991): 14; Pepper Schwartz, *Peer Marriage: How Love Between Equals Really Works* (New York: Free Press, 1994).

70. Communitarian position papers have been issued on gun control, character education, the family, health-care reform, organ donation, and diversity.

71. Among those whom the press has cited as supporting communitarian ideas are President Bill Clinton (Michael Kranish, "Communitarianism: Is Clinton a Convert?," *Boston Globe*, 22 May 1993; Charles Trueheart, "At Death's Door—And Back Again," *Washington Post*, 11 February 1992); Housing and Urban Development Secretary Henry Cisneros (Michael D'Antonio, "I or We," *Mother Jones*, May/June 1994); Jack Kemp (*Guardian*, 13 March 1995); Senator Bill Bradley (Jacob Weisberg, "All Together Now," *New York*, 24 July 1995); Vice President Albert Gore ("Communitarian Conceits," *Economist*, 18 March 1995); and William J. Bennett (*Guardian*, 13 March 1995). See also "The False Politics of Values," *Time*, 9 September 1996.

72. Among them were German Chancellor Helmut Kohl; British Prime Minister John Major and his opposition leader, Tony Blair; and former European Union president Jacques Delors.

73. Data available from the Communitarian Network.

74. Michael D'Antonio and Michael Krasney, "I or We?," *Mother Jones*, May/June 1994, 23.

75. Forst, "Sentencing," 377–78.

76. Lawrence W. Sherman, "The Police," in *Crime*, ed. Wilson and Petersilia, 328; and Forst, "Sentencing," 377.

77. U.S. Department of Justice, Federal Bureau of Investigation, *Crime in the United States, 1994: Uniform Crime Reports* (Washington, D.C.: GPO, 1995), 5.

78. Ibid., 10, 38, 49.

79. Ibid., 14.

80. Carol J. De Vita, "The U.S. at Mid-Decade" *Population Bulletin* 50, no. 4 (March 1996): 34.

81. Ibid., 34.

82. "Rate of Births for Teen-agers Drops Again," *New York Times*, 22 September 1995.

83. *A disclaimer:* Societies are complex beings, that as a rule change direction gradually; and on some fronts before others. One can always find indicators that point in different directions, and hence both reasonable people

and social scientists can reach different conclusions as to their meanings. However, just as economists can draw a picture when seven (or even six) out of eleven leading indicators point one way, and so can the Federal Reserve when it receives conflicting reports from different parts of the country, so can a sociologist.

84. Justin Burke, "Germans Voice Concerns about Rising Crime," *Christian Science Monitor*, 6 May 1994.

85. For 1960–1980: B. R. Mitchell, *British Historical Statistics* (Cambridge: Cambridge University Press, 1988), 776–78; for 1981–1991: Home Office Criminal Statistics, as quoted by Himmelfarb, *De-Moralization*, 226, 231.

86. James Lynch, "Crime in International Perspective," in *Crime*, ed. Wilson and Petersilia, 15–26.

87. Wolff, *Where We Stand*, 232, 237.

88. Ibid., 175.

89. Communitarian circles were formed in Canada, Great Britain, Germany, and Spain. There was an explosive increase in the number of press items and scholarly books on the subjects, as well as numerous meetings and briefings. Details are available from the Communitarian Network, Washington, D.C.

90. See Jeffery Sachs, Oliver J. Blanchard, and Kenneth Froot, *The Transition in Eastern Europe* (Chicago: University of Chicago Press, 1994).

91. Nicholas D. Kristof, "Who Needs Love! In Japan, Many Couples Don't," *New York Times*, 11 February 1996.

92. "The rule that 'a person is presumed innocent until he (or she) is proven guilty' seems to be disregarded not only in practice but also in existing regulations," Peter J. Herzog, *Japan's Pseudo-Democracy* (New York: New York University Press, 1993), 50. See also "Case Closed in Japan?," *New York Times*, 17 May 1995.

93. Ronald Bayer, *Private Acts, Social Consequences: AIDS and the Politics of Public Health* (New York: Free Press, 1989). Bayer does not argue for quarantine, but he discusses calls for one.

94. See Amitai Etzioni, *The Active Society: A Theory of Societal and Political Processes* (London: Collier-Macmillan, 1968).

95. Zbigniew Brzezinski and Samuel P. Huntington, *Political Power: USA/USSR* (New York: Viking, 1964).

96. In discussing the steering of a society, no teleological assumptions are made or intended. No claim is made that societies consciously pursue a purpose or multiple ones, let alone that—as suggested by the terminology of statecraft—societies have a captain who steers them. The government does play something of this role, but even government's capacity to drive the economy is rather limited and its effects on societal processes and values and institutions is even more limited though not nil. The processes at work are often not highly visible and not centralized: various societal groupings pull in one direction (e.g., leaders of minorities in the United States pull for more diver-

sity) or another (e.g., the movement to enhance character and core values education in public schools helps build unity). Each of these groups responds to its analysis of societal conditions and to its notions as to how these are to be corrected if "our way of life" is to be protected, or "our needs are finally taken into account," and so on, without necessarily to a full or accurate analysis of the societal tilt or how it may be corrected (or exacerbated). Societal direction is much affected by the combined results of all these groups vying with one another, although the government does serve as some kind of articulating and combining factor, one that has some effects of its own.

97. Barnaby J. Feder, "Bigger Roles for Suppliers of Temporary Workers," *New York Times*, 1 April 1995.

98. The New York Times, *The Downsizing of America* (New York: Times Books, 1996); Susan J. Tolchin, *The Angry American: How Voter Rage is Changing the Nation* (Boulder, Colo.: Westview Press, 1996).

99. Ralf Dahrendorf, "A Precarious Balance: Economic Opportunity, Civil Society, and Political Liberty," *Responsive Community* 5, no. 3 (Summer 1995): 13–39.

100. Joan Warner, "Clinging to the Safety Net," *BusinessWeek* (Industrial/Technology Edition), 11 March 1996, 62. "Australia, and John Howard, Opt for Change," *Economist* , 9 March 1996, 31–32.

101. Amity Shlaes, "Germany's Chained Economy," *Foreign Affairs* 73, no. 5 (September/October 1994): 109–24. See also Amitai Etzioni, *A Compassionate Approach: Community Jobs and Prevention* (Washington, D.C.: Communitarian Network, 1995); and Jeremy Rifkin, *The End of Work: The Decline of the Global Labor Force and the Dawn of the Post-Market Era* (New York: Putnam, 1995).

102. James P. Pinkerton, *What Comes Next: The End of Big Government—And the New Paradigm Ahead* (New York: Hyperion, 1995), 313–17.

4. SHARING CORE VALUES

1. Alexis de Tocqueville, *Democracy in America*, trans. George Lawrence, ed. J. P. Mayer (Garden City, N.Y.: Doubleday, 1969), 433–34.

2. Lee Hockstader, "The Baltic Evolution: Westward Ho!," *Washington Post*, 28 March 1996.

3. William A. Galston, *Liberal Purposes* (Cambridge: Cambridge University Press, 1991), chapters 4–7; Michael J. Sandel, "Moral Argument and Liberal Toleration: Abortion and Homosexuality," in *New Communitarian Thinking*, ed. Amitai Etzioni (Charlottesville, Va.: University Press of Virginia, 1995); and Michael J. Sandel, *Democracy's Discontent: America in Search of a Public Philosophy* (Cambridge, Mass.: Belknap, 1996), chapters 1–4.

4. For a full discussion of this example, see Tamar Lewin, "On Common Ground: Pro-Life and Pro-Choice," *Responsive Community* 2, no. 3 (Summer 1992): 48–53.

5. Michael Walzer, *Spheres of Justice: A Defense of Pluralism and Equality* (New York: BasicBooks, 1983).

6. Philip Selznick, *The Moral Commonwealth: Social Theory and the Promise of Community* (Berkeley, Cal.: University of California Press, 1992), 387–90.

7. Robert N. Bellah, Richard Madsen, William M. Sullivan, Ann Swidler, and Steven M. Tipton, *Habits of the Heart: Individualism and Commitment in American Life* (Berkeley, Cal.: University of California Press, 1985); Amitai Etzioni, *An Immodest Agenda: Rebuilding America Before the 21st Century* (New York: McGraw-Hill, 1983).

8. Daniel A. Bell, *Communitarianism and Its Critics* (Oxford: Clarendon Press, 1993); Michael J. Sandel, *Liberalism and the Limits of Justice* (Cambridge: Cambridge University Press, 1982); Galston, *Liberal Purposes*; Amitai Etzioni, "Liberals and Communitarians," *Partisan Review* 57, no. 2 (Spring 1990): 215–27; Etzioni, *New Communitarian Thinking*, 16–34.

9. Galston, *Liberal Purposes*, 221–27.

10. Jeff Weintraub and Kumar Krishan, eds., *Public and Private in Thought and Practice: Perspectives on a Grand Dichotomy* (Chicago: University of Chicago Press, forthcoming). See also Ronald Thiemann, *Religion in Public Life: A Dilemma for Democracy* (Washington, D.C.: Georgetown University Press, 1996) and Stephen L. Carter, *The Culture of Disbelief: How American Law and Politics Trivialize Religious Devotion* (New York: BasicBooks, 1993).

11. Carole Pateman, *The Sexual Contract* (Stanford, Cal.: Stanford University Press, 1988); Elizabeth Frazer and Nicola Lacey, *The Politics of Community: A Feminist Critique of the Liberal-Communitarian Debate* (Toronto: University of Toronto Press, 1993), 125–27.

12. Galston's argument in *Liberal Purposes* (see chapter 1).

13. David Miller, "Community and Citizenship," in *Communitarianism and Individualism*, ed. Shlomo Avineri and Avner de-Shalit (New York: Oxford University Press, 1992), 87.

14. Compare this position to the one taken by Dennis Wrong, who points out that mores are "generated spontaneously in the interplay of mutual expectations that constitute recurrent social interaction." Dennis Wrong, *The Problem of Order* (New York: Free Press, 1994), 107.

15. John Rawls, *Political Liberalism* (New York: Columbia University Press, 1993).

16. Thomas A. Spragens Jr., "The Limitations of Libertarianism, Part II," *Responsive Community* 2, no. 2 (Spring 1992): 46.

17. Robert Putnam, *Making Democracy Work: Civic Traditions in Modern Italy* (Princeton, N.J.: Princeton University Press, 1993); Adam Seligman, *The Idea of Civil Society* (New York: Free Press, 1992); Don E. Eberly, *Restoring the Good Society* (Grand Rapids, Mich.: Baker Books, 1994); Bill Bradley, "Civil Society and the Rebirth of Our National Community," *Responsive Community* 5, no. 2 (Spring 1995): 4–10; David S. Broder, "Civic Life and Civility," *Wash-*

ington Post, 1 January 1995; George F. Will, "The Frontier and Civic Virtue," *Washington Post*, 3 March 1991); and Arnold Beichman, "In Search of Civil Sociality," *Washington Times*, 3 February 1993.

18. Bradley, "Civil Society."

19. Gertrude Himmelfarb, "Beyond Social Policy: Re-Moralizing America," *Wall Street Journal*, 7 February 1995.

20. For a particularly cogent discussion of the role of reason in deliberations of ends and not just means, see Selznick, *Moral Commonwealth*, 524–26.

21. Dennis Wrong illustrates the tendency toward reason in stating, "Many sociologists confine themselves, implicitly at least, to the cognitive rather than the motivational or emotional aspects of interaction, often making tacit assumptions about the latter or simply taking them for granted. Berger and Luckmann explicitly call their vivid account of how actors construct an objective social world that then confronts and constrains them a contribution to the 'sociology of knowledge.'" Wrong, *Problem of Order*, 60. Although Wrong speaks directly of sociology, the affinity for the rational applies to many disciplines.

22. Miriam Galston, "Taking Aristotle Seriously: Republican-Oriented Legal Theory and the Moral Foundation of Deliberative Democracy," *California Law Review* 82, no. 329 (1994): 355.

23. James H. Kuklinski, Ellen Riggle, and Victor Ottati, "The Cognitive and Affective Bases of Political Tolerance Judgments," *American Journal of Political Science* 35, no. 1 (February 1991): 22. Jack Knight and James Johnson write, "[D]emocratic legitimacy accrues to political outcomes insofar as they survive a process of reasoned debate sustained by fair procedures." Jack Knight and James Johnson, "Aggregation and Deliberation: On The Possibility of Democratic Legitimacy," *Political Theory* 22, no. 2 (May 1994): 289.

24. Knight and Johnson, "Aggregation and Deliberation," 285. Furthermore, Knight and Johnson stress the importance of reason, "[D]eliberation involves reasoned argument. Proposals must be defended or criticized with reasons. . . . [T]he crucial point is that parties to deliberation rely only on what Habermas calls the 'force of the better argument'; other forms of influence are explicitly excluded so that interlocutors are free to remain unconvinced so long as they withhold agreement with reasons." Ibid., 286, italics omitted.

25. Philip Selznick, "Defining Democracy Up," *Public Interest* no. 119 (Spring 1995): 106–7; Amy Gutmann, "The Power of Deliberation," *Responsive Community* 6, no. 2 (Spring 1996): 8–10.

26. Kuklinski et al., "Cognitive and Affective Bases," 1–27. See also James Q. Wilson, "Interests and Deliberation in the American Republic, or Why James Madison Would Have Never Received the James Madison Award," *PS: Political Science and Politics* (December 1990): 559; James H. Kuklinski et al., "Thinking about Political Tolerance, More or Less, with More or Less Information" in *Reconsidering the Democratic Public*, ed. Russell Han-

son and George E. Marcus (University Park, Pa.: Pennsylvania State University Press, 1993), 227; Benjamin R. Barber, "An American Civic Forum: Civil Society Between Market Individuals and the Political Community," *Social Philosophy and Policy* 13, no. 1 (Winter 1996): 275, 276; James S. Fishkin, *Democracy and Deliberation* (New Haven, Conn.: Yale University Press, 1991).

27. Samuel P. Huntington, *The Clash of Civilizations? The Debate* (New York: Foreign Affairs, 1993).

28. For further discussion, see Etzioni, *Moral Dimension*, 136–50; Charles Lindbolm, *The Intelligence of Democracy* (New York: Free Press, 1965); Kenneth E. Boulding, review of *A Strategy of Decision: Policy Evaluation and as a Social Process*, by David Braybrooke and Charles E. Lindblom, *American Sociological Review* 29 (1962): 930–31.

29. ACLU membership letter; emphasis in original.

30. Bette Hileman, "Fluoridation of Water," *Chemical and Engineering News* 66, no. 31 (1 August 1988): 26, 27, 42.

31. Louis Uchitelle, "Politicians May Be up in Arms about Government Deficits, but Economists Aren't," *New York Times*, 8 January 1996.

32. James Davison Hunter, *Culture Wars: The Struggle to Define America* (New York: BasicBooks, 1991).

33. Michael Cromartie, "Listening to Mr. Right," *Christianity Today* 39, no. 11 (2 October 1995): 36.

34. Hunter, *Culture Wars*, 67–86; Todd Gitlin, *The Twilight of Common Dreams: Why America Is Wracked by Culture Wars* (New York: Metropolitan Books, 1995); *New Encyclopedia Britannica*, vol. 7 (Chicago: Encyclopedia Britannica, 1993), 30.

35. James Davison Hunter, *Before the Shooting Begins: Searching for Democracy in America's Culture War* (New York: Free Press, 1994), 4–5. See also Gitlin, *Twilight*.

36. Jane J. Mansbridge, *Beyond Adversary Democracy* (New York: BasicBooks, 1980), especially chapter 5, "The Town Meeting," 47–58.

37. Robert E. Goodin, *No Smoking: The Ethical Issues* (Chicago: University of Chicago Press, 1989).

38. Stephen Carter, *Integrity* (New York: BasicBooks, 1996).

39. See Michael Lerner and Cornel West, *Jews and Blacks: Let the Healing Begin* (New York: Putnam, 1995).

40. "Advertising, through and through, according to the Chicago economists, is information, not persuasion," Jerry Kirkpatrick, *In Defense of Advertising* (Westport, Conn.: Quorum Books, 1994).

41. *The Religious Right: The Assault on Tolerance and Pluralism in America* (New York: Anti-Defamation League, 1994), 30.

42. Sidney Blumenthal, "The Newt Testament," *New Yorker*, 21 November 1994, 7.

43. Courtney Leatherman, "Whither Civility?," *Chronicle of Higher Education*, 8 March 1996, A21.

44. Closely related is drawing a line between one's legal right to free speech, which allows one to say most things, however offensive, and the communitarian merit of not voicing whatever offensive thoughts come to mind. See William A. Galston, "Rights Do Not Equal Rightness," *Responsive Community* 1, no. 4 (Fall 1991): 78. Also Etzioni, *Spirit of Community*, 192–206, especially 201–4. Several of the leading hosts of radio call-in shows were blamed for ignoring this distinction and undermining values discourse as a result. See discussion in chapter 1.

45. Mary Ann Glendon, *Rights Talk: The Impoverishment of Political Discourse* (New York: Free Press, 1991), 9. She adds, "The most distinctive features of our American rights dialect [are] its penchant for absolute, extravagant formulations, its near-aphasia concerning responsibilities, its excessive homage to individual independence and self-sufficiency, its habitual concentration on the individual and the state at the expense of the intermediate groups of civil society, and its unapologetic insularity. . . [E]ach of these traits make[s] it difficult to give voice to common sense or moral political discourse." Glendon, *Rights Talk*, 14.

46. See Bruce A. Ackerman, *Social Justice in the Liberal State* (New Haven, Conn.: Yale University Press, 1980), especially chapter 11. See also discussion of the ideas of Jürgen Habermas in chapter 8 of this volume.

47. Hunter, *Before the Shooting Begins*, 239, italics omitted.

48. Jane J. Mansbridge, *Beyond Adversary Democracy* (Chicago: University of Chicago Press, 1983).

49. David Lamb, *Death, Brain Death, and Ethics* (London: Cromm Helm, 1985), 4.

50. "[It] would probably not be difficult to reach agreement, even among persons of diverse value orientation, that the following values are conspicuous parts of American culture." The list follows: monogamous marriage, acquisitiveness, democracy, education, monotheistic religion, freedom, and science. Robin M. Williams Jr., *American Society: A Sociological Interpretation* (New York: Alfred A. Knopf, 1952), 389.

51. Marc Mowery and Tim Redmond, *Not in Our Backyard* (New York: William Morrow, 1993), 39.

52. Daniel Yankelovich, *Coming to Public Judgment: Making Democracy Work in a Complex World* (Syracuse, N.Y.: Syracuse University Press, 1991).

53. Ibid., 59–65.

54. Seymour Martin Lipset, *Continental Divide: The Values and Institutions of the United States and Canada* (New York: Routledge, Chapman & Hall, 1990).

55. Aaron Wildavsky, "Representative vs. Direct Democracy: Excessive Initiatives, Too Short Terms, Too Little Respect for Politics and Politicians," *Responsive Community* 2, no. 3 (Summer 1992): 31–40.

56. James S. Fishkin, *The Voice of the People: Public Opinion and Democracy* (New Haven, Conn.: Yale University Press, 1995).

57. Howard Rheingold, *The Virtual Community: Homesteading on the Electronic Frontier* (Reading, Mass.: Addison-Wesley, 1993).

58. Walter Goodman, "And Now, Heeeeeeeere's a Referendum," *New York Times*, 21 June 1992.

59. Richard Morin, "Numbers from Nowhere: The Hoax of the Call-In Polls," *Washington Post*, 9 February 1992.

60. Amitai Etzioni, *Capital Corruption: The New Attack on American Democracy* (San Diego: Harcourt Brace Jovanovich, 1984); also Elizabeth Drew, *Politics and Money: The New Road to Corruption* (New York: Macmillan, 1983).

61. Ray Moseley, "Across Europe, Corruption Scandals Are Filling Jails, Emptying Offices," *Chicago Tribune*, 18 September 1994; Daniel Singer, "The Stench of Corruption," *Nation* 260, no. 1 (January 2, 1995): 16–20; Elizabeth Neuffer, "Europe's Leaders Find Unity in Woes," *Boston Globe*, 24 January 1995.

5. THE MORAL VOICE

1. For a study that shows values that have survived but have been hollowed out and have rather little effect on behavior, see Robert Wuthnow, *God and Mammon in America* (New York: Free Press, 1994).

2. The social psychological mechanisms involved, from shame and guilt to the desire to win approval, are not explored here. One example, however, of the use of shame is New York State's publication of a list of the top-ten deadbeat dads. For two fine treatments of shame, out of many that could be cited, see John Braithwaite, *Crime, Shame and Reintegration* (New York: Cambridge University Press, 1989); and Stuart Schneiderman, *Saving Face: America and the Politics of Shame* (New York: Alfred A. Knopf, 1995).

3. Jonathan L. Freedman, "Transgression, Compliance and Guilt," in *Altruism and Helping Behavior*, by J. Macauly and L. Berkowitz (New York: Academic Press, 1970), 156.

4. The inner voice is often referred to as a conscience. It is a term moralists and religious people use, but it has long been avoided by most social scientists.

5. Etzioni, *Moral Dimension*, 51–58.

6. For more discussion on value affirmation, see ibid., 45.

7. Brian Barry, *Sociologists, Economists and Democracy* (Chicago: University of Chicago Press, 1978), 17; Kenneth Godwin and Robert Cameron Mitchell, "Rational Models, Collective Goods and Nonelectoral Political Behavior," *Western Political Quarterly* 35, no. 2 (June 1982): 161–81.

8. Paul C. Stern, *Improving Energy Demand Analysis* (Washington, D.C.: National Academy Press, 1984), 62, 72; J. S. Black, "Attitudinal, Normative, and Economic Factors in Early Response to an Energy-Use Field Experi-

ment" (Ph.D. diss., University of Wisconsin, 1978); Thomas A. Heberlein and G. Keith Warriner, "The Influence of Price and Attitude on Shifting Residential Electricity Consumption From On- To Off-Peak Periods," *Journal of Economic Psychology* 4 (1983): 107–30. For additional documentation, see Etzioni, *Moral Dimension*, 64–66, 162–63.

9. Alan Lewis, *The Psychology of Taxation* (New York: St. Martin's, 1982), 5–6.

10. For additional discussion, see Amitai Etzioni, *A Comparative Analysis of Complex Organizations*, revised and enlarged edition (New York: Free Press, 1975).

11. The term "social network" captures this concept of the multiple attachments that make up a community. John Barnes evokes this sense of community when he writes, "[T]he image I have is of a set of points some of which are joined by lines. The points of the image are people, or sometimes groups, and the lines indicate which people interact with each other." Quoted in Colin Bell and Howard Newby, *Community Studies: An Introduction to the Sociology of the Local Community* (New York: Praeger, 1973), 52.

12. Robert Booth Fowler, *The Dance with Community: The Contemporary Debate in American Political Thought* (Lawrence, Kans.: University Press of Kansas, 1991), 3–4.

13. Walter Goodman, "Working with a Girl's Best Friend," *New York Times*, 25 July 1995.

14. Paul H. Robinson, "Moral Credibility and Crime," *Atlantic Monthly*, March 1995, 75.

15. Edward C. Banfield, *The Moral Basis of a Backward Society* (Glencoe, Ill.: Free Press, 1958).

16. See Evan Schwartz, "Looking for Community on the Internet," *Responsive Community* 5, no. 1 (Winter 1994/1995): 54–58.

17. Cited in Bell and Newby, *Community Studies*, 49.

18. Colin Bell and Howard Newby, *The Sociology of Community: A Selection of Readings* (London: Frank Cass, 1974), xliii.

19. Bell and Newby, *Community Studies*, 15.

20. "To earn the appellation 'community,' it seems to me, groups must be able to exert moral suasion and extract a measure of compliance from their members. That is, communities are necessarily, indeed, by definition, coercive as well as moral, threatening their members with the stick of sanctions if they stray, offering them the carrot of certainty and stability if they don't." David E. Pearson, "Community and Sociology," *Society* 32, no. 5 (July/August 1995): 47.

21. Linda C. McClain, "Rights and Irresponsibility," *Duke Law Journal* 43, no. 5 (March 1994): 1029.

22. Will Kymlicka, "Appendix I: Some Questions about Justice and Community," in Daniel Bell, *Communitarianism and Its Critics* (Oxford: Clarendon Press, 1993), 208–21.

23. Derek L. Phillips, *Looking Backward: A Critical Appraisal of Communitarian Thought* (Princeton, N.J.: Princeton University Press, 1993), 195.

24. Amy Gutmann, "Communitarian Critics of Liberalism," *Philosophy and Public Affairs* 14, no. 3 (Summer 1985): 319.

25. Phillips, *Looking Backward*, 183.

26. Fowler, *Dance with Community*, 142.

27. Michael Taves, "Roundtable on Communitarianism," *Telos* 76 (Summer 1988): 7–8.

28. Judith Stacey, "The New Family Values Crusaders," *Nation*, 25 July 1994, 119–22.

29. The Communitarian Network, *The Responsive Communitarian Platform: Rights and Responsibilities*, (Washington, D.C.: Communitarian Network, 1991).

30. McClain, "Irresponsibility," 1030.

31. R. Bruce Douglass, "The Renewal of Democracy and the Communitarian Prospect," *Responsive Community* 4, no. 3 (Summer 1994): 55.

32. See, for instance, Myron Magnet, *The Dream and the Nightmare: The Sixties' Legacy to the Underclass* (New York: William Morrow, 1993).

33. This notion is attributed to Robert Bork in a keen analysis by Martha Nussbaum, "Human Functioning and Social Justice: In Defense of Aristotelian Essentialism," *Political Theory* 20, no. 2 (May 1992): 210–11.

34. John Stuart Mill, *On Liberty*, ed. David Spitz (New York: W. W. Norton, 1975), 71.

35. Ibid., 10–11.

36. Steven Kautz, *Liberalism and Community* (Ithaca, N.Y.: Cornell University Press, 1995), 193.

37. Ibid., 215.

38. Gertrude Himmelfarb, *The De-Moralization of Society: From Victorian Virtues to Modern Values* (New York: Alfred A. Knopf, 1995), 240–41.

39. Jean Bethke Elshtain, "On Moral Outrage, Boycotts, and Real Censorship," *Responsive Community* 2, no. 4 (Fall 1992): 12.

40. Ibid.

41. Joseph Losco, "Understanding Altruism: A Critique and Proposal for Integrating Various Approaches," *Political Psychology* 7, no. 2 (1986): 323–48.

42. For other such reductionist arguments and responses, see Etzioni, *Moral Dimension*, 51–52.

43. Dale Carnegie, *How to Win Friends and Influence People* (New York: Simon & Schuster, 1936).

44. See Mark E. Courtney and Harry Specht, *Unfaithful Angels: How Social Work Has Abandoned Its Mission* (New York: Free Press, 1994). Also see Douglas Besharov, "The Moral Voice of Welfare Reform," *Responsive Community* 3, no. 2 (Spring 1993): 13–18.

45. John Leo, "The Psychologizing of Crime," *U.S. News & World Report*, 7 December 1992, 22.

46. Robert Bellah, Richard Madsen, William M. Sullivan, Ann Swidler, and Steven M. Tipton, *Habits of the Heart* (Berkeley, Cal.: University of California Press, 1985), 333–34.

47. Ibid., 139.

48. William Doherty, "Bridging Psychotherapy and Moral Responsibility," *Responsive Community* 5, no. 1 (Winter 1994/1995): 42.

49. Quoted in ibid., 43.

50. Quoted in ibid., 44–45.

51. William Damon, the director of Brown University's Center for the Study of Human Development, points out that claims that self-esteem causes many positive consequences are based on the simple correlation between self-esteem and positive development. Damon explains, however, that correlations do not prove causality; self-esteem is just as likely to be a result of positive development outcomes as it is to cause them. William Damon, *Greater Expectations: Overcoming the Culture of Indulgence in America's Homes and Schools* (New York: Free Press, 1995), 70–71. Also see, Ruth C. Wylie, *The Self-Concept: A Review of Methodological Considerations and Measuring Instruments* (Lincoln, Neb.: University of Nebraska Press, 1974).

52. The psychologists Richard Bednar, Gawain Wells, and Scott Peterson suggest that unconditional love and praise actually lead to low self-esteem. That is, people who are praised for inappropriate behavior fail to develop the mechanisms for coping with their real shortcomings. Richard L. Bednar, M. Gawain Wells, and Scott R. Peterson, *Self-Esteem: Paradoxes and Innovations in Clinical Theory and Practice* (Washington, D.C.: American Psychological Association, 1989), 264–65.

53. Dennis Byrne, "Correcting Kids," *Ethics: Easier Said than Done* 29 (1995): 33.

54. M. P. Baumgartner, *The Moral Order of a Suburb* (New York: Oxford University Press, 1988), 11.

55. Ibid., 10.

56. Ibid., 74.

57. Himmelfarb, *De-Moralization of Society*, 240.

58. Quoted in Irwin M. Stelzer, "The Stakeholder Cometh," *Weekly Standard*, 5 February 1996, 16–17.

59. Jacob Weisberg, "All Together Now," *New York*, 24 July 1995, 21. See also Robert Wright, "The False Politics of Values," *Time*, 9 September 1996, 42–45.

60. "Down with Rights," *Economist*, 18 March 1995, 59.

61. See exchanges between Harry C. Boyte and Amitai Etzioni, "Community vs. Public?," *Responsive Community* 2, no. 4 (Fall 1992): 75–78; Harry C. Boyte and Amitai Etzioni, "Redefining Politics, Part II," *Responsive Community* 3, no. 2 (Spring 1993): 83–88.

62. Alan Wolfe, *Whose Keeper?: Social Science and Moral Obligation* (Berkeley, Cal.: University of California Press, 1989), 189.

63. This theme is also found in John Gray, *Beyond the New Right: Markets, Government, and the Common Environment* (London: Routledge, 1993).

64. Wolfe, *Whose Keeper?*, 189.

65. Ibid., 188.

66. Benjamin Barber, *Strong Democracy: Participatory Politics for a New Age* (Berkeley, Cal.: University of California Press, 1984), 217.

67. "Die Stimme der Geimenschaft," *Frankfurter Allgemeine Zeitung*, 8 March 1994.

68. Bill Bradley, "Civil Society and the Rebirth of Our National Community," *Responsive Community* 5, no. 2 (Spring 1995): 4–10.

69. Amitai Etzioni, *An Immodest Agenda: Rebuilding America Before the 21st Century* (New York: McGraw-Hill, 1983), 130; Amitai Etzioni, *The Spirit of Community: Rights, Responsibilities, and the Communitarian Agenda* (New York: Crown, 1993), 145, 263–64; Daniel Yankelovich, "The Revitalizing Power of Reciprocity," *Responsive Community* (forthcoming).

70. For a fine, recent discussion of laws and social mores, see Richard A. Epstein, "Norms: Social and Legal," *Good Society* 6, no. 1 (Winter 1996): 1–7; William A. Galston, "When Should Norms Be Legally Enforced? A Response to Epstein," ibid., 8–9; and Richard A. Epstein, "Postscript on Galston," ibid., 9.

71. Claiming to be following the War Department's directives against discrimination, Col. Noel Parrish desegregated the Tuskegee Army Air Field in 1943. Stanley Sandler, *Segregated Skies: All-Black Squadrons of WW II* (Washington, D.C.: Smithsonian Institution Press, 1992), 38–39.

72. Nicholas Lehmann, "The Unfinished War (I)," *Atlantic Monthly* 262, No. 6 (December 1988).

73. Rochelle L. Stanfield, "Earning Their Stripes in the War on Poverty," *National Journal* 11, No. 9 (3 March 1979).

74. Charles F. Westoff and Norman B. Ryder, *The Contraceptive Revolution* (Princeton, N.J.: Princeton University Press, 1977), 22–23.

75. Robert M. Ackerman, "Tort Law and Communitarianism: Where Rights Meet Responsibilities," *Wake Forest Law Review* 30, no. 4 (1995): 661–62.

76. Mary Ann Glendon, *Rights Talk: The Impoverishment of Political Discourse* (New York: Free Press, 1991), 88.

77. In a March 22, 1993, Time/CNN poll that asked, "Should laws be passed to eliminate all possibilities of special interests giving huge sums of money to candidates?," 80 percent responded yes, 17 percent no, and 3 percent not sure; a December 1992 poll conducted by the Center for a New Democracy indicated that 86 percent of voters wanted to limit campaign spending in general; 75 percent of voters want to lower the amount of money that political action committees are allowed to contribute, from $5,000 to $1,000. Gordon Black and Benjamin D. Black, *The Politics of American Discontent: How a New Party Can Make Democracy Work Again* (New York: John Wiley, 1994), 205.

78. According to a Gallup poll that asked, "In general, do you feel that the laws covering the sale of firearms should be made more strict, less strict, or kept as they are now?," 70 percent favored more strict; 67 percent favored limiting the number of guns an individual can purchase to one gun per month; 66 percent favored banning the manufacture, sale, and possession of semiautomatic assault guns, such as the AK–47. *Gallup Poll Monthly* (March 1993): 3.

79. In a November 26, 1991, Time/CNN poll that asked, "Do you think that agricultural subsidies should be reduced and/or eliminated for farmers who earn net incomes of $100,000 or more?," 60 percent responded yes, 31 percent no, and 9 percent not sure.

80. It might be argued that the French are generally less inclined to accept government authority. Actually, the opposite case can be made rather readily. Surely they are much more regulated than Americans in numerous areas of conduct, from hiring and firing practices to what is taught in various schools, from ID papers to advertising regulations, than Americans. For further information on the reaction to smoking laws in France, see Sharon Waxman, "French Take Tobacco Ban with a Puff of Smoke," *Chicago Tribune*, 30 June 1994.

81. The U.S. Department of Justice estimates the recidivism rate of untreated sex offenders at 60 percent. Art Caplan, "Sentence Sex Offender to Life, Not Castration," *Houston Chronicle*, 6 May 1995. A 1973 Swiss study found the recidivism rate of sex offenders to be 76.9 percent. Anon., "A New Approach to Sex Offenders," *Responsive Community* 4, no. 4 (Fall 1994): 13.

82. Seymour Martin Lipset and Amy Bunger Pool, "Balancing the Individual and the Community: Canada versus the United States," *Responsive Community* 6, no. 3 (Summer 1996): 37–46.

83. Pam Belluck, "In Era of Shrinking Budgets, Community Groups Blossom," *New York Times*, 25 February 1996.

84. National Fire Protection Association Survey of Fire Departments for U.S. Fire Experience (1983–1994).

85. For a case study on drug patrols, see Suzanne Goldsmith, *The Takoma Orange Hats: Fighting Drugs and Building Community in Washington, D.C.* (Washington, D.C.: Communitarian Network, 1994). For numerous other case reports, see "Community News," *Responsive Community* 5, no. 2 (Spring 1995) and 6, no. 2 (Spring 1996).

86. Leo Srole, "Measurement and Classification in Socio-Psychiatric Epidemiology: Midtown Manhattan Study (1954) and Midtown Manhattan Restudy (1974)," *Journal of Health and Social Behavior* 16, no. 4 (December 1975): 347–63.

87. For a highly relevant discussion about volunteerism, especially among American youth, see Robert Wuthnow, *Learning to Care: Elementary Kindness in an Age of Indifference* (New York: Oxford University Press, 1995).

88. Theda Skocpol, "What if Civic Life Didn't Die?," *American Prospect*, no. 25 (March 1996): 17–28.

89. Ernesto Cortes Jr., "Changing the Locus of Political Decision Making," *Christianity and Crisis* 47, no. 1 (February 2, 1987): 18–22; Barber, *Strong Democracy*; Harry C. Boyte, *CommonWealth: A Return to Citizen Policies* (New York: Free Press, 1989); John W. Gardner, *On Leadership* (New York: Free Press, 1990). See also Jeffrey M. Berry, Kent E. Portney, and Ken Thomson, *The Rebirth of Urban Democracy* (Washington, D.C.: Brookings Institution, 1993), chapter 11.

90. Alison MacIntyre, "Guilty Bystanders? On the Legitimacy of Duty to Rescue Statutes," *Philosophy and Public Affairs* 23, no. 2 (Spring 1994): 138, n.4.

91. Ibid., 137, n.1.

92. Ackerman, "Tort Law."

93. Organizers of block parties are often required to pay insurance fees to cover themselves and/or the city for liability. For example, see Charlise Lyles, "Creating a Community Holds a Hefty Price Tag," *Virginian-Pilot*, 5 August 1995; Collin Nash, "Whose Fault Is It, Anyway? Town Facing Lawsuit After Block Party Shooting," *Newsday*, 4 June 1995.

94. Kris Mayes, "Door-to-Door Demise: Block Parties, Inspections Make Halloween Safer," *Phoenix Gazette*, 31 October 1994.

95. Dan Coats, *The Project for American Renewal* (Washington, D.C.: Office of U.S. Senator Dan Coats, 1995).

96. Milt Freudenheim, "Charities Aiding Poor Fear Loss of Government Subsidies," *New York Times*, 5 February 1996.

97. For a discussion of a new division of labor between the federal government and the states, see Alice M. Rivlin, *Reviving the American Dream: The Economy, the States, and the Federal Government* (Washington, D.C.: Brookings Institution, 1992); and Alice M. Rivlin, "Making Responsibilities Clearer: A New Federal/Local Division of Labor and Resources," *Responsive Community* 2, no. 4 (Fall 1992): 17–23.

98. Jeremy Rifkin, *The End of Work: The Decline of the Global Labor Force and the Dawn of the Post-Market Era* (New York: Putnam, 1995).

99. See Etzioni, *Spirit of Community*, 184–85.

100. Herman Goldstein, *Problem-Oriented Policing* (New York: McGraw Hill, 1990), 66. See also Robert Sampson, "The Community," in *Crime*, eds. James Q. Wilson and Joan Petersilia (San Francisco: Institute for Contemporary Studies Press, 1995), 199.

101. *Responsive Community* 5, no. 4 (Fall 1995): 5.

102. Floyd Abrams, "Why Lawyers Lie," *New York Times Magazine*, 9 October 1994, 54–55.

103. American Bar Association, "Model Rules of Professional Conduct" (Washington, D.C.: American Bar Association, 1995), 62, 64; *Federal Civil Procedure and Rules* (St. Paul: West Publishing, 1996), Rule 11, p. 62.

6. THE IMPLICATIONS OF HUMAN NATURE

1. For a discussion on this issue, see Elizabeth Frazer and Nicola Lacey, *The Politics of Community: A Feminist Critique of the Liberal-Communitarian Debate* (Toronto: University of Toronto Press, 1993), 121.

2. For a rich and elaborate discussion of human nature and references to other works, see Benjamin Barber, *Strong Democracy: Participatory Politics for a New Age* (Berkeley, Cal.: University of California Press, 1984), chapter 4.

3. For a clear explanation of the views of some theorists who have argued that crime is a matter of incentives, and a refutation thereof, see Ralph Andreano and John J. Siegfried, eds., *The Economics of Crime* (New York: John Wiley, 1980); and Simon Rottenberg, ed., *The Economics of Crime and Punishment* (Washington, D.C.: American Enterprise Institute, 1979).

4. See George J. Stigler and Gary S. Becker, "De Gustibus Non Est Disputandum," *American Economic Review* 67, no. 2 (1977): 76–90.

5. John Stuart Mill, *On Liberty*, ed. Elizabeth Rappaport (Indianapolis: Hackett, 1978), 56–57. Emphasis added.

6. Gertrude Himmelfarb, *On Liberty and Liberalism* (New York: Alfred A. Knopf, 1974), 321.

7. Ivan Illich, *Deschooling Society*, vol. 44 of *World Perspectives*, ed. Ruth Nanda Anshen (New York: Harper & Row, 1970–1971), 99.

8. John Holt, *What Do I Do Monday?* (New York: Dutton, 1970), 70–71.

9. Russell Kirk discusses "the corrupt nature of mankind" in Russell Kirk, *The Roots of American Order* (La Salle, Ill.: Open Court Publishing, 1974), 272.

10. B. V. Miller, "The Fall of Man and Original Sin," *The Teaching of the Catholic Church: A Summary of Catholic Doctrine*, vol. 1, ed. George D. Smith (New York: Macmillan, 1949), 159, 320–59.

11. Bernard Lohse, *Martin Luther: An Introduction to His Life and Work*, trans. Robert C. Schultz (Philadelphia: Fortress Press, 1986).

12. For the Calvinist Jonathan Edwards, we are "sinners in the hands of an angry God." Harold P. Simonson, ed., *Selected Writings of Jonathan Edwards* (New York: Frederick Ungar, 1970), 96.

13. Donald G. Bloesch, *God, Authority, and Salvation*, vol. 1 of *Essentials of Evangelical Theology* (San Francisco: Harper & Row, 1978), 88.

14. Solomon Schimmel, *The Seven Deadly Sins: Jewish, Christian, and Classical Reflections on Human Nature* (New York: Free Press, 1992), 12. The community rule scroll from Qumran, the 1QS, also speaks at great length about the twin spirits in humanity. 1QS 3:17, for instance, explains that God "set in him [man] two spirits for him to set his course by them until the set time of his visitation. They are the spirits of truth and perversity. In a dwelling of light are the generations of truth and from a well of darkness come the generations of perversity." For an excellent discussion of 1QS in terms of the divided soul, see A. R. C. Leaney, *The Rule of Qumran and Its Meaning* (Philadelphia: Westminster Press, 1966), 37–56.

15. "Education in America: How We See It," *The Public Perspective* 6, no. 6 (1995), 32.

16. Alasdair MacIntyre, *After Virtue* (Notre Dame, Ind.: University of Notre Dame Press, 1981), 263.

17. Oswald Spengler, *The Decline of the West* (New York: Alfred A. Knopf, 1962).

18. Russell Kirk, *The Conservative Mind: From Burke to Eliot* (New York: Discus Books, 1953), 18.

19. Russ Rymer, "Annals of Science: A Silent Childhood," parts 1 and 2, *New Yorker,* 13 April 1992, 41–81, and 20 April 1992, 43–77. Susan Curtiss, *Genie: A Psycholinguistic Study of a Modern-Day "Wild Child"* (New York: Academic Press, 1977). For documentation of other cases of neglected/wild children, see Jean Marc Gaspard Itard, *The Wild Boy of Aveyron*, trans. George and Muriel Humphrey (New York: Appleton-Century-Crofts, 1962); Harlan Lane and Richard Pillard, *The Wild Boy of Burundi: A Study of an Outcast Child* (New York: Random House, 1978); and J. A. L. Singh and R. M. Zingg, *Wolf-Children and Feral Man* (London: Harper, 1942).

20. Douglas Candland, *Feral Children and Clever Animals* (New York: Oxford University Press, 1993), 14–15.

21. Ibid., 9.

22. Ibid., 18.

23. Ibid., 60.

24. Talcott Parsons, *Social Structure and Personality* (New York: Free Press, 1964), 85–86; and John Finley Scott, *Internalization of Norms: A Sociological Theory of Moral Commitment* (Englewood Cliffs, N.J.: Prentice Hall, 1971), 89.

25. See, for instance, "New Men for Jesus," *Economist,* 2 June 1995, 21–22.

26. Dennis Wrong, "The Oversocialized Conception of Man in Modern Sociology," *American Sociological Review* 26, no. 2 (1961): 183–93.

27. "Weight Control," *Mayo Clinic Health Letter* Supplement (1994): 1–8.

28. Harry Frankfurt, "Freedom of the Will and the Concept of a Person," *Journal of Philosophy* 68, no. 1 (1971): 6.

29. Ibid., 7.

30. See also Albert O. Hirschman, "Against Parsimony: Three Easy Ways of Complicating Some Categories of Economic Discourse," *Bulletin: The American Economic Review* 74 (1984): 89–96.

31. Charles Taylor, *Sources of the Self: The Making of the Modern Identity* (Cambridge, Mass.: Harvard University Press, 1989), 36. See also Taylor's discussion of "strong evaluations" and Daniel Bell's profound commentaries on it in his *Communitarianism and Its Critics* (Oxford: Clarendon Press, 1993).

32. Taylor, *Sources of the Self*, 35.

33. Ibid., 36.

34. James Fishkin defines heroic actions as those "things we 'ought' to do but which we would not be morally blameworthy or wrong for failing to

do. .... [I]t would be admirable or virtuous if we were to do what we 'ought,' but no one could reasonably blame us if we did not." James Fishkin, *The Limits of Obligation* (New Haven, Conn.: Yale University Press, 1982), 11.

35. The deep and multiple connections between commitments to core values and shared meanings cannot be examined in the province of this book. They have been explored in the works of Michael Lerner and the publication he edits, *Tikkun*.

36. Katherine Griffin, "Sex Education That Works," *Health* 9, no. 3 (May 1995): 62–64.

37. Emile Durkheim, *The Elementary Forms of Religious Life*, trans. Karen E. Fields (New York: Free Press, 1995); Cf. Leigh Eric Schmidt, *Consumer Rites: The Buying and Selling of American Holidays* (Princeton, N.J.: Princeton University Press, 1995).

38. Robert Bellah, Richard Madsen, William M. Sullivan, Ann Swidler, and Steven M. Tipton, *The Good Society* (New York: Vintage, 1991), 260.

39. See, for instance, Neil Postman, *Technopoly: The Surrender of Culture to Technology* (New York: Vintage, 1992).

40. John R. Gillis, *A World of Their Own Making: Myth, Ritual, and the Quest for Family Values* (New York: BasicBooks, 1996), 18.

41. For a discussion of the communitarian position toward the moral infrastructure in general, please see "The Responsive Communitarian Platform," 4–20. For a more specific explanation of communitarian thought on each aspect of the moral infrastructure, see Amitai Etzioni, *The Spirit of Community: Rights, Responsibilities, and the Communitarian Agenda* (New York: Crown, 1993). For in-depth views of the communitarian position on each building block of the moral infrastructure, please see the relevant position papers published by the Communitarian Network: "A Communitarian Position Paper on the Family," "Character Building for a Democratic Society," and "The Community of Communities."

42. Embodiment is the main subject of Bellah et al., *Good Society*. See also William Sullivan, "Reinstitutionalizing Virtue in Civil Society," in *Seedbeds of Virtue*, ed. Mary Ann Glendon and David Blankenhorn (New York: Madison Books, 1995), 185–200. For an encompassing treatment by a public authority see Hillary Rodham Clinton, *It Takes a Village* (New York: Simon & Schuster, 1996).

43. Edward Zigler as quoted by Kenneth Labich, "Can Your Career Hurt Your Kids?," *Fortune*, 20 May 1991, 49.

44. For a study in such families, please see Pepper Schwartz, *Peer Marriage: How Love Between Equals Really Works* (New York: Free Press, 1994). Cf. David Blankenhorn, *Fatherless America: Confronting Our Most Urgent Social Problem* (New York: BasicBooks, 1995).

45. James H. Bray and Ernest N. Jouriles, "Treatment of Marital Conflict and Prevention of Divorce," *Journal of Marital and Family Therapy* 21, no. 4 (October 1995): 461–73. Using a number of prior studies as evidence, E.

Mark Cummings and Patrick Davies argue that marriages can be strengthened by argument if it serves to resolve problems. Negotiation and compromise yield a higher level of satisfaction for couples who use these techniques for conflict resolution. E. Mark Cummings and Patrick Davies, *Children and Marital Conflict: The Impact of Family Dispute and Resolution* (New York: Guilford, 1994), 32.

46. James H. Bray and Ernest N. Jouriles report that premarital counseling has a positive effect by "preventing relationship dissolution prior to marriage." Bray and Jouriles, "Treatment of Marital Conflict," 467.

47. Amitai Etzioni, "How to Make Marriage Matter," *Time*, 6 September 1993, 76.

48. For a call for fault divorce, see David M. Wagner, "Taming the Divorce Monster: The Many Faults of No-Fault Divorce," *Family Policy* 7 (April 1994): 5–6.

49. U.S. Department of Education, *Digest of Education Statistics* (Washington, D.C., 1995), 5.

50. William Peters, *A Class Divided: Then and Now* (New Haven, Conn.: Yale University Press, 1987).

51. Ibid., 24–25.

52. Adam Smith, *Theory of Moral Sentiments* (New York: Garland, 1971).

53. Bellah and colleagues point out that even the most laissez-faire minded will admit to "public values" when pressed. Bellah et al., *Good Society*, 136–37.

54. Etzioni, *Spirit of Community*, 183–84; Bruce Miller, "Student Advocates, Teachers' Rights," *American Educator* (Spring 1981): 30–33.

55. The rather telegraphic discussion provides pointers that are discussed in much greater detail in position papers available from The Communitarian Network. Those interested may send e-mail to comnet@gwis2.circ.gwu.edu, or may call 1-800-245-7460.

56. Robert D. Putnam, "Bowling Alone, Revisited," *Responsive Community* 5, no. 2 (Spring 1995): 18–33.

7. PLURALISM WITHIN UNITY

1. See, for example, Kent E. Portney, *Siting Hazardous Waste Treatment Facilities: The NIMBY Syndrome* (New York: Auburn House, 1991).

2. John Darnton, "Nationalist Winds Blow Hot in the Highlands, Warming Scots to Separatism," *New York Times*, 17 October 1995.

3. See "Racial and Ethnic Tensions in American Communities: Poverty, Inequality, and Discrimination—A National Perspective," *Hearing Before the United States Commission on Civil Rights* (Washington, D.C.: GPO, 1992), especially "Panel Three—Hate Incidents."

4. Howard Erlich, testimony, "Racial and Ethnic Tensions," 71.

5. Danny Welch, testimony, ibid., 77.

6. Arthur Schlesinger Jr., *The Disuniting of America: Reflections on a Multicultural Society* (New York: W. W. Norton, 1992), 10.

7. See ibid.; Shelby Steele, *The Content of Our Character: A New Vision of Race in America* (New York: St. Martin's Press, 1990).

8. Technically the term "melting pot" refers to merging different substances into a *new* brew while "assimilation" refers to absorbing various new groups into the mainstream culture. However I follow here the tendency in public dialogue to equate the two.

9. Roberto Suro, *Remembering the American Dream: Hispanic Immigration and National Policy* (New York: Twentieth Century Press, 1994), 64.

10. Mark Helprin, "Diversity Is Not a Virtue," *Wall Street Journal*, 25 November 1994.

11. *Time*, special issue, Fall 1993, cover graphic.

12. Sheldon Hackney, the chairman of the National Endowment for the Humanities, suggested that "jazz [is] the ideal metaphor for America." Sheldon Hackney, "Organizing a National Conversation," *Chronicle of Higher Education*, 20 April 1994.

13. Martha Farnsworth Riche, "We're All Minorities Now," *American Demographics* (October 1991): 26.

14. *Time*, special issue, Fall 1993, 20.

15. John A. Porter coined the term "vertical mosaic" with reference to Canada. John A. Porter, *The Vertical Mosaic: An Analysis of Social Class and Power in Canada* (Toronto: University of Toronto Press, 1965).

16. Suro, *Remembering the American Dream*, 65.

17. "People, Opinions, and Polls," *Public Perspective* 6, no. 5 (August/September 1995), 15.

18. Michael Wolff et al., *Where We Stand: Can America Make It in the Global Race for Wealth, Health, and Happiness?* (New York: Bantam, 1992), 210.

19. Calculated from George Thomas Kurian, *Datapedia of the United States 1790–2000: America Year by Year* (Lanham, Md.: Berman Press 1994), 16–17.

20. Ursula Casanova and M. Beatriz Arias, "Contextualizing Bilingual Education," in *Bilingual Education: Politics, Practice, and Research*, eds. Ursula Casanova and M. Beatriz Arias (Chicago: University of Chicago Press, 1993), 15–17. (Estimates were first made only in the late 1970s.)

21. U.S. Department of Education, cited in *U.S. News & World Report*, 25 September 1995, 45.

22. Personal communication with Raul Yzaguirre, president of the National Council of La Raza.

23. Rosalie Pedalino Porter, *Forked Tongue: The Politics of Bilingual Education* (New York: BasicBooks, 1990), 211 (table). Six states have English-only constitutional amendments, and eleven have English-only statutes or resolutions.

24. Ibid., 173–74. The law was struck down by the Canadian Supreme Court in December 1988, but a few days later, Robert Bourassa, the premier of Québec, used the legislative override power of the Canadian Charter of Rights and Freedoms, claiming a unique duty to protect French culture in Quebec.

25. James Bryce, *The American Commonwealth*, vol. 2 (London, 1888) 328, 709: quoted by Schlesinger, *Disuniting*, 7.

26. Schlesinger, *Disuniting*.

27. Cf. Glenn C. Loury, "Individualism Before Multiculturalism," *Public Interest*, no. 121 (Fall 1995), 101.

28. Lewis A. Coser, *The Functions of Social Conflict* (Glencoe, Ill.: Free Press, 1956); Ralf Dahrendorf, *Class and Class Conflict in Industrial Society* (Stanford, Cal.: Stanford University Press, 1959).

29. Rupert Wilkinson, *The Pursuit of American Character* (New York: Harper & Row, 1988), 1. See also Wilkinson, *American Social Character: Modern Interpretations* (New York: Iron Editions, 1992). Better-known examinations of the American character include: David Reisman et al., *The Lonely Crowd: A Study of the Changing American Character* (New Haven, Conn.: Yale University Press, 1950); Geoffrey Gorer, *The American People: A Study in National Character* (New York: W. W. Norton, 1948); D. W. Brogan, *The American Character* (New York: Alfred A. Knopf, 1944); and F. J. Turner, *The Frontier in American History* (New York: H. Holt and Company, 1921).

30. Seymour Martin Lipset, *American Exceptionalism: A Double-Edged Sword* (New York: W. W. Norton, 1996).

31. Melinda Fine, *Habits of the Mind: Struggling over Values in America's Classrooms* (San Francisco: Jossey-Bass, 1995), 9.

32. Ibid.; emphasis added.

33. Benjamin Barber, *Strong Democracy: Participatory Politics for a New Age* (Berkeley, Cal.: University of California Press, 1984), 119.

34. Article 1, Section 2, of the United States Constitution refers to "the . . . number of free persons, including those bound to service for a term of years, and excluding Indians not taxed, three fifths of all other persons."

35. Emile Durkheim, *The Division of Labor in Society* (Houndmills, Eng.: Macmillan, 1984).

36. Dan Morgan, "House Reverses EPA Stance," *Washington Post*, 1 August 1995.

37. Kevin Merida, "House Absentees Hand Democratic Leaders Another Disappointment," *Washington Post*, 2 August 1995.

38. George Gallup Jr., and Frank Newport, "Americans Back Bush on Flag-burning Amendment," *The Gallup Poll Monthly*, June 1990, 2.

39. In contrast to the Supreme Court, several recent progressive educational guidelines and documents reverse the reference and systematically refer to the American *peoples* instead of the American *people*. John Fonte, "We the Peoples: The Multiculturalist Agenda Is Shattering the American

Identity," *National Review*, 25 March 1996, 47–49. And various leaders of racial and ethnic groups strenuously object to the introduction of a new category into the U.S. Census for 2000 which would enable Americans to classify themselves as not of this or that race, but as multiracial.

40. Malcolm X, "Minister Malcolm X Enunciates the Muslim Program," *Black Nationalism in America*, ed. John H. Bracey Jr. (Indianapolis: Bobbs-Merrill, 1970), 419. This speech was originally given at the Harlem Unity Rally in 1960, and was reprinted in *Muhammad Speaks* (September 1960), 2, 20–22.

41. John Leo, "Cash the Check, Bob," *U.S. News and World Report*, 18 September 1995, 43.

42. David Boaz, "Don't Forget the Kids," *New York Times*, 10 September 1994; David Boaz, "Domestic Justice," *New York Times*, 4 January 1995.

43. People for the American Way, "The Two Faces of the Christian Coalition," released 16 September 1994, 9.

44. James Davison Hunter, *Before the Shooting Begins: Searching for Democracy in America's Culture War* (New York: Free Press, 1994).

45. See Betty Friedan, "To Transcend Identity Politics: A New Paradigm," *Responsive Community* 6, no. 2 (Spring 1996): 4–8. There is a rich literature on the politics of difference, which is not reviewed here. See Amy Gutmann, ed., *Multiculturalism and "The Politics of Recognition": An Essay by Charles Taylor with Commentary* (Princeton, N.J.: Princeton University Press, 1992); Michael Walzer, *What It Means to Be an American* (New York: Marsilio, 1992); Iris Marion Young, *Justice and the Politics of Difference* (Princeton, N.J.: Princeton University Press, 1990); and Will Kymlicka, *Multi-Cultural Citizenship: A Liberal Theory of Minority Rights* (Oxford: Oxford University Press, 1995).

46. Lewis H. Lapham, "Who and What Is American?," *Harper's*, January 1992, 43.

47. Quoted in Louis Aguilar, "Latinos, Asians Seek a Voice in Emerging National Discussion on Race," *Washington Post*, 15 October 1995.

48. Janet Saltzman Chafetz, "Minorities, Gender Mythologies, and Moderation," *Responsive Community* 4, no. 1 (Winter 1993/1994): 42.

49. Ibid., 42.

50. David A. Hollinger, *Postethnic America: Beyond Multiculturalism* (New York: BasicBooks, 1995).

51. Rodolfo O. de la Garza, "Introduction," in *Ignored Voices: Public Opinion Polls and the Latino Community*, ed. Rodolfo O. de la Garza, (Austin, Texas: Center for Mexican American Studies, 1987), 4.

52. Lena H. Sun, "Cultural Differences Set Asian Americans Apart: Where Latinos Have Common Threads, They Have None," *Washington Post*, 10 October 1995.

53. Rodolfo O. de la Garza, "Researchers Must Heed New Realities When They Study Latinos in the U.S." *Chronicle of Higher Education*, 2 June 1993, B1–3.

54. Michael Tomasky, "The Left Lost Touch," *Washington Post*, 20 November 1994.

55. See, for example, the study done by the Washington Post, Kaiser Family Foundation, and Harvard University cited in Sun, "Cultural Differences."

56. Betty Friedan, "To Transcend Identity Politics," 4–8.

57. Nicholas Tavuchis, *Mea Culpa: A Sociology of Apology and Reconciliation* (Stanford, Cal.: Stanford University Press, 1991), 15–44.

58. Ibid., 21–22.

59. Ibid., 62–63.

60. Ibid., 106–7.

61. Gary L. Carter, "Southern Baptists Apologize for Having Condoned Racism," *Boston Globe*, 21 June 1995.

62. Tavuchis, *Mea Culpa*, 107–8.

63. Harlon Dalton, *Racial Healing: Confronting the Fear Between Blacks and Whites* (New York: Doubleday, 1995), 42.

64. Bjorn Krondorfer, *Remembrance and Reconciliation: Encounters Between Young Jews and Germans* (New Haven, Conn.: Yale University Press, 1995), 95.

65. Tavuchis, *Mea Culpa*, 56–57.

66. Krondorfer, *Remembrance*, 16.

67. Porter, *Tongue*, 214–16.

68. Ibid., 193–221.

69. Ibid., 217.

70. The *National Latino Political Survey* reported that 94 percent of Puerto Rican Americans, 93 percent of Cuban Americans, and 90 percent of Mexican Americans agree or strongly agree that all Americans should learn English. De la Garza, "Researchers Must Heed New Realities," B1–3.

71. Porter, *Tongue*, 212–13.

72. Ibid., 218.

73. See Lynne V. Cheney, "The End of History," *Wall Street Journal*, 20 October 1994.

74. Ronald Takaki, *A Different Mirror: A History of Multicultural America* (Boston: Little, Brown, 1993). In his book *Dictatorship of Virtue*, Richard Bernstein reports that in many schools children are taught that America has no common culture, nor anything important to offer the world; educators refuse to concede that not all cultural styles have been equally successful, often by ignoring the less savory aspects of non-Western cultures, while highlighting such shortcomings in the West. Richard Bernstein, *Dictatorship of Virtue: Multiculturalism and the Battle for America's Future* (New York: Alfred A. Knopf, 1994).

75. See, for example, the speech by Louis Farrakhan during the Million Man March and commentary in *Washington Post*, 17 October 1995.

76. The examples are from Terence Cooper, "The Rewards of Racial Prejudice," *Journal of Housing* 46, no. 3 (May/June 1989): 105–7.

77. Douglas S. Massey and Nancy A. Denton, *American Apartheid: Segregation and the Making of the Underclass* (Cambridge, Mass.: Harvard University Press, 1993), 98–109.

8. THE FINAL ARBITERS OF COMMUNITY'S VALUES

1. As Galston shows, "this defense of liberalism is fundamentally misguided. No form of political life can be justified without some view of what is good for individuals." William A. Galston, *Liberal Purposes: Goods, Virtues, and Diversity in the Liberal State* (Cambridge: Cambridge University Press, 1991), 79. His argument for this extends over most of Part II of his book. Michael J. Sandel has also argued that attempts to take a procedural, value-neutral stance on issues are doomed. See Michael J. Sandel, *Liberalism and the Limits of Justice* (Cambridge: Cambridge University Press, 1982).

2. John Rawls, *A Theory of Justice* (Cambridge, Mass.: Belknap Press, 1971), 62.

3. Daniel A. Bell, *Communitarianism and Its Critics* (Oxford: Clarendon Press, 1993), 38. For additional discussion, see ibid., 37–39, 55–78.

4. Michael J. Sandel, "Morality and the Liberal Ideal," *New Republic*, 7 May 1984, 17. Emphasis added.

5. Michael J. Sandel, *Democracy's Discontent: America in Search of a Public Philosophy* (Cambridge, Mass.: Belknap Press, 1996), 321.

6. Ibid., 322.

7. Ibid., 323.

8. Michael J. Perry, *Morality, Politics, and Law: A Bicentennial Essay* (Oxford: Oxford University Press, 1988), 40.

9. Amy Gutmann, "The Challenge of Multiculturalism in Political Ethics," *Philosophy and Public Affairs* 22, no. 3 (1993).

10. Reported in "New Philosophy Urges a Social Commitment," *Press-Enterprise*, 30 January 1993.

11. Glasser interview, "Your Rights vs. My Safety: Where Do We Draw the Line?," *BusinessWeek*, 3 September 1990, 56.

12. Peter Singer, "Is There a Universal Moral Sense?," *Critical Review* 9, no. 3 (1995): 326.

13. Gutmann, "Challenge," 180–81.

14. See Michael J. Sandel, in Bill Moyers, *A World of Ideas II* (New York: Doubleday, 1990), 155.

15. Benjamin Barber, *Strong Democracy: Participatory Politics for a New Age* (Berkeley, Cal.: University of California Press, 1984), 224.

16. As Gutmann notes, "A complete social consensus on slavery, assuming one ever existed, would not in itself justify slavery." Gutmann, "Challenge," 177.

17. Derek L. Phillips, *Looking Backward: A Critical Appraisal of Communitarian Thought* (Princeton, N.J.: Princeton University Press, 1993): 183.

18. Stephen Holmes, *The Anatomy of Antiliberalism* (Cambridge, Mass.: Harvard University Press, 1993), 178–79.

19. Ronald Beiner, "Liberalism: What's Missing?," *Society* 32, no. 5 (1995): 19.

20. David Willetts, *Modern Conservatism* (London: Penguin, 1992), 157.

21. Ibid., 154.

22. Ibid., 154–55.

23. Seymour Martin Lipset, *American Exceptionalism: A Double-Edged Sword* (New York: W. W. Norton, 1996).

24. William A. Galston, "Two Concepts of Liberalism," *Ethics* 105, no. 3 (1995): 518–21. Cf. Stephen Macedo, *Liberal Virtues* (Oxford: Oxford University Press, 1990).

25. Galston, "Two Concepts," 528.

26. See especially Galston, *Liberal Purposes*, 165–190, 241–56. See also Galston "Two Concepts"; and Galston, "Liberal Virtues and the Formation of Civic Character," in *Seedbeds of Virtue: Sources of Competence, Character, and Citizenship in American Society,* ed. Mary Ann Glendon and David Blankenhorn (Lanham, Md.: Madison Books, 1995).

27. Galston, "Two Concepts," 525.

28. The Qur'an is the official constitution of Saudi Arabia—the government claims that all its laws derive from the principles of the Qur'an. Fouad Al-Farsy, *Modernity and Tradition: The Saudi Equation* (London: Kegan Paul International, 1990), 39–42.

29. Jürgen Habermas, *Moral Consciousness and Communicative Action* (Cambridge, Mass.: MIT Press, 1990), 14.

30. Jürgen Habermas, *Justification and Application: Remarks on Discourse Ethics* (Cambridge, Mass.: MIT Press, 1993), 9.

31. Habermas, *Moral Consciousness*, 89.

32. Bruce Ackerman, "Why Dialogue?," *Journal of Philosophy* 86, no. 1 (1989): 9.

33. Ackerman does not think it necessary to make Habermas's claim that moral truths are ontologically based in dialogue (though at times he is inclined toward this view) in order to reach this conclusion. Ibid., 7. But it does mean that we have to give up the idea that politics is about moral truth. Ibid., 9, 10.

34. Ibid., 16.

35. Ibid., 17–19.

36. Ibid., 16–17, 19.

37. Dennis H. Wrong, *The Problem of Order: What Unites and Divides Society* (New York: Free Press, 1994), 59. See also Edna Ullman-Margolit, *The Emergence of Norms* (Oxford: Clarendon Press, 1977).

38. Mark Gould, "The Wrong Problem of Order" (paper presented at

the 1995 Annual Meeting of the American Sociological Association, Washington, D.C., August 1995), 33.

39. Gareth Porter and Janet Welsh Brown, *Global Environmental Politics* (Boulder, Colo.: Westview Press, 1996), 69–105.

40. Steven Greenhouse, "Ecology, the Economy and Bush," *New York Times,* 14 June 1992.

41. For an excellent discussion of relativism by a communitarian, see Philip Selznick, *The Moral Commonwealth: Social Theory and the Promise of Community* (Berkeley, Cal.: University of California Press, 1992), chapter 4.

42. Carolyn Fluehr-Lobban, "Cultural Relativism and Universal Rights," *Chronicle of Higher Education,* 9 June 1995.

43. James Q. Wilson, "Liberalism, Modernism, and the Good Life," in *Seedbeds,* Glendon and Blankenhorn, 23.

44. A. M. Rosenthal, "Fighting Female Mutilation," *New York Times,* 12 April 1996. Even the name of the procedure has been "relativized." To avoid implicit Western value judgments, an article in Hastings Center Report refers to the procedure as "female genital surgery" (Sandra D. Lane and Robert A. Rubinstein, "Judging the Other: Responding to Traditional Female Genital Surgeries," *Hastings Center Report* 26, no. 3 [May/June 1996]: 31). And the fine copy editor of this book recommended "ritual circumcision." (Neither seems aware that, far from coming up with a nonjudgmental term, they actually suggest terms that have positive connotations.)

45. Daniel A. Bell, "The East Asian Challenge to Human Rights" (unpublished), 9.

46. Communitarians have been taken to task for avoiding issues of cross-cultural values, especially for neglecting universal human rights. See Gideon Sjoberg, "The Human Rights Challenge to Communitarians: Formal Organizations and Race and Ethnicity," in *Macro Socio-Economics: From Theory to Activism,* ed. David Sciulli (Armonk, N.Y.: M. E. Sharpe, 1996).

47. See Abdullahi Ahmed An-Na'im, "Toward a Cross-Cultural Approach to Defining International Standards of Human Rights: The Meaning of Cruel, Inhuman, or Degrading Treatment or Punishment," in *Human Rights in Cross-Cultural Perspectives: A Quest for Consensus,* ed. Abdullahi Ahmed An-Na'im (Philadelphia: University of Pennsylvania Press: 1992).

48. Bell, "East Asian," 11; see also Abdullahi Ahmed An-Na'im, *Toward an Islamic Reformation: Civil Liberties, Human Rights, and International Law* (Syracuse, N.Y.: Syracuse University Press, 1990).

49. Joanne Bauer, "Three Years after the Bangkok Declaration: Reflections on the State of Asia-West Dialogue on Human Rights," *Human Rights Dialogue* 4 (March 1996): 1.

50. See Joseph Chan, "The Task for Asians: To Discover Their Own Political Morality for Human Rights," *Human Rights Dialogue* 4 (March 1996): 5; see also Chan, "The Asian Challenge to Universal Human Rights: A Philo-

sophical Appraisal," in *Human Rights and International Relations in the Asia-Pacific Region,* ed. James T. H. Tang (New York: St. Martin's, 1995).

51. Michael Walzer, *Thick and Thin: Moral Argument at Home and Abroad* (Notre Dame, Ind.: University of Notre Dame Press, 1994), 7.

52. Ibid., 8.

53. Michael Walzer, *Spheres of Justice* (New York: BasicBooks, 1983), 313.

54. Stephen Mulhall and Adam Swift, *Liberals and Communitarians* (Oxford: Blackwell, 1992), 140.

55. Ronald Beiner, *What's the Matter With Liberalism?* (Berkeley, Cal.: University of California Press, 1992), 28–29.

56. A. L. Kroeber and Clyde Kluckohn, *Culture: A Critical Review of Concepts and Definitions* (New York: Vintage, 1963), 349.

57. Alison Dundes Renteln, *International Human Rights: Universalism versus Relativism* (Thousand Oaks, Cal.: Sage Publications: 1990), 88ff.

58. See also Wendell Bell, "World Order, Human Values, and the Future," *Futures Research Quarterly* 12, no. 1 (spring 1996): 5–24; and Rushworth M. Kidder, *Shared Values for a Troubled World* (San Francisco: Jossey-Bass, 1994).

59. Rhoda E. Howard, *Human Rights and the Search for Community* (Boulder, Colo.: Westview Press, 1995), 54. Emphasis added.

60. Robert Wright, *The Moral Animal: The New Science of Psychology* (New York: Pantheon, 1994); James Q. Wilson, *The Moral Sense* (New York: Free Press, 1993).

61. See Wright, *Moral Animal,* 200–201.

62. Sociological work finds several crosscultural value similarities. See especially Shalom H. Schwartz, "Beyond Individualism/Collectivism: New Cultural Dimensions of Values," in *Individualism and Collectivism: Theory, Method, and Applications,* ed. Uichol Kim and Hanguk Simni Hakhoe (Thousand Oaks, Cal.: Sage Publications, 1994).

63. This point is stressed by Wilson, *Moral Sense,* 200–207. See also Amitai Etzioni, "The Responsive Community: A Communitarian Perspective," *American Sociological Review* 61 (February 1996): 1–11.

64. Marcus Singer, as quoted by James Gaffney, "The Golden Rule: Abuses and Uses," *America,* 20 September 1986, 115.

65. George Weigel, "Are Human Rights Still Universal?," *Commentary* 99, no. 2 (February 1995), 43–44.

66. Howard, *Human Rights,* 165ff.

67. See, for example, UNESCO, *Our Creative Diversity: Report of the World Commission on Culture and Development* (1995).

68. Walzer, *Spheres of Justice,* 314.

69. Minerva Etzioni, *The Majority of One: Towards a Theory of Regional Compatibility* (Beverly Hills, Cal.: Sage Publications, 1970).

70. Reported by Erik Kuhonta, "On Social and Economic Rights," *Human Rights Dialogue* 2 (September 1995): 3.

71. Julius O. Ihonvbere, "Underdevelopment and Human Rights Violations in Africa," in *Emerging Human Rights: The Africa Political Economy Context*, ed. George W. Shepherd and Mark Anikpo (Westport, Conn.: Greenwood Press, 1990), 57.

72. *1993 Britannica Book of the Year* (Chicago: Encyclopedia Britannica, 1993), 796.

73. George Thomas Kurian, *Datapedia of the United States 1790–2000* (Lanham, Md.: Bernan Press, 1994), 90.

74. Seymour Martin Lipset, "A Comparative Analysis of the Social Requisites of Democracy," *International Social Science Journal*, no. 136 (1993): 155.

75. Rhoda E. Howard, *Human Rights in Commonwealth Africa* (Totowa, N.J.: Rowman and Littlefield, 1986).

76. Kishore Mahbubani, "The Dangers of Decadence," *Foreign Affairs* 72, no. 4 (1993): 14.

77. Mohamed Elhachmi Hamdi, "The Limits of the Western Model," *Journal of Democracy* 7, no. 2 (1996): 82.

78. Amitai Etzioni, *The Spirit of Community: Rights, Responsibilities, and the Communitarian Agenda* (New York: Crown, 1993).

79. Joanne Bauer, "International Human Rights and Asian Commitment," *Human Rights Dialogue* 3 (December 1995): 1.

80. Ibid., 1–2.

81. Bilahari Kausikan, "Asia's Different Standard," *Foreign Policy*, no. 92 (Fall 1993): 24.

82. Readers may wonder why I do not use the term "deontology," which is derived from the Greek *deon*, meaning a binding duty, which is what I am writing about. My reason is that the term brings much baggage with it, and is deeply associated with the individualistic philosophy, which I do not share.

83. On the concept of the moral sense, see Wilson, *Moral Sense*.

84. Charles Taylor, *Sources of the Self: The Making of the Modern Identity* (Cambridge, Mass.: Harvard University Press, 1989), 5.

85. Ibid., 5–8.

86. Ibid., 7.

87. See, for example, C. K. Ogden and I. A. Richards, *The Meaning of Meaning: A Study of the Influence of Language upon Thought and the Science of Symbolism* (New York: Harcourt, 1946).

88. See the Josephson Institute of Ethics, *Making Ethical Decisions* (Marina Del Rey, Cal.: 1996).

89. William J. Bennett, ed., *The Book of Virtues: A Treasury of Great Moral Stories* (New York: Simon & Schuster, 1993).

90. Colin Greer and Herbert R. Kohl, eds., *A Call to Character* (New York: HarperCollins, 1995).

91. Galston, *Liberal Purposes*, 221–27.

92. Martha Nussbaum reports that an unnamed French anthropologist expressed regret that the introduction of the smallpox vaccination in India

by the British led to the end of the Cult of Sittala Devi, to whom one used to pray for protection from the disease. When Nussbaum wondered if health is not to be preferred to illness, the anthropologist chided her for thinking in Western, binary terms, where life and death, well-being and illness, are in sharp opposition. Martha C. Nussbaum, "Human Functioning and Social Justice: In Defense of Aristotelian Essentialism," *Political Theory* 20, no. 2 (May 1993): 203.

93. Immanuel Kant, "Grounding for the Metaphysics of Morals," in *Ethical Philosophy* (Indianapolis: Hackett Publishing Company, 1983), 36. This connection to Kant is made most explicit by a leading libertarian, Robert Nozick, in *Anarchy, State and Utopia* (New York: BasicBooks, 1974), 32.

94. Joseph de Maistre, *Considerations on France*, Richard A. Lebrun trans. (Montreal: McGill-Queen's University Press, 1974), 97.

95. Hans Joas, "The Communitarian Experience." Paper presented at the Communitarian Summit, Geneva, Switzerland, July 1996.

96. The complex relationship between social and individualist virtues is exceptionally well explored in Miriam Galston, "Taking Aristotle Seriously," *California Law Review* 82, no. 329 (1994): 331.

97. For additional discussion, see Robert E. Goodin, "Making Moral Incentives Pay," *Policy Sciences* 12 (August 1980): 131–45.

98. Philip Selznick's paper on communitarian social justice and Alan Wolfe's on social welfare, presented at the July 1996 communitarian summit in Geneva, Switzerland, take us giant steps forward, but were presented too late to be included in my deliberations. Philip Selznick, "A Communitarian Perspective on Social Justice" (paper presented at the 1996 Communitarian Summit, Geneva, Switzerland, July 1996); Alan Wolfe, "Turning Point for the Welfare State" (ibid.). See also Charles Derber, "Communitarian Economics: Criticisms and Suggestions from the Left," *Responsive Community* 4, no. 4 (Fall 1994): 29–42.

99. Elizabeth Frazer and Nicola Lacey, *The Politics of Community: A Feminist Critique of the Liberal-Communitarian Debate* (Toronto: University of Toronto Press, 1993), 66–67.

100. See Herman E. Daly and John B. Cobb Jr., *For the Common Good: Redirecting the Economy Toward Community, the Environment, and a Sustainable Future* (Boston: Beacon Press, 1989).

101. Benjamin R. Barber, *Jihad vs. McWorld* (New York: Times Books, 1995); Samuel P. Huntington, "The Clash of Civilizations?," *Foreign Affairs* 72, no. 3 (1993).

102. Chuck Colson, "Can We Be Good Without God?," *Imprimis* 22, no. 4 (1993): 2.

103. Patrick Robertson, *The Turning Tide* (Dallas: Word Publishing, 1993), 158.

104. Peter Steinfels, "Beliefs: Battling for the Backing of Judaism," *New York Times*, 4 November 1995.

105. "The National Prospect," *Commentary* 100, no. 5 (November 1995): 23–116. Irving Kristol raises this issue in his book *Reflections of a Neoconservative: Looking Back, Looking Ahead* (New York: BasicBooks, 1983).

106. Michael S. Joyce, "The New Impulse Toward Self-Government," *Wall Street Journal*, 19 April 1993.

107. Joshua Abramowitz, "The Tao of Community," *Public Interest*, no. 113 (Fall 1993), 121. Several people have criticized the relationship between communitarianism and religion, while others have been complimentary. See Matthew Melton, "The Communitarians," *Focus* (Fall/Winter 1992): 18–21; Brandy Dutcher, "Communitarians and the Christian Right," *Focus* (Fall/Winter 1992): 20–22; Charles J. Sykes, "Liberal Angst," *The World and I* (August 1993): 309–13; "The Communities Missing from 'Communitarianism,'" *First Things* (February 1994): 55–56.

108. Robert Wuthnow, *God and Mammon in America* (New York: Free Press, 1994), 241.

109. Ibid., 129.

110. Ibid., 58.

111. Ibid., 6.

112. Amitai Etzioni, *Demonstration Democracy* (New York: Gordon and Breach, 1970).

Index